FREEDOM AND THE SPIRIT

NICOLAS BERDYAEV

Freedom and the Spirit

Translated by
Oliver Fielding Clarke

 BOOKS FOR LIBRARIES PRESS
A Division of Arno Press, Inc.
New York, New York

First Published 1935
Reprinted 1972

Library of Congress Cataloging in Publication Data

Berdíâev, Nikolaĭ Aleksandrovich, 1874-1948.
  Freedom and the spirit.

  ([BCL/select bibliographies reprint series])
  Translation of Filosofíâ svobodnago dukha.
  1. Religion--Philosophy. 2. Apologetics--20th
century. I. Title.
BL51.B5244 1972   201   72-2567
ISBN 0-8369-6848-4

Contents

Introduction

AS Léon Bloy has well said in *Le Pèlerin de l'Absolu*, " Souffrir passe, avoir souffert ne passe jamais "[1]. This is a remarkable aphorism demanding the broadest possible interpretation. Victory may indeed be achieved over what has been experienced, and yet that experience is still in our possession as a permanent enhancement and extension of the reality of our spiritual life. What has once been lived through cannot possibly be effaced. That which has been continues to exist in a transfigured form. Man is by no means a completely finished product. Rather he moulds and creates himself in and through his experience of life, through spiritual conflict, and through those various trials which his destiny imposes upon him. Man is only what God is planning, a projected design.

Victory can indeed be won over the past, and Christianity teaches us that it can be redeemed and forgiven. Rebirth into a new life is possible, but into every new and transfigured life there will return those former experiences which cannot disappear into oblivion without leaving traces behind them. A period of suffering can be overcome, joy and happiness can be born anew, but into every fresh joy and happiness there will enter again, in some mysterious way, that suffering which has already been endured. Joy and happiness will henceforth be different. The torment of doubt may be defeated, yet even in the new-found faith the depths of previous uncertainty are revealed. Such a faith will possess quite a different quality from that belonging to those who have not had these doubts, and who have inherited their beliefs from tradition. The man who has travelled far in the realms of the spirit, and who has

[1] " Suffering disappears, but the fact of having suffered remains always with us."

vii

passed through great trials in the course of his search for truth, will be formed spiritually along lines which must differ altogether from those pertaining to the man who has never shifted his position and to whom new spiritual territories are unknown. Man is tied to his destiny and has no power of renouncing it. It is in what I experience of life, in the trials I suffer, and in my search for reality, that my spirit is formed and moulded. Everything I have lived through is part of the highest acquisition of my spiritual life and of the faith and truth which I possess. I am enriched by my experience even if it has been fearful and tormenting, even if to cross the abyss which lay before me I have been forced to address myself to powers other than human.

When a man returns to God after an experience of apostasy he knows a freedom in his relations with Him untasted by one who has passed his life in the peace and security of his traditional faith and who has remained within the borders of his spiritual inheritance.

" Suffering disappears, but the fact of having suffered remains always with us." That is the exact truth of the matter whether we are considering individuals or aggregates of human society. We live in an age of transition and of spiritual crisis, in which many erring pilgrims are returning to Christianity, to the faith of their fathers, to the Church, and to Orthodoxy. These men return, having passed through the ordeal of the new age, to the extreme limits of which they have now penetrated. These souls who belong to the end of the nineteenth and the beginning of the twentieth centuries are tragic souls indeed. They are souls new-born, it is true, but from their lives the consequences of past experience can never be uprooted.

How, one may ask, are these travellers returning to the Father's House received ? Too often not in the way in which the Prodigal Son in the parable was welcomed. The voice of the Elder Son who boasts of having remained with the Father and of serving Him is far too much in evidence. And yet among these pilgrims of the spirit there are not only the depraved : there are also those who are hungering and thirsting after the truth. These will be accounted more righteous in the sight of God than numberless " bourgeois Christians " who pride themselves on their pharisaical religion and who imagine that they are " men of property " in the religious sphere.

The human soul has developed into something quite different from what it was when the message of Christianity was first received or when the great Doctors of the Church flourished, when the Œcumenical Councils were making their dogmatic decisions, when monasticism was passing through its formative stages, or in the days when theocracy was in power and mediæval and Byzantine piety took shape. This transformation and the purifying of the human soul have been brought about especially by the influence of the mysterious action of Christianity itself, often invisible and profound in character, which triumphed inwardly over the rude barbarity of man's spirit in the process of educating him.

We find in the instructions of the Elders no answer to the agonized questions of Nietzsche which demand from Christianity a creative completion. The whole movement of Russian religious philosophy in the last few decades has passed through an experience which cannot be effaced and which cannot fail to enrich Christianity. It is not the result of any process of individual growth in perfection or acquiring of sanctity. Nevertheless the spirit of reactionary ecclesiasticism (not the Church itself) is opposed to the creative thought of religious philosophy, and denies its significance. The Orthodox world imbued with traditionalism does not yet understand that Christianity is ceasing to be, *par excellence*, the religion of simple people, and that it must turn towards more complex souls and discover a more profound spirituality.

Those who have known a limitless freedom of spirit, and who have returned in freedom to the Christian faith, cannot efface from their souls this experience or deny its existence. Freedom, with its own interior dialectic, that tragic destiny which it bears within itself, is an experience of a particular order inherent in Christianity itself. A man who has achieved a definite victory over the seductive temptations of humanism, who has discovered the hollow unreality of the deification of man by man, can never hereafter abandon the liberty which has brought him to God nor the definitive experience which has freed him from the power of evil. It is impossible to entertain the question of religious liberty upon any abstract ground, and to treat it from a static point of view. I have come to Christ through liberty and through an intimate experience of the paths of freedom. My Christian faith is not a faith based on habit or tradition. It was won through an experience of the inner life of a most painful character. I knew no compulsion in my religious life, and I had no experience of authoritarianism either in faith or in the sphere of religious devotion. Can one oppose to this fact dogmatic formulas or abstract theologies ? I answer No, for in my case they will never be really convincing.

Freedom has brought me to Christ and I know of no other path leading to Him. Nor am I the only one who has passed through this experience. No one who has left a Christianity based on authority can return to anything but a Christianity which is free. That is a truth born of vital and dynamic experience, which need not be linked up with any particular conception of the relations between grace and freedom. That is a question of an entirely different order. I admit that it is grace which has brought me to faith, but it is grace experienced by me as freedom. Those who have come to Christianity through freedom bring to it that same spirit of liberty. Their Christianity is of necessity much more spiritual, for it is born of the spirit and not of flesh and blood. The experience of the liberty of the spirit is one which nothing can efface, though it is true that arbitrariness in freedom is an evil to be overcome. Those whose religion is authoritarian and hereditary will never understand properly those who have come to religion through freedom, and through the tragedy immanent in their life's experience.

The religious life passes through three characteristic stages. Firstly there is the stage of objective religion which is both popular and collective, natural and social. Secondly there is the subjective stage which is individualistic and psycho-spiritual. In the third stage the opposition between the objective and subjective is transcended and the highest degree of spirituality is reached. A condition of the emergence of Christianity is this movement from an objective and popular religion to one which is subjective and individual. But in actual practice Christianity has not developed in this way; it has crystallized into a religion which is at once objective and popular, social and collective. It is precisely this form of Christianity which is undergoing a crisis at the present time. Religious life is passing through a subjective and individualistic phase which cannot be final and which is bound, in its turn, to give way to something else.

There are two types which confront one another all through the course of man's history, and they are types which find it hard to enter into any mutual comprehension. The former belongs to the collective, to the majority of society, which outwardly predominates in history; the other belongs to the sphere of "spiritual individuality", to the elect minority, and its significance in history is much harder to discover. These two types or states of mind may be called, respectively, the "democratic" and the "aristocratic". Now socialists are in the habit of affirming that throughout the course of history the privileged minority has exploited the disinherited majority. But there is another truth which, though at first sight less obvious, is more profound. The collective, the "quantitative" majority, has always oppressed and persecuted in history the "qualitative" minority, that which possesses the divine Eros and is composed of truly spiritual individuals whose lives are directed towards the highest aims. History works out habitually in favour of the average man, and of the collective. It is for such that the State, the family, the law, and our educational institutions have been created, no less than the whole fabric of custom and convention and the external organization of the Church. It is for such that knowledge and morality, dogma and cult have been adapted. It is the average man, the typical product of the mass, who has dominated history, and who has always insisted that everything should be done for him and that everything should be brought down to the level of his interests.

The right wing and the left, conservatives and revolutionaries, monarchists and socialists, all alike belong to this collective " democratic " type. The conservatives and the monarchists, who are the partisans of authority, are not less " democratic " than those who actually bear the name " democrats ". For this social collective, for mankind in the mass, the hierarchy of authority is maintained and ancient institutions are preserved. It is for them also that they are abolished, and for them that revolutions are made. Absolute monarchies and socialist republics are alike necessary to the masses, and are equally well adapted to the average man. It is, in fact, the average man who has dominated among the nobility no less than among the middle classes, the peasants, and the workers. It is never for the aristocracy of the spirit that governments are established, constitutions elaborated, and systems of learning or the technique of creation evolved.

Saints, prophets, geniuses, men, in short, who live on the higher planes of the spiritual life and who are capable of authentic creation, have no need of monarchy or republicanism, conservatism or revolution, nor yet of constitutions and educational establishments. For the aristocracy of the spirit does not bear the burden of history for itself. On the contrary it is made to submit to institutions, reforms, and systems whether old or new, in the name of the so-called people and of the collective, or, in other words, of the happiness of the average man. Evidently the aristocracy of the spirit, the elect who are alive with the divine Eros, belong to the fallen race of Adam and suffer in this way the consequences of the sin which they have to expiate. They cannot isolate themselves from " the world " and must therefore bear its burden, and serve the universal cause of freedom and of civilization. One can only deplore the pride of men who, while believing that they share in that which is highest, regard with contempt lesser men, and will not help the world to progress. But those who belong to the aristocracy of the spirit, who are not responsible for the qualities they possess, have in reality a bitter and tragic destiny in the world, for they cannot adapt themselves to any of the social conventions and systems of thought which belong to average men. They are a race of men who have always been oppressed and persecuted.

Those who are of the " democratic " type, whose orientation is towards the masses and the organization of the life of the collective, may be endowed with great talents and may number among them great men, heroes, geniuses, and saints. On the other hand those who are of the " aristocratic " type, whose interests are centred on other worlds and the creation of values which are of no use to the average man, may be completely lacking in genius and may be less powerful and talented than men of the former type. Nevertheless they possess a different spiritual organization which is at once more sensitive, more complex, and more subtle than that of the " pachyderms " of democratic breed. Such men suffer more from the " world " and from its ugliness, barbarity, and decadence than the men whose attention is focussed upon the masses and the collective. Even the great men of the " democratic " type possess this simple kind of psychology, which places them under the protection of that very world which is so inimical to spiritual personalities less adapted to it. Cromwell and Bismarck belong to this type, as in a certain sense do all men of action, as well as the great statesmen and revolutionaries. This simple psychological make-up can also be found among many of the Doctors of the Church, who have often belonged to the democratic type.

From this point of view the Gnostics are of particular interest. A great number of them truly belong to the " aristocracy " of the spirit, but they seem to have been unable to reconcile themselves to the " democracy " of the Christian Church. The question is not whether they were in the right. The Church had profound reasons for opposing and condemning them, for had the Gnostics won the day Christianity would never have been victorious. It would have been transformed into an aristocratic sect. But the question which Gnosticism raises is a profoundly disturbing one which is always with us, and has its importance even to-day. Revelation and absolute truth are both distorted and assimilated, according to the make-up and spiritual development of the persons receiving them.

Are we bound to consider as absolute and unchangeable that form of the Christian revelation which was intended for the average man ? Must the more spiritual, complex, and subtle type of man, who has in some measure received the great gift of Gnosis, be brought down to a lower level and perforce rest content with a reduced spirituality for the sake of the masses, and in order that he may share in the fellowship of the whole Christian people ? But is it possible to identify *sobornost* [1] with the popular collective ? Can the path which leads to the acquiring of the gifts of the Holy Spirit and to spiritual perfection and holiness be regarded as the sole criterion of spiritual life and the only source of religious Gnosis ?

The question of the religious significance of human gifts and giftedness is a profoundly difficult one. It was a question which the Gnostics had to face and it also confronted Clement of Alexandria and Origen, who were themselves also Gnostic Christians. It was a question too for Solovyov, and in our own time it is still there for the Christian consciousness to grapple with. It is part of the problematics of Christianity. Must the question of Christian consciousness and knowledge be solved in a " democratic " spirit with a view to the requirements of average humanity, or will a more " interior " solution, beyond the comprehension of the masses, be possible and allowed by authority ? " I have given you milk," says St. Paul, " not solid food, for ye could not bear it : and ye cannot bear it even now, for ye are yet carnal."

" Democratic " Christianity feeds on " milk ", because it attends to " the flesh ", and, moreover, the Church, is right in acting thus. But this fact does not solve the problem of the possibility of other fare for those whose spiritual hunger is still unsatisfied. The history

[1] In Russian the adjective *soborny*, corresponding to the noun *sobornost*, translates the word " Catholic " as applied to the Church in the Creed. As *sobornost* and *soborny* have a wealth of meaning not found in any equivalent English words, I have used them wherever the symphonic character of Catholic consciouness seems to be indicated. (Translator.)

of the human spirit testifies to the fact that the quality of spiritual aspirations and aptitudes is by no means proportional to the degree of perfection and holiness achieved, as the Church, on the whole, seems to think. There is a natural hierarchy of spiritual temperaments and gifts. In some beings the " spirit " predominates, in others the " natural " man. Nor does this mean that the former are more perfect and have obtained a greater measure of holiness and grace. The " spiritual " man has no right to be proud of the fact and to boast of his own superiority over the " natural " man. He is, in fact, no better nor is he endowed with greater merit. Such persons are, in the majority of cases, more unhappy in this world ; they are made to shoulder heavier responsibilities and they are torn within by greater contradictions. They attain with greater difficulty to a harmonized personality, and at the same time find it harder to reach a state of poise and balance in relation to the world which surrounds them. They are also more lonely. But the difference between spiritual gifts and temperaments is determined by God and not by man. The error of the ancient Gnostics which the Church denounced lay in their spiritual pride. They could not accept the fact that the good news of salvation and the coming of the Kingdom of God was brought by Christ for the whole of mankind. According to them those who were " spiritually minded " were eternally separate from merely " natural " and " carnal " men. The latter could not raise themselves towards a higher spiritual world and were condemned to remain in the shallows of existence. For them no redemption and salvation were possible. The idea that the lower might be transfigured and moulded into something higher lay outside the consciousness of the Gnostics, and it is for this reason that they never became real Christians. In this matter they really go back to the pagan Plotinus, although this last great representative of the Hellenic spirit would certainly have been opposed to them. As Vladimir Solovyov has very clearly shown, the whole process of the universe remained barren of results as far as the Gnostics were concerned, because of their inability to conceive of the lower being transformed into the higher. The

" spiritual " element, detached from the rest of the world, soars upwards to the heavenly places, while the " carnal " element lies imprisoned in the depths. But nothing is achieved as a result of this process for the " spiritual " element belongs, *ipso facto*, to a higher world and the " carnal " to a lower one.

The Gnostics did not understand the mystery of freedom, that is, of freedom in Christ, any more than they understood the mystery of love. There was in all this a hopeless dualism which upset the true hierarchy of values. The Gnostics were without a glimpse of the order of values upon which the world of the Christian rests, where the highest elements are organically linked with the lowest and thus assist the process of transfiguration and of universal salvation. Their interpretation of the hierarchic principle was a false one. The supreme Gnosis of " spiritual " persons is necessary for the salvation and transfiguration of those who are " carnal ". " Spiritual " persons must not remain proudly upon the mountain-tops in separation from the " carnal " world, but they must devote their energies to its spiritualization and to raising it to the highest levels. Moreover the source of evil is spiritual and not carnal. The Church has rightly condemned the pride of the Gnostics, their hopelessly dualistic point of view, and the unbrotherly and unloving attitude which they displayed towards their fellow men and the world at large. But the consciousness of the Church was absorbed by preference with the problems of the average man, of the typical product of the mass. The Church was anxious to guide aright the ordinary man and was preoccupied with the task of effecting his salvation. In condemning Gnosticism, the Church in some measure affirmed and made lawful agnosticism. Even the problem which had given rise to such sincere and tormenting perplexity among the Gnostics was regarded as one which could not and indeed ought not to be raised. The highest aspirations of the spirit, the thirst for a deeper knowledge of divine and cosmic mysteries, were brought down to the level of average humanity. Not only the Gnosis of Valentinian but also that of Origen was regarded as inadmissible and dangerous, in the same way as that of Solovyov is to-day. A system of theology was elaborated which became an obstacle to the higher Gnosis. Only the great Christian mystics succeeded in cutting their way through these well-nigh impregnable defences.

It must be recognized, however, that one of the difficulties connected with " the higher knowledge " in those days was that men could not disassociate it from its connection with the worship of demons, and here Christianity found itself entangled with pagan cults and with the " wisdom " of pagan religion. And yet it is possible for a higher Christian knowledge of spiritual things to exist which is at once more penetrating, less exoteric, and less moulded to the needs of the collective than that of the dominant systems of official theology. There is room in Christianity not only for St. Thomas Aquinas but also for Jacob Boehme, not only for the Metropolitan Philaret but also for Vladimir Solovyov. If spiritual persons ought not to boast of the heights they have reached, and to separate themselves from those of the " natural " and " carnal " order, it must not, on the other hand, be supposed that such men do not exist, nor must the aspirations of their spirit and their almost frenzied thirst for truth be denied satisfaction on the grounds that there is no such thing as " a higher spiritual know-ledge ". This would be equivalent, in an opposite direction, to that very destruction of the organic hierarchy of values which we have noticed already in Gnosticism. The world finds it easy to deny and despise every form of spiritual life, every aspiration of the spirit, and every sort of higher learning or knowledge. It readily asserts that such things are a clog upon the progress of the world towards its more complete organization and that they can perfectly well be left on one side. This is a point of view which is held and expressed by millions. Furthermore, nothing can be more heart-rending than to find the Church itself subscribing to that denial of the spirit which is professed by the State, a denial which at the opposite pole in atheistic Communism means the definite crushing out of the spirit and the extermination of every form of spiritual aristocracy.

" Quench not the spirit " it has been said ; but to deny the problem presented to us by the Christian consciousness is to forget this command. The task which has as its object the enlightenment of the world will ask for no diminution in the quality of the spirit. Thus the problem which above all is confronting us to-day is the problem of the spirit and of the spiritual life.

I should like what I intend to say in this book to be clearly understood. I recognize that there is something essential which I cannot put into words, and that I cannot adequately develop my inmost thoughts. It is very difficult to find a form of expression which exactly suits the essential idea as it appears to oneself. Everything I have written in this book is bound up with that most difficult of problems, the problem of the spirit, and, in conformity with the peculiar characteristic of my own turn of mind, I restate the questions that trouble me in a form which, though affirmative, also in a measure conceals them. I put my problems in the form of affirmations. But my thought as it moves within my own being is that of a man who, without being a sceptic, is putting problems to himself. In the solution of these problems of the spirit, or, rather, of the special problem of the relations between man and God, no exterior assistance is possible. Here no Elder, however advanced in the spiritual life, could be of any help to me. For the whole problem lies just here, in the very fact that I must discover for myself that which God has hidden from me. God expects from me a free creative act. My freedom and my creative activity are my obedience to the secret will of God, Who expects from man something much more than what is usually meant when we speak of His will. Perhaps one should be occupied not with abstract metaphysics about God, but rather with the concrete psychology of God. May it not mean, if we can so put it, a sweat of blood and agony for God when He sees in how slavish a spirit men interpret His will and how utterly formal is the manner of their obedience to it ? The divine will must be carried out to the very end, yet has not God willed that man should be also a free creator ? And does He not also love a Nietzsche who fights against Him ?

Introduction

My book is not a theological work, nor is it written according to any theological method. It belongs to no school of philosophy; rather it forms a part of " prophetic " as distinct from " scientific " philosophy, if one may employ the terminology which Jaspers has suggested. I have consciously avoided the language of the schools. It is a book of what may be called " free philosophy ", written in the spirit of a free religious philosophy and Gnosis. In it I have deliberately passed beyond those limits of philosophical, theological, and mystical knowledge so dear to the Western mind, as well in Catholic and Protestant circles as in the sphere of academic philosophy.

I regard myself as being a Christian theosophist, in the sense in which Clement of Alexandria, Origen, St. Gregory of Nyssa, Cardinal Nicholas of Cusa, Jacob Boehme, St. Martin, Francis Baader, and Vladimir Solovyov were Christian theosophists. All the forces of my spirit and of my mental and moral consciousness are bent towards the complete understanding of the problems which press so hard upon me. But my object is not so much to give them a systematic answer, as to put them more forcibly before the Christian conscience. There is no need to see in this book anything directed against the holiness of the Church. I may be much mistaken, but my purpose is not to introduce heresy of any kind nor to promote fresh schism. I am moving in the sphere of Christian problematics which demands creative efforts of thought and where the most divergent opinions are naturally allowable.

Paris—Clamart, 1927.

CHAPTER ONE

Spirit and Nature

I

WE have lost all confidence in the possibility and fruitfulness of an abstract metaphysic. For abstract metaphysics are based upon the hypostasizing of the phenomena of man's psychic life and of the material world, or still more of the categories of thought, that is to say, of the world of ideas. It is in this way that metaphysical spiritualism, materialism, and idealism come into existence. But concrete living realities have always eluded these metaphysical doctrines. Abstractions of reality or the abstract ideas of the knowing subject were taken as constituting the essence and fulness of reality. Abstraction and the hypostasizing of abstractions created both spiritual and materialistic metaphysical systems. Life was objectified as material or spiritual nature, and the essential category of knowledge of this metaphysical nature was that of substance. Being is an objective substance whether spiritual or material. God is conceived of as substance, a thing, nature. Ideas are also substances. Metaphysics in all its dominant tendencies was naturalistic and hypostasizing. It understood reality on the analogy of that of material objects. God and spirit are a reality of the same order as the material world. To the metaphysics of naturalism was opposed that of phenomenalism, which recognized the existence of phenomena but not that of noumena, and which denied the possibility of knowing life at its source.

Nineteenth-century German idealism played a preponderating part in the work of liberation from every form of naturalist metaphysics and marked a step forward in the knowledge of the spirit.

A   I

But Hegel's idealism hypostasized the categories of thought, and in spite of its claims did not reach the concreteness of the spirit. The metaphysics of the universal reason are just as far from the concreteness of the spirit as are those of naturalism. The hypostasization of the knowing subject no more achieves this end than does the hypostasizing of the known object. The reality of life eludes one whether one sets up as an absolute the concept of the subject or the nature of the object. But the metaphysics of German idealism are more dynamic than the naturalism of pre-Kantian philosophy, and it is to this fact that their undoubted success is due. This dynamic quality has its roots in the freedom achieved from all static and substantialist conceptions of nature whether material, spiritual, or divine. German idealism, in spite of all the defects of its " monophysitism " and its abstractness, has stated the problem of the philosophy of spirit and of the spiritual life and has cleared the ground for it. It has grasped this truth : that being is action and not substance, movement and not immobility, life and not thing. Naturalist metaphysics, which have taken the most varied forms, insisted on the subjection of " spirit " to " nature ", and have certainly had a powerful influence on the religious consciousness and on various systems of theology.

We have to recognize that theological systems bear upon them the fatal imprint of objective and naturalist metaphysics. They witness in fact to the naïve realism inherent in the naturalist conception of the world according to which God is an object, an objective reality, in the same sense as all other realities in nature. Thus God is known under the categories of nature, not those of spirit, and the reality of God is thus made to resemble that of material substances. But God is spirit, and spirit is activity. Spirit is liberty. The nature of spirit is the opposite of passivity and necessity ; it is for this reason that spirit cannot be a substance. The Aristotelian conception of God as *actus purus* deprives God of that interior active life, and transforms Him into a lifeless object. God is left without power, that is to say, He is no longer the source of movement and life. It is vain for Thomism to distinguish between the natural and the supernatural, for it is enslaved to a naturalist metaphysic of divinity. The supernatural is simply the natural on a higher plane and possessing a greater range. The very word " supernatural " is composed of two terms which in themselves have no positive implication. It is in vain also that philosophers strive to persuade themselves that a philosophy is possible which is absolutely free and independent of all living religion and of every sort of connection with " life ". Such attempts are instinct with a pride which inevitably brings its own punishment. In freeing itself from religion philosophy has only succeeded in passing under the yoke of science. There never has been and there never will be an absolutely autonomous philosophy which is completely emancipated from " life ". For philosophy is a function of life which knows life and sheds light upon it. The task of philosophy is fulfilled in and for life, and it is always dependent upon what is going on in its deeper currents. It is quite useless for philosophy to seek to disguise its true nature, for it is always positively or negatively religious. Greek philosophy, which has been considered to be the model of a completely autonomous philosophical system, was religious in its origins and its pathos, and it reflected the religious ideas of the Greeks. The philosophy of the Ionians can only be understood against the background of the Greek religious view of nature. Platonism is an enigma without Orphism and its mysteries through which men sought for freedom from sin and death. Plotinus and the Neo-Platonists are also confessedly religious. Again German idealism is linked on to Protestantism and to a particular stage in the inner development of Christianity. Kant and Hegel found themselves unable to break with Christianity in spite of the considerable differences between them and the mind of the Church. Even eighteenth-century rationalism as well as nineteenth-century positivism and materialism show themselves to be negatively religious by their very pathos. They reflect the struggle against God and against Christianity, and there is accordingly no real achievement of autonomy or of pure freedom. Rationalism, criticism, empiricism, all alike maintain a conflict with religion, but they cannot escape from the ties which bind them to life. Atheism is quite

3

as much a state of life and a religious conflict as faith itself. Almost the whole of the science of objective biblical criticism as well as that concerned with historical enquiry into Christian origins bring in their train a religious conflict, and are instinct with a negatively religious pathos. Such science has never yet succeeded in becoming a body of pure knowledge completely detached and apart. Unbelief is a premiss on which we may base our lives just as much as faith. Positivism has always had its own faith by which it was directed along the paths of knowledge and understanding. For philosophy is just spirit becoming conscious of itself, and it cannot claim to be independent of this or that spiritual aspiration. It is determined by the nature of spirit, by its quality, its aspiration towards higher or lower worlds, by the fact that spirit is restricted or free in its expression. We may conclude therefore that philosophy is determined by life, because spirit is life, and because the knowledge which spirit has of itself is the knowledge that life has of itself.

The orientation of spirit determines the character of consciousness, which in its turn decides the nature of knowledge. Knowledge is spiritual life, the activity of spirit. But the fact that philosophy depends upon life does not in the least degree justify relativism. In spirit and in life itself are revealed qualities from which spring the light of knowledge, and these qualities are not relative.

Knowledge is dynamic, and it has its destiny, its spiritual history, its great periods, and its stages of development. That which we call metaphysics or naturalist theology is the expression of the orientation of spirit, the reflection of the religious idea of the world, and it represents a period of great inner significance in the history of knowledge. Naturalist metaphysics and theology are not simply to be regarded as errors. They constituted an essential stage in the destined development of knowledge and in that of religious life. It is by this path that man travelled towards the light. It has not been realized before that spirit is creative becoming. Spirit has been conceived of as something achieved, that is to say, as something substantial. Naturalist metaphysics with its substances and rigid objects reflects, relatively it is true, certain aspects of being seen from a particular

4

orientation of spirit and structure of consciousness. It gives us our direction but cannot claim to give expression to the final and absolute truth about being. The process of hypostasization beloved of metaphysicians and theologians, and the objectification and erection into absolutes of certain moments of spiritual life, cannot acquire that perfect significance to which the dogmas of faith lay claim. These last are neither metaphysics nor theology but facts of spiritual experience and spiritual life.

A new spiritual orientation becomes possible, and a new movement begins, when naturalist metaphysics and theology with their rigid substances no longer express the truth about life, when spirit becomes self-conscious in a different way and is open to other influences, and when the spirit strives to free itself from bondage to substantial nature and from the yoke of objectivity to which it had yielded itself. Faith and the dogmas of religion cannot lose their absolute significance because of this, but they appear in a different light and new depths of meaning are disclosed in them. Religion cannot be dependent upon philosophy nor can philosophy limit and alter religion to suit itself. The mistake of modernism consists in the attempt to subordinate religion to reason and contemporary knowledge. In reality the problem is of a totally different order. Religion has always had its own philosophy and its religious metaphysics, which are in themselves only the expression of a particular epoch of man's spiritual development and not an absolute and definite embodiment of religious truth. Along this path of spiritual development, and even where the original spiritual life is concerned, modifications may supervene which will demand the use of different symbols to express knowledge and another form of consciousness. It is not philosophy which will change religion, but within the sphere of the original life itself certain events may demand the transcending of the naturalist and objective phases of the mysteries of religious life. Throughout the history of Christianity there have been those who were dominated by naturalist metaphysics and theology, for whom the mysteries of their religion bore different meanings. To rise above naturalist metaphysics and theology, and to get beyond that static conception of the religious life which sees in it nothing but substances and objects, is to understand what spirit and spiritual life really are and the true difference between spirit and nature. An abstract metaphysic cannot exist, but a philosophy or a phenomenology of the spiritual life is possible.

II

It is not the distinction between spirit and matter, between the " psychical " and the " physical ", which is the fundamental and ultimate one. Yet it is on this distinction that both spiritual and materialist metaphysics, alike naturalist, are based. Within " nature " a distinction is made between the " psychical " and the " physical ", while " spirit " is identified with " soul ". Religious metaphysics and theology indeed go even further by maintaining an opposition between the Creator and creation and between grace and nature. But in making this opposition, which from a purely pragmatic standpoint is of course profound, creation is naturalized and objectified, with the result that the Creator Himself is subjected to the same process. In the natural created world spirit is no longer to be found, for the world is completely naturalized and deprived of any deeper meaning. The Creator in opposition to the world is alone regarded as possessing in Himself any element of profundity, while spirit consists merely in the action of divine grace ; from which it follows that only the Divine Spirit has any existence. Man is regarded from the angle of naturalism, and though he is allowed to possess soul, he is denied spirit. Man is entirely a natural being and it is only by the action of grace that he becomes a spiritual being. Christian theology has generally affirmed that man is composed of soul and body, and that spirit is only the result of the work of the Holy Spirit within him. St. Thomas Aquinas in his philosophical system has given very clear expression, in a form now classical, to the antithesis between the natural and the supernatural.[1] Thomism

[1] See the works of contemporary French Thomists : *Réflexions sur l'Intelligence*, by Jacques Maritain ; *Le sens commun, la philosophie de l'être et*

definitely naturalizes the being of the created world and of man, thereby reducing philosophy to a mere natural knowledge of the natural. In this conception of the natural creature there is indeed a truth relative to the lines along which mankind had developed, a truth born of authentic experience. Nevertheless both the religious metaphysic and the theology which claim to state the final truth about being are naturalist. Not only nature but grace is naturalized because it is objectified and because it is put " outside " and not " in the depths ".

The antithesis between spirit and nature must be considered as primary,[1] and it is the mark of a dualistic metaphysic however established. This antithesis is affirmed in a sphere which is not that of objectified, that is to say, naturalized, being. Spirit is not reality and being in the sense in which nature is recognized as both real and existent. Moreover naturalist theology makes exactly the same mistake. The extreme dualism of Creator and creation, and of supernatural and natural, is allied here to an extreme monism with regard both to reality and being. The supernatural is on the same ascending scale as the natural, for it too is natural, though at a higher, and indeed an immeasurably higher, level. The antinomy existing between spirit and nature does not provide us with a dualistic metaphysic of being, but it introduces a distinction in the comprehension of reality itself. It is above all things the antithesis between life and thing, between liberty and necessity, between creative movement and passive submission to exterior impulses.

The first and most elementary point which must be established if there is to be any understanding of spirit is the distinction of principle between " spirit " and " soul ". Soul belongs to nature and its reality is of the natural order, for it is not less natural than body.

les formules dogmatiques, by Garrigou-Lagrange, and *The Philosophy of St. Thomas Aquinas,* by the best historian of mediaeval philosophy, E. Gilson.

[1] Some very interesting ideas on the subject of the distinction between spirit and nature may be found in the writings of the Italian philosopher Gentile (see his book, *Spirit, Pure Action*). But one is too conscious of the influence upon him of Fichte's idealism.

Yet soul is not the same entity as body or matter.[1] On the other hand, however, spirit cannot be opposed to body and to matter, as though it were a reality of the same order as that of body and of the material world. It is from within, from the depths, that spirit absorbs into itself body, matter, and likewise soul, but spirit belongs to another order of reality and to a different scheme of things. Nature is not denied but rather illuminated by spirit. Spirit unites itself inwardly to soul and transfigures it. The distinction between spirit and soul does not imply their separation. But all " psychologism " in philosophy is but a form of naturalism. Metaphysical spiritualism is not the philosophy of spirit but rather a naturalist metaphysic which tends to see the substance of being in the objectified phenomena of soul.

The distinction between spirit and soul is a very old one. It is to be found as early as Plato himself. St. Paul later gave expression to it with a certain profound religious pathos. " The ' natural ' man (*i.e.* the man who is mere ' soul ' or ' psyche ') receiveth not the things of the Spirit of God, for they are foolishness unto him, and he cannot know them because they are spiritually judged. But he that is ' spiritual ' judgeth all things and he himself is judged of no man." " It is sown a ' natural ' body (*i.e.* a body of ' soul ' or ' psyche '), it is raised a ' spiritual ' body." The categories of " spirit " and of " soul " are religious and not metaphysical, but the difference between them was exaggerated by the Gnostics and brought into disrepute. Yet the difference was recognized by Hegel, and he considered the knowledge of spirit as knowledge in its most concrete form. The distinction between spirit and soul is proper to all kinds of mysticism. All mysticism has as its object the instruction of the

[1] E. Röde in the course of his remarkable researches analyses the process by which the mind of ancient Greece conceived the idea of the soul and of immortality. The Greeks did not regard immortality as a natural attribute of the human soul ; immortality was enjoyed only by gods, heroes, and demons. It was only later that the soul was recognized as an integral part of man. But even in Christianity the existence of spirit was recognized only in God. Only the mystics see spirit in man. In romanticism spirit is imprisoned in soul. See E. Röde : *Psyche.*

8

spiritual man in the experience of the spiritual life and in the paths by which it is achieved. The spiritual for the mystics was never an abstract metaphysical category, it was the authentic life itself. The confusion of spirit and soul within the categories of objectified metaphysical being was one of the causes alike of a false naturalism and a false " spiritualism " in philosophy. Spirit is not a substance, an objective reality, in the same sense as other substances. Spirit is life, experience, destiny. A purely rational metaphysic of spirit is impossible. Life is only disclosed in experience. Spirit is life and not an object, and in consequence it can only be known in concrete experience, in an experience, that is, of spiritual life and in the accomplishing of its destiny. In the knowledge of spirit subject and object are not opposed to one another. Spirit as the knowing subject is at the same time the known object. Spiritual life is not an object of knowledge, it is the knowledge itself of spiritual life. Life is only open to life. Knowledge of life is life itself. The life of the spirit is not set over against knowledge as an objective thing, such as nature. Everything that transpires in the life of the spirit and in its own knowledge of itself lies within the unfathomable depths of spirit. Everything that takes place in the spiritual world takes place in me.

III

Spiritual life is the most real kind of life. Spirit and the natural world are utterly unlike one another, and exteriorly they do not meet and there is no interaction between them. It is only at inconceivably deep levels that spirit absorbs the world into itself and reveals it in a new light. Spiritual life is not an objective reality : still less is it something purely subjective. The attempt to comprehend spirit either objectively or subjectively is equally erroneous, for in the natural world the problem of reality is always a matter of subject-object relationship. Is there, for example, something real in itself and by itself, which corresponds to the world as we know it and conceive it ? Does physical and psychical being really exist ? Similarly, when we come to consider God from the naturalist point

9

of view, the question of the reality of God must be stated in the same form. Is there anything really existing which corresponds to our idea of God ? The ontological proof of the existence of God tends to deduce the divine reality of the idea of God from the idea of the Perfect Being. In a word all the proofs of the existence of God are naturalist in character and conceive of God as an objective reality similar to that of the natural world. In the same way all the arguments urged *against* the existence of God are naturalist and naïvely realist. For naïve realism consists precisely in transferring to the spiritual and divine sphere that quality of reality which properly belongs to the natural world. The arguments for unbelief which deny the existence of God and of the spiritual world are always linked to this naïve and naturalist realism.

The idea of God and the consciousness of God exist, but is there any reality corresponding to this idea and perception ? Here indeed we have the psychological question which is the bane of so many men and of so many philosophers, and it is on this point that the fiercest controversy rages between those who seek to prove the existence of God and those who would refute it. But the truth is that the reality of the spiritual world and of the divine do not correspond in any way to the reality of our sense-perceptions and our thoughts. The reality of the spiritual world and of God exist, not by virtue of any relationship or comparison with other things, but rather in their own right, as a reality of a different quality infinitely greater than the perceptions and thoughts of the world of psyche and the phenomena of the natural world. It is only in the experience of the soul and in the thought-life which is connected with it that men seek for proof of the existence of the divine and of the spiritual life. Within the sphere of spiritual experience such a question does not arise ; for spiritual experience is spiritual life itself, the reality of spirit, the reality of the divine. Spiritual realities are revealed in spiritual life, and in consequence doubt cannot arise on the basis of the relationship of the realities themselves to the revelations of the spiritual life. In the spiritual world objective realities do not correspond to experience, but spiritual experience is itself a reality of a higher order. Spiritual life is not the reflection of any other reality whatsoever, it is reality itself. It is impossible to ask the question whether there is a reality which corresponds to the experience of the great saints, to that of the mystics, to that of men who live on a higher spiritual plane, for that is a question arising only within the sphere of psychology, naturalism, and a naïve, and non-spiritual, realism. The spiritual experience of the saints, mystics, and those who possess a higher type of spirituality, is reality itself, the appearance and manifestation of the Spirit of God. Spirit is real existence, and spiritual life does in fact appear and manifest itself. It is a basic fact which can be undeniably established but which cannot be proved. Spiritual experience is the greatest reality in human life. The divine is manifested in it, but its existence cannot be demonstrated. God and His divinity, spirit and the spiritual, are given to us in the experience of life ; they reveal themselves but they cannot be established by ratiocination.

To ask oneself whether the reality of mystical experience is merely an illusion and the result of auto-suggestion is to detach oneself from spirit and spiritual experience. Such reflections belong simply to the sphere of soul and disclose the frailty of human thought when it attempts to grapple with the reality of life itself. For the man who possesses spiritual life and has experienced the things of the spirit, the question of their reality does not arise ; for him reality does not involve extrinsic relationships and exterior objectivity. There is nothing " corresponding " to my spiritual life, for it exists in its own right. My own spiritual life is limited, but there is a spiritual life which has no limits and this is in no sense something exterior to that which I enjoy myself. Nothing in the world can possibly prove to me that my own spiritual life does not exist. It may be that the world has no real existence, but my spiritual life, my experience of the divine, does exist, and it is a manifestation of the divine reality which is incontestable. Intense exaltation and ardour of spirit have a real existence ; they are, in fact, the very reality of the spirit and the manifestation of the spiritual world. Those who say that this elevation and fervour of spirit are an illusion and simply the result of auto-suggestion merely prove that they are without any knowledge of its existence. But the absence of spiritual life cannot prove that there is after all no such thing and that exaltation of spirit is an illusion. The divine Eros in me is the reality of the divine itself. The experience of the divine does not demand proof of its reality, for it is itself reality. In the spiritual world reality is not determined by anything given from without, for it is the result of a fervent orientation of the spiritual life itself. The discovery of reality depends upon the activity of the spirit, its intensity and its ardour. We cannot expect that spiritual realities should be revealed to us in the same way as objects in the natural world which are presented to us exteriorly like stones, trees, tables, chairs, or like the principles of logic. In the spiritual life it is the force of spirit which determines reality. In the realm of spirit reality is not extrinsic, for it proceeds from the heart of spirit itself. The question of illusion and of the non-reality of the life and experience of spirit only arises from the fact that they are identified with the life and experience of the psyche or soul.

But, it may be objected, is not spiritual experience after all only another name for the emotional life of the soul ? Is not the spiritual life purely subjective, and for that very reason unconvincing ? To which it may be replied that it is impossible to prove the existence of spiritual experience to one who knows nothing but the soul-life, for one cannot compel such a person, immersed as he is in an isolating subjectivism, to recognize the existence of spiritual realities. Spiritual experience alone can provide us with proofs of its existence ; only the manifestation in man of spiritual realities can prove to him the existence of these realities. The man whose life is not turned towards God cannot demand to be shown God or to have His reality demonstrated. The reality of God cannot be " inserted " or demonstrated from without. It is quite impossible to compel a man to recognize the reality of the spiritual life in the same way as he can be compelled to admit the reality of the natural world. The spiritual life must first reveal itself in a man. On the other hand the non-existence of the spiritual life is equally incapable of proof, nor can it be shown that spirit and God are illusions to which nothing in actual fact corresponds. Spiritual life is an extra-objective reality, it is not determined by time, space, or matter, it is an ideal reality as compared with that of the objective world, it is the reality of " initial " life.

Space and time, within which is the givenness of the natural world, are created by spirit and merely denote a particular condition of the spiritual world. The reality of the spiritual life is not determined by a series of causes in the physical and " psychical " world, it is determined at much deeper levels at the very heart of " initial " life. If there had only been a few men in history in whom a higher spiritual life had been kindled and in whom a thirst for the divine had been aroused, it would have been sufficient proof of the reality of spirit and of God, and the natural world would have been raised above itself.

How then can the existence of spiritual experience be proved and justified ? There are too many people who deny the qualitative originality of spiritual experience and who reduce it entirely to an experience of a purely psychological nature. But the objections urged against the possibility of the existence of spiritual experience are always based upon its absence in the lives of those who deny it. From the fact that the qualities of spiritual experience are unrealized by, it may even be, the majority of mankind, it by no means follows that this experience is either non-existent or impossible. The fact that the consciousness of a particular man is limited gives him no right to suppose that that limitation applies to all other human beings. If X or Y have never had any mystical experience that only proves that their experience is limited, but it does not give them the justification in any shape or form for denying it in the case of other people. A genuine, rational, and absolute empiricism does not give the right to set limits to experience. If in the experience of my life a particular thing is not revealed, I may not conclude that it will not be revealed to others. It is essential to have great humility and a greater consciousness of the limitations of our own nature, without extending them to human nature in general ; that is an

a lot like James

indispensable condition of knowledge, the *docta ignorantia*. But men of limited experience pride themselves on their limitations and actually propose them as a standard for others. The "average mind" creates a sort of tyranny and its limitations are identified with those of human nature in general. Spiritual experience is actually denied and the possibility of the miraculous and all forms of mysticism are rejected. This attitude finds its way into the religious life and even there affirms its positivism. This "average mind", which is the consciousness of the natural man, is in fact the affirmation of the natural world which it regards as the sole reality, while it denies at the same time the spiritual man and the world of spiritual experience. It manifests itself in a certain complacency and self-sufficiency, a "bourgeois" state of consciousness, which believes itself to be master of the situation in this world. Thus it comes about that both the existence and the experience of the spiritual world are revealed to us only by those who possess them. Those who do not possess this experience or who have not been able to rise to the perception of it have no authority to pronounce upon this subject. It is more fitting to speak of what one knows rather than of what one is ignorant.

Positivism erects ignorance into a very principle of knowledge and confers the prerogatives of the latter upon those who are destitute of spiritual experience. Positivism sees in this ignorance and in the absence of experience a guarantee of scientific objectivity. One presumes that it is just those who are without any religious experience or faith who can most fruitfully occupy themselves with the science and the history of religions. Surely there can be no more monstrous error. The spiritual sciences are distinguished by their very character from the natural sciences in that they require a real affinity between the knowing subject and the known object. The sciences which relate to spirit rest upon a foundation of spiritual experience, and a man who has not known this experience, and who has always denied its existence, can make nothing of them. The experiences of the spirit are not the same as those of the soul, which are purely psychological, being concentrated within the self and in which the personality remains self-absorbed. It is, rather, a liberating experience which opens the door into the spiritual and suprapersonal world, revealing those hidden links which bind the microcosm to the macrocosm. It corresponds always to a breach in the structure of the psycho-corporeal monad, to a leaving behind of self through immersion in the deepest levels of selfhood ; it is the mark of victory over all that divides and is extrinsic.

The denial of the reality of the spiritual world commonly proceeds from the fact that it is conceived of as metaphysical substance and objective reality. Now substance is a monad, finished and finite. A substantialist conception of the soul therefore involves its isolation from the spiritual world and renders spiritual experience an impossibility. Substance is thereby imprisoned in its own soul-world, for a world concentrated upon itself is always one of the soul and not of the spirit. For in relation to soul-substances spirit is in some way a transcendent reality set over against them and removed far above them. Man is placed in the natural world and subordinated to its laws. Metaphysical spiritualism still remains naturalist and is forced to deny the reality of spiritual experience. Besides this it is ordinarily connected with a rationalist theory of knowledge. The soul is regarded as a reality, analogous to that of the material world. Here we find ourselves up against a static view of the soul and of the world which places the dynamic of life outside the sphere of knowledge. In such a system of metaphysics God is regarded as an inert substance ; God, the world, and the soul are separated from one another, and in consequence spiritual experience becomes impossible, for it can only exist when man is regarded as a microcosm in which the whole universe is revealed and in which there are no transcendent limits isolating man from God and from the world. God is spirit, and for that very reason, therefore, cannot be substance. The nature of spirit is Heraclitic and not Parmenidean. Spirit is fire and energy.

It is not true to suppose that personality must necessarily be a substance and therefore limited and isolated in character, or that to deny that it is a substance involves the negation of personality.

15

Concrete and living personality has actually no resemblance to substance, for the nature of personality is essentially dynamic. Personality is above all a spiritual energy of qualitative originality, a spiritual activity which is the very centre of creative power. The existence of personality does not necessarily imply its separation from God and the world. To admit the existence of the suprapersonal element within personality does not mean the denial of personality, but rather its affirmation. The existence of personality, in the truest sense of the word, is only possible through the manifestation in it of spiritual principles which assist in liberating it from a state of isolation while uniting it to what is divine. Personality is the divine idea, God's design. To conceive of personality as a naturalist substance is tantamount to limiting its possibilities of spiritual development and experience. Every form of authentic, religious, and mystical experience testifies to the fact that personality is not an isolated substance, but, rather, that it conceals within itself unheard of possibilities, and that there lies before it a world of infinite extent containing vast stores of spiritual energy.

In the spiritual life the personal and supra-personal are united in a somewhat paradoxical fashion, for, while the personal is not annihilated or denied, it is raised to the level of the supra-personal. Being reveals itself in its inner nature as life, spiritual experience, destiny, divine mystery, and not as mere substance or objective nature. Spiritual life is dynamic in the highest degree, bearing the closest resemblance to life in the more general sense. Leibniz's view of the human soul as a closed monad, and of God as a supreme monad existing on the same plane as others, is a good example of naturalist metaphysics, though containing certain elements of a true spiritual conception.

In the life of the spirit there is no absolute heterogeneity and there are no impenetrable substances opposing to one another insurmountable barriers. Substances are the creation of space, time, and matter, and souls which are in bondage to the corporeal world acquire its character. Substantiality is only a state of the world representing, as it were, both its enslavement and its "ossification" and not its interior and essential being. This natural world is but the child of hatred and division, which in its turn engenders bondage and servitude. But spirit is liberty. This definition of Hegel's remains unshakably true, confirmed as it is by the spiritual experience of humanity. Constraint and exterior limitations result from the rejection of life, as it were, from without, and the adoption of an " extrinsicist " attitude towards the things of this world. For that is exactly what a " thing " is, namely, that which is outside ourselves and not within. Spirit, on the other hand, always remains in the inner depths, for it is itself " depth ", it is within not without, and its life can never owe its origin to the purely external, the superficial, and the extrinsic, or in fact to anything which is lifeless and impenetrable. Depth is the symbol of spirit. The natural world, in itself, knows nothing of this depth, for it can only be revealed in the spirit by regarding this natural world as the symbol of the spirit and as an interior moment of its mystery. But the true understanding of the spiritual world demands a delimitation of its sphere in relation to the natural world, the resolution of all its confusions, and the refusal to accept that naturalizing of the spiritual world which is proper to metaphysics.

Just as there is in the life of the spirit nothing extrinsic or capable of division or separation, so also there is no place in it for that antithesis between unity and multiplicity upon which the life of the natural world is based. Unity is not opposed to multiplicity as to some exterior reality, for it penetrates the latter and creates its life while at the same time leaving it as multiplicity. " I am in my Father, ye are in me, and I in you." " It is no more I who live, it is Christ who lives in me." It is on this interior victory over the extrinsicity of the one and the many that spiritual life is based. The antithesis between the one and the many has its origin in space, time, and matter, which are simply the result of the Fall and of separation from God. Spiritual life is lived outside time, space, and matter, although it is bound to them as symbolic images of the interior divisions of spirit. In spiritual life and experience there is given to me the interior unity of my destiny as well as that of the world, and of God Himself. In spiritual experience my destiny ceases to be divisible and isolated, which means that spiritual life reaches the highest degree of concreteness. The reality of nature is an abstract and divisible reality in which neither integration, completeness, nor absolute unity, can be found. In the spiritual life, however, there is integration and completeness, while every degree of being is transformed and transfigured as a part of it. At the same time also hatred and heterogeneity are ended and objectivity is banished. The spiritual life is not detachment from the life of the natural world, and the meaning of the asceticism and self-purification which are indispensable to it is not to be sought in this direction. Abstract spirituality is spirituality in a very imperfect form. Infinitely superior to this is that concrete spirituality which transfigures and enlightens the life of the world.

Spiritual life is not a reality of the same order as the physical or " psychical ", or yet again as that of the natural world, for it absorbs into itself the whole of reality, regarding it as the symbol of itself and as the reflection of its own various phases, of all that happens within it, and of the general trend of its development. Spirit is by no means opposed to flesh ; rather, flesh is the incarnation and symbol of spirit. The spiritual life is a historical life, for the latter is concrete in character. But the exterior reality of history is only the image of spiritual life under the conditions of time and divisibility. Everything without is but the symbol of that which is within. Matter itself is only the " symbolization " of the inner states of the spiritual world, that is, of its hatred and its divisibility, and is not a substance existing by itself. It is therefore not a metaphysical spiritualism or an abstract spirituality that I would affirm, but rather " symbolism ", that is, a spirituality which is concrete.

Spiritual life cannot be discovered by any psychological analysis of the workings of the soul, for psychology is a science which treats of nature and not of spirit. Spiritual life, in so far as it is a special quality inhering in the life of the soul, must always elude the science of psychology. The majority of psychological processes must be related to the phenomena of the natural world, for they are con-

18

nected with the body and material things, they occur in time, and have a certain relation with space, taking place as they do in the sphere of isolation, divisibility, and externality. Psychology analyses spiritual life in an abstract fashion, and therefore finds itself faced with a purely abstract reality. But spiritual life is concrete and demands concrete study, since it is manifested in the knowledge of a concrete spiritual culture, and not in that of the abstract elements of the soul-life. The knowledge of spiritual life is a historical science which deals with culture and not a natural science, if we may use Rickert's [1] imperfect terminology. The materials of a philosophy of a spiritual life are contributed by the spiritual life of humanity itself as it has developed in history ; it is always with life as concrete that religion, mysticism, philosophy, science, morality, and artistic creation are concerned. And what a thing it would be if men would only reflect upon the great achievements of the spirit and the noble manifestations of spiritual life ! But this historic, spiritual, experience of mankind can only be approached from the angle of spiritual experience, through the medium of which alone a comparison becomes possible.

The soul of one who intends to acquire this knowledge is able to do so in so far as there flows into him something of that unique spiritual life which is manifested in the history of the spirit. In the highest flights of spiritual culture there is revealed the genuine experience of spirit, and through these there is acquired a spiritual life which is supra-temporal. But the man who is seeking the spiritual life must join himself to all those who have participated in the development of the knowledge of spirit in history. That is why a philosophy of the spirit inevitably contains within itself a traditional element and presupposes fellowship with tradition. An isolated individual by himself cannot know, still less commence, the spiritual life.

[1] We owe to Dilthey some sound and interesting ideas on the subject of the science of spirit. See his *Einleitung in die Geisteswissenschaft.* But he is wrong in excluding the possibility of a philosophy of history which must be placed at the very core of spiritual philosophy.

The point from which Descartes begins his philosophical system cannot be considered as a favourable one so far as the knowledge of spiritual life is concerned. The anterior recognition of the authenticity of the spiritual life in mankind is an indispensable premiss to the philosophy of that life. Plato, for example, is not only for us the subject-matter of our investigation, for we share with him a common life and experience and we meet him in the inner depths of our spiritual life. The spiritual world does not reveal itself in the exterior world of nature, but rather in the human spirit and in the spiritual life of mankind, and the knowledge of it presupposes a " soborny " [1] spirit in humanity.

This " sobornost " is something completely outside the sphere of psychology and metaphysical spiritualism, for it is a genuine spiritual culture. The lives of the saints, the great creative efforts of the pioneers of religion, and the great thinkers and artists which constitute the monuments of man's spiritual life, are of infinitely greater importance than the deductions of purely abstract thinking. The spiritual life has been manifested in a real and concrete form in the spiritual experience of humanity, and it has bequeathed to us innumerable evidences of its creative energy. Here we have, not a manifestation of nature, but rather a manifestation of spirit. The profound intuition of religious tradition consists precisely in its having discovered the spiritual life not in external nature or in abstract thought but in " sobornost ".

IV

Religious life is a spiritual experience not a psychological one, nor is it a reality which comes to us from without. Spiritual life is the awakening and the manifestation of the soul. That is why the religious life is an acquiring of kinship, a victory over heterogeneity and " extrinsicism ". Religion can be defined as an experience of intimacy and kinship with being. In the religious life man ceases

[1] Cf. footnote page xiv Introduction.

to be aware of his strangeness and isolation. But intimacy and kin-ship with being are only possible within the sphere of spiritual experience ; in the domain of the life of the senses and the soul being suffers from isolation and disintegration. When being appears to us strange and remote, and when it fills us with a sense of oppression, then we are no longer in the spirit, for we are in an isolated world of mere body and soul. That is why spirit is not only liberty but also love and the union and interpenetration of the different parts of being in a unique and concrete life. That is also why Christianity is the revelation of the life of the spirit.

It is in the spiritual world and not in the natural and " psychical " that the drama of being and the mutual relations between God and man and between God and the world transpire. Nevertheless spiritual life does not at present imply a life of perfection which is free from sin. Within it there lie hidden those sources of sin and those divisions which give rise to our natural world. The spiritual life is capable of a falling away from its true nature. In it there take place and are revealed all those religious occurrences which remain invisible in the natural life. Spiritual life is a symbolic life, that is to say, one which unites two spheres, which unites God and the world, and in which there are numerous encounters and conflicts. It is according to a spiritual plan and within the spiritual life that the creation of the world took place ; God desired another self and a reciprocal answer to His love. Then came the Fall, and the New Adam was the restorer of fallen human nature. All these occur-rences within the spiritual world are only symbolically reflected in the world of nature and of history. Naturalist theology which at the same time confuses and separates the two spheres of being, regards all the events of the spiritual world as taking place upon this earth, that is, within time and space. The world was created by God in time as a fact of the natural order, an objective occurrence, Paradise existed on this earth between the Tigris and the Euphrates, and it was this that produced the Fall.

Such is the character of that naïve biblical science which by re-flecting a primitive naturalism has failed to reach any conception of the difference between nature and spirit. Scholastic theology by assimilating itself to this " infantile " biblical science regarded the mysteries of the spiritual life as events in the natural order. The natural world appears so "obdurate" that religious thought has great difficulty in escaping beyond its limits, and finds it hard to conceive that this natural world is itself but the reflection of the spiritual world, an event in spiritual life, and that even this very obduracy is a spiritual state which may not endure. The Fall could not have taken place in the natural world, because this world is itself the result of the Fall. The Fall is an event in the spiritual world, and in this sense it is anterior to the world, for it took place before time began and, in fact, produced time as we know it. It is mere intellectualism to suppose that realities exist apart from spirit and are, as it were, external to it. But intellectualism means a false theory of knowledge.

The ideas and beliefs of religion bear no relation to the abstract truths of metaphysics, for they are linked to the facts and to the events of the spiritual world which are revealed in spiritual experience. These facts and these events have no resemblance to the categories of abstract thought nor to natural substances. Religious ideas and beliefs can only be expressed through the categories of spiritual experience and by the inner tragedy of life and of destiny. We see spiritual life as a paradox. The events in which the deepest reality of being is revealed are paradoxical for reason and the rational consciousness and give rise to antinomies because they are incapable of reduction to concepts. In the religious life, in so far as it is genuinely spiritual and not natural, there is revealed to us an identity of contraries, namely the identity of monism and dualism, of unity and multiplicity, of immanence and transcendence, of God and man. All the attempts which have been made under the various systems of naturalist and rationalist theology to eliminate the paradox of spiritual life are entirely exoteric, and whatever value they possess is purely temporary and pedagogic. They correspond to the naturalist stage in the history of the religious consciousness and in the apprehension of Christianity. Theological naturalism is a naive form of realism in which spirit, regarded as objectified in nature, is thrust back again into the natural objective world ; but the true revelation of the spiritual world involves a supersession of naturalism which is achieved in the sphere of religious mysticism. For the mystics everything happens at the deepest levels, or in other words within the spiritual world. All religions may be divided into two classes, the natural and the spiritual. Christianity is the religion of the spirit, though not in the sense in which Hartmann employs the phrase.[1] For example we cannot help appreciating the spirituality of India, but it is, nevertheless, an abstract spirituality which ignores concrete personality.

A naturalist attitude towards God, conceived of as a metaphysical transcendent Being, an immobile Substance, represents the latest form of idolatry in the history of the human spirit. Monotheism can indeed be a form of paganism. Man in bondage to the natural world conceives of God as a great exterior force, as a " supernatural " power in every respect comparable to " natural " power. God is merely the highest and most perfect of all forms of power, or in other words the projection of natural being. This supreme Power demands to be appeased. The transcendent God avenges Himself like the gods and men of the natural world. But Christianity appeared in the world to conquer decisively both idolatry and servitude. It affirmed the religion of the spirit and the spiritual life, the religion of the Trinity as the home of the spirit in which God reveals Himself as a Father who loves all and is near to all. But natural humanity has put the mark of naturalism upon both the perception and the revelation of Christian verities. The very dogmas of the Christian faith, which are really mystical facts and discoveries of the spiritual world, were translated by the various systems of theology into the language of reason and of the natural world. But God is life and cannot be expressed in terms of categories of thought which were framed to deal with nature, for He differs from the realities of the natural world. He cannot even be conceived of as

[1] E. Hartmann's *Die Religionen des Geistes* is simply antichristian monism.

" supernatural ", for the " supernatural " is a category which itself resembles too closely the " natural ". God is life and He can only be revealed in spiritual life. But the mysteries of divine life can be expressed only through the interior language of spiritual experience, by a living language and not that of objective nature and reason. As we shall see later on, the language of spiritual experience is inevitably symbolic and mythological, and it is always concerned with events, with real mutual contacts and with the destiny of things, nor do we find here any trace of rigid categories or substances. The ideas of the soul and of the spirit have themselves a mythological origin.[1] All truths relative to God must be shaped in the depths of the spiritual life. The God of religious naturalism still remains an object of idolatry. He represents the deifying of nature in its latest form, alike when He is conceived of in the perspective of an extreme theism and when He is regarded as created, and as not divine.

The relation between God and man is an inward one revealing itself in the spiritual life, and not an exterior relation between the supernatural and the natural manifested in this world. So at least the Christian mystics used to understand the matter, and it is to them that we must go to learn the knowledge of the mysteries of the spiritual life. For this life is made known to us not in a theology which has never yet freed itself entirely from naturalism, but in mysticism which is always absorbed in the spiritual world. Christianity has always flourished while it remained at this deep level and found its true nourishment here, but, when it has become externalized and lived on the surface through an assimilation with the natural world, it has degenerated and fallen into decay.

V

The question of the criterion of truth, and of the principle underlying the sanctions of the knowledge, of truth, and of authority in

[1] H. Cohen is right when he speaks in his *Ethik des reinens Willens* of the mythological origin of the idea of the soul, but he draws from this false conclusions, for he wishes to exclude all forms of mythology.

matters of faith, is not a spiritual question. It is, rather, character-istic of that type of reflection proper to the religious and scientific thought which arises within the sphere of purely natural existence.

The setting up of hard and fast distinctions and antinomies does not belong to the life of the spirit. It is only the soul which can regard itself as opposed to the known object and can interrogate the criterion of its own knowledge. But no object can be set in oppo-sition to the spirit, and in the spiritual world the question of a criterion does not arise. Only an object which appears to us as something alien and impenetrable can raise a question as to the criterion of our knowledge of it. In the spiritual life, however, there are neither objects of knowledge nor of faith, because here there is possession, an interior rapprochement, a kinship with the object perceived, an absorption of the object at the very deepest levels. The criterion of truth where the spirit is concerned lies in the manifestation of the spirit itself, the intuitive contemplation in the spirit of this truth as of reality and life itself. Truth in the spiritual life is neither the reflection nor the expression of any other reality, for it is reality, the spirit in the inner life. In the spiritual life there is, in the gnoseological sense of the word, neither object nor knowing subject.

In the spiritual life that life is itself everything and everything is identified with it. Within it there is neither the idea nor the per-ception of God ; there is just the revelation of God Himself and the manifestation of the divine. That is why in the spiritual life there is no such thing as an isolated soul or an isolated subject. Spiritual experience is precisely the escape from a state in which objects are everywhere extrinsically opposed to one another. Truth in the spiritual life is the life itself. Those who know the truth become truth in it. " I am the Way, the Truth, and the Life." That is neither an abstract truth nor a mere statement of a relationship. The truth is also the way and the life, and there can be no question as far as the truth is concerned about authority and outward criteria, for no guarantee is demanded. Truth is revealed in the way and in the life. In the spiritual life we discover that knowledge is something which transpires within us, an illumination of being and of life itself. Being is not opposed to knowledge as an object, but within being itself the light springs up which illuminates its darkness. In the natural world, which is the result of separation and division, the knowing subject is separated from the known object ; it is separated from being. The true quality of spirituality is reached when there is no longer any separation, when the knowing subject finds itself at the very heart of being. The spiritual man lives here on the deepest levels and from his knowledge comes illumination.

It is in the spiritual life that truth itself is found, for it can neither be perceived nor known from without. Reflection is entirely a function of the objective world ; it seeks laboriously for the criteria of truth outside the truth which it fails to possess, and outside the life which is lived in truth. But outside this truth and on a lower plane it is impossible to find such criteria. The truth itself is its own criterion. The question is sometimes asked whether a criterion of our faith in God and of our knowledge of Him can be discovered. But such a question can only be asked by the " natural " man. For the criterion of our faith and the knowledge of God cannot be found apart from God and His manifestation in us and our relations with Him. He cannot exist in this lower natural world. In demanding an authoritative criterion which will convince us of the existence of God and enable us to discern what is divine in the world, we are looking for support not to God Himself and to divine reality, but to the lower natural reality of the exterior world. Thus man is engulfed by the natural world and the spiritual becomes enslaved to the natural.

Authoritarianism in the religious life is precisely the search for criteria of truth in a lower world to serve the purpose of a higher one. It is the attempt to draw from the natural world the standards of the spiritual world, a process which shows that the ultimate ground of confidence is exterior rather than interior, belonging to the constraint of what is natural rather than the liberty of what is spiritual. The infallibility of the Pope and Kantian gnoseology are in a certain sense phenomena of the same order, namely, the search for a justification and a criterion of truth apart from its actual possession. "Papo-caesarism" and "Caesaro-papism" are alike extreme manifestations of this quenching of the spirit by nature and of the search for visible evidences of the divine in tangible reality upon which greater reliance is placed than upon spiritual life and experience. Thus the lower becomes a criterion of the higher, and the truth is perceived not by the way and the life, nor yet by truth itself, but merely by an "extrinsicist" reflection of it. But in the spiritual world, the Truth, that is, God Himself, is alone the authority and the sole criterion of the truth, and man possesses it because it lives within him and because of his experience and his relations with it.

In the spiritual world everything happens in a manner different from that in which things occur in the natural world; yet these two worlds mingle with one another and are interdependent. Man is a complex being, for he is at once spiritual, supra-natural, and psycho-corporeal, and also natural. Man is the point where two spheres intersect, the place at which they meet, and he belongs to two different orders. It is for this reason that human life is infinitely complex and difficult. There is a spiritual man and there is a natural man, and yet the same individual is both spiritual and natural. The spiritual world is manifested in the natural or "psychical" man as his peculiar quality, but the natural man does not disappear in the process. It is for this reason that the spiritual life is not exhibited in man in all its purity. It is not given to man to raise himself easily above the natural level of his being and to deny himself. The way of the spiritual life is an arduous one, and no man can regard himself as entirely spiritual. Every man is organically related to the whole structure of the universe and has his duty towards the natural world. To imagine in one's pride that one is entirely spiritual, as the Gnostics did, is to imagine a lie in the sight of God. Man must work for the illumination and spiritualization, not only of his own soul and body, but also of the soul and body of the whole universe. The spiritual must not be separated from the "psychical" and natural; rather, it must illuminate it and spiritualize it. That is why Christianity was unable to be entirely spiritual in character and had also to concern itself with the soul, the " psychical " element. Herein lay the great truth of the Church's descent into the sinful world. Christianity is at work in the natural world and it is from this very fact that there arise those obstacles which it has encountered in the course of its history. The correlation of spirit and soul has been seldom achieved in the history of Christianity, and Christian truth has been distorted in the natural world. But this weakness is of course common to all forms of activity in the world.

In various systems of theology we do not find, generally speaking, any opposition between nature and spirit, but rather between nature and grace, and between the natural and the supernatural. Spirit possesses no independent properties ; or, rather, it is incorporated with nature and is scarcely to be distinguished from soul, that is to say, it is naturalized ; or, again, it is referred to the Divine Being and regarded as the grace of the Holy Spirit. For the process of naturalization consists precisely in banishing, as it were, the divine and the spiritual from the created world, so that man comes to be regarded as an exclusively natural being, as a psycho-physical monad. Man is allowed to possess soul and body, but the spirit is relegated to a transcendent sphere in which it is a mere appendage of Divine Being. Spirit finds itself exiled from the depths of man's being into a far-off transcendent sphere, into the world beyond. Thus it is that it is only from without that spirit is conferred upon man. It is only by grace that he can become a spiritual being for he is by nature exclusively psycho-corporeal. Thus there is set up an extreme dualism between the Creator and creation and between the state of grace and the state of nature. Man and the world are essentially and in origin non-spiritual and non-divine.

Such metaphysical and theological doctrine, however, which denies the divine image in man, never played a prominent part in Christianity. Christian mystics have always held that man is spiritual and the pathway into the spiritual lies all around us and within. That system of theology and metaphysics which is based on an extreme dualism between the Creator and creation, between grace and nature, and which denies the spirituality of man, is not the only possible doctrine definitive of being within Christianity. It is in reality nothing more than a particular phase in the history of the human soul, corresponding to a certain moment in the spiritual development of man which reflects a particular experience of the spiritual life. The absence of spirit and of spiritual life in man is not a normal condition, but rather a state of sin and a debasement of the divine image, and in such a state spirit assists man as a transcendent and extrinsic principle. The empirical personality immersed in the natural world and separated from God finds itself condemned to a divided existence. Thus spirit is always in such circumstances an "extrinsicism".

The consciousness of sin is transformed into the consciousness of the transcendence of spirit. Sometimes, indeed, we get the impression that official theology and the precepts of the Church refuse to consider man as a spiritual being at all, and thus guard him against any temptations towards spirituality. "Natural" Christianity is even recognzed as being truer and more orthodox than the Christianity of the spirit. To be conscious of oneself as a spiritual being is to challenge the accusation of pride ; on the other hand to recognize oneself as unworthy to possess spirit or spiritual life is to qualify for a title to humility, and it is on this basis that Christian positivism and a bourgeois spirit suitable to the consciousness of the average "natural" man was originally based. Spirituality is regarded as the particular preserve of saints, ascetics, and elders. The spirituality of men who have not reached the higher levels of perfection and who have not acquired the grace of the Holy Spirit always provokes suspicion, for it is not regarded as having its origin in God. Thus there is a distrust of all spiritual life which does not find a place within the conception of the Church regarding the acquisition of the gifts of the Holy Spirit. Spirit is the Holy Spirit, the Third Hypostasis of the Holy Trinity, and there is no other spirit, nor can there be. No spirit exists in man and the consciousness of spirit within him is due to a lack of humility and to pride. To be thoroughly wrapped up in the life of the soul and body is at once more pious and more humble. For theologians and Church dignitaries the higher spirituality was often more suspect than the sins of the body and the soul. Here, indeed, we are confronted by a very difficult problem. The Church forgave the sins of the flesh and was infinitely indulgent towards the weaknesses of the soul, but it manifested the most implacable rigour towards the temptations and the pretensions of the spirit. This was the reason for its intransigent attitude towards Gnosticism, and towards any theosophical tendencies within Christianity, as well as for the distrust of the creators of a spiritual culture, philosophers, poets, spiritual reformers, and so forth. This was the origin of a kind of Christian materialism and positivism, Christianity being proclaimed as a religion of the soul and not of the spirit.

Such was the character of Christian exotericism. In theology it found static expression in the doctrine of grace and nature, in the doctrine of spirit as exclusive of grace, and in that of man and the world as entirely natural. Thus the religious mysteries of life and of experience were objectified, were symbolized in a purely external manner, and materialized. Life and experience, the Way and the Spirit, were transformed into substances, into abstract truths and principles of metaphysical theology. God and the life divine were regarded as static and inert things, and the mystery of the spiritual life within Christianity was unrecognized. The course of my spiritual life, its very essence, becomes in this way exteriorized as rigid substance and objective existence.

There was, however, in the distrust which the Church manifested towards the spirit and spiritual life an essential truth, for pride and satisfaction are sins which are inimical to the truth as it is in Christ. There is, indeed, a false spirituality, in which there is no real acquiring of the spirit. We find it frequently, for example, in contemporary theosophical circles. There is also a false mysticism and a purely fictitious spiritual knowledge. There is again a pretended spirituality which has undergone no purification and which has been vitiated by its contact with the natural world. It is this sort of spirituality, from which demonolatry has not been expelled, which used to exist among the Gnostics. There is also a form of mysticism in which certain states of the soul and even of the body are regarded as spiritual. It is necessary to try the spirits, for we cannot give credence to every spirit. More must be expected of the spiritual than of the "natural" man. Spirituality makes no claims ; in fact it imposes a task upon us. There are regions of the spiritual life which must at certain times remain closed to us, for they are inaccessible to the "natural" man. Nothing is more lamentable than to claim a measure of spiritual elevation or a continuous degree of spirituality which is in reality nothing of the kind, a claim which is at the same time accompanied by a contempt for the simple life of the soul and for the "natural" man. The Church is right in its insistence upon simplicity and humility, but a simple spiritual attitude does not necessarily imply the existence of a spiritual life. In the practice of the Church there was, undoubtedly, an essential truth. Nevertheless a theological system, which denies the qualitative originality of the spiritual life and the fact of its inherence in man, cannot lay claim to possess absolute and incontestable truth. It is exoteric and can be superseded. Spiritual life is victory over sin. The subjection, therefore, of sinful human nature to sterile ontology is a form of mental aberration. Man becomes worthy of the spiritual life in so far as he is in effective communication with it.

VI

The mystics all tell us that there is a spiritual rebirth. We are born originally as the children of the first Adam, the progenitor of natural humanity, and this birth involves disunion and separation, and at the same time submission to necessity and to generic sonship. But the second birth is spiritual, by which we become the children of the second Adam, the Head of spiritual humanity, and this is a birth into union and into liberty. Here is victory over the constraint of material and generic necessity, for it is rebirth into Christ and into a new life. The first birth involves a purely external form of existence, while the second means that all is now lived on a deep, interior, level. The spiritual second birth in its pure form is known to the mystics, and they have given descriptions of it, pointing out for us the way by which it is approached. But a rebirth into Christ is possible for every Christian and the paths of the spiritual life are open to all.

Christianity is the religion of the spirit and of the new birth. " Except a man be born again, he cannot see the Kingdom of God." Every Christian, then, must be born again. " The wind bloweth where it listeth and thou hearest the sound thereof, but thou canst not tell whence it cometh or whither it goeth. So is everyone that is born of the Spirit." " But the hour cometh, and now is, when the true worshippers shall worship the Father in spirit and in truth : for the Father seeketh such to worship Him. God is Spirit, and they that worship Him must worship Him in spirit and in truth." And St. Paul says, " And as in Adam all die, even so in Christ shall all be made alive." " If ye are led by the Spirit, ye are not under the Law."

But the Christian revelation of the spiritual life and of the new birth, of the worship of the Father in spirit and truth, operates within the sphere of natural humanity, among the children of the first Adam, and among average men. It thus becomes embodied in the forms of a Christianity which is at once spiritual and " natural ". Christianity, a religion which is not of this world, suffers humiliation in the world for the sake of the general mass of humanity, and so spiritual life becomes merely symbolic and is no longer realized in practice. Christianity, the religion of a truth which is not from below, by entering into the world in order to save it, is always running the risk of becoming weakened and losing its true spirit. Herein lies its dramatic quality, the origin of its success and of its activity, as also of its failure in history. Christianity must perforce descend into the natural world, while remaining the truth which is not of this world, that is, the truth of the spirit and of spiritual life. The whole tragedy of spiritual humanity lies in this fact. Spirit is not of this world, for spirit is precisely that which is not of this world. To live in the spirit and to attain to the spiritual life is to cease to love the world and the things that are in the world. But the spirit is shed abroad in the world, only to leave it again, and then to descend once more, taking upon itself a symbolic form within the world. The world is the symbol of that which transpires within the spiritual sphere, the reflection of God's " abandon " as fulfilled in the spirit.

To live in the world compels all men to partake of the common destiny, to become involved in the sin which exists even among spiritual persons, and makes it impossible for them to stand apart and work out their own destiny. For there is a unity in the process of the universe and in human destiny. " Love not the world, neither the things that are in the world. If any man love the world, the love of the Father is not in him." Thus writes St. John. But he also says, " He that loveth not his brother abideth in death ". " He that loveth not, knoweth not God, for God is love." Here we have the whole painful inner contradiction of Christianity. Love for our brother and not merely self-love compels us to live in the world and to share his destiny. Yet love for our brother may mean the enslavement and subjection of our spirit to the world. Christianity has lived through this tragic antinomy but finds no easy solution of it. But such is man's destiny. Man is condemned to a reciprocal activity, to the attraction and repulsion of the spirit and of the world, and of spiritual and natural humanity.

Spiritual and mystical apprehension within Christianity is truer and more real than the objective and "psychical" apprehension which is given symbolic expression on the natural and historical plane. The inner depths of Christianity and the mysteries of the spiritual life are revealed within Christian mysticism. But these depths remain hidden so far as theological systems and Christian rationalism are concerned, for the mysteries of the divine life are rejected by them or else conceived on the analogy of the natural life. Christianity is the revelation of the mystery of spiritual life, within which all is mysterious, and the hidden depths of being are unveiled as a divine mystery ; within it all is life, all is vital tragedy.

The mystery of Redemption and of Calvary is an inner mystery of the spirit which is accomplished in the secret depths of being.

Calvary is an interior moment of life and of spiritual development, the submission of all life to crucifixion and to sacrifice. The Christ is born in the depths of the spirit, He passes through life, dies upon the Cross for the sin of the world, and rises again. This is the inner mystery of the spirit. It is revealed in spiritual experience, and everyone who is born of the spirit knows it ; it is described for us by the mystics as the way of the inner life. The Christ must be revealed in the interior life of the spirit before He is revealed in the exterior world of nature and history. Without the inward and spiritual acceptance of Christ the truths set out in the Gospel remain unintelligible facts of the empirical, exterior, world.

But the Christian mystery of the spirit is objectified and ex-teriorized in the natural world and is symbolized in history. Christ is born, He dies, and rises again, not only in the depths of the spirit but in the natural, historical, world. The birth of Christ, His life, His death upon the Cross, and His Resurrection are authentic facts of the natural world. That which we read in the Gospel really happened in history, and in space and time. But the reality of the truth which happened in history, in space and time, is the same in this case as in that of all reality in the natural world, that is to say, it is a symbolic reality reflecting the happenings of the spiritual world.

But it must not be supposed from this that the events of the Gospel story are mere symbols, while other events are realities for which historical science can vouch. All historical events which have taken place in the natural objective world are but symbolic realities and reflections of the spiritual world. The life of Alexander of Macedon and of Napoleon, the emigration of peoples, and the French Revolution are only symbolic realities and merely possess the character of reflections.

But the life of Christ revealed in the Gospel symbolizes and re-flects events of the spiritual world of an importance, a unity, and a determining value, infinitely greater than anything else in world history. These facts bring before us the very essence of the spiritual in its initial mystery and divine significance. It might be said,

34

indeed, that the Gospel history is meta-history, that is, mythological in the sense in which the whole of history is, that is to say, in the sense that the inner mystery of the spirit is symbolically reflected upon the natural and objective plane.

A conception of this kind has nothing in common with docetism, which did not recognize the reality of Christ's human life and for which His sufferings and death were illusory. Docetism, so far from avoiding a naturalistic conception of Christianity, introduced into it a false spiritual philosophy which impoverished by undue simplification the richness and the mystery of the spiritual life. For docetism and monophysitism spiritual and divine nature are real in the naturalist and objective sense of the word, while the life of the flesh and human nature are merely illusory appearances. We, on the other hand, affirm that the life of the flesh in this world possesses symbolic validity and that man is quite as real as God Himself, not only as a symbolic reflection, but also in the spiritual world itself. All forms of docetic and monophysite heresy set the spirit and the flesh in opposition, and this opposition is bound up with the naturalization and objectification of the spirit.

In reality the " flesh " of this world is completely absorbed by the spirit and symbolically reflects its life. The spiritual conception of Christianity, while concerned with the inner mystery of life, does not reject the " natural ", objectified, conception, but, rather, gives to it an inner significance by illuminating it and penetrating it deeply from within. The esoteric approach does not mean that we must reject or eliminate the exoteric, for its object is not to combat the latter but to render it more profound. Esoteric and mystical Christianity does not rule out the exoteric Christianity of an objectified and more external type ; its aim is only to understand it more deeply and to illuminate it from within, for it recognizes, even in the lowest forms of its objectification, the reflections of authentic spiritual realities. If we may so put it, the " carnal " element represented by exoteric Christianity is not less real than the " spiritual " element, for both reflect symbolically and to an identical degree the true realities of the spiritual life and its divine mysteries.

The events of the spiritual world, though subject to the limitations neither of space nor time, are reflected symbolically in space, time, and matter. This is the reason why the material and carnal elements in history of Christianity have acquired a sacred significance. For sacred significance means symbolic significance. The " holy flesh " exists in so far as it is " symbolic flesh ", but it is not " matter ", that is, a substantial reality in the naïve, realist, sense of the word.

Spiritual and mystical Christianity is poles apart from the attitude of those iconoclasts who deny the symbolical reflection of the spiritual in the natural world ; for really profound Christianity always sees in material objects the symbols of the spiritual world and finds itself in perfect agreement with the mind of the Church on this subject. All Christian worship, with its " carnal " externalism, is the genuine reflection in symbolic form of the mystery of the spiritual life and as such cannot be rejected by Christianity. There is, indeed, a certain type of " spiritual " Christianity of Protestant origin (exemplified in the writings of Schleiermacher) which ignores realistic symbolism, and recognizes only an idealistic and psychological form of symbolism which contributes only to disunion. It is one of the features of a naturalistic Christianity that by opposing " spirit " to " flesh " it ends by placing both on the same level.

A true Christianity of the spirit recognizes a concrete form of spirituality, capable of symbolical expression and embodiment at all levels, which gives a real and ever-deepening meaning to things, which suppresses nothing and denies nothing. But the philosophical spiritualism which is commonly described as " spiritual Christianity ", and has produced a number of sects of that name, is really nothing but an abstraction. It represents what one might call a mutilation, not to say an " amputation " of Christianity, for it thrives on negation and suppression.

The most profound mystics who attained to the Christianity of the spirit were never " spiritual " Christians in the limited and sectarian sense of the word. Master Eckhart, one of the greatest of Christian mystics, who interpreted Christianity as a mystery of the spirit and as an inner, spiritual, way of life, remained a Dominican and a fervent Catholic, recognizing, as he did, every concrete embodiment or symbolization of spiritual reality. Mysticism had a great effect on Luther, which manifested itself as much in sectarian circles as in certain movements within Catholicism. The most daring of the German mystics, Angelus Silesius, for whom Christianity was undoubtedly a mystery of the spirit, who aspired even beyond the divine, and to whom we owe the phrase, "Without man God Himself could not exist even for an instant", was a fanatical Catholic who never broke with the symbolism and "incarnationalism" of Church Christianity.

VII

Spiritual life does not mean an abstract and indeterminate unity : rather, it is within this life that the concrete, that is to say, qualitative, unity is revealed. A monistic interpretation of spirituality, such as to be found in Indian religious philosophy and in certain forms of German idealism (as, for example, in Hartmann's religion of the spirit), is simply a form of monophysite heresy, for it involves the denial of the reality of human nature, coupled with the affirmation of the divine as the alone-existing. But in spiritual life and experience two natures are given us, namely, God and man. The spiritual world is precisely the meeting place of divine and human nature, and this is its basic and original characteristic. Within the depths of the spiritual life there is unfolded before us the religious drama of God's dealings with man, and man's with God. Without God and within human nature alone there can be no spiritual life. That quality of life which is called spiritual can only exist in man if there is something to deepen his life and towards which he can raise himself, that is, it demands for its existence a higher and a divine nature. Did man possess merely his own human nature he would be cut off from the spiritual life. On the other hand, if there were nothing but the divine nature, if God had, as it were, no other self, there would be no original phenomenon in the spiritual life and all would disappear into an abyss of undifferentiated abstraction.

The Divine Being must exteriorize Itself in order to penetrate its other self, that is, the being of man. Within the sphere of concrete spirituality the personality of man is neither eliminated, nor reduced, nor yet obscured in an indeterminate unity. Two natures, God and man, exist side by side in the very depths of the spiritual life.

Human personality provides no evidence for an individuation of spirit effected by matter. Individuation, the manifestation of personality, is effected by spirit itself within the depths of the spiritual life, for it is a property of that life. In the spiritual life beings, personalities, act and manifest their powers. Spiritual life is the arena in which concrete beings encounter one another. Within it there are no abstractions or abstract principles, there is, simply and solely, life. Beings, and not substances, are revealed in the spiritual life, and the Christian revelation is the revelation of the spiritual life of being. In Christianity there is only a series of beings in a graded hierarchy. Beings, human personalities, with their eternal destiny, are given without any intermediary in the sphere of spiritual experience. But we cannot elaborate abstract ontological and metaphysical doctrines about the nature of beings and that of personality.

The truth is that the mystery of human personality can be expressed only in the language of spiritual experience and not in that of abstract metaphysics. The philosophy of pluralism is equally abstract and rationalistic and corresponds as little to the life of spirit as monism ; metaphysical spiritualism in its own way is not less defective than materialism ; Duns Scotus protested against the doctrine of St. Thomas Aquinas regarding the individuality and immortality of the soul, and showed that this doctrine really amounted to the denial both of the immortality and the very existence of human individuality. Nevertheless the scholasticism of Duns Scotus, though in certain respects more refined than that of St. Thomas, was open to equally well-founded objections.

The mystery of the Christian revelation concerning human personality and its individual destiny can be expressed neither through the medium of Thomism, nor through the pluralism of Leibniz with its monadology, nor yet through the monism of Hegel or of

Hartmann. It is neither scholastic philosophers nor metaphysicians but rather the mystics who have given expression to the mystery of the divine-human life and of its ways and ends. The experience of the saints gives to us a deeper understanding of human personality than the whole of metaphysics and theology put together. None of the attempts which have been made to base the certainty of a future life on the substantiality of the soul are at all convincing, nor can they bring us any real proof of it. They have their origin in a naturalist outlook upon the mysteries of the spiritual life, and life itself eludes this mode of thought. Human personality is immortal not because the human soul possesses substantiality, nor because the idea of personality necessarily involves the assumption that it is immortal, but because there is a spiritual experience of eternal life, because that spiritual life is divine-human, and because Christ exists as the source of that life. It is proved and demonstrated by the manifestation of immortality itself in the spiritual life. Immortality is indeed a spiritual and religious category, and not a category of naturalist metaphysics. It is not a natural property inherent in man, it is an acquisition of the spiritual life, a result of the new spiritual birth in Christ Who is Himself the source of eternal life. The immortality of man is not a prolongation into infinity of his metaphysical nature ; it is a rebirth into a higher life whereby man becomes the offspring of the second Adam. It is eternal life which has conquered death. Immortality, that is, eternal life, is the revelation of the Kingdom of God and not merely another name for the metaphysical nature of being. Thus it is that Christianity does not regard the immortality of the soul in the same way as naturalism does. Rather, it points us to the Resurrection as an occurrence in the sphere of spiritual life and the victory of spirit over corruption and death.

The Christian Church lays bare the falsehood which underlies all monophysitism, that is to say, the error which distorts the whole meaning of the spiritual life by leaving no place for the mystery of the two natures, divine and human, and which expresses itself in a rationalist way through monistic theories. The unity and duality of

39

the two natures which cannot be confused lies at the very heart of the mystery of religion and of the original experience of things spiritual, and this can only with difficulty be expressed by a rationalist metaphysic which always runs the risk of falling into the abstractions of either monism, dualism, or pluralism. The mystery of the eternal life of the two natures is the mystery of Christ, the God-Man. Even the greatest of the scholastic philosophers were incapable of expressing this mystery in the language of substantialist metaphysics and theology. Pagan Greek thought maintained only the immortality of the gods and of the divine principle ; but though immortality could also be attributed to heroes and demi-gods, it was not regarded as the common heritage of man. And here we find the expression of an undoubted truth. The natural man, the psycho-corporeal monad, does not possess immortality as an inherent quality. Only spiritual life merits immortality, for only spirit possesses the quality of eternal life.

Immortality means an entering into the life of the spirit and a laying hold upon it. It means the restoration of spirit to man who has been separated from it. The source of immortality is in God and not in nature, and it is impossible to conceive of immortality apart from the life in God and apart from the divine. The way to eternal and immortal life is given to us in Christ. Eternal life is the Kingdom of God, and without it and without the Holy Spirit there is no immortality or eternal life. In the Kingdom of Christ there is revealed an immortality for man of which neither Jews nor Greeks could conceive. Spirit is restored to man and thus he ceases to be a self-contained, psycho-corporeal, monad. Moreover, this restoration and this entry upon the spiritual life does not imply either the suppression or the mortification of soul and body, but, rather, their transfiguration, their illumination and spiritualization, their absorption into the higher spiritual life. That is why Christianity teaches the resurrection of the flesh. To understand this mystery there is no need to employ naturalist metaphysics nor to regard the flesh and the body as a substance. The " flesh " is a religious category, that is to say, it is spiritual and not naturalist. Moreover, the attempts which have been made to express the mystery of the flesh and its resurrection in terms of naturalist metaphysics are always exoteric, for they involve a subjection of the mystery of Christianity to material nature which is closely bound up with the collective symbolizations of the masses. The mystery of the resurrection of the flesh is a spiritual and concrete mystery and it can only be expressed by life itself, that is to say, by spiritual experience. The naturalism, not to say the materialism, of certain systems of theology reveals only one thing, and that is that at certain levels of spiritual life, spirit is conceived of as transcending man, while man himself is regarded as a merely natural and psycho-corporeal being.

The fundamental distinction between spirit and nature, as between realities and orders of being of different quality, does not imply any denial of the unity of the cosmos, or a separation of spiritual man from the life of the universe. The cosmos, the divine world, and the divine nature are only revealed in spiritual experience and in spiritual life. In fact it is only in the spirit that man encounters the cosmos, and man is not separated from it but, rather, united to it thereby. Concrete spirituality contains within itself the fulness of cosmic life in all its varying degrees. It is only in the interior, spiritual, world that the cosmos is presented to us in all the beauty of its inner life. In the natural world man in his isolation regards the cosmos as exterior to himself, as something strange and unfathomable, as an object capable of subjection to a " technique " and of being studied by mathematical and physical science. He sees in the cosmos his own subordination to lower sense-elements.

The contemplation of beauty and order in nature is in itself a form of spiritual experience and a means of penetration into the inner life of the cosmos which is manifested in spirit. To love nature, whether it be the mineral, vegetable, or animal kingdom, is already to have experienced the spiritual, and to have triumphed over the sense of disunity and " extrinsicism ". The mystical and theosophical doctrine of nature such as we find in the writings of Paracelsus, Jacob Boehme, and Francis Baader and in part at least in Schelling, looks at nature from the spiritual point of view, as the inner life of the spirit, and as the merging of nature in spirit and spirit in nature. The cosmos is regarded as a particular degree in the hierarchy of the spirit and as the symbol of its inner life. The naturalization of spirit in Boehme is only the counterpart of the absorption of nature in spirit. The natural and cosmical elements are also the elements which make up the soul of man and they are united in the spiritual world. The microcosm and macrocosm are revealed in spiritual life, not in separateness and in " extrinsicism ", but in unity and in interpenetration.

When man lost Paradise it meant his separation from the cosmos and from the divine nature, and at the same time the formation of a strange, new, exterior nature bringing with it dissension and subordination. But the winning of Paradise means the return of the cosmos to man and of man to the cosmos, a consummation achieved only in a really spiritual life and in the Kingdom of God. This experience begins in the experience of love and in the contemplation of beauty. A purely external concept of nature means a hardening and a drying-up of the spirit. For the cosmos is life, and not merely a collection of hard, material, objects and inert substances.

The acosmism of an abstract metaphysical spiritualism is totally foreign to Christianity which comprehends a concrete spirituality containing within itself the plenitude of the divine. The " world ", in the Gospel sense of the term as something which we have to treat as hostile, is not the same as the divine creation, the cosmos, which on the contrary we are expected to love and with which we are to be united. The " world " or " nature " in the above-mentioned sense does not stand for the cosmos, but, rather, for the deadly torpor of sin, and the " hardening " produced by the passions which involve subordination to the lowest elements and the distortion of all that is divine.

VIII

In the course of the long struggle which is waged in the natural world on behalf of the higher spiritual life and in the name of God,

of love, of liberty, and of knowledge, the means employed to
secure these spiritual realities often become ends in themselves, and
here we have the origin of the greatest of all tragedies in the
spiritual life.

In the history of the world nothing has ever been fully realized,
in the true and ontological sense of the word, because the means to
which recourse was had in order to attain to the spiritual life obscured in some measure the ends to be achieved. Mankind was
pent up within the defences of the spirit without ever being able to
attain to the spiritual life itself. In their endeavours to reach God
men made use of every kind of profanity, as, for instance, when hate
and animosity were appealed to for the realization of the purposes
of love, and violence and oppression were employed in the service
of liberty. In civilized societies the state and the external organization of the Church gained the upper hand by methods which were
totally opposed to the true goals of the spiritual life and of the divine
world. Violence and hate were justified by an appeal to the lofty
ends which they were intended to achieve. God Himself was
forgotten in favour of the approach designed to lead men to Him.
Men set themselves to hate in the cause of love, to use compulsion
in the name of freedom, and to become practising materialists for
the vindication of spiritual principles.

In the external organization of the Church, in its canons and in
the doctrines of its theology, God was, in a measure, relegated
to the background, and often disappeared completely in the process. Freedom perished in the organization of the state, love was
buried under a mass of custom and tradition, while in the sciences
and the academies created for them the zeal for knowledge was
extinguished and the very end of knowledge was lost to sight. On
every side the outworks of the spiritual life effectually concealed
from men's gaze the life itself, and so they acquired a quite independent existence. The processes employed in the attainment of the
spiritual life, the means by which its principles were safeguarded,
were in truth an obstacle to its realization. The symbols of religion
underwent a hardening process and ended by becoming substitutes

43

for reality itself. The natural world, the kingdom of Caesar, triumphed over the spiritual world, the Kingdom of God, by means of its own acts of violence, its internal divisions, and by the methods of struggle which it employed, and, the victory once achieved, the spiritual world was rendered indistinguishable from the natural world. Men had proposed to enter the Kingdom of the Spirit not by spiritual but by material means, and they ended by forgetting it altogether. By ceasing to be interested in it they lost even the faculty of perceiving it.

Tolstoy, in spite of the limited rationalism of his religious outlook, had a real understanding of this tragedy and felt profoundly the great lack of proportion which existed between means and ends in religion, between the methods with which men busied themselves and their real appreciation of the meaning of life, between that which justified itself in actual existence and that which gave authority to this justification. The organization of the world and of mankind, based upon a forgetfulness of the life of the spirit and upon the use of spiritual principles as the mere instruments of this organization, can never bring men to the enjoyment of the spiritual life. Spirit cannot allow itself to be employed simply as an instrument, for nothing can come of such a process since it is utterly opposed to the very nature of spirit.

In the spiritual life there can be no antithesis between the means and the ends of life, for such an antithesis only exists in the natural world. A disharmony of this kind is the creation of evil, and it cannot be explained by reference to the sinfulness of human nature and the necessity of this disunion for victory over sin. Such an attempted justification is far from the truth and contains an element of hypocrisy which constitutes an obstacle in the way of attaining spiritual life.

As men move towards the attainment of the spiritual life there is an identification of means with ends ; the methods by which the divine objective of life is realized, as for example the exercise of love, freedom, and knowledge, are themselves the realization of the divine, in love, freedom, and in an enlightened understanding of the true nature of being. But the barriers must be thrown down in order that the way which leads to the spiritual life may be opened up. For the latter remains inaccessible to man, not only because of his sin and his subordination to the lower natural world, but because of those things which, though they are supposed to preserve the spiritual life, are in truth so little conformed to its principles. A religious life founded on respect for outward observances, an academic science, and the hallowing of pagan customs, is simply an edifice of lies and shams, an obstacle to the development of the true spiritual life and of the knowledge of divine reality.

The world of nicely calculated symbolisms conceals that of the spirit and of true reality, and the symbols themselves lose all connection with what they are supposed to represent. The natural world is the symbol of the spirit, but the latter can be mistaken for the reality itself and can become hardened and materialized. Thus the centre of gravity of life, and, most serious of all, that of the religious life, is shifted into the hard, material, world to which there has been accorded a symbolic sanctity. Man is not absorbed by the contemplation of the infinite and the spiritual, but is thrown back into the natural and material world with all its limitations. It is here that he places the centre of his life and he becomes united to it by numerous invisible attachments.

Man creates for himself a species of Church-positivism which is at once distrustful and fearful in its attitude towards the spiritual world. For such positivism the other world is simply a means to the consolidation and subjection of this world here below, since it dreads any changing and softening of the natural order and fears every revolution of the spirit. It does not believe that it is capable of manifesting those events in the spiritual world which require a new symbolic expression and a new embodiment " in the flesh ". For positivists regard the symbolic expression of the spirit as absolute and unchangeable and consider the ancient symbols as sacred, since spirit is for them something inert and static, a substance and not life itself.

But the ancient forms of symbolization and of spiritual technique can in fact become out of date and useless, for we have to remember that the nature of spirit is dynamic. Thus the search for some new system of symbols becomes inevitable, in order that the means may be better adapted to the ends in view and the symbolism employed may correspond more closely to the realities of the spiritual world. Even God Himself has been regarded as finite, for sinful humanity is ever haunted by the fear of the infinite. This obsession finds its reflection in a finite symbolism.

Terrible upheavals and revolutions, manifestations of evil hitherto unknown, are inflicted upon Christendom solely in order that this sinful world, having betrayed what is sacred, may at last move towards the realization of a true and free spiritual life. At the present time barriers which divide and restrict are crumbling into ruin, everything is changing and dissolving in the natural historic world, and even its rigid symbolism is being subject to alteration. It is therefore a propitious moment to put the Christian life into serious practice, and to bring about a new relation between the means and ends of life, between symbols and the realities which lie behind them. At a time of catastrophe a process of ascetic purification takes place within history in the absence of which there can be no spiritual life whether for society or for the individual. The fate of Christianity depends upon this, for a new type of spirituality must arise in the world.

Either a new epoch in Christianity is in store for us and a Christian renaissance will take place, or Christianity is doomed to perish— although this cannot for a moment be admitted, since we know that " the gates of hell shall not prevail against it ". Christianity simply cannot return to the state it was in prior to the catastrophe which has occurred. The image of man has become defaced as a result of the disasters which have overtaken the world, and his lost dignity must be restored to him. But man's dignity is not determined by his situation or by his power in the natural world but by his spirituality, that is to say, by the divine image within him, by the Eros which turns him Godwards towards the life in truth, goodness, and beauty, that is, towards the spiritual life. For this spiritual

46

life is precisely the life in God, in truth, goodness, and beauty, and not in the natural isolation of soul and body. God is immanent in spirit, but He transcends psycho-corporeal man and the natural world. In the future Christians will have to prefer God to those defences of the basic principles of life which really belong to this world and only succeed in obscuring that which they are intended to establish.

IX

Spiritual life is infinite and contains within itself a variety of quality. It is something far greater than that which, canonically speaking, is usually called " the spiritual " in Christianity. Spirit cannot be identified simply with the Holy Spirit, the third Hypostasis of the Trinity. Spirit is the sphere in which the divine and the human are united and it includes all man's aspirations after God and the whole spiritual culture of man. The grace of the Holy Spirit, in the theological sense of the word, is a particular quality of spiritual life and constitutes its highest aspiration. Revelation which represents the profoundest element in this spiritual life is the revelation of the Holy Spirit and the hope of a future spiritual life which will transfigure the natural world. It is the hope of a more fruitful activity of the Holy Spirit.

But spiritual life is revealed by degrees and in a diversity of qualities. All the intellectual, moral, and artistic life of humanity, all fellowship in love, forms a part of it. The nature of the Holy Spirit, dogmatically speaking, has always been insufficiently expressed in the thought of the Church. The Fathers and Doctors of the Church, as well as the general religious consciousness of Christendom, have failed to get beyond the idea of subordination in the doctrine of the Third Person of the Trinity. This applies particularly to Catholic theology. But indeed it had to do so during the period when Christianity was making its first attempts to influence natural humanity. Nevertheless the incomplete revelation of the nature of the Holy Spirit bears witness to the fact that the

47

most profound elements of the spiritual life are only imperfectly disclosed in Christianity, that the spirit is still imprisoned in the soul, and that men fail to realize that all spiritual life and all genuine culture have their roots in God and in the Holy Spirit.

In the Holy Spirit God becomes immanent in the world and in man, for the spirit is closer to man than God the Father and even than God the Son, in spite of the fact that in theology the doctrine of the Spirit may be less prominent. It is only in the new birth that the true, that is, the non-subjective and non-psychological, nature of spiritual life is revealed. The natural man possesses also some of the rudiments of the spiritual life, but they lie hidden in the soul and their real meaning remains obscure. And yet, though submerged in his racial environment and primarily living the life of " flesh and blood ", the natural man does possess as well a religious life and there is a possibility of his salvation. But the real depths of the spiritual life are not revealed in traditional Christianity for spirit is opposed to race and to racial customs. To bestow a symbolic and sacred character upon racial traditions is to give a false revelation of the Christian life and of the life of the spirit. The man who before all else desires a religious justification for his traditional customs and the carnal elements of his being is not yet spiritual.

To subordinate the infinite spirit to the finite natural world leads inevitably to the enslavement of the spirit. In a hereditarily acquired Christianity man holds on before everything else to that which is of " flesh and blood ", to his person, his family, his nation, and his state. He attaches no little importance to the religious justification of tradition and custom where these things are concerned. But spirit is being, not this mass of codes, habits, and customs. The life of the spirit consists precisely in breaking free from these things and in penetrating into true being. The man who is Christian by tradition desires before everything else that his own " flesh and blood " shall be recognized as sacred. A spiritual life which transcends race and custom appears to him as something abstract and as an abandonment of life. He sees the spiritual life and the spiritual man as a positivist does. In fact this subjection of the infinite spirit to the limitations of flesh and blood in the natural world, this enslavement of the divine to the racial element, is nothing more nor less than positivism in the religious life.

Thus it is we find treated as an absolute that which is merely temporal in a particular form of symbolism which has come to be recognized as unique and definitive. It is thus that monarchy has been regarded as sacred and that the life of the Church has been subordinated to it. This too is one of those cases in which Christianity sinks beneath the burden imposed upon it till it is itself engulfed. It exchanges the wings of the eagle for the claws of the lion. It succumbs to the domination of the natural world. Man is not recognised as a spiritual being and is excluded from the life of the spirit with its limitless horizons. The spiritual life is reserved for saints, while the rest of mankind see themselves condemned to remain natural beings belonging to this or that particular level of existence, who from birth to death achieve nothing but the symbolic sanctification of their earthly life.

Religious positivism is quite as much an obstacle to the spiritual renaissance of humanity as that of a materialist order. Both involve the enslavement of the human spirit, and the big spiritual revolution which is bound to take place in the world will mean the liberation of man from this slavery to his own " flesh and blood " and from his oppression by collectivity. The greatest spiritual leaders have looked forward to this revolution and have already had a prophetic vision of it. They looked forward to a coming of the Spirit upon Christianity. But the road to the higher levels of spirituality and spiritual freedom is an arduous one, for it is that of purification and creative inspiration which involve an ascetism and sacrifice which is not only individual but more than individual, being in fact both historic and social. We live in an age in which on every side the Christian world is being summoned to asceticism and to sacrifice, and where even to dream of the old sanctification of " flesh and blood " would mean their being accorded a position of more importance than the truth of Christ.

The fact that within me the spiritual life is born, that I seek for

God, that I aspire to the divine, and that I love God in this life, is of all facts the most important and is the very justification of existence. No power on earth can persuade me that that is an illusion, a product of auto-suggestion, and not life itself. For in truth it is the only life, without which all is but dust and phantasy. We do not live in a real world, but in a world where existence and non-existence are confused, and our spiritual awakening is an awakening to true existence.

X

The Platonic tradition is more favourable to the philosophy of spirit and the spiritual life than the Aristotelian. Scholasticism, in the person of its most illustrious representative St. Thomas Aquinas, made use of the teachings of Aristotle in order to affirm that man and the world belong exclusively to the natural order in opposition to the supernatural. According to him they are created by God, but not rooted in God. Divine power does not function directly in creation. The action of God upon the world operates by means of grace and by the official channels which have been established by the Church. God is conceived of as *actus purus*, without potentiality, for potentiality is an imperfection of created being, a proof of its confusion with non-being.

Thus we have a system of thought which at once restricts and isolates the natural world and in which the spiritual nature of man is denied. But the patristic literature of the East in its classic form managed to preserve the Platonic tradition. Thus it was easier for these writers to recognize that man and the world are both rooted in God and the divine ideas, and to admit the existence not only of a terrestrial world and humanity but also of a celestial. If Aristotelianism is extremely unfavourable to a symbolic conception of the world, Platonism on the other hand is capable of providing the necessary foundation for it.

In Platonism the earth is only the symbol of the heavenly and spiritual. Man is at once an earthly and heavenly, a natural and supernatural and spiritual being ; in him two worlds meet. Spirit-uality and the spiritual life are inherent in human nature in so far as it is the image of the divine. Spiritual life and spirit are immanent in man and not transcendent. Christian thinking is not necessarily subordinated to those ancient thought-forms which give rise to naturalist metaphysics and theology, but a philosophy of the spirit is capable of becoming a true Christian philosophy.

CHAPTER TWO

Symbol, Myth, and Dogma

*" All that we see is simply the reflection and the
shadow of that which is invisible to our eyes."*

VLADIMIR SOLOVYOV

I

ETYMOLOGICALLY speaking the word " symbol " conveys
the sense of something intermediary which has the function of
a sign, and at the same time it suggests a relationship between
the sign and the thing signified.[1]   Symbols presuppose the existence
of two worlds and two orders of being and they would not exist
were there only one order.   A symbol shows us that the meaning
of one world is to be found in another, and that this meaning itself
is revealed to us in the latter.   Plotinus understood by a symbol the
union of two things in one.   A symbol constitutes a bridge which
links together two worlds.   Being is not completely isolated ; a
symbol suggests to us not only the existence of two worlds, but
also the possibility of an alliance between them, since it proves that
they are not in a state of irrevocable separation.   While delimiting
both worlds it also unites them to one another.

Our natural empirical world does not possess in itself either significance or orientation ; its qualities are dependent upon the extent
to which it functions as a symbol of the spiritual world.   It does not
possess in itself any source of life capable of giving meaning to its
existence, for it receives life symbolically from the spiritual world.
The Logos which exists in the latter can only reflect Itself in sym-

[1] See Max Schlessinger : *Geschichte des Symboles*, 1920.

bolic form in the natural world. Everything which possesses
meaning in our life is but the index and symbol of another world
in which alone that significance inheres. Everything of importance
in our lives is significative and symbolical of this other world. The
symbolic connection between facts in our life and in the life of our
meaningless and empty world does not appear unless it is seen in
relation to the other world, which possesses significance simply
in virtue of the fact that it is spiritual.

In the natural world and in the life of nature, which constitutes a
closed system, everything is accidental, unconnected, and destitute
of meaning ; for man in so far as he is a natural being is deprived of
any deep significance and his natural life is devoid of a significant
connecting principle. In the life of man, considered as a fragment
of the natural world, the Logos cannot even be discerned, and even
man's reason is nothing but the faculty by which he adapts himself
to the world-process. Thinking which is directed exclusively towards the contemplation of the natural and self-contained world is
bound to be overcome by a sense of the absurdity and futility of
existence, and is incapable of dissipating the oppressive obscurity of
the natural world in which it is unable to discern the indications of
another.

But man, in so far as he is the image of the Divine Being, that is,
in so far as he is a symbol of divinity, has a precise and absolute
meaning and significance. When his mind is turned towards the
divine world he discovers everywhere an inner connection and
meaning ; the indications of another world are apparent to him.
Such a state of consciousness is free and it brings some measure of
significance to the apparent meaninglessness of natural world. It
is impossible to demonstrate the existence of a meaning underlying
the life of the universe, for it cannot be established by rational in-
duction from a scrutiny of the natural world. Finality in the
processes of nature appears to us a very debatable hypothesis. The
meaning of things can only be discovered by living out that meaning
in spiritual experience and by an appeal to the spiritual world. It
can be demonstrated only by a life which is itself full of meaning,

and through a symbolic attitude of mind which itself imparts significance as an active uniting principle.

The symbolic conception of the world is the only profound one and it alone manifests and makes clear the deep mysteries of being. The whole of our natural life here below is devoid of meaning save when there lies upon it a symbolic sanctity, but of this men may be either conscious or entirely unconscious. It is possible to experience this sense of the symbolic character of natural life in a superficial manner, for it can be objectified in consciousness and perceived in a naïve and realistic fashion. It is possible to live a symbolic existence while at the same time mistaking symbols for realities, for in this way the symbolic character of all that is significant and sacred in life disappears. Men become so immersed in the natural, objective, world, that although they see in it clearly the incarnation of the holy they enslave the spirit to this world through the medium of a naïve realism.

To the naïve materialism and realism, often inherent not only in the non-religious but also in the religious mind, we must oppose not merely philosophical spiritualism or idealism of an abstract nature, but rather a philosophy of symbolism. "Spiritualism" and idealism are not religious attitudes of mind nor religious orientations of the spirit but metaphysical theories, whereas symbolism is religious by the mere fact of its existence. But a distinction must be made between realist and idealist symbolism. The latter, which is frequently to be found in cultured circles in contemporary society, is not a genuine symbolism which unites and links together two worlds, but is rather the symbolism which results from a hopeless dualism and from the isolation of our own inner world. The philosophy of Kant, more than any other, is based on this kind of symbolism ; it is the expression of a state in which man finds himself detached from all that is profound in existence and immersed in subjectivity. It is the symbolism of that deep spiritual solitude of the modern man, with all the inner conflict by which he is torn asunder. It finds a striking expression in contemporary art. The symbolic conception of the world was that of the Middle Ages, a characteristic example of which is to be found in the mysticism of Hugh and Richard of St. Victor.

Our age has lost the meaning of things. Idealist symbolism is subjective and conventional, it can only see in everything a reflection of the experiences of the soul-life, that is, the states of the knowing subject detached from the spiritual world and the sources of life. We find in Schleiermacher this same expression of subjective idealist symbolism which the " symbolo-fideism " of Sabatier also affords us. There is no ontological necessity in these symbols ; in reality they contradict profoundly the very nature of a symbol which is a link, a bond of union with, and the sign of, another world which really exists. When idealist symbolism attempts to explain the truths of religion it is always inclined to attribute to them nothing more than a subjective value ; and, where spiritual experience is concerned, it leaves man shut up within himself and separated from the realities of the world of spirit, for it does not understand the nature of spiritual life and experience.

Realist symbolism is the only authentic one which links together two worlds while testifying to the existence of the spiritual world and divine reality. In it there are given to us not merely the conventional indications of man's affective life, but the indispensable signs of an original life and of the spirit itself in its primitive reality. In them we discern the paths which lead from the natural to the spiritual world. For realist symbolism, the outward form of the world is neither a phenomenon devoid of reality nor a subjective illusion, but rather a symbolic incarnation of spiritual realities. Realist symbolism is a liberating and not an enslaving influence, a uniting and not a disruptive force. It is fundamentally opposed to naïve, objective, realism, but it is also equally opposed to subjective idealism and idealist symbolism. It transcends the gnoseological distinction between subject and object and the absorption of reality into the world of either of them.

Spiritual experience, upon which realist symbolism rests, lies altogether beyond the antithesis between subject and object and the substantialist conception of them. Spiritual life is no more subjective than it is objective. The symbolization of it, that is, its embodiment in forms belonging to the natural world, may be understood as an objectification, but that is precisely why it is not objective in the rationalist sense of the word. The symbolic mode of thought includes both subject and object within itself, and that at an infinitely deeper level of consciousness. If objectification is nothing more than a process of symbolization, then for that very reason all objective rationalism and all naïve conceptions of an object-substance cease to possess justification. What are called objective realities are in fact only realities of a secondary order, for they are merely symbolic and possess no reality in their own right. But subjective realities, such as the reality of the affective life and that of the subject and its subjective world, are likewise merely secondary and symbolic in character. This, however, is no mere restatement in a different form of the old distinction between noumenon and phenomenon underlying that whole theory of knowledge which is based upon an antithesis between subject and object. It would be very inexact to say that the spiritual world is a thing in itself (*Ding an sich*) and that the natural world is a mere appearance. In making this sort of distinction and antithesis the noumenon is conceived of from the point of view of naturalism, from which this type of thinking is inherited. The noumenon appears as a reality analogous to those of the objective, natural, world. The thing in itself is not life nor is it given in the experience of life, it is a mere thing, an object. The spiritual life has nothing in common with the noumenon of metaphysicians and epistemologists. The doctrine of " the thing in itself " does not presuppose the existence of spiritual experience as the primary experience of life, and it has its origin in naturalist metaphysics and in a failure to discover a rational answer to the riddle of life. When Fichte eliminated the conception of the noumenon as useless a big step forward was taken. He sought to discover the primary activity of life, of activity as opposed to " thing ". But in this the danger of hypostasizing the subject lay close at hand. Subjective idealism is incapable of producing a doctrine of the spiritual life. On the other hand, symbolism is directed towards a true comprehension of spiritual life and experience. But the classic examples of symbolism are to be found not in the philosophers but in the mystics and the artists, and in the literature of spiritual experience.

II

There are two conceptions of the world both of which leave upon religious thinking their particular characteristics. One of these sees everywhere in the world " realities in themselves ", completely circumscribing the infinite by the finite, and subduing the spirit to the flesh so far as the natural world is concerned. By thus subordinating the divine to the limitations of the flesh it always tends to see the absolute and the permanent in what is transitory, and transforms the processes of life into rigid ontological categories. This conception of the world forms the foundation of religious positivism and materialism and is the determining factor in our dominant systems of theology.

The experience which lies at the heart of this conception becomes the source of those reactionary and conservative opinions which are hostile to any forward movement. Those who are wedded to such opinions are lovers of authority and have an inveterate distrust of all creative genius. We have here an idea of the world which is naïvely realist and materialist, and, in spite of the religious form which it takes, a positivist conception, incapable of rising above the finite and distrusting the infinite, regarding the outward processes of nature and history (which are in themselves relative and transitory) as absolute and divine.

This conception of the world is static and hostile to every form of dynamism. It is the result of transferring the centre of gravity of life into the natural world. It gives to the outward forms of the historical process an absolute justification. National habits and customs, various forms of monarchy and of ecclesiastical authority which divide church and state, the differing systems of theology, have acquired a sacred significance which is absolute and unchangeable ; and to these the divine element is subjugated. The outward form of these things is regarded as sacred and this often leads to the quenching of the spirit. It is here that we must look for the origins of anti-religious and atheistic materialism and positivism. The spirit departs and disappears, while the outward embodiment remains and is regarded with veneration. The kind of experience through which we are now passing means the subordination of the spirit to the external world, and accustoms us to look for reality primarily in the finite and in the natural and historical world.

But the time comes in which the external embodiment of monarchy, once regarded as sacred, decays, and in which the outward forms of socialism acquire a new sanctity, since they are regarded with all those feelings of reverence which formally gave a hallowed significance to monarchy. Thus there will arise between the concrete embodiments of these two forms of government a fierce struggle, from which, however, the spirit will remain aloof since it can admit of no confusion of the absolute with the relative. The spirit is infinite and " bloweth where it listeth ". Its symbolism is transformed in accordance with the dynamic processes of the spiritual life. It is dynamic by its nature, it cannot tolerate any subordination to the static. The spirit cannot be imprisoned within custom and tradition. The organic process constitutes precisely a correlation between the outward and the inward, between the natural and historical symbolism of the external embodiment of things and the life of the spirit. When a " carnal " and exterior symbolism no longer gives expression to the inner life of the spirit its sanctity disappears, and the kingdoms and the civilisations which were based upon its support fall into ruin, dragging with them all those forms of life which were founded upon them. A new form of symbolism becomes henceforth indispensable which will give expression to a spiritual state which is different, and, in fact, organically new, that is to say, which will correspond to the reality of the inner life. The external forms in which the world is embodied may grow old and decay, but the spirit can free itself from them. It is then that the quenching of the spirit, that is, the sin against the Holy Ghost, manifests itself in a desire to safeguard at any cost those outward forms which are suffering from decay and to which the spirit is subordinated. Spiritual life will not submit to the domination of what is natural and "carnal"; its infinite reality cannot manifest itself completely in the sphere of history where its presence is never more than symbolic.

But there is another conception of the world which *is* capable of expressing the dynamic nature of spirit. It is that which sees everywhere in this world the signs and symbols of another world, and which perceives the divine as the mysterious and infinite, beyond that which is finite and transitory. Nothing relative and impermanent is regarded by it as absolute and abiding. It is a symbolic conception which places the centre of gravity of life in that other world which is spiritual, dynamic, and infinite. It refuses to see any final reality in this world, and in its natural exterior "body".

This aspiration towards the infinite has found a remarkable expression in Ibsen's play *The Lady from the Sea*. The limitless immensity and mystery of the divine and spiritual world do not admit of anything but a symbolic comprehension of all that is finite and natural. The conception of which we are speaking demands the sanctification of natural and historical life, but it must be symbolic in character. Such a sanctification cannot, however, regard the exterior "body" of the world as an absolute and sacred reality containing within itself all the divine fulness.

All spiritually creative human life and all really dynamic Christianity has been bound up with this latter conception of the world. The whole life of the Church of Christ is a myth created within history, a realist symbolism expressing and incarnating the dynamic energy of the spirit. The life of the spirit has been intense and powerful in the Church only in so far as there has been taking place this process of creating myths and symbols ever more and more rich in character. The dogmas of the Church, its worship and its traditions, the lives of saints and ascetics, alike proclaim this dynamic energy of the spirit. Nevertheless its traditional customs, the subjection of its life to the dominion of Caesar, the crystallizing process within theology, the undue erection of its canons into absolute laws, the creation in short of an unchangeable and sacred embodiment of its inner quality, all this has too often meant a drying-up of the spiritual life in the Church, indeed, an extinction of the spirit and an arrest of its dynamic energy. Thus the life of the Church becomes a mere reflection of the creative forces active in former periods.

Only the symbolic conception of the world is capable of directing us in the ways of the spiritual life, for it alone renders possible a continuity in the process of the creation of myth by maintaining that traditional life which links the past to the future. According to Creuzer symbolism is the vision of the infinite in the finite. It is the visible image of invisible and mysterious things. A symbol by its very nature does not subject the infinite to the finite. On the other hand it renders the finite transparent and allows us to see the infinite through it. In the finite world our horizons are by no means completely restricted, for, when the whole outward order is symbolically sanctified it is freed from the intractability, the inertia, and the isolation of the natural world. Authentic reality is always more remote and at a deeper level of existence than that which appears in the natural, outward, order of things. The creative movements of the spirit cannot be fettered by the immobility of " the flesh " which claims for itself final reality.

The incarnation of God, the coming of the Son of God into the external order of this world, shows that the physical world is not a closed system incapable of being influenced from without. It demonstrates rather the power of the infinite to enter into the finite, the penetration of the spiritual world into the natural world, the divine manifestation of the bond which unites the two, the victory of grace over the intractability of the natural world, and the breaking of the spell which holds it in bondage. The coming of Christ as a child of Adam constitutes the kenosis, the humiliation of God, which has taken place in order that the flesh may be freed from its intractability and its subordination, and in order that it may be illumined and transfigured, but not that it may be affirmed or sanctified in any absolute fashion.

The religious materialism which puts an absolute value upon the flesh distorts the mystery of the divine incarnation and is a negation of its symbolic character. The birth of the Son of God into the world, His life, His death upon the Cross, and His Resurrection, are so many facts constituting by their significance a unique and absolute symbol of the true issues of the spiritual world and of the inner life of the spirit. This symbol frees us from the power of the world. The fact that the Son of God has lived in the flesh enables us to hope that it will be subdued in all its fearful realism and that it is at the same time capable of being illumined by another world and transformed into " spiritual flesh ".

All flesh is a symbol of the spirit, the reflection, the image, and the sign of another far off, yet much more profound, reality. All that we call created nature is by no means a reality in itself, rather it is a symbolic reality and a reflection of the light which belongs to the spiritual world. The obstinacy of the flesh is only the symbol of a fall in the spiritual world. But the illumination of the flesh manifested by the earthly life of the Son of God is the indication of a fresh uprising in the spiritual world. The flesh is not a snare and an illusion ; it is the symbolic reflection of the realities of the physical world. The alliance of these two worlds, the possibility of their interpenetration, the transfusion of energy from one world into the other, are all communicated to us by means of this symbolic sign. This symbol unveils for us the life of God and signifies for us the entrance of divine energy into the life of this natural world. But on the other hand it guards for all time the sense of infinite mystery and affirms the impossibility of reducing to a common denominator the life of the world and the life of the spirit. Symbolism does not admit the validity of that hard isolation of the flesh and the natural world which results from transforming them into entities incapable of permeation by the infinitude of God and the Spirit.

The substantialist conception of the natural world, immutable in its non-divine principle, is simply a religious form of naturalism, which engenders in consequence a materialist and positivist naturalism, since God has been definitely isolated from the natural world and the spirit irrevocably quenched. In the process of its development naturalist metaphysics led to a dualistic theism which, by rejecting the symbolic tie uniting the divine to the natural world, produced first of all an " atheism " with regard to the world and then an " atheism " in respect of God Himself. To this we must oppose the symbolic conception which, admitting the link existing between the two worlds, does not consider the natural as nondivine, but on the contrary see within it the signs of the divine world, reflections of events, whether they be falls or uprisings, in the spiritual life. The natural order is not eternal and immutable. It is but the expression of a moment which symbolizes the life of the spirit. Consequently forces can arise in the depths of the spirit capable of transfiguring it and freeing it from the power which holds it in bondage.

III

There are three possible conceptions of the relations between the divine world and our natural world. Firstly, there is the dualistic conception which sets God over against the world, a form of agnosticism, a subjective idealism which shuts itself up within the subject, an idealistic symbolism which admits only the symbolization of the subjective world, of the affective life detached from the core of being. Secondly, there is the rationalist hypothesis which supposes the mystery of the Divine Being is accessible to itself, an objective realism which considers the realities of the natural world as absolute. Thirdly, there is the symbolism which admits the possibility of the transfusion of divine energy into this world, which binds together and unites two worlds, and recognizes that the Divine Being can only give symbolic expression to Itself while it remains inexhaustible and mysterious.

Dualism and rationalism, false dualism, and false monism, alike separate man from the divine world, imprison him in this world and prepare the way for positivism and materialism. For these systems of thought there exist no mysterious relations between the two worlds, no transfusion of energy from one to the other, no signs given from other worlds. But the divine world is shut up within itself and is banished from human sight quite as much when it is considered as comprehensible by rationalism as when the natural world is regarded as an objective reality, and when the Divine Being and the subjective world are separated from one another, thus condemning man to the isolation of his emotional life. Subjective idealism and objective realism are gnoseological tendencies which equally reflect (though in diametrically opposite ways) a separation between the divine and the natural worlds and a division of the human spirit. The objectification of the divine life and its identification with the natural world is the denial of the mystery and the infinitude of God's Being. We find this same denial when the divine life is regarded as a subjective reality and assimilated to the affective life. Dualism gives rise to agnostic positivism and to " psychologism " in philosophy. Rationalism engenders naturalism and materialism.

These two conceptions which attempt to explain the relations between the two worlds predominate in thought to-day, and religion is in danger of becoming an exclusively psychological category. But the judgment of the soundest contemporary opinion is protesting against the attempt to explain the Divine Being by means of rational concepts. Through deism and through natural religion reason brings us to atheism and the negation of religion. Deism is the fatal product of a rationalist theism which combines within itself an abstract dualism and an abstract monism. Only symbolism is capable of expressing and safeguarding the infinite depth and mystery of the divine world, while maintaining both its distinction from and its close alliance with the natural world. The spiritual life is only perceived in this world by means of symbolism. While it is difficult to conceive of, and may be distorted through the presence of heterogeneous principles both rationalist and dualist, it yet remains organically inherent in the religious life.

God can only be perceived symbolically for it is only by means of symbols that it is possible to penetrate the mystery of His Being. Divinity cannot be rationally determined and remains outside the scope of logical concepts. This is what the great religious thinkers, mystics, and theologians have always affirmed, and it is impossible for scholastic or metaphysical theology to refute it. At the back of the religious idea of God there is always the irrational and supra-rational element.[1] This mystery of the irrational determines the nature of symbolism which is the only means through which men can attain divine knowledge and wisdom. There are no rational and conceptual categories, nor any categories of affirmative theology, which can express the final truth about the divine, for they are all relative to this world and to the natural man and are adapted to their limitations.

The rationalist way of looking at things is simply the positivist reaction of man to the natural world, and is only a refraction of the divine within the finite. For the divine life in itself, in its inexhaustible mystery, bears no relation to what is affirmed through the medium of rational concepts. Logic is not the same thing as the Logos. Between these two there is a great gulf fixed and a radical discontinuity. It is impossible to imprison the infinite in the finite, and the divine in the natural. But St. Paul has himself given us an unforgettable description of what true symbolism in the knowledge of the divine does involve : " For now we see in a mirror darkly ; but then face to face : now I know in part ; but then shall I know even as also I have been known ".

We know God as in a mirror, in an obscure, that is to say, a symbolic fashion. A definitive knowledge of God, a vision of Him face to face, belongs to another sphere, to the mystical life in God. Rationalism, where the knowledge of God is concerned, refuses to admit that this mirror is obscured ; for it believes that

[1] This is an idea expressed in that remarkable book on the philosophy of religion, *Das Heilige*, by R. Otto.

rational concepts are capable of reflecting the real essence of God's Nature and of comprehending the Divine Being. The negative theology of the Pseudo-Dionysius the Aeropagite is opposed to this doctrine. The greatest religious thinkers adhere to the truth enunciated by Nicholas of Cusa who saw in divinity the *coincidentia oppositorum*. The identity of contraries is an antinomy for the rational faculty. Our human reason is not adapted to a form of reality in which contraries are compatible with one another. They are subject to the laws of logic governing identity and contradiction, but these rules of logic can never express the nature of divinity. Moreover all the dogmas of Christianity giving expression to the facts and events of spiritual experience have a supra-logical and supra-rational character and are above the law of identity and contradiction.

Religious knowledge has always been symbolical in contradistinction to all rational theology and metaphysics and to scholasticism. The knowledge of God has never been and could never have been a rational, abstract, intellectual form of knowledge, for it has always had its origin elsewhere.

All systems of scholastic theology and rational metaphysics have but a limited character, being adapted to this world and to the natural man, so that they possess only a pragmatical and juridical value. Only the facts of mysticism within Christianity are absolute, and our thought about them is always relative.

Symbolism is justified by the fact that God is both knowable and unknowable. Divinity is an object of knowledge both infinite and inexhaustible, eternally mysterious in the unfathomable depth of its being. Thus it is that the knowledge of the divine is a dynamic process which finds no completion within the fixed and static categories of ontology. The limits which are imposed by agnosticism do not exist. The gnosis which searches for truth ever further and further afield and ever more deeply is an effective possibility, for the process of knowing of God is a movement of the spirit which has no end. But the mystery always remains and can never be exhausted. This truth is expressed by means of symbolism and escapes all attempts at comprehension by our understanding, which is always a limiting factor demanding an end beyond which there is no more mystery. It is there, where the domain of rational knowledge and logical understanding which apply only to the natural finite world terminates, that the domain of symbolic knowledge and of the symbolism applicable to the divine world begins.

It is impossible to elaborate a positive concept of absolute being, for all possible concepts dissolve in irreconcilable contradictions as soon as they are applied to it. It is impossible also to think about the inner life of the Divine Being along lines similar to those which we use where the human affections are concerned. The attributes of God as stated in affirmative theology are logically contradictory and are open to criticism from the standpoint of reason. Conceptual thinking, by its sheer inadequacy for reaching any knowledge of God, inevitably becomes atheistic in character when the existence of other methods of knowledge is denied.

Academic theology is powerless in face of the criticisms which reason brings against it. Rationalism and naturalism, when transferred from the religious and theological sphere to that of natural being, are definitely affirmed there, and so a conflict arises between knowledge and. faith, and between science and religion. And here science will win and will continually extend its domain. Nor can this process be artificially controlled, for the activities of a natural and rationalist theology cannot be limited. By affirming a dualism between the two worlds Kant attempted to defend the sphere of faith and religion by transferring it to the sphere of the knowing subject. But along this line faith soon comes to an end, for religion is placed in a subordinate position by being restricted and obscured. Symbolism alone, by a delimitation of the spheres of spirit and nature, by putting a barrier to the competence of rational knowledge, and by opening up new ways of knowledge, safeguards the inalienable rights and eternal truths of the religious life.

Academic "rational" theology transgressed the limits of its

competence in one direction by regarding the mysteries of divine life as entirely accessible to itself, and, in the other, by supporting agnosticism, assigned fixed limits to spiritual experience, and the knowledge of the divine. Dogmatic and systematic theology of the academic type, being naïvely realist and non-symbolist, never expresses the final ontological truth of the divine life. Behind the concepts and formulas of dogmatic theology there lies the infinite mystery of the divine life perceptible only in spiritual experience and in its symbolic expression. Symbolism restricts the pretensions of rational knowledge with its dominating concepts, but it places no limits on spiritual experience itself ; it does not affirm agnosticism as a principle ; and it admits of an infinite diversity in the paths of knowledge. The wisdom and knowledge of Jacob Boehme penetrated deeply into the mysteries of the divine life, and he discovered a gnosis which knew of no limitations : but it was a symbolic and not a conceptual knowledge of divinity.

Knowledge has a considerable importance and an illuminating value in the spiritual life. We are to love God with all our minds, but we must do so freely and no limit can be imposed on us from without. Knowledge must be capable of infinite development as much in the sphere of positive science as in that of religious and philosophical gnosis.

The symbolic knowledge of God is deeply rooted in the soil of Christian tradition. The negative theology which is to be seen in the works of Dionysius the Aeropagite is symbolic. This symbolic and mystical theology teaches us that God is unknowable and that positive definitions cannot express the mysteries of the divine life. The mystery of divinity can only be approached by way of negations. God is nothing that is ; He is non-being. The greatest thinkers have expounded the negative theology, whether pagans like Plotinus, or Christians like Nicholas of Cusa. Negative theology demonstrates precisely that the Divine Being is *not* being in the sense in which that word is used with regard to the natural world, where everything is positively and limitatively determinable. The Divine Being is a reality of another order, and, if the natural world is being, then God is non-being or nothingness; He is superior to being, for He is " super-being ". Negative theology recognizes the unfathomable mystery of God, and the impossibility of exhausting His nature by affirmative definitions; it recognizes the opposition and the antinomy which the divine nature necessarily presents to our reasoning faculty. In a word it is opposed to the naturalization and rationalization of the Divine Being.

But " affirmative " theology predominates in the academic sphere, and it is a rationalist and anti-symbolic theology, for it admits the possibility of attaining a perfect system of divine knowledge by means of positive statements. It understands the Divine Being in a naturalist sense, for it conceives its reality as similar to that of the nature of the world, and regards God as being and not non-being. It refuses to see the " super-being " of divinity, and it denies its unfathomable mystery. Affirmative theology is the theology of the finite and not the infinite. It is an exoteric theology which confuses the reflection and even the refraction of God in the natural world with the divine nature itself. Its affirmative definitions borrowed from the natural world are transferred into the divine world. It takes symbols for realities.

The knowledge which belongs to affirmative theology is pragmatic, juridical, exoteric, and social, but, though it is the organizing principle of the collective religious life of the masses, it is far from being a genuine gnosis. Gnosis penetrates more profoundly the mysteries of the divine life by recognizing them just where positive theology denies them. The symbolic knowledge of mystical theology penetrates into the very heart of the mystery and at the same time safeguards it. Affirmative theology is not real knowledge for its objective is already perceived in advance, it precedes, as it were, the very process of knowledge, and such theology is but a codifying of the dogmatic truths of revelation. The knowledge of God can only be given in an experimental and symbolic theology of the spirit, for all real advance in the knowledge of God always rests upon spiritual experience and its symbolic expression. The theology of Christian mystics has always been experimental and is symbolic of the actual course of their spiritual life. Symbolism presupposes the abyss, the " groundlessness " (*Ungrund*) of the divine life, the infinite hidden beyond the finite, the esoteric life of God which cannot be grasped by the mind of man and is incapable of logical and juridical formulation. The absolute of the philosophers is not the God of religion, neither is the God of the Bible the absolute of philosophy.

IV

The foundation of mystical and symbolic knowledge is not formal philosophical statement but mythological representation. Concepts are the basis of philosophical statement, while symbols give rise to mythological representation. Philosophical and religious knowledge, having reached the culminating point of gnosis, ceases to be dominated by concepts and turns to mythology. Religious philosophy is always bound up with myths and cannot break free from them without destroying itself and abandoning its task. For religious philosophy is in itself a creation of myth, an " imagination ".

From Plato and Plotinus to Schelling and E. de Hartmann, all thinkers of the gnostic type have employed mythological representation. The whole of Boehme's gnosis is mythological, and the whole of E. de Hartmann's philosophy of the unconscious, which attempts to build up a purely spiritual religion free from myth, is likewise entirely mythological. It rests upon the myth of an unconscious Divinity which, having created the evil of being in a fit of madness, would free itself from the sufferings of this being by the full consciousness that man could acquire of himself. Plato in his best and most finished dialogues, in the *Phaedrus*, in the *Symposium*, and in the *Phaedo*, and in others too, affirms the truth that myth is the path to knowledge. The philosophy of Plato is steeped in Orphic mythology. At the heart of Christian philosophy too, though it does develop conceptually, we find the most important of all the myths of mankind, namely that of Redemption and

of the Redeemer. The most arid rational theology and metaphysics derive their sustenance from the myths of religion. A
metaphysic which is pure, abstract, and entirely free from all
mythology means the end of any living knowledge and a complete
detachment from existence. Living knowledge is mythological
in character. That is something which we must grasp quite
clearly if we are to have any understanding of what myth really
means.

Myth is a reality immeasurably greater than concept. It is high
time that we stopped identifying myth with invention, with the
illusions of primitive mentality, and with anything, in fact, which
is essentially opposed to reality. For that is the sense which we give
to the words " myth " and " mythology " in ordinary conversation. But behind the myth are concealed the greatest realities, the
original phenomena of the spiritual life. The creation of myths
among peoples denotes a real spiritual life, more real indeed than
that of abstract concepts and of rational thought. Myth is always
concrete and expresses life better than abstract thought can do ; its
nature is bound up with that of symbol. Myth is the concrete
recital of events and original phenomena of the spiritual life symbolized in the natural world, which has engraved itself on the
language, memory, and creative energy of the people. The original
reality pre-exists in the spiritual world in deepest mystery. But
the symbols, signs, images, and reflections of this primitive reality
are not given to us in the natural world. Myth presents to us the
super-natural in the natural, the supra-sensible in the sensible, the
spiritual life in the life of the flesh ; it brings two worlds together
symbolically.

The great Aryan myth of Prometheus symbolizes in a sensible
manner and on the natural plane certain events of the spiritual life
of man, of his destiny, and of his relations with nature. The Promethean principle is the eternal principle of the spiritual nature of man.
The same may be said of the Dionysian myth, which is reflected
mythologically in the sensible world. The myth of the fall of
Adam and Eve, a fundamental one for the Christian consciousness,

expresses the greatest of all realities in the spiritual world. The separation of man and of the world from God is one of the original phenomena of the spiritual life, it belongs to the deep things of the spirit which are before creation. But this spiritual happening is symbolized in the natural and sensible world. While the meaning of the Fall is revealed in spiritual experience this event is nevertheless expressed in a concrete myth, that of Adam and Eve, which speaks of something as having taken place in time and on this earth. Myth always represents a reality, but its reality is symbolic.

Schelling has an ingenious theory about mythology, for he regards it as the pre-history of the human race, and as the reflection of a theogonic and cosmogonic process in the human consciousness.[1] The philosophy of mythology associated with the works of Creuzer is out of date in the light of more recent research in this direction, but the philosophical core of Schelling's teaching on the subject of mythology maintains its significance unimpaired.

When knowledge claims to be entirely free from religious myths it falls a prey to the myths of anti-religion. For materialism also offers a form of mythological creation and lives by the myth of matter and material nature. Positivism, again, lives by the myth of science considered as universal knowledge. These myths do not express the really deep things of spiritual life, but only certain phases of man's development. Christianity is entirely mythological, as indeed all religion is, and Christian myths express the deepest and most central realities of the spiritual world. It is high time to cease being ashamed of Christian mythology and trying to free it from myth. No system of theological or metaphysical concepts can destroy Christian mythology, and it is precisely this collection of myths which constitutes its greatest reality, for it becomes an abstraction as soon as it is freed from them. But it is essential to grasp the inner meaning of the myth and symbol in a spiritual manner in order to free oneself from that naïvely realist influence which they may possess as a result of a superstition which has

[1] See *Schellings sämmtliche Werke*, Zweite Abteilung. Erster Band. *Einleitung in die Philosophie der Mythologie*, 1856.

enslaved the spirit. It is then only that the way will be opened up which cannot fail to lead us to spiritual realities.

Mythology had its origin in the dawn of human consciousness when spirit was enveloped in nature, when the natural world had not yet become a rigid system, and when the frontiers between the two worlds had not been clearly defined. The consciousness of man was not yet fully awake, and our language and ideas still bear the imprint of this primitive mythological consciousness. The core of man's being was still unconscious, and it is to his subconsciousness that mythological creation owes its origin. The delimitation of the spheres of spirit and nature is the product of later evolution, and a revival of mythological creation can only take place through a new spirituality.

A pure philosophy free from myth and religious experience and likewise conceptual theology cannot know God. Every attempt at a rational knowledge of divinity runs the risk of falling into abstract monism or dualism. Every conception of the divine nature which is not contradictory and paradoxical is hopelessly far removed from the mysteries of the divine life. Neither a dualist theism with its radical antithesis between the Creator and creation, nor a monistic pantheism which identifies them, are capable of expressing the mysteries of the divine life, for the relations between the Creator and the creation are contradictory and paradoxical so far as reason is concerned. Natural understanding cannot grasp nor translate into concepts the nature of God and His relations with the world. The divine life, the esotericism of the Diving Being, does not admit of being handled by the reason. But reason can perceive the paradox and antinomy with which the Divine Being presents it ; it can admit the existence of the supra-rational. That is what Nicholas of Cusa means by his teaching on the subject of learned ignorance.

The great merit of German thought, which is linked on here with mysticism, consists precisely in the fact that it recognized the un-fathomable nature of God and His " irrationality ", as a primary ground of existence. There is, for example, " the essential Deity "

(*Gottheit*) of which Eckhart speaks, deeper than God Himself, and "the groundlessness" (*Ungrund*) of Boehme. Divinity is not perceived by the categories of reason, but by the revelations of spiritual life. The Trinitarian nature of God lies beyond rational thought. Reason, without the illumination of faith, tends naturally towards monism or dualism, and the mythological character of the Christian Trinity is an offence to the reason, which is too ready to see in it a form of polytheism. With regard to the mystery of the Trinity, myth and symbol alone can be used, and conceptual thinking is out of the question. But this myth and this symbol reflect, not my religious sentiments, nor the inner states of my soul, as the neo-symbolists of the subjective idealist type suppose, but rather the very heart of existence and the deepest mysteries of life. It is only in the divine Trinity than an inner life exists which cannot be reduced to concepts.[1]

For the same cause it is impossible to form a conception of the dual nature of Christ. Reason leans quite naturally towards monophysitism or the recognition of a single nature ; the mysteries of the union of two natures in one single personality is inconceivable by reason. That is why myth and symbol alone can be employed where the nature of the God-Man is concerned.

When thought forces itself to penetrate into the final mysteries of the divine life it necessarily involves a drastic revolution in our consciousness, which brings with it a spiritual illumination transforming the very nature of reason itself.[2] And a reason thus illuminated is now a reason of another kind, belonging neither to this world nor to this age. God is immanent in reason when it is illuminated and spiritually integrated, but He remains transcendent and inaccessible so far as the old reason of the natural man and

[1] The remarkable German Catholic theologian Mathias Scheeben said with great justice, " God would be a lifeless Monad, a rigid and motionless Unity, if He were not regarded as a Trinity of Persons."

[2] St. Bonaventura comes very near to the truth : " For the knowledge of God, the illumination of the intellect by faith is essential." See Gilson : *The Philosophy of St. Bonaventura.*

the first Adam is concerned. Only the wisdom of Christ renders possible an immanent perception of divinity. But the acquiring of this wisdom involves a breach of continuity in our natural thinking. This discontinuity in our thought about God consists precisely in the abandonment of concepts in favour of symbols and myths. From the point of view of our natural reason our very thought becomes mythological ; but this only goes to prove that true realities are beginning to be revealed in our consciousness. The Trinitarian nature of God, and the divine-human nature of Christ, are initial realities of the spiritual life. These realities are disclosed when our minds turn from the natural world towards another one, when our thought, through being conformed to these changes in our minds, ceases to be enslaved by concepts. Then it is that life reveals itself. But it is only myths which can explain life, which is always inexhaustible and unfathomable. In spiritual experience and in the spiritual life there is a continual movement in the direction of the deepest things in the divine life, and this movement can never come to rest in concepts and in the rigid categories of theology and metaphysics. But this does not imply either the denial of religious and philosophical knowledge and its effective value, or on the other hand the affirmation of agnosticism. *Docta ignorantia*, according to the ingenious teaching of Nicholas of Cusa, is the knowledge of ignorance.[1] There is a possibility of knowledge by way of paradox and antinomy. In admitting the unapproachable character of divinity, and the impossibility of any rational knowledge of the divine life, we do at the same time allow for a religious knowledge and philosophy of the divine. Negative theology is also a knowledge of divinity. The assertion that there are certain limits to reason presupposes its acuteness and intensity ; reason when enlightened by the spirit is raised to a higher level, not annihilated.

But in order to live again we must first die ; a sacrifice is necessary. Religious gnosis has been and always will be symbolical and mythological, and the task of Christian gnosis consists in expressing Christian symbolics and in making use of Christian myth.

[1] See Nicholas of Cusa : *Vom Wissen des Nichtwissens*.

In the gnosis of Valentinian and Basilides Christian myth was still too much overlaid by pagan myth, and the spiritual was enveloped in the natural and in cosmic infinity. It was here that the confusion of gnosis began.

But in our own time when we speak of the symbolism of religious truths we are up against a danger of a different kind, namely that of modernism, or the symbolo-fideism of Sabatier, which sees in symbols only the reflection of faith, that is, of our subjective feelings. Schleiermacher too had already perceived in dogmas the symbolics of religious sentiment. But this conception means a breach between the two worlds, for it confines man within his own subjective world, that is, within his own faith and feelings. But symbols and myths do not in reality reflect faith nor the religious feelings of mankind, but rather the divine life and the depth of being which lie within the experience of the spirit, this last being distinguished from the experience of the soul in that it presents to us, not man's faith in the divine, but the divine itself. When the mere symbol is taken for the final reality the spiritual world is subordinated to the natural.

V

The dogmas of the Church must not be confused or identified with dogmatic theology or theological doctrines. Dogmas possess absolute and indefectible truth, but this truth is not necessarily attached to a particular doctrine. The truth of dogmas is the truth of religious life and experience. Their significance is not moral and pragmatical, as certain Catholic modernists think, but religious and mystical, for they express the principle which underlies the spiritual life. Dogmas acquire a rationalist character only when enshrined in theological doctrines, where they are frequently bound up with a naïve realism and naturalism. Dogmas are useful and salutary because they mark out the way of the spirit which is the truth and the life, and not because salvation and life demand the acceptance of certain doctrines.

It cannot be a matter of indifference for my life and destiny whether that human being which is dearest to myself does or does not exist. Similarly, too, it is not a matter of indifference whether Christ, my Saviour, does or does not exist. But Christ exists only if He is the Son of God and consubstantial with the Father (homo-ousios). The dogma of the consubstantiality of the Father and the Son is not a doctrine, but the expression of a mystical fact indispensable to my life. Dogmas are not theological doctrines, but mystical facts belonging to spiritual life and experience which refer to real religious contacts with the divine world. Dogmas are symbols which point out for us the way of the spirit, myths which give expression to the events of the spiritual world of an absolute importance.

I cannot be indifferent as to whether an event on which my life and my very fate depend, not only in time but in eternity, may or may not have happened in the spiritual world. Does God exist, or does He not ? Is He a living reality, or an abstract idea ? That is a question of life and death for me, and not merely a question of accepting this or that theological or metaphysical doctrine. If God does not exist, neither does man, nor do I exist myself, and all my life becomes a meaningless illusion arising from certain obscure moments of the natural process. If Christ be not risen, then I cannot hope for victory over death and the life of nature. What is essential to me for my own resurrection to eternal life is not the *doctrine* of Christ's Resurrection, but rather the *fact* that this event has actually taken place. I cannot be indifferent as to whether this mystical fact did or did not occur, whereas I can be quite indifferent with regard to the theological or metaphysical doctrine of the Resurrection. The denial of the mystical fact of Christ's Resurrection is for me a denial of eternal life, and that is not something which I can calmly admit.

No, dogma is not doctrine but symbol and myth giving expression to events in the spiritual world of absolute and fundamental importance. Dogma symbolises spiritual experience and life by mythological representations and not by concepts. But this experience and this life are not states of man's soul, nor his faith, nor his religious feeling, but rather ontological realities, original life itself and original existence. When St. Athanasius fought the heresy of Arius he was not defending mere doctrines, but the true way of life and certain real points of contact with the spiritual world.

The annals of the human spirit tell of one particularly striking event in the spiritual career of one man, namely the meeting of Saul with Christ. This mystical encounter, which transformed Saul into Paul the Apostle, is the very foundation of Christian faith in the Redeemer and in Redemption, and is one which all men may experience for themselves. The transforming of Saul into Paul is the new birth, the second or spiritual birth. But a true meeting with divine reality is not a state of the soul nor a psychological experience. The emotions of the soul leave man shut up within himself, absorbed in his own feelings and beliefs, which are distinct from divine realities. Only spiritual experience can liberate the human soul and transform his subjective feelings into real ontological contacts with the spiritual world. Dogmas possess a spiritual not a psychological and naturalist character.

Dogmatic formulas in the history of the Church's thinking have a pre-eminently negative rôle. They anathematize not erroneous doctrines but a false orientation of spiritual experience, a deviation from the spiritual path. They show us what the fruits of death and of life are. Dogmas in fact have primarily a spiritual and pragmatical, not a doctrinal and " gnostic " value. The evil consists not in the fact that heresies are false doctrines, but rather in their testimony to a distorted spiritual experience. The denials of Christ's consubstantiality with the Father as the God-Man uniting in one unique Personality two natures and two wills, divine and human (namely the denials of Arianism, monophysitism, monothelitism, and Nestorianism), represent a complete distortion of spiritual experience. They contain a false symbolism of the events of the spiritual world, an ill-omened spiritual tendency which will permit of no perfect union between man and God. The evil consists not in the fact that Gnostic doctrines are false and incapable of providing men with authentic knowledge, but rather in the fact that they disclose a spiritual experience and a way of life in which the lower world cannot be illuminated and transfigured by the higher one.

A symbol is important in so far as it points to things which take place in the spiritual world and which bring men into the Kingdom of God, to a union between man and God, and to the transfiguration and deification of the world. But dogmas do not give expression to any final knowledge of the Divine Being ; by themselves they do not yet constitute a definitive gnosis, in spite of their preponderating importance, for the latter has to be sustained by the facts of spiritual experience. To reconcile gnosis and dogma is not to subject knowledge to the external control of certain theological doctrines, but rather to have recourse to spiritual experience and the vital sources of divine knowledge. Gnosis is free, but freedom in knowledge must bring it to the sources of life. Dogmas are symbols of the spiritual world, and the events of this world play an important part in the knowledge of it, for they disclose its unity and integrality in opposition to the desultory and accidental character of events in the natural and " psychical " world.

It matters little that theological systems and dogmas are exoteric and that they direct the spiritual experience of mankind with social organization as the end in view ; for it is also an esoteric truth that the spiritual world is the *soborny* world, that spiritual experience is not individual and isolated, and that in the spiritual life there is vital contact with a single divine reality in which the one Christ is revealed. *Sobornost* proceeds from the very nature of spirit.

Harnack's theory, which attempts to prove that the elaboration of the dogmas of the Church represents a process of Hellenization and the introduction of Greek philosophy into Christianity, does not correspond with the truth. The dogmas of the divine Trinity, of the dual nature of the God-Man Christ, and of Redemption through the mystery of the Cross, have always been folly so far as

Greek thought was concerned and will always remain so. There is nothing in these dogmas which is rational or capable of being grasped by the intelligence. On the other hand heresy is a good deal more conformable to reason. Arianism, particularly, is perfectly rational, and its supporters were all to be numbered among those who found it impossible to escape from the influence of Greek thought and philosophy. It is certainly easier to hold with the monophysites and the monothelites that there is in Christ but a single nature and a single will than to maintain with the Church a paradoxical coalescence of two natures and two wills. Christianity sets forth the folly of the Cross which is incompatible with natural reason. That is why it is a revelation of another world, a truth which is from above and not from below.

The adaptation of Christianity to the mind of this world constitutes an esoteric element within it, and is the result of its pathetic endeavour to reach the natural world and the mass of average humanity. It is for the masses that systems of theology and of rigid canonical regulations have been elaborated. Authoritative forms of thinking are inevitable where masses have to be directed in the ways of religion. The purpose and nature of the external control of the religious consciousness is social and exoteric, and involves a failure to give expression to final truth within itself. All men have not reached that spiritual level on which there is immediate contact with divine realities. A really deep, spiritual, experience is only revealed by degrees and assumes a graded order of different levels of experience. The religious life of Christian nations presupposes the existence of some men who, having no personal spiritual experience of their own, live on that of others. This also is a form of religious experience, though of a very primitive kind. Esotericism is always the justification and presupposition of exotericism.

The consciousness of the Church expresses and safeguards the unity of spiritual experience belonging to all generations of Christians through the medium of its organization, it guarantees the same points of contact with Christ and marks out the way to salvation for the mass of mankind and all who are still at a lower level of spirituality. That is why the mind of the Church always holds to a middle course ; for there is in the Church both a revelation and a mystery at the same time. It is this fact which explains the difficulty experienced by the Church in maintaining a balance between conservative and creative elements.

VI

The struggle against the Gnostics was a struggle against pagan mythology and demonolatry and not against myth, against a false form of knowledge and not against gnosis in general ; it was a struggle also for the true and pure expression of the occurrences of the spiritual world. The mind of the Church is always afraid of the premature where the mass of mankind is concerned, and so it preserves a balance by forbidding too much elevation or too much depression of spirit.

The conservatism of the Church is democratic by nature ; it " preserves " for the sake of the average man and the masses. On the other hand creative spirit in the religious life possesses an aristocratic quality, daring to assert what is only revealed to a minority of the very elect. The former element is *par excellence* sacramental, the latter essentially prophetic ; while one is manifested in collectivity, the other is individual. Creative development in the Church is always effected by upsetting the balance between the minority and the majority, and by the action of creative personalities who break free from the mass of average Christians. Priesthood is the conservative principle of religious life while prophecy is the creative element. The prophetic mission is always realized by means of individual inspirations. The prophetic spirit is hostile to every theology and metaphysic of the finite, and to every attempt to materialize the spirit and to transform the relative into the absolute. To deny creative development in the life of the Church and its dogmatic system is to deny the prophetic spirit, and to reserve to the priesthood exclusively all initiative in the religious life. The divine spirit works differently through the priest and through the prophet. In the consciousness of the prophet and in the exercise of his mission the infinite perspective of the spiritual world is disclosed, and the limits of the finite world recede.

The dogmas, in which the absolutes of spiritual life have their adequate symbolic expression, cannot be modified and changed. The Trinitarian character of the being of God, the dual nature of the God-Man Christ are mystical and eternal facts ; Christ is the only begotten Son of God from all eternity. But the meaning of these dogmas can be given a deeper significance and can be thrown into relief by a new form of gnosis, for certain happenings in the spiritual life can find their symbolic expression in new dogmatic formulas.

The process of mythological creation in the life of the Church is a continuous movement which marches irresistibly forward. It is a process of life itself. For we cannot go on living exclusively on the experience of others and on the myths created by former generations ; we must have our own personal life. But our own life and our mythological creation cannot be separated from the life and creative achievements of our forefathers. It is, rather, a creative life which proceeds without interruption, at once individual and supra-individual, a life in *sobornost* in which the past and the future, tradition and creation, are bound together in eternity.

Only symbolic thinking can do justice to the facts of the spiritual world, and to the ineffable and original quality of its life. Symbolic thinking brings freedom to the spirit by delivering it from the influences of the finite world, for " all that is fleeting is but a parable ". We can be bound by nothing transitory.

The true centre of our life is transferred to another world. As we turn aside from the life of this world our whole attention is fixed upon the unfathomable and the ineffable : everywhere we are in contact with the mysterious and we see the light of another world, in which nothing ever comes to an end, and which knows no subordination. This world is open to the light, it has no limits, it penetrates into other worlds, and they in turn penetrate into it. Here there is nothing hard or rigid which cannot be subdued. Its apparent intractibility and obscurity are not objectively real ; they are but the outward signs of that which takes place in its inmost depths. For every outward event of the natural and objective world also occurs within the depths of the spiritual life, and within us, too, in so far as we are spiritual beings ; consequently we cannot regard such things as alien to ourselves. The whole realm of nature and history is comprised within the depths of the spirit where it acquires fresh meaning and significance. The outward is only the external sign of that which lies within. The whole historic process of the universe is simply the symbolic reflection of that which takes place within the sphere of our inmost spirit, and this is not a mere subjective experience of the soul but something genuinely belonging to the spiritual world, in which the self and being are not separated nor extrinsically opposed to one another, for we are in being and being is in us.

Hence in the new light which comes from within one sees Christianity as a mystery of the spirit which can only be reflected symbolically in the natural and historic world. Mystical Christianity does not deny nor seek to eliminate the Christianity of a more external kind, but it sees it in a new light and gives it another meaning. The whole natural world is only an interior moment of the mystery of the spirit and of its basic and original life reflected in oneself. It ceases to be an exterior reality involving the subordination of the spirit. A mystical and symbolical conception of the world does not deny the world, it " absorbs " it. Memory is simply the interior link which mysteriously binds the history of one's own spirit to the history of the world, the latter being nothing more than the symbol of the pre-history of one's spirit. The process which created man and the cosmos is unfolded in and through us so far as we are spiritual beings. Nothing is entirely exterior, superficial, or alien so far as one's spirit is concerned, for it knows and possesses all things from within.

Heterogeneity and superficiality are only symbols of spiritual

division and of the inner conflicts which occur within the spiritual
life. Everything that happens above happens below as well. Even
the Holy Trinity Itself is to be found in every part of the world.
It is in the inmost depths that superficiality has its origin, and it is
the lack of unity in the inner life which creates heterogeneity. The
world, nature, and history are only the highway of the spirit, a
moment of its mysterious inner life. The life of the spirit is our
own life, but it is at the same time the life of all men, the divine
life, and that of the whole universe. As we pursue the course of
our spiritual development we launch out into the objective world
of symbols, and then return again to achieve a fresh integration of
ourselves in the inmost depths and at the very centre of life and
reality. It is in this way that life's mystery proceeds. At first
it looks as if the relation between symbols and realities was an
entirely paradoxical one. Nevertheless it is just precisely a symbolic
mode of thought which brings us face to face with ultimate realities,
whereas a naïve realism conceals reality from us and makes symbols
our masters. A truly symbolic way of thinking prevents us from
accepting symbols as external realities.

This way of thinking makes a distinction between symbol and
reality, and so can direct us towards the realization of the spiritual
life. True symbolism marks a return to a genuine spiritual
realism, in which symbols are exchanged for realities, and it is a
return to the transfiguration of life and to the spiritual perfection
of our heavenly Father. It is precisely symbolism which strives
after realism for it is in the domain of symbols that realism is to
be found.

A realist way of thinking confuses symbols with realities. It
binds us to symbols and prevents us from attaining to realities or
to a real transfiguration of life. This truth, paradoxical though it
may appear, is essential, if we are to understand the spiritual life.
Naïve and objective realism is compelled to live within a frame-
work of natural symbols ; it does not believe in the possibility of
any effective achievement of the spiritual life because it regards
spirit as transcending man.

Religion in culture and history has a symbolic character and reflects the spiritual life in the natural and historical world. Dogmas and forms of cultus are symbolic by nature. Such a symbolism is realist and conceals the realities of the primal spiritual life, but it remains symbolism none the less, though it is not a mystical realism. A final realism is only reached through a mysticism which has penetrated to the inmost depths of the primal spiritual life. The whole of spiritual culture is symbolic by its very nature ; its importance consists in the fact that it enables us to observe within this world that which emanates from another. But culture does not transfigure life nor raise men to the highest levels of existence, it is in fact nothing more than a preliminary to these things, and that art which is in a peculiar degree symbolic is of special significance for the symbolism of culture. So-called realist art, which is in fact not seeking for reality, is in a naïvely unconscious way dominated by symbols, while it is the art of a consciously symbolic character which aspires to mystic realism and to a share in that life which is primary and original. The art of Dante and Goethe brings us nearer to this life than the realist art of the nineteenth century. Cultural symbolism endeavours to break through the limitations of the symbol and to escape to primal reality.

The essential goal is the transfiguration of culture into being and of symbols into realities, that is to say, the illumination of the world. Even our religious culture is only relatively speaking an entry upon a higher plane of existence and a symbolic sanctification of life, but it should be noted carefully that even this symbolization is often deceptive. The outward signs of the basic and original life are given to us, but the life itself is not there, for the natural world cannot contain it ; it is impossible within this lower sphere to achieve the transfiguration of life at all effectively. It is only within the spiritual world that a real regeneration of life becomes possible, which involves the absorption of nature into spirit, and the overcoming of the intractability, inertia, impenetrability, and divisiveness of the natural world.

The spirit clothes itself here on earth with the outward forms of culture, that is to say of symbolism, and the mystery of the spirit is objectified in public worship. In the sacrament of the Eucharist the bread and wine are changed into the Body and Blood of Christ. But this is a realist and symbolic transubstantiation behind which there lies the mystery of the basic and original life, for it is in the inmost depths of existence that the Lamb of God is offered in sacrifice for the sins of the world. It is by means of the sacrament that the other world penetrates into ours, but the divine energy is only *reflected* upon the plane of this natural world : the Body and Blood of Christ are offered under the forms of bread and wine.

Transubstantiation must be understood in the spirit of a realist, not of an idealist and subjective symbolism. This sacrament is the reflection of an event in the spiritual world of absolute significance, which belongs, not to my subjective world, but to that of basic and original life itself. Nor can it be regarded from the angle of a naïve objectified realism. The sacrifice of Christ and redemption from sin is something which takes place eternally in the spiritual world. It is in fact the initial phenomenon of all spiritual life. The matter of the sacrament is not accidental, for it is symbolically linked with the original spiritual phenomenon itself. The symbolic view of the sacrament has no relation to modern symbolism which denies its reality and sees in it only the conventional expression of the religious emotions of the soul. The true symbol is not an allegory and the sacrament possesses a cosmic nature, for its significance is not confined merely to the human soul. Its symbolism is real and absolute, but its reality originates in the spiritual world and not in our natural world. "The flesh" which has been sanctified, everything on earth in fact which is sacred, possesses merely a symbolic reality and does not constitute reality in itself.

The sacred forms in which theocratic monarchy is embodied are only symbols of the sacred and do not constitute that real regeneration in which life is transfigured in the Kingdom of God. Original and authentic reality is only given in the transfigured life of the spirit. But when a transitory symbolism is regarded as an eternal reality, when nature and the flesh dominate at the expense of the sacred, then the way is closed to any real transfiguration of life and the attainment of spiritual realities. A false conservatism which overrides the creative forces of the spirit reveals the fact that symbols have been substituted for reality and that the spirit is subdued to the flesh. But as soon as symbolism ceases to express the events of the spiritual world and the power of the spirit is no longer present in it, a fatal disintegration sets in, catastrophes follow, and the existing régime collapses.

The truth which lies behind " laicization " is this. Conscience demands that what is holy should be definitely freed from outward impostures. A new system of symbols must then be established and a moment arrives when a return to reality, the transfiguration of life, and the attaining of true being, become possible. It is at such moments that great crises, in the state, and in civilization as a whole, occur, and that spiritual revolution takes place on a big scale. The conventional symbolization of the perfect life is impossible, for that life must be realized in the effective transformation of the natural into the spiritual world. In such a process the ideal form of " the flesh " is preserved, while its intractibility and materiality disappear. A merely symbolic theocracy displaying only the outward signs of the Kingdom of God is no longer satisfying. The Kingdom itself must be realized and a perfection similar to that of the Heavenly Father attained. Then the age of existing symbolism will come to an end and a new age will begin for the world.

The coming of this new era of spirituality and fresh realism will demand a symbolism which will deliver the human spirit from a false realism and from its subjection by means of symbols to the natural world. A true symbolic mental approach gives a meaning to life because it sees the outward signs of another world everywhere, and because it also permits of our being freed from the bondage and misery of this vain world. Nothing absolute, nothing sacred, can be fettered by this world which is itself incapable of anything like a complete comprehension of the spiritual. The Kingdom of God is not of this world, it is not the kingdom of nature and cannot be manifested within its limits, for there only the symbols of other worlds are possible.

And yet the Kingdom of God is being realized at every instant of our lives !

CHAPTER THREE

Revelation and Faith

I

THE traditional distinction between revealed and natural religion is exoteric and not very profound. Every religion in which we can see a measure of divine illumination is a revealed religion. Where the divine is manifested, there is revelation. The divine is revealed in pagan religions as well as in Christianity, and it is manifested through nature in natural religions.

The old-fashioned teaching of the seminaries which sought to prove that God was revealed in the pre-Christian world only to the people of Israel under the Old Covenant, and that paganism was wholly sunk in the darkness of demonolatry, can no longer be maintained to-day. The whole of the varied religious life of mankind has been nothing less than a continuous ascent towards the unique revelation made in Christianity. For when specialists in the science of religion attempt to prove that Christianity is not original, that pagan religions already had the idea of a suffering God (such as Osiris, Adonis, Dionysos, and so forth) that Totemism had its eucharist in the form of communion through the body and blood of the animal, that most of the elements of Christianity can be found in Orphism and the ancient religions of Persia and Egypt, they are failing completely to understand the significance of what they observe. The Christian revelation is universal, and everything analogous to it in other religions is simply a part of that revelation. Christianity is not a religion of the same order as others ; it is, as Schleiermacher said, the religion of religions. What does it matter if within Christianity, supposedly so different from all other faiths,

88

there is nothing original at all apart from the coming of Christ and His Personality ; for is it not precisely in this particular that the hope of all religions is fulfilled? Former revelations were but anticipations foreshadowing the Christian revelation which was to come.

Egypt was drawn irresistibly towards the idea of immortality and in the mysteries of Osiris the death and Resurrection of Christ were prefigured.[1] But the Resurrection is an ontological reality and was only accomplished in Christ ; it is by Him alone that death has been overcome and the way opened up to everlasting life. Yet in Egyptian religion there was a divine revelation, and a symbolic anticipation of the truth was reflected upon the plane of the natural world. Christianity appeared in the world precisely as the realization of all these expectations and prefigurings.

When people speak of natural religion as opposed to revealed religion they mean that the former contains no revelation of other worlds and that it merely represents certain natural states of human consciousness, the illusions of primitive thought and of mythological creation, the reflection of the fear and the sense of oppression aroused by the menacing powers of nature, or perhaps the manifestation of natural and non-divine forces within the mind of man. But a nature totally devoid of any divine element does not exist, for the whole world is but the symbol of other worlds. The revelation of nature is only a stage in the revelation of God.

But the distinction between natural and spiritual religions is a deeper and truer one, for these religions belong to different stages of revelation in the world. The difference between them corresponds to the fundamental distinction which exists between the natural and the spiritual world. God is revealed in nature and in spirit, and He is revealed in man as natural and spiritual being. The revelation of divinity in nature is only the reflection, the projection, and objectification, of an event which has taken place in the spirit-world, for revelation is in essence an event of the spiritual life and religion is a manifestation of the spirit.

[1] Reading A. Moret's book on *Egyptian Mysteries* one is struck by the close analogy between these mysteries and the Christian liturgy.

89

Religion is the revelation of God and of the divine life in man and in the world. Religious life is the obtaining by man of kinship with God by which he escapes from his state of isolation, solitude, and separation from the fundamental elements of his being. But though God can be revealed in the religious life, He can also be hidden within it. Revelation does not abolish mystery ; in fact it discloses its very depths in all their ineffability. Revelation is poles apart from rational thought ; it does not imply that God is capable of being grasped by reason and by conceptual thinking, and that is why an element of mystery always remains. Religion is a para-doxical combination of that which is revealed and that which remains hidden. Parallel to the exoteric there is always the esoteric. Now the goal of exotericism in religion is a finite one while eso-tericism always presupposes the infinite. The interpretation of revelation in a spirit of naïve realism and naturalism is always of an exoteric nature in which the really profound elements of revelation are concealed. The revelation of God is not a transcendent event taking place on the objective and natural plane of reality, nor is it an illumination from without. It is on the contrary something which transpires within us, a light springing up in our inmost depths, a fact of the spiritual life which has no connection with exterior realities.

Revelation does not proceed from the object to the knowing subject, nor is it by any means something subjective in character. The antithesis between subject and object is not basic in the religious life and it vanishes altogether in the inner depths of spiritual ex-perience. The objectivist, transcendent, and realist interpretation of revelation is a form of naturalism which really amounts to a re-jection from without of spiritual experience. Revelation does not take place in the objective sphere, nor for that matter in the subjective sphere of the soul which is merely a part of the natural world. Revelation takes place in the spirit, for it is a true integration of the spiritual in the world of nature and in our natural life. But the spiritual world, within which the light of revelation shines forth, is not something objective and unconnected with our subjective world. Its proper relationship cannot be identified with the sort of thing which exists on the plane of natural and " psychical " reality, for it can be grasped only by a symbolic form of thinking.

Where revelation is concerned there is no distinction between that which comes from without and that which comes from within, between that which emanates from the object and that which proceeds from the knowing subject, for everything is contained in the innermost depths of being and can only be symbolized externally. Revelation cannot be regarded either as entirely transcendent or as entirely immanent for it is both, or rather, neither, for the distinction between transcendence and immanence is a purely secondary one. It was for example in the inmost depths that God revealed Himself to Moses when he heard the voice of God speaking to him at an ineffable distance. But when this revelation is projected and objectified in a naturalistic manner within the sphere of unregenerate human nature the voice of God is heard echoing from Sinai, as though the revelation had come from something external.

In the earlier stages of the development of man's religious consciousness revelation is regarded from the point of view of naturalism and as something which takes place in the natural and objective world. The Father is revealed in nature objectively before He is revealed by the Son at the deepest spiritual levels. He is manifested pre-eminently as " power " and not as " truth ". But while power is a natural category, truth is a spiritual category. It is only in the Son, in Christ, that the inner nature of the heavenly Father is revealed. But for naturalistic thinking He is the personification of the Master and the Sovereign Lord, and the traces of this old conception remain in Christianity even to the present day. The revelation of the Trinity is, however, not that of a heavenly monarchy (which would be a heresy) but that of heavenly love, the divine *sobornost*. In the Son there is revealed another aspect of the Father than that which is given to us without the Son. The Son proclaiming the Father's will, the Christ enshrined in the objective and historical incidents of the Gospel and in the natural world, can be truly known only if He is revealed also in the inmost depths of spiritual experience ; and this knowledge of Christ by man's spirit presupposes the action of the Holy Spirit. Nevertheless the natural world and the natural man leave the imprint of their essential limitations upon the revelation which the Spirit of God makes to the spirit of man.

Distortion caused by the limitations of the natural world and the unregenerate nature of man is responsible for the different degrees of revelation which are to be observed, and it is the limitations of revelation which produce exotericism. The light of absolute truth is refracted as it passes through the distorting medium of human nature. The words which express the truths of revelation are all imperfect and inadequate. The absolute of revelation is limited by the subject–object relationship which, though it is the reflection of a certain element within the spiritual world, does not express the primary phenomenon of revelation. God is compelled to conceal Himself in a measure from the natural world, for the divine illumination would blind the eyes of mortal man were it to shine upon him in full strength. Man under the Old Covenant was unable to look upon God. The light came by degrees, and it grew feebler as man proved himself unprepared to receive it.[1]

The God of the Old Testament, Jahveh, was not a revelation of the Divine in Its inner secrecy, for He was only an exoteric expression of the Divine Countenance as it appeared to the Hebrew mind. The wrath of God described in the Bible is simply an exoteric *motif* reflecting the wrath of the Jewish people. God the Father reveals Himself in the Son as infinite Love. Heathen polytheism was also a revelation, but one in which the nature of the divine became, as it were, divided into separate fragments in the mind of the ancient world. A monotheistic conception was impossible because of the inner condition of human nature at the time. The esoteric life of God can only be revealed exoterically in the religious life of natural humanity.

[1] From this point of view it is possible to recognize an element of truth in Spinoza's *Theologico-Political Treatise* in spite of its narrow rationalism.

There was, in fact, not a single corner of the world in which the secret, esoteric, life of the divine Trinity was even partially disclosed : it was made known to man only in the Son, as infinite Love, as a drama of love and of freedom. Yet even this mystery of Christianity remained for a time, as it were, subject to a certain legalism and an exoteric comprehension which sought to limit the infinite by the finite. The Christian revelation in its absoluteness continues to work within the natural and relative world, and through its acceptance by the natural man receives the impress of his limitations. Even within Christianity the light-penetrates only by degrees and is distorted by the obscurity of the medium which receives it. This is why we find in Christianity a number of different periods which are on a variety of levels. Christianity cannot be comprised within any juridical system nor reduced to any one simple doctrine. The spiritual constitution of man is flexible and dynamic so that it is impossible to regard as in any sense finally true that which belongs to a spiritual constitution of a finite and mediocre type. The supremacy of the finite indicates a " bourgeois " spirit in the religious life.

Inner, spiritual, revelation ideally precedes the outward and historical revelation, though not necessarily chronologically. Man cannot understand or receive a revelation of religion from the historical sphere if there is at the same time no revelation within the inmost depths of his spirit, and if the historical itself is not realized as a spiritual manifestation. Every event and indeed every word and action in the external world remain unintelligible as far as we are concerned if they do not reveal to us that which speaks and acts within, and if there is no clue to their meaning in the inmost depths of the spirit. There can be revealed to us only that which is revealed *in* us, for only that which happens within can have any meaning for us. Religious revelation is not merely something which is done for us, it demands our co-operation ; it is something spiritual and catastrophic which is accomplished within our being ; if we had not ourselves lived through the experience of what others call divine revelation it would have no meaning for us. We cannot under-

93

stand the Gospel except in the light of our own inner spiritual experiences. Apart from these inner happenings the Gospel has no more meaning than any other series of historical events.

Indeed we may go further and say that history cannot be understood except through spiritual experience of it, and when it is regarded entirely as a reflection of certain spiritual manifestations. If we refuse to grant this inner, spiritual significance to history it becomes something purely material and empirical, devoid of any connected meaning. Revelation is always a revelation of meaning and does not consist of outward events in themselves apart from a spiritual interpretation. That is why faith always has spiritual precedence over authority. It is simply a form of materialism to regard revelation as authority. The acceptance of Christian dogmas by the consciousness presupposes that this consciousness, that is to say the spirit in its inner life, precedes the external revelation of these dogmas.

When men oppose freedom of thought on the ground of the objective necessity of revelation they forget that God can only be revealed in religious consciousness, that Spirit can only be revealed to spirit, and Meaning to meaning, and that revelation involves inner illumination. God cannot be revealed to impenetrable matter or to inanimate objects. Revelation is a bilateral Divine-human process, the meeting together of two natures which are inwardly allied to one another, and in order to be received it requires a favourable medium to which the divine element is not alien ; for a nature which had nothing divine about it could not receive it. It is a mistake to regard the relation between God who reveals and man, to whom the revelation is made, as being of a transcendent character. God cannot reveal Himself to the man who will not come to Him. Revelation presupposes faith in man and in his higher nature which renders possible that religious upheaval which we call revelation, the birth of God in man, and the meeting of man with God. This means that revelation implies the immanence of the divine within the human spirit—not of course within the human soul. In revelation the transcendent becomes immanent. The denial of a higher spirit-

94

ual nature in man which renders him God-like is tantamount to a denial of the very possibility of revelation, for there would be nothing to which such a revelation could be made. God would no longer have another self and would remain isolated and solitary.

Catholic theologians assert that man is only a spiritual being resembling God by grace and not by virtue of his proper nature, but such language is a mere convention and makes a distinction which only exists on the natural and outward plane. Man has been created in the image and likeness of God. Revelation, because it is a spiritual phenomenon of the inner life, can only be understood in the light of the indwelling spirit, which is itself the affirmation of the divine image in man. To deny completely the immanence of spirit and to regard it as something purely transcendent is practically to commit oneself to deism, that is to say, to a denial of the inner relationship between God and man. Pure transcendence involves a complete dualism between the divine and the human and makes impossible any real union between them. This is the reason why both theology and philosophy must refuse to take either God or man as their starting point, but must rather begin with the God-Man whose theandric nature is beyond and above this antithesis.

Revelation for man means in some way a release of the spirit which has been imprisoned in his consciousness and in material nature. Revelation unveils the inmost depths of the spirit, at the same time uniting them with the surface life of the soul. Our personal religious experience is always immanent. That alone is transcendent which we have neither lived through nor experienced for ourselves, and transcendence of such a kind only exists in the experience of the soul-life, for on the spiritual plane there are no impassable barriers between our experience and that of others. Our spiritual experience is that of St. Paul and it belongs to one and the same spiritual world, whatever differences there may be between us. Mystical experience which is the highest form of spiritual experience means a definite overcoming of transcendence and the attainment of a perfect state of immanence.

The affirmation of the transcendent in the religious consciousness is a form of naturalist objectification which severely restricts the inner life of the spirit. But immanentism is not characteristic of contemporary thought, which, on the contrary, in its best acknowledged forms, manifests a very strong tendency towards the transcendent. It separates God and man, isolating man in himself and dividing the spirit from the soul ; it is, in fact, a form of agnosticism. Spiritual and mystical immanentism has no connection whatever with that of contemporary philosophy which affirms that being is immanent in consciousness and is a form of phenomenism and positivism.

But there is another kind of immanentism in which consciousness is regarded as immanent in being. The knowing subject is merged in the infinite life of the spirit. The limits of consciousness recede, the barrier between the soul and the spirit is removed, and each world alike penetrates the other. That which transpires within the sphere of the knowing-subject, that is, within our consciousness, transpires also in and with the sphere of being, in the depths of the spiritual life. The transcendent is only part of the immanent, an incident in the course of spiritual development, a separation of spirit from spirit, constituting an antithesis to itself. In the process of this antithetical division of the spirit revelation appears to possess a transcendent and objective character, but actually in its inner nature revelation is entirely immanent in the spirit within which it cocurs.

II

Revelation is a catastrophic transformation of consciousness, a radical modification of its structure, almost, one might say, a creation of new organs of being with functions in another world. Revelation is not evolution but revolution. It produces a change in the reciprocal relationships between the sub- or supra-conscious ; it brings the sub-conscious into the conscious. In the piercing light of revelation the barriers of consciousness dissolve, and its hard crust is melted in the fire of revelation. The conscious is raised to the level

of the supra-conscious and is widened and deepened to an unlimited extent. The isolated psycho-corporeal monad begins to
open up and the slumbering spirit awakes. Revelation always
means a spiritual awakening and it is accompanied by a fresh
orientation of consciousness towards another world. The general
structure of consciousness and the elaboration of its organs are
always directed and determined by spiritual causes and by the will
of the spirit which chooses or rejects. The limits of consciousness
are dependent upon the degree of spiritual experience achieved.
The forms which it takes are secondary and not primary, and are
conditioned by the contraction and expansion of the different
spheres as determined by the initial will of the spirit. The particular
orientation of consciousness is the result of occurrences in the basic
and original life itself which involve the revealing of one sphere
and the obscuring of the other.

The fact of revelation and the possibility of religious experience,
of the entry of the other world into ours, can only be understood
through the medium of a dynamic consciousness. Nevertheless
most schools of philosophy and theology have a static conception
of the nature of consciousness and are afraid of dynamism. The
average type of consciousness, which is entirely dominated by
reason and shut up within the natural order of the psycho-physical
monad, is not incapable of transformation, nor is it the only form of
consciousness.[1] Personal consciousness is not a limitation of the
spirit by the body as E. Hartmann, Drevs, and others think. The
border line between the conscious and the unconscious is not absolutely fixed and static. Being is prior to consciousness and that which
takes place within its sphere modifies its structure in addition. The
Logos, the meaning of the world, is absolute, while consciousness
is subject to change and is within its limits relative. The understanding of the rationalized consciousness cannot be identified with

[1] Modern science which has made a study of the sub-conscious considers
this latter an established fact. It recognizes to-day phenomena which a few
decades ago would have been regarded as the result of lunacy or due to
fraud. See, for example, Charles Reibet : *Treatise on Metapsychics.*

the Logos. Consciousness is active and dynamic. In the basic and original life and in the spiritual will an orientation towards a new world is possible which will create new organs of consciousness.

Positivism, materialism, and rationalistic naturalism identify a limited area of consciousness with the whole of being. Consciousness having put limits to the receptivity of being, regards itself as reflecting it in its totality. Kantian philosophy, which is more spiritually refined than positivism and materialism, postulates the existence of a fundamentally static type of consciousness irrevocably limited in its scope, to which it gives the name transcendental. Thus we find ourselves in a completely closed circle. So far as it is concerned being becomes either a thing in itself (*Ding an sich*) or disappears completely. Spiritual experience cannot pass beyond the limits of transcendental consciousness without escaping from the sphere of obligatory logical forms. But transcendental consciousness is not responsible for the limitations which are imposed upon the spiritual life of man ; it only reflects the state of life, the experience, and the orientation of the primary will.[1]

Theology, even while combating Kantian philosophy, really moves in the same isolated sphere and fails to recognize the infinitude of spiritual experience and the possibility of any enhancement of consciousness. The unlimited possibilities of spiritual experience and of raising consciousness to a higher level were recognized only by the mystics. Official theology reduces the mysteries of the divine life to the average level, that is to say, to the universally imposed transcendental consciousness. But it would be a mistake to suppose that naturalist evolutionism gives a dynamic interpretation of consciousness. It admits a modification and a development only within the limits of the rigid forms of the natural order. The evolution of man does not mean freedom from a static rigidity of consciousness. This static rigidity guarantees that everything will take place strictly within the limits of the natural order. A con-

[1] Du Prel is right when he speaks of the mobility and evolution of the transcendental consciousness.

sciousness incapable of variation determines the intangible boundaries of this order and hence guarantees the natural character of all evolution and every modification in the world. Naturalist evolution refuses to admit that the limits of consciousness and being can be enlarged. It foresees in advance quite definitely what can and what cannot be accomplished within the sphere of being, by which it means that of nature as bounded by normal consciousness. For such a line of thought all evolution in the direction of other worlds is in principle out of the question.

Theosophists, as distinguished from evolutionists of the naturalist type, admit that consciousness can evolve, that is to say, can be concerned with other worlds. This idea of theosophy contains in itself an undoubted element of truth, though it does not owe its discovery to theosophy but merely its popularization. We can admit a modification of the individually isolated consciousness and also the possibility of a cosmic consciousness and of a supra-consciousness. The spiritual experience of humanity witnesses to the existence of a cosmic consciousness possessing organs different from those of the individual consciousness.

The empiricism which is so common to-day is no more dynamic in its attitude towards consciousness than the equally common theories of evolutionism. It also places limits to experience in advance and claims to know what is and what is not possible within such experience. These limits are not determined by experience itself, which is infinite, but rather by the rationalist consciousness. Empiricism is completely rationalist in character and regards only rationalist experience as admissible ; " original " experience possessing unlimited possibilities is outside its scope. It knows nothing of the experience of the infinite spiritual world and recognizes only the sensible experience of the soul with its orientation towards the natural world and limited by the rational consciousness. Empiricism as well as evolutionism considers the structure of consciousness from a static point of view, for both these systems are characterized by the conviction that the limits of being correspond to the limits of a fixed and rigid consciousness, and, like rationalism, they move in a vicious circle.[1] Only mystical empiricism admits the possibility of a full and unlimited experience and brings us back to basic and original life itself.[2] But this has little to do with the prevailing form of empiricism which denies all possibility of communication between the two worlds.

Rationalism, transcendental idealism, empiricism, evolutionism, theological positivism are so many tendencies in which the repressive characteristics of a static consciousness are manifested. None of them admit that consciousness is capable of being enlarged, and that it can be in touch with the cosmic and divine life ; they also deny the possibility of spiritual experience of an original quality. They are different expressions of one and the same process, of a single course of development, and the reflection of the same limited experience. It is this which gives rise to a transcendent and external interpretation of revelation which is the product of a naïve and naturalist realism.

A dynamic conception acknowledges the existence of different degrees of consciousness, and revelation indicates precisely a new and dynamic modification of its limits. For consciousness is not passively determined by reality ; it is rather actively directed towards one reality or another. Diverse realities correspond to different orientations of consciousness, and Zimmel explains very clearly why there are many of these, showing that science, art, and religion all possess their own. This theory, though it takes on a relativist character in Zimmel, manages to preserve its cogency in spite of its relativism. We move in different worlds and we depend on the particular orientations selected by the spiritual will. The world of day-to-day experience is created by the active orientation

[1] This inability to admit any essential modification in consciousness shows itself in the analysis of the religion of uncivilized peoples. Taylor and Frazer attribute to savages the characteristics of their own mentality and their own spiritual make-up. Levy Bruhl in his book on *The Mentality of the lower Races* treats this question in a very interesting manner.

[2] The empiricism of Losky and of James does, however, support religious experience.

of our consciousness, by the choice of some things and the rejection of others, and it cannot claim for itself a reality higher than that of other worlds.

The consciousness of average humanity is determined by its subjection to normal reality, and by its incapacity for concentrating on any other reality and for turning its attention towards another world. The world of religion is created by a different aspiration of the spirit and by a different choice of the will ; and, it might be added in this connection, consciousness becomes attached to the object to which it habitually turns while it rejects the object upon which it was previously focussed. The structure of consciousness always implies a selection, and it is determined by the reality to which it aspires ; it obtains what it wishes, while remaining blind and deaf to the things from which it turns away.

Our consciousness responds to certain worlds and elaborates receptive organs adapted to them ; but it is also closed to others against which it desires to protect itself. We are always surrounded by an infinite world of which we are extremely afraid because we are unable to bear the vision of it, and we defend ourselves against this " redoubtable infinite " by a certain deafness and blindness. We are so afraid of being blinded and deafened by our contact with it that we try to oppose it, partly by imposing on it certain rigid limitations, and partly by our own inertia ; and surely nothing but fire from Heaven can melt such hardness.

The widely-held supposition that reality in itself can be grasped by a static and passive type of consciousness is false. Being precedes consciousness and does not determine it in that naïvely realist sense which always implies the belief that it is static and passive. Being determines consciousness from the innermost depths and not from without. That which precedes consciousness is not the limited fragment of being revealed to an equally limited consciousness as *par excellence* objective reality, but, rather, the fullness of being which is the infinite life of the spirit. But this fullness of being is incapable of perception by a passive and static consciousness. As spiritual life it can be revealed only to the spiritual, that is, to a consciousness directed towards the life of the spirit, and which has created for itself new powers of receptivity ; in a word, it can be revealed only to supra-consciousness. The faculty of intuitive contemplation constitutes a new organ non-existent in the average consciousness and it is revealed only as the result of an intense activity of the spirit. It is impossible to envisage the existence of an objective reality by looking at things from the angle of a static and passive consciousness, for a reality of this kind has no true existence in itself. Reality is a life which knows no limits, which is always active and dynamic, and it can only be revealed to a life possessing the same characteristics. The reality of the spiritual world cannot originate from without, for it comes only as the result of deep spiritual life within. We must discover the reality of the spiritual world for ourselves in our own experience of life, and not merely wait for it to be communicated to us from without. Experience depends upon the limits of consciousness, but the latter are the result of an attitude of the spirit, that is to say, of a process which takes place in the basic and original life itself. Whole worlds remain outside our experience because our consciousness acts as a barrier to them, and because our attention has been focussed elsewhere and we have chosen another and more limited world. But if these other worlds are to be revealed to us our consciousness must undergo a catastrophic change and must be purified in the fire of the spirit.

In the inmost depths of the spirit, where the barriers created between oneself and the spiritual world cease to exist, an event occurs which involves the shattering of one's whole being to its foundations and the transformation of the very structure of consciousness. And in this, the basic phenomenon of the religious life, two processes are at work, namely the movement of the divine towards the human and the movement of the human towards the divine. Revelation is the fire which proceeds from the divine world, which kindles our souls, reshapes our consciousness, and removes its limitations. Revelation comes from the divine world, but is directed towards the world of humanity and implies the existence of some inner movement within it. It requires for its perception a certain degree of maturity and a spiritual hunger and thirst in man which, having a profound conviction of the vanity of this world, is seeking that which is above. The divine life is revealed by a double process having its origin in both natures and through a change in the human consciousness which presupposes both the action of divine grace and man's freedom. The phenomenon of revelation requires the phenomenon of faith. Revelation is impossible without that fact of spiritual experience which we call faith, just as faith is impossible without that fact of the spiritual world which we call revelation. Real and objective faith presupposes revelation, the movement which originates in the divine sphere, but revelation cannot itself penetrate into this world save in so far as it is received by faith and is a fact of man's spiritual life.

III

The phenomenon of faith in the spiritual life of humanity pre-supposes a dynamic quality of consciousness as well as its detachment from the natural world and its return to the other world. If it is impossible to deny the existence of the object of faith, it is certainly quite out of the question to refuse to recognize it in the inner life of man. Moreover, as its very great importance in the history of the human race shows, this fact proves that a change in the structure of consciousness is possible. The fact that the world of religion is created and revealed by a certain particular orientation of man's spirit is quite as undeniable as the fact that the empirical world is also created and revealed by a different one. Religious experience is not inferior to empirical experience. The empirical world cannot claim a particular reality of its own. The truth is that man is haunted by empirical reality, and, if he is to concern himself with the reality of other worlds than this, he must be aroused from what is really a state of trance. The direction given to the human will has created an irresistible and magnetic attraction towards this rigid empirical world, the experience of which is perforce a limited one. For the world means just this hard rigidity of a particular experience.

The basis of the phenomenon of faith is the redirection of the primitive will latent in the original life of the spirit towards another world, involving an extension of experience to an unprecedented degree. The primitive will exercises at all times the power of choice, selecting one world while rejecting others and modifying the boundaries of experience. The origin of faith is to be found in the primitive spiritual will, not in the " psychical " will, for the direction of consciousness and the extent of experience are not determined in the sphere of the soul, but in that of the spirit. Faith is not directed towards that reality which is the product of the hardening and constraining process of habitual and indefinitely repeated experience. It is not a clog upon reality. It is, according to St. Paul's immortal definition, " a demonstration of things invisible ", but one, be it noted, which does not compel recognition on our part. Faith is always directed towards the mysterious and hidden world.

The knowledge of reality which is revealed to the ordinary mind is a demonstration of things visible. The empirical world which surrounds us compels us to recognize its existence ; it forces itself upon us and we cannot refuse to see it. The world of visible things which is demonstrated in daily experience persists within the sphere of scientific experience and leaves us no freedom of choice. Faith is a free act of the spirit and is the work of free election and love. No visible and objective reality can compel in us an act of faith, for faith is an appeal to the mysterious and intimate world of spirit which is conditioned by freedom and not by necessity.

Knowledge and perception of the natural and empirical world of visible things do not demand a radical transformation of consciousness nor a fresh " election " of the world on the part of the spiritual will. This knowledge and perception take place not in the primary but in the secondary sphere which has been predetermined by the original life of the spirit. The knowledge and perception of the palpable and visible reality which surrounds us on every side does not require an intense spiritual freedom in order to establish the existence of the known object or of the reality itself.

If we are to direct our faculties towards the other world we must detach ourselves from this world by free spiritual action. We must break loose from the crushing bondage of visible things by which the things invisible are obscured. When we are confined within the rigid limits of normal consciousness we can perceive only the empirical world, while the spiritual world remains a sealed book to us. The unseen, mysterious, world cannot force itself upon our attention. The very possibility of atheism, of that state of consciousness which denies the reality of God Who is the source of all being, would be unbelievable did it not exist. I cannot deny the reality of the table at which I am writing nor that of the chair upon which I sit, and yet it is possible for me to deny the reality of God. But while we can regard solipsism as a mere *jeu d'esprit*, atheism determines a man's whole life. God does not force us to recognize Him, for His purpose lies in the freedom of the spirit, and He is only revealed in the freedom of its life.

" Blessed are they which have not seen and yet have believed." This blessedness is unknown to those who see only the visible world and who believe only what they are compelled to believe. But blessed are those who have believed in the invisible world which compels no belief in itself. It is in this freedom of choice and in the liberty of the spirit that that heroic act of faith lies which presupposes mystery and cannot even exist without it. The knowledge of visible reality constitutes complete safety and protection, and this is guaranteed to us by compulsion, whereas faith in an invisible and mysterious reality is a dangerous thing requiring from us a leap into the abyss of mystery. Faith knows nothing of external guarantees, that is, of course, faith as an original experience of the life of the spirit. It is only in the secondary exoteric sphere of the religious life that we find guarantees and a general attempt to compel faith. To demand guarantees and proofs of faith is to fail to understand its very nature by denying the free heroic act which it inspires. In really authentic and original religious experience, to the existence of which the history of the human spirit bears abundant witness, faith springs up without the aid of guarantees and compelling proofs, without any external coercion or the use of authority ; its source is within ; it prefers folly to the wisdom of this world ; it accepts antinomies and paradoxes no matter how great. Faith necessitates the sacrifice of the lower reason, and it is only by this sacrifice that man attains the higher reason and that the Logos, the meaning of the world, is revealed.

" If any man thinketh that he is wise among you in this age, let him become a fool that he may become wise. For the wisdom of this world is foolishness with God."

" The wisdom of this world " is associated with a normal consciousness directed towards visible things. This consciousness is liquidated through the spiritual experience which we call faith, and man of necessity becomes a fool.

The phenomenon of faith is often described as a condition of absolute passivity in which the grace of God is alone active while man remains silent and spellbound. We find this interpretation of the phenomenon of faith in certain forms of Protestantism and Quietist mysticism but it is far from being the whole truth. It is rather a description of the phenomenon of faith in terms of the soul, that is, of the " natural " man who remains silent and passive before God. But deep down beyond this there lies concealed the intense creative activity of the spiritual man. In the basic and original life of the spirit faith presupposes tremendous action, and an intense and infinite creativity. The " natural " man is paralyzed, and abandons his natural will. But the inner spiritual man maintains his activity and his primitive freedom at a maximum degree of intensity, and it must be remembered that an outwardly passive condition is sometimes only the expression of inward activity. The action of divine grace presupposes the action of human freedom. It is only in Calvin's teaching on the subject of predestination that we find a trenchant denial of this activity of human freedom and of the bi-lateral character of faith. In the depths of the spirit and in the hidden recesses of spiritual life and experience a reciprocal interaction between the divine and the human is always taking place. To be obsessed by either the divine or the human is to remain shut up within the restricted sphere of the soul. However, the reciprocal action between the two natures in the sphere of the spirit must not be held to involve the transcendence of one by the other. This external transcendence does not exist in the spiritual world and belongs entirely to the exoteric world of the soul.

Faith is a free spiritual act for without freedom faith is an impossibility, and it is in this respect that faith differs from knowledge. Yet knowledge also presupposes faith or a primitive intuition with regard to the reality towards which the spirit's choice is directed. Before we know the natural and empirical world of visible things we believe in it. The world of visible things compels us to recognize its existence because in the first place we have deliberately chosen it and have linked our own destiny to it. Being separated from the divine world we find ourselves in the natural world, which becomes for us the only visible and accessible one capable of compelling our recognition. It is because we believe so firmly in this world that we find it so easy to grasp. We have turned our backs on the divine world and thus it has closed its doors upon us and is now lost to sight. We have in some way forfeited the spirit that is ours and have become mere creatures of body and soul ; our consciousness is conformed to the natural world and we have adapted ourselves to the task of dealing with it. We have forgotten the spirit and have ceased to know it, for like can only be known by like.

It is by faith, by a voluntary re-direction of our power of choice, that we can once more address ourselves to the divine and spiritual world. God is only revealed in the experience of liberty and free love, and He expects such love from man. Faith proceeds from the depths of the subconscious or from the heights of the supra-conscious and destroys all previously existing forms of consciousness. It is this experience which creates fresh possibilities of knowing the spiritual and divine world. The higher gnosis is not restricted by faith, which, on the contrary, opens up the way to this experience, but of course, a gnosis of this kind is by no means the same thing as a rational and logical proof of the Divine Being. Such a proof of the divine would at once identify It with those objects of the visible and natural world which compel us to recognize their

existence. God is spirit and is revealed in the intuitive contemplation of spirit. Gnosis is precisely spiritual knowledge based upon a
living contemplation of the spiritual world which is totally different
from the world of nature.

IV

The existence of a universal logical compulsion and of rational
proofs is a function of a certain degree of spiritual unity, of a certain
" catholicity " of consciousness. When a logical proof is demanded
in matters of religious faith, then faith is dragged down to the lowest
level of spiritual unity. Scientific and also juridical necessity represent a lower degree of spiritual unity, or, to put it more accurately,
a state of disunity which belongs to the natural world. Only those
who are far removed from the spiritual and who are victims of
interior conflict have recourse to scientific and juridical proofs in
order to achieve mutual conviction. For example, I have no need
to prove certain things to a friend who is spiritually dear to me nor
to compel him to believe, for we both see the same truth, and it is
that which unites us to one another.

But even for the natural world with all its divisions there must
exist some kind of unity in truth and a certain possibility of mutual
understanding and common life. What is logically and scientifically speaking conclusive, in those truths of the natural and historical
world from which we take our bearings, only provides us with a
lower measure of unity or at least a unity of a rudimentary kind.
The truths of mathematics, of the natural sciences, and of history,
are convincing and conclusive because they must be accepted
indifferently by men who are spiritually opposed to one another
and who are inwardly in a complete state of disharmony. A
scientific and logical unity is possible in the realm of mathematical
and physical truth between those who are in spirit hostile to one
another. The recognition of these truths necessitates only an
elementary and inferior type of unity. The laws of logic, the ideal
being of Husserl, also belong to the visible world, that is, to the

world of universal necessity. The believer and the atheist, the conservative and the revolutionary, are alike forced to recognize the truths of mathematics, logic, and physics, and the same may be said of juridical necessity.

Unity, *sobornost*, and spiritual fellowship are not necessary for a recognition of a bare minimum of rights among human beings. There is no need of a spiritual fellowship in love in order that the general truths of science and of law may be recognized. Their necessitarian character is exactly suitable to a society in which men have no love for one another, and are not united in spirit but on the contrary are mutually hostile. Proofs are necessary for our opponents, but with friends unity is achieved simply by the contemplation and realization of truth. Universally recognized logical validity and the demand for proof which accompanies it have a social significance. They provide a means of restoring unity to a divided world and of maintaining it by coercion, thus preserving it from disintegration. Positive science and positive law arise in the atmosphere of a divided world and their object is to preserve unity within a dominating environment of divisive hostility. The obligation of submitting to the truths of legal science could never have arisen in an atmosphere of spiritual love and unity where knowledge is the contemplation of truth in *sobornost* and where the relations between men are determined not by juridical standards but by love itself and by the unity of the spirit. In such an atmosphere there would be no need of proving anything to anybody, nor yet of putting compulsion on anybody, for each person would be in contact only with beings spiritually akin to himself instead of with distant strangers.

As it is, truths of the moral order or the teachings of the philosophers presuppose a greater degree of spiritual unity and have a less obligatory character than the truths of mathematics, of positive science, or of law. Interchange of ideas where philosophy is concerned demands a greater degree of spiritual affinity than it does in the sphere of scientific knowledge. In philosophy those who are mutually strange and remote cannot convince one another of a single truth, for in this matter a certain unity of intuition is essential. For example the Platonists in every age constitute as it were a single spiritual society in which the contemplation of the world of ideas is always identical, but they are unable to demonstrate the existence of this world to those who do not form part of their spiritual circle. The truths of the moral order rest upon a common spiritual foundation and on the vision of a single truth, and it is difficult to convince those who remain outside this particular experience of spiritual unity. The truths of religion and revelation presuppose a maximum degree of fellowship and *sobornost*. They are not very convincing, and indeed they are highly debatable and even useless, to those who remain strangers to spiritual fellowship and keep themselves aloof from it. In fact, apart from this single common spiritual experience, these truths are no longer vital.

To give a logical and juridical meaning to the truths of religion is simply to place an exoteric social valuation upon them, and it is in this way that the spiritual world is reduced to the level of the natural and adapts itself to those forms of unity which are typical of this divided world. The natural man still has need of logical and juridical coercion and he identifies religious life with the life of this world, and the Kingdom of God with the empire of Caesar. But in the spiritual world things are in fact altogether different. The doctrine of authority as the chief criterion of truth springs from the identification of the other world order with that of this, and from the need for preserving some kind of basis for it. The doctrine of authority is perhaps a necessity for the " natural " man and the natural world at certain stages of their evolution, but it indicates weakness of faith, a lack of spiritual experience, and an incapacity for contemplating truth and facing up to reality.

The fact is that there can be no criterion of the truth of the knowledge of God outside God Himself, and it is the same with spiritual experience, which can rest only upon a deep personal foundation. But spiritual experience is at once individual and supra-individual, and it is never entirely personal. The search for transcendent criteria is the result of the isolation of the " natural " world.

In the phenomenon of faith man's love, his activity and his powers
of choice are given, and they mysteriously unite with the action of
divine grace and with the outpouring of the divine love upon him.
Faith is the acquiring of grace which knows nothing of necessity in
the logical or juridical sense ; it reveals to us a unity of quite a
different order and is the very opposite of law and logic. Above all
the vision of God is given in freedom and not under authority.

V

Revelation is adapted to the structure of consciousness and is pro-
portioned to the degree of development which it has reached. It
follows therefore that there are degrees also in revelation. The
pouring forth of the divine illumination corresponds to the changes
to which consciousness is subject and to the various tendencies and
manifestations of the spirit. In the different stages of revelation not
only man but the world changes, and whole new periods come into
existence in the original universal life of the spirit. The Old Testament revelation was limited by the life of the Hebrew people and
corresponds to the degree of consciousness attained by the ancient
people of Israel. The light of revelation only spreads in proportion
to the capacity of consciousness and to the degree of receptivity
which the natural man possesses for the spiritual world. Jacob
Boehme said that the divine love suffers distortion through the
darker elements of existence and thus appears as the divine wrath
and as a consuming fire. God in Himself, in the divine Trinity, is
absolute love, but it is possible to regard Him as the wrath of, as it
were, " an element separated from God " and devoid of love. The
ancient image of Jahveh is only an exoteric revelation of God distorted by obscure natural elements.

Yet even in the primitive and naturalistic revelation of the Old
Testament there are different stages, for at first the revelation of
God to the Hebrews was polytheistic as among all ancient peoples.
Monotheism is the fruit of a later development. The advent of
monotheism was in some kind of a way ante-dated, and it was only

at a later period that it was assigned to the past. But even in the revelation of the one God there are also different stages and degrees. The revelation of Moses represents a totally different historic period from that of the prophets. The religious consciousness which regarded the one God as the Jewish national Deity was of quite a different order from that which saw in Him the God of the whole world and of every nation. Old Testament religious consciousness passed through the stage of naturalistic nationalism as well as through that of heathen polytheism.

A very deep spiritual crisis had to take place in prophetic circles, for the consciousness of the Jew had to pass through a period of individualism, by freeing itself from religious nationalism and racialism, and by experiencing those spiritual processes which are reflected in the books of Job and of Solomon, while, parallel to the increasing rigidity of the religion of the Law, an intense apocalyptic strain had also to make its appearance. Then, on the basis of individualism, during the Hellenistic period a feeling for universalism had to arise in order that a spiritual environment might be created in which it was possible for the light of the New Testament to shine. We have here an extremely complex history of the development of the religious consciousness, reflecting many spiritual struggles and a great deepening and widening of spiritual experience. There is nothing static here ; everything is dynamic. We notice, too, that the higher stage of revelation always includes the spiritual creations of the previous stage. Revelation necessarily presupposes development in the world and implies also a dynamic development of consciousness.

Similar processes of spiritual evolution took place in the pagan world also. There too changes in the structure of the religious consciousness and a deepening and widening of its experience prepared the ground for the reception of the Christian revelation which is the central event of the spiritual life of the whole world. In the great spiritual moments of Greek paganism, in the cults of Dionysos and Orpheus, in the Mysteries, in Greek tragedy and philosophy, in the works of Heraclitus, Pythagoras, and Plato, pagan naturalism met its defeat, the religious consciousness developed, and the spirit was revealed. Paganism also had its contacts with the spiritual world, and there were stages in its revelation of God. The eager longing for resurrection among the Egyptians, the religious dualism of the Persians, the denunciation of the evil, deceitfulness, and vanity of the natural world by the religious mind of India, are important moments in the history of the spirit, in the development of consciousness, and in the revelation of the divine to the world.

Even Christianity itself has its degrees of revelation, and the history of Christianity has its special epochs. The fullness and depth of Christian truth are not adequately revealed owing to the existence of diverse structures of consciousness and the different degrees of spirituality. There are different periods of Christianity not only in the life of individuals but also in world history. There are different degrees of development of consciousness and manifestations of spirituality, which are by no means due to different individual achievement in the way of sanctity. There is a perfection and sanctity of spirit, and also a perfection and sanctity of soul, an esoteric and an exoteric consciousness. Christian truth is revealed in a dynamic and creative process in the world which is still unfinished nor can it be finished before the end of time. The revelation of Christian truth to man demands an eternally dynamic state of consciousness and an eternal creative tension of spirit.

But the New Testament revelation is still hampered by unregenerate human nature and by pagan forms of consciousness. The spiritual world has not definitely entered into the natural. The infinite remains imprisoned within the finite. The mystery is made known in exoteric fashion, and thus it is that Christianity is still too often a paganized Christianity (so far as this world is concerned). The revelation given in the Bible and the symbolic stories of the creation of man and the world are interpreted in the spirit of the Old Testament. Christianity for the most part remains enslaved to the Law and is converted by the natural man into a legal religion instead of a religion of grace and freedom ; it has moulded itself to the natural life of this world and its iron necessities. Even the mystery of grace is naturalized, objectified, and rationalized by being assimilated to the forces operating in the natural world—a process clearly apparent in the systematizing of Catholic theology.

Thus Christianity in its development passes through a sort of legalistic phase, a kind of "Jewish-paganism" where law predominates. The spirit of the prophets is not seldom denied, and so Christianity is transformed into a rigid and static system of theological doctrines, canons, and external organization. We picture the Church as a finished building, spire and all. The infinite horizons of the spiritual world are cut off from our gaze and a Christian legalism and pharisaism begin to dominate everything. Creative energy of mind only arouses fear, and restrictions are placed upon its activity. Church Christians often resemble the positivists in their static view of consciousness as something severely limited and incapable of change.

VI

The various stages and periods of revelation are not only a manifestation of changes in consciousness and its receptive capacity, but they also reflect a theogonic process. Various periods of revelation disclose the inner life of the Divine Being and the relationships existing within the Trinity. The mysterious and hidden life of God is reflected in our human world. The essential and fundamental moments in the development of the human consciousness, that is to say, the periods of man's creation, also indicate moments of the divine life. Man is born in revelation ; and not only the divine nature but also human nature is there disclosed. Degrees of revelation imply also degrees in the development of man.

Revelation is always the revelation both of God and of man ; it is divine-human by nature, and it is this aspect which finds its definitive expression in Christianity. In Christ the God-Man there is a revelation not only of God but also of His other-self, that is to say, of man ; for the Second Hypostasis of the Holy Trinity is Man in the absolute sense, and His revelation means the appearance of a new spiritual and eternal man.

But this new spiritual man is not definitively manifested, and in principle a new revelation is possible within Christianity. Nor can any real objections be urged against this possibility. One thing alone can be said against it, and that is, that the new revelation might possibly destroy the earlier one ; but this, of course, would be far from the case, for in reality the new would be the continuation and the fulfilment of the old. The creative process of the world must continue its irresistible forward march, for any arrest of progress would mean the paralysis and extinction of the spirit. Revelation is life, it is a divine-human process which has as its object the limitless world of the spirit, and not the mere imparting of abstract truths and rigid formulas. But while the consciousness of man is capable of attaining the infinitude of the divine and of the cosmic, man protects himself against these unlimited forces as well as against nature by jealously guarding the isolation of his consciousness. In the pagan world man was more open to the influences of the inner life of nature and to the mysteries of the universe than in the Christian world where he wins freedom for his spirit from the powers of nature by setting limits to his consciousness. But if at one time it is necessary to protect man from the infinitude of the cosmos, and if, thanks to this, his spirit is free to turn towards God, a time may also come when man runs the risk of increasing his isolation and separation from the divine world. The natural world owes it origin firstly to a transcendental conception of revelation and secondly to the succeeding denial of this revelation. But to-day the naturalistic view of the world is undergoing a crisis and there is a return to the spiritual world-view.

Between the West and the East there is a fairly fundamental difference. In the East, for example in India, there is a greater flexibility in the structure of the human consciousness, and the emergence of a cosmic consciousness is not as unlikely as it is in the West. Man for this very reason finds himself lost in the infinite cosmos. On the other hand, Western culture rests upon an intense historical dynamism and upon immutability of consciousness. Eastern culture knows nothing of historical dynamism though it does admit the dynamism of the human consciousness, that is to say, of a change which makes the discovery of spiritual worlds possible. But such a divergence cannot exist for ever. In the West, man has been moulded through the possession of a perfectly stable consciousness which has protected him from the infinitude of the cosmos and at the same time through the pressure of a historical dynamism which has continually thrust him forward into the future.

But this course of development has brought mankind to a crisis. The Christian revelation, which surpasses all others in existence, has become far too rigid and it looks sometimes as if the spirit had departed from the Christian world. A unique spiritual world must be created in which dynamism of consciousness and the appearance of a cosmic consciousness will not make man the plaything of the universe. Faith in the Christian revelation guarantees the fact that man is not destined to disappear. When the Christian revelation itself is understood more esoterically and more mystically some real progress will have been made in the manifestation of the spiritual man, and a new period in Christian history will begin. While a true intellectual culture and genuine knowledge will contribute to the coming of this epoch, there is an artificial sort of culture which always has a destructive effect on the religious life ; and there is also a true form of knowledge, a real illumination of consciousness, and a triumph over that obscurantism which still forces Christianity down to the lowest levels and which ministers to superstition and prejudice. The truth of revelation must be freed from the trammels of a restricted field of consciousness, and an illumination infinitely more radiant in character must shine forth from the spiritual world.

CHAPTER FOUR

The Freedom of the Spirit

I

SPIRIT is freedom unconstrained by the outward and the objective, where what is deep and inward determines all. To be in the spirit is to be in oneself. So far as the spirit is concerned the constraint of the natural world is only the reflection of inward processes. The religious pathos of freedom is the pathos of spirituality; to win true freedom is to enter into the spiritual world.

Freedom is the freedom of the spirit and it is mere illusion to search for it exclusively in the natural world. For the order of freedom and the order of nature are opposed to one another, and the deepest thinkers have always been aware of the difference between them. Nature is always a deterministic system, and our own nature therefore cannot be the source of our freedom. The attempts which have been made to base freedom upon naturalistic metaphysics have always been superficial, and they are analogous to those which seek to establish immortality upon a similar foundation. But it is quite as difficult to find liberty as immortality within the human soul or within the world of nature. Freedom must be discovered and revealed in the experience of the spiritual life, for it is impossible to demonstrate it or deduce its existence from the nature of things. In every object known to us, in so far as it is a natural object, freedom eludes our grasp and disappears. Rationalization in all its forms is the death of freedom.

The religious and spiritual problem of freedom must not be confused with the question of free-will. Freedom has its foundations not in the will but in the spirit, and man is made free not by abstract will-power but by the efforts of his whole conscious being. When men seek for proof of the existence of free-will the true pathos of freedom is entirely overlooked. For the motive behind such attempts has been the desire to establish the moral responsibility of man by justifying the merit of good works and the existence of punishments in this world and the next. The interest attaching to the question of free-will has been pedagogic and utilitarian and not in essence spiritual.

Spiritual metaphysics which have frequently been the predominating official philosophy always included in their system the defence of free-will, but they have never been a philosophy of freedom.[1] The substantialist doctrine of the soul claimed to provide a foundation for immortality and free-will, but it was a form of naturalism and involved a rationalist conception of the spiritual life. Substantialist nature was the source of determinism not of freedom.[2] The doctrine of the freedom of choice in the sense of a freedom of indifference is clearly the least satisfying of all.

It is interesting to note that in the controversies on the subject of the reconciliation of grace and free-will, which have divided Western religious thought from the days of St. Augustine and Pelagius, it was the Jesuits, who knew nothing of the pathos of spiritual freedom and who rejected liberty of conscience, who became the most ardent champions of free-will. The Jansenists, however, who like Luther denied free-will and attributed everything to grace, recognized religious liberty far more than the Jesuits did. Pelagius, the fanatical upholder of a natural and invariable free-will, was a rationalist quite incapable of understanding the mystery of freedom. The very antithesis between freedom and grace is false and vicious, for it involves a rationalization of freedom which subjects it to the natural world order.

This false antithesis between grace and freedom was the pre-

[1] One of the most interesting books on this subject is that of C. Secrétan, *The Philosophy of Freedom*.

[2] Substance is a category of naturalist metaphysics, not of the natural sciences, which can do without it.

cursor of the division between Catholicism and Protestantism, in which certain quite paradoxical divergences are to be observed. Protestantism always proclaimed the principle of liberty of conscience and defended religious freedom, while at the same time it denied free-will in favour of grace ; it refused to recognize the freedom of man in relation to God.[1]

Catholicism, on the other hand, denied liberty of conscience in religion (indeed the very principle was formally condemned by the Vatican as the principle of liberalism) and yet maintained free-will on an equality with the action of grace. It was round this point that the controversy on faith and works took place. Without intending it Protestantism and Catholicism opposed freedom to grace and works to faith. The religious problem of the freedom of the spirit was thus badly stated, and with insufficient clearness. The question of freedom has nothing whatever to do with the question of the freedom of willing in the sense in which a naturalist psychology or a moralizing pedagogy use the term. It is, rather, the question of the fundamental principle of being and of life. The very perception of being depends on freedom which is itself prior to being. Liberty is a spiritual and religious category not a naturalistic or metaphysical one. On the question of freedom philosophical tendencies and religious doctrines are divided. In Dostoievsky this problem of the freedom of the spirit appears in its deepest and most acute form.[2] But what troubled Dostoievsky so profoundly was not the question of free-will but something infinitely deeper.

The idea of freedom is one of the leading ideas of Christianity. Without it the creation of the world, the Fall, and Redemption are incomprehensible, and the phenomenon of faith remains inexplicable. Without freedom there can be no theodicy and the whole world-process becomes nonsense. A spirit of limitless freedom pervades the Gospels and Epistles. Freedom must not only be an object of investigation, but in our researches we must manifest the

---

[1] See Luther's remarkable book : *De Servo arbitrio*.
[2] See the author's *Dostoievsky*.

freedom of the spirit and state the problem of freedom in a spiritually favourable atmosphere.

" Then are the children free " (St. Matthew). " If then the Son shall make you free, ye shall be free indeed " (St. John). " Ye shall know the truth and the truth shall make you free " (St. John). " Henceforth I call you not servants, for the servant knoweth not what his lord doeth, but I have called you friends, for all things that I have heard of My Father I have made known unto you " (St. John). " But whoso looketh into the perfect law of liberty . . ." (St. James). " Ye are bought with a price, be not yet the servants of men " (St. Paul). " Where the spirit of the Lord is there is liberty " (St. Paul). " Thou art no more a servant but a son " (St. Paul). " Brethren, ye have been called unto liberty " (St. Paul). " He will have no man be His servant against his will or by con- straint ; but He wills that all men serve Him freely and voluntarily and know the sweetness of His service " (St. John Chrysostom). " But I never compel any who are not willing, for I desire that the service of those who obey Me may be free and spontaneous " (St. Simon the New Theologian). In Dostoievsky the Grand Inquisitor says to Christ : " You desired the free love of man in order that, beguiled and captivated by You, he might come to You freely."

Here we are dealing not with a special question about free-will, but with the whole question of the freedom of the spirit. Here freedom is the whole atmosphere of the spiritual life and its essential principle. For there is a certain quality of feeling and of under- standing of life connected with freedom. Christianity presupposes both the spirit of freedom and the freedom of the spirit. Without this spiritual atmosphere it cannot exist and becomes utterly meaningless.

II

The religious problem of the freedom of the spirit cannot be solved by a rational philosophy. The best thinkers have always been conscious of its unfathomable mystery. Bergson tells us that all definitions of freedom rationalize it and lead to its disappearance. It is impossible to elaborate a logical and positive concept of freedom which is capable of completely elucidating its mystery. Freedom is life which can only be grasped in the experience of life, for in its inner mystery it eludes the categories of reason. Rational philosophy involves a static view of freedom, while the latter is dynamic in its very essence and can only be conceived dynamically. Freedom must be analysed from the point of view of its inner destiny, in its tragic dialectic, in the various spiritual epochs through which it passes, and in those departures from its true nature in which it suffers decay and may even be transformed into its very opposite.

Freedom is not a rigid and static category, it is the inner dynamic of the spirit, the irrational mystery of being, of life, and of destiny. But this does not mean that it is unknowable and that we must reconcile ourselves to agnosticism, though the path to such knowledge is a difficult one and has no resemblance to that which naturalistic metaphysics follows and which leads us to the doctrines of determinism and free-will. Actually determinism is right in so far as the physical and metaphysical world is concerned, and it is almost impossible to refute it rationally.

Apart from Christianity there is no freedom, and determinism is always supreme. Freedom of spirit, like immortality, is not natural to man ; it is rather a new birth in which the spiritual man makes his appearance and which is only revealed in the experience of the spiritual life. Its source is not in the soul, and, of course, still less in the body of man, in that natural being of his which is always subject to the laws of nature and restricted on every side by external determining forces, but in the spirit, and in the acquiring of spiritual life. To be free is to have entered upon another order of being which is spiritual in character.

There is a classic definition of freedom which remains indisputably true in spite of its inability to give us a positive clue to its mystery. According to this freedom is self-determination in the inmost depths of being and is opposed to every kind of external determination which constitutes a compulsion in itself. Hegel defined it as follows, namely, " Freedom is to be in possession of oneself." Self-determination is precisely that which proceeds from the inmost depths of the spirit where spiritual forces are at work and not from some exterior natural impulse, nor from man's own nature. In a state of freedom man is not determined from without under the compulsion of a nature alien to himself, but he is self-determined in the depths of his spiritual life and out of his own spiritual energies ; he finds himself in his own spiritual world.

Physical causality offers no explanation of the inner relation between cause and effect, for it remains simply an external law. It is therefore not without reason that Mach proposes to replace the principle of causality which is of a purely mythological character by that of functional relationships. The sciences concerned with the physical world do not succeed in penetrating to the real nucleus of being, for their researches are directed to ascertaining the causes underlying the phenomena of the external world. The natural world appears to us as devoid of any internal energy, and there is no such thing as being acting through its own internal resources so far as it is concerned. In our search for the efficient causes of physical reality we find ourselves increasingly on the circumference of things. In fact the reign of necessity in the physical world is exactly this sort of determination by means of external origins or causes. We regard phenomena as belonging to the physical and material world because they are determined by external causality and because they show no sign of creative energy acting from within. But when we see within nature an inner force and we regard natural events as manifestations of an intimate creative energy, nature itself ceases to be purely material and physical and becomes part of the spiritual world. Material nature with its intractability, its impenetrability, and the mutual exclusiveness of its component parts, is indeed far removed from the real centre of being, for it involves a disintegration of the totality of things into elements which are at once inert in relation to one another and reciprocally coercive. The material world is constituted by the loss of the freedom of the spirit. This is why external physical causality operates within it, creating that determinism which is the indispensable order of nature.

In the psychical causality to be observed in those phenomena of the soul which still form part of the natural world, the inner relation between things and the connection between cause and effect is to be seen more clearly. But psychical reality being still subject to material reality and to the life of the body, external causes continue to operate within it ; it is still a divided reality, isolated in itself, and that is why it meets opposition at every turn from a nature alien to its own and sees itself subject to the action of necessity. Freedom is manifested in psychical reality in proportion to the degree in which the spiritual world is revealed in it.

The human soul is an arena in which there takes place the interplay of freedom and necessity, the spiritual and the natural world. When the spiritual is operative within the psychical, the freedom of the spirit is revealed ; when it is the natural which is active, then necessity once more asserts its sway. Man is determined from within, from the inmost depths of his being, in so far as the spirit subdues in him the psychical and natural elements and the soul is absorbed by the spirit and the spirit enters into the soul. Freedom belongs only to those phenomena of the life of the soul which can be called spiritual.

Psychical causality is only a form of natural causality. Within its sphere one phenomenon of the soul determines another, and this means that necessity still operates, though it is more complex and inward in character than that of the natural world. Psychical causality does not reveal the inmost depths of the interior activity of being ; it involves only the distinction of one psychological phenomenon from another. Since the two events which it links together belong to the life of the soul the connection between them is, of course, of a more inward nature than that of physical phenomena, but we still see nothing of the real freedom of the spirit in it.

That inner, deep, hidden, and mysterious energy which creates life is only apparent in spiritual causality. Here the antithesis between freedom and causality disappears ; in the determination of events and phenomena in life of this kind there is no longer room for extrinsicism. In the spiritual life the cause of activity lies within, for it is self-determining. Here the mysterious relationships underlying the life of the whole are revealed, and the inner nucleus of being, hitherto concealed by the symbols of the natural world, appears.

The freedom of the spirit, which is itself the origin of the effects we observe and which creates life, is revealed to us as something completely unfathomable. It is impossible for us ever to plumb its depths ; nowhere is the ground firm beneath our feet ; there is literally nothing by which it can be determined from without. Nor can our substantial nature provide us with a foundation,[1] for, on the contrary, it is the freedom of the spirit from which all nature springs. Freedom does not raise us up towards nature, but towards the idea of the divine, and towards the void which is prior to being. It is rooted in non-being. Free activity is original and entirely irrational, for all rational conceptions of it involve its identification with the phenomena of nature. The determined world of physical and psychical causality is a secondary sphere and is the product of freedom, for freedom is not the result of necessity, as many thinkers assert, but rather it is necessity which results from freedom as a consequence of its own peculiar orientation. The natural, psychical, and physical world is the result of events and actions in the spiritual world. Separation from God and from the original sources of spiritual life, the disunion and division of being produced by an irrational orientation of it, are reflected in the psychical and material world. We live in a secondary world of reflections and the necessity which binds us is the natural result of our own evil freedom.

It is in freedom that the inward activity of all life is made perceptible. The experience of freedom is known to every being

[1] It is by an appeal to nature that Lopatine imagines he can find a basis for freedom in the second volume of his *Positive Problems of Philosophy*, a work remarkable from many points of view.

possessing a spiritual life. The mystery of action and of the relation between cause and effect is not revealed to us through physical causality and only in part through psychical causality. The original phenomena of action and creation in their essentially dynamic character are given in the life of the spirit, and it is only in their secondary aspect that we catch a glimpse of them in the natural and determined world of external causality. This means that freedom is dynamic in a higher degree. It is perceptible only in its interior activity and cannot be discovered apart from it. For a static sort of freedom degenerates into necessity and this fact compels us to recognise that there are not only different conceptions but also different stages of freedom.

III

As early as St. Augustine we get the distinction between two kinds of freedom, namely *libertas minor* and *libertas major*. In fact we can see that the word " freedom " possesses two different meanings, for by " freedom·" is understood either that initial and irrational liberty which is prior to good and evil and determines their choice, or else that intelligent freedom which is our final liberty in truth and goodness. Consequently freedom is regarded either as a starting-point and a means to an end, or else as an aim and object.

Socrates, and the Greeks generally, recognized only the existence of the second kind of freedom, which comes to us through reason, truth, and goodness. In the words of the Gospel, " Ye shall know the truth, and the truth shall make you free," it is the same kind of freedom which is referred to, that is to say, freedom in the truth and by the truth. When we say of a man that he has attained a true liberty by having overcome the lower part of his nature and having submitted it to the control of the highest spiritual principles, that is, to truth and goodness, it is always this second kind of freedom that we refer to. Similarly when we say of an individual or a whole people that they must free themselves from spiritual slavery and attain a true liberty, it is again the same sort of freedom that we have in mind. It is the freedom to which man is making his way, the very summit of his life's activity and its final goal ; it is the freedom which must one day be achieved through the triumph of the highest principles of life.

But there is another kind of freedom, the kind from which man starts and by which he makes choice of his direction in life and through which he acquires truth and goodness. There is a sort of freedom which is, in some kind of way, the mysterious source of life, the basic and original experience, the abyss which is deeper than being itself and by which being is determined. Man feels within himself this irrational and unfathomable freedom in the very fibre of his being, and it is closely bound up with his potential energies. But Thomism with its Aristotelian doctrine about potentiality is led to deny freedom in the end as being a species of imperfection.

This idea of freedom has received brilliant expression in the hero of Dostoievsky's *Spirit of the Underworld*. Man is an irrational being and he tends more than anything else to live according to his own will. He puts up with suffering for the sake of this free-will. He is ready to upset the whole rational order and unity of life if they menace his freedom of choice or are imposed upon him by force.

If we admit only the freedom which is the gift of truth and has its source in God, and if we reject our freedom to choose and to receive the truth, we are inevitably and fatally impelled towards tyranny, and the freedom of the spirit is replaced by the organization of the spirit. Let us face the fact that true freedom is only possible in and through Christ ; that Christ, whatever may be said, must be freely accepted and that it is by a free spiritual act that we must come to Him. He wants us to accept Him freely, He desires the unforced love of man, and He can never compel anyone for He always has regard for our freedom. God can only accept the free. God expects the free love of man and man expects freedom from God, that is to say, the divine truth which will make him free.

God expects freedom from man ; He waits for his free response to the divine call. True liberty is that which God demands from us and not that which we demand from God. It is upon this deep foundation that man's freedom is based ; it is latent in the deepest recesses of his being. Truth gives us the highest kind of freedom but freedom is necessary for the acceptance of this truth. Truth can neither constrain nor compel, and it cannot give freedom to man through violence. It is not enough to accept Truth, that is to say, God ; It must be freely accepted. Freedom cannot be the result of constraint even were this constraint divine. Freedom cannot be expected from an organized, harmonious, and perfect condition of life, for such a condition itself must be the result of freedom. Salvation comes through the Truth which brings us freedom, and salvation imposed from without is impossible and useless. Salvation cannot be achieved without man's freedom, for it *is* his freedom in Truth and in God. This freedom therefore cannot be realized by means of compulsion and in the absence of liberty.

When we affirm the existence of the second kind of freedom as unique we affirm the divine freedom. But the freedom of the spirit is not only the freedom of God, it is also that of man. Human freedom is not only freedom in God, but also freedom in relation to God. Man must be free in respect of God, the world, and his own nature. Freedom in the acceptance of Truth cannot be won from Truth itself, for it is prior to it. Freedom is not identical with goodness and perfection of life ; it is this compulsion and this identification which have been the cause of its being misunderstood and denied. Goodness and the perfection of life must be freely achieved, for it is just the fact that they are freely accepted and achieved which gives to the spiritual, religious, and moral life its quality of originality and true dignity.

The great mystery of freedom is not to be discovered in that direction in which men generally seek for it or where they often seek to establish its existence, for man's freedom is not something which is constituted by any claim which man asserts to it. Man easily forgoes his liberty for the sake of peace and happiness, he bears the heavy burden of it with difficulty and is only too ready to shift it on to stronger shoulders. In his individual and historic destiny he too often renounces freedom, preferring quietness and happiness under the conditions of necessity. We see examples of this abdication of freedom by man and this preference for compulsion as well in the old theocratic theories as in the new ideas of socialism.

The freedom of the spirit presupposes a kindling of the spirit, but such a kindling is not often met with nor is it on this that human societies are usually based. Morality, custom, and society generally become enfeebled and their very crystallization is due to the quenching of the fire of the spirit. Man can get on without freedom, and the demand for spiritual liberty which is the cause of so much tragedy and suffering in life is not a human but a divine claim. It is not man but God who cannot get on without human freedom. God demands from man the freedom of the spirit, for He only wants the man who is spiritually free. The divine plan for man and for the world cannot become incarnate apart from the freedom of man and the freedom of the spirit. Human freedom has as its foundation the demands of the divine Will.

It is not enough to say that man must carry out the divine Will, for we still have to discover in what this Will consists. If it is God's pleasure that man should be free, then the affirmation of man's liberty is the fulfilling of the divine Will. It is in the name of God and of the fulfilling of His plan for man and the world that man's freedom is to be affirmed, and it is not only the second kind of freedom, but the first also, which must be affirmed ; that is, not only liberty in God but also liberty in the acceptance of God.

It is upon this very deep foundation that freedom as a principle of being prior to all organized and perfected life rests. Liberty is bound up not with the form but with the matter of life, to the irrational in life ; it is associated with what is infinite, with the very depths of being and of life. These infinite depths were still undiscovered by the mind of Greece and that is why it could not conceive of the idea of freedom. But it is within the sphere of Christianity and in the spiritual world which it reveals that this infinitude is disclosed. Freedom is bound up with the potential energies of the spirit. The denial of freedom always means subjection to the finite.

St. Augustine really only recognized the second kind of liberty, namely, that which God who is the Truth has given to us. Our initial liberty, according to him, had been definitely lost by reason of the Fall, and he could discuss the problem of freedom only in relation to sin. *Posse non peccare, non posse non peccare, non posse peccare.* His struggle with the rationalistic naturalism of Pelagius tended to make him depreciate freedom. And so later on the semi-Pelagianism of the Jesuits inevitably provoked the reaction associated with Pascal and the Jansenists. The very problem of freedom was minimized and its significance distorted, for to compel one to state a question falsely is tantamount to inducing one to give a false answer to it. Pelagius looked at the problem of freedom from a rationalistic point of view and St. Augustine denied freedom. Freedom and grace were opposed to one another. Those who had a rationalistic cast of mind pronounced in favour of freedom while those who were mystically inclined supported grace.

But there is a true mysticism of freedom because freedom is a mystery belonging to the inmost depths of the spirit. It is not grace which is opposed to freedom but necessity. The realm of the spirit is the realm of freedom and grace, as opposed to the realm of nature, necessity, and compulsion. Thus the error into which St. Augustine fell in his solution of the problem of freedom had disastrous consequences. It amounted to a justification of compulsion in questions of faith, to the denial of freedom of con-science, to the possibility of punishing heretics, and, in a word, to that general course of development which led in time to the establishment of the Inquisition. It was his experience of the struggle against the Donatists which impelled St. Augustine along this dangerous path. Freedom led him into temptation.

St. Thomas Aquinas also completely rejected freedom, for which his scholasticism leaves no place whatever. Love for God is for him a necessity. Freedom is the badge of imperfection. And such an idea of freedom had, of course, fatal results in the denial of the freedom of the spirit in religious and social life. It was thought that the imperfection resulting from liberty must come to an end, in order that the love of God might be forced to manifest itself. The second kind of freedom was here confused with divine necessity. It is along this line of the denial of freedom that humanity fell a victim to the spirit of the Grand Inquisitor. Catholic and Byzantine theocracy, as well as atheistic socialism, are naturally inclined to deny human freedom, to control and to organize for good the life of man, that is to say, to identify freedom with the necessity either of divine organization or of the social organization of life. The denial of liberty by the Christian consciousness is an extreme consequence of the doctrine of the Fall, and of the denial of spiritual nature and the divine image in man. Catholic theology tends to believe that man has not been created in the likeness of God and that Adam received his higher qualities through a special operation of grace. In separating himself from God man lost his initial freedom and it is only by the action of grace that he can again acquire it. Grace acts upon him, and by its organized action he can recover his freedom, that is to say, he can receive it from the truth and from God.

All this goes to prove that freedom has been understood entirely in the second of its two senses. The first kind of human freedom consists in what St. Augustine characterized by the words : *Non posse peccare*. There is really no human freedom, only that of God. The antithesis between freedom and grace is maintained because grace is considered as a transcendent force acting upon man from without. In this way it is in some sort objectified and excluded from the inner life of the spirit. There is held to be a great gulf fixed between the creative activity of God which is responsible for nature and the activity of God as the Author of grace. Christian thought has never gone sufficiently deeply into this problem.

If human nature was definitively perverted and the freedom of the spirit definitively impaired, there would be no faculty in man capable of receiving the truth of revelation and he would be insensible to the operations of grace. But man though wounded and broken remains a spiritual being and has preserved his religious consciousness, for the Word of God could not be addressed to a being who was deprived of it. Liberty in man precedes the action of revelation and grace. The operation of grace presupposes freedom in man, and is distinguished by this very fact from the activity of creation. A consistent transcendentalism pushed to its logical conclusions is an impossibility ; it denies the possibility of a religious life, and the juridical comprehension of the relations between God and man illustrates its consequences only too forcibly. The very fact of religious experience presupposes a certain degree of immanence, the existence of the religious consciousness, and of the freedom of the spirit in human nature.[1]

Man bears upon him the mark of the divine image, he is the divine idea, the divine plan, without, however, being divine by nature, for had he been so he would not have been free. The freedom of man presupposes the possibility of his divinization as well as the possibility of the destruction of the divine idea and image. Man deprived of the freedom to do wrong would be merely a good automaton.

IV

Freedom is dynamic by nature. It has its own destiny and cannot be understood except by those who have entered into its tragic dialectic. The existence of two kinds of freedom has been revealed to us and each possesses its fatal dialectic through which it degenerates into its opposite, that is, into slavery and necessity. Indeed the destiny of freedom is tragic and so is that of human life. The first kind of freedom, which is in itself irrational and unfathomable, by no means alone guarantees that man will follow the right path, that he will come to God, that truth will dominate in his life and that freedom will in the long run be supreme in the world. Unlimited force makes possible the most varied and opposite actualizations.

The first kind of liberty does not necessarily mean an adherence to the life in truth and in God. It may mean the choice of the

[1] The diatribes against the Protestants on the subject of freedom in Moehler's *Symbolics* and Denifle's *Luther and Lutheranism* are superficial, and are devoid of any ontological profundity.

path of discord and hatred, of the affirmation of one part as against another, the way of disunion in the spiritual world, that is to say, the way of evil. Initial freedom has not been sanctified in love, it has not been illuminated by the inner light of truth.

When freedom precipitates man into the world of division and egoistical self-affirmation, he necessarily falls under the domination of the laws of natural necessity and becomes a slave of the lower elements. For freedom contains hidden within it certain poisonous and destructive influences, of which we are only too well aware from having experienced them in our own individual destinies. We know how our irrational freedom brings us into a condition of slavery and forces us to submit to ineluctable necessity. The historic destiny of nations tells the same story ; destructive revolutions, born of man's irrational liberty, precipitate us into anarchy which in turn brings slavery and tyranny. The doom of necessity strikes down the nations with fearful blows. We know in our own experience that the anarchy of our passions and the lowest impulses of our nature which live each for its own ends bring us into a real state of slavery, deprive us of the freedom of the spirit, and bring us under the domination of necessity and our lower nature. The danger of anarchy, that is to say, of definite disintegration, is always lurking in the background when our initial freedom is centred upon itself.

Incalculable forces both for good and evil are latent in the first kind of liberty, for it is in that unfathomable obscurity which lies behind good and evil that the energy actualized by this freedom lies dormant. The myth of the Fall is bound up with this initial freedom and it could not be explained apart from it. This freedom, and the separation from the divine centre of which it is the cause, are the first stages in the dynamism of the spirit, and a mysterious moment of the basic and original life. This process takes place in the most intimate depths of the spiritual world and is only reflected in our natural world. This world, which is subject to the laws of necessity, and which is at the same time a world of disunion, division, and purely mechanical relationships, is a secondary product of the interior dialectic of freedom in the spiritual world. The dialectic of initial freedom is the source of the tragedy of the world-process, a tragedy which issues in nothing, neither through this liberty itself, nor through the necessity in which it results.

The second kind of liberty also possesses in itself a fatal destiny and its own ineluctable interior dialectic ; it is also threatened by the danger of degenerating into its opposite. Without the first kind of freedom it leads to arbitrariness and constraint where truth and goodness are concerned, and to a virtue imposed from without, that is to say, to a denial of the liberty of the spirit and to the tyrannical organization of human life. If the first kind of freedom spells anarchy which ends by annihilating liberty, the second gives rise to an arbitrary organization of life, whether theocratic or communistic, in which the freedom of the spirit and of the conscience is entirely destroyed. An authoritarian type of society is a product of this second kind of liberty understood in an abstract sense.

Human life, whether individual or social, is constrained by force to submit to truth and goodness. Whether this truth be theocratic, papal, imperialist, or communist, the freedom of the spirit is equally denied and the free choice of truth and goodness becomes an impossibility. The freedom resulting from the arbitrary organization of life is the only sort recognized. Communists even admit that a definitely higher type of liberty will be gained by the whole of mankind, but it will be by the careful training of human nature and by its submission to the truth and goodness of Communism apart from which there is no freedom. Catholics are actuated by the same considerations when they deny liberty of conscience. They reject the liberty of evil but they affirm the liberty of goodness in the good. Thus freedom results from necessity ; for some, that of divine necessity and of organized grace, for others, again, that of social necessity and of an organized and rationalized society subjected to a system of rules and regulations. Goodness becomes automatic. The second kind of liberty is dogged by the temptation of the Grand Inquisitor who may belong either to the extreme " right " or to the extreme " left." Man is freed from the burden of freedom of choice in the interests of the peace and happiness of society and the organization of human life. The spiritual world ceases to possess the quality of infinitude and the organization of the merely finite becomes a substitute for its true pathos.

Communism is as much the product of the tragedy of freedom as anarchy. While revolutions within national life start with the affirmation of the unrestricted character of the first kind of liberty, they end by making the same claims for the second. This means that freedom in its dynamism and its inner dialectic leads to tyranny and self-destruction. The first kind of liberty means division and disunion. The second strives to subject this division and disunion to the control of organized truth and goodness and by this means to reduce the world to order and to a series of arbitrary and mechanical relationships ; in a word its object is to create necessitarian freedom in and through necessity. There appears to be no end to this tragedy of freedom, and it seems doomed to perish, for it contains within itself the seeds of its own destruction. The dialectic of both the first and the second kinds of freedom belongs to a world already divorced from its divine centre. But a more disturbing consideration is that Christianity itself has been constantly led into error by freedom, examples of which are to be seen in Pelagianism, in St. Augustine, in Jansenism, and in Calvinism, in the denial of the principle of freedom of conscience in the Church. The tragedy of the universal process is the tragedy of freedom.

V

No system of naturalistic metaphysics can reveal the natural issue of this tragedy of the self-annihilation of liberty. The natural man moves from the first kind of freedom to the second and from the second to the first, but everywhere freedom is poisoned from within and dies. The conflict between freedom and necessity appears to be insurmountable, for freedom itself is the origin of necessity. Necessity does not counteract the deadly effects of freedom for necessity itself arises immediately from freedom. And how can it be rendered innocuous unless some kind of external limitation is placed upon freedom ?   How, in a word, can freedom be separated from the evil it brings in its train except by the destruction of freedom itself ?

To this universal problem there is no solution save in the coming of Christ.   Only the coming of the new Adam, the spiritual man, can end this tragedy of freedom and can overcome the conflict between freedom and necessity.   The Son of God descends into the void of original freedom.   Only the New Adam can take from freedom its deadly effects without compromising freedom itself ; it is an impossibility for the children of the first Adam.   For them the victory over evil means the destruction of freedom.   In Christ there is revealed to us a third kind of liberty which is a reconciliation of the two other kinds.   The grace of Christ is the inner illumination of freedom without any outward restraint or coercion.   The truth of Christ which makes men free constrains no one ;   it differs in this respect from the truths of this world which seek to organize the life of man by constraint and end by depriving him of the freedom of the spirit.   The light of Christ illuminates the dark irrationality of freedom without imposing external limitations upon it.   The grace of Christ triumphs over the evil of freedom and the beneficence of necessity.   The mystery of Christianity, the religion of God made man, is above all the mystery of liberty.

Rational metaphysics are incapable of providing either foundation or justification for the freedom of the two natures, divine and human, and they can make nothing whatever of their union. There are altogether too many theories of liberty which by erring in the direction of monophysitism affirm the freedom of God at the expense of that of man.   Only the Christian revelation, the religion of the God-man, can reconcile the two kinds of freedom.   It is precisely Redemption which frees human liberty from the evil which destroys it, and that, not by means of constraint and necessity, but by grace, which is a force acting from within freedom itself. That is why the Christian doctrine of grace is the true doctrine of freedom.

The source of human freedom cannot be found in the natural man, for he is not an absolute self-sufficient being possessing in himself the source of life. The source of all life goes back to the original fount of being, that is, to God. Thus we reach the conclusion that the origin of man's freedom is in God, man's freedom having the same source as his life. By separation from God, that is to say, from the original source of life, man loses his freedom too.

But if we proceed further along this line of argument we reach a monophysite position in which the freedom of God is recognized while that of man is denied. Man receives a certain kind of freedom from God, but he does not possess that which leads him to God. The free response that man has to make to the divine call becomes impossible, God responds to Himself. The tragedy in which two beings participate is transformed into a tragedy which involves action on the part of one being alone. With such a conception of freedom the original phenomenon of the religious life becomes incomprehensible. How then can man's liberty be saved ? Does he possess in himself as a creature the unfathomable source of being ? May it not be that man is only a creature, and would not human life then simply have value as an event occurring at the centre of the divine life ?

Pantheism, which regards man as a manifestation of divinity, is not only incapable of helping us but it means a definite annihilation of freedom. Pantheism is monophysitism pure and simple for which there is no liberty but that of God, a liberty which is identical with necessity ; it is a system which leaves no place for human freedom. But freedom is also denied in theistic dualism which sees in man simply a creature not possessing in himself the source of being ; it is denied also in pantheistic monism which sees in man nothing but a fragment of the divine. Thought refuses to discover any foundation for human freedom. Dualism, the philosophy of transcendence, as well as monism, the philosophy of immanence, have to refer freedom back to God as the original source of being.

It is Christianity alone which can comprehend the fundamental mystery of human freedom which is inseparably linked with the union of the two natures of Christ the God-Man, a union which, however, does not in any way exclude their distinction. The source of man's freedom is in God, and that, not in God the Father, but in God the Son. But the Son is not only God but man in the absolute and spiritual sense of the word, that is the Eternal Man. The freedom of the Son is that in which and by which the free response to God is effected. It is the source of the freedom of the whole human race, for this freedom is not only that of the natural Adam but also that of the spiritual Adam, that is, of Christ. It is in the Son that the free response is given to the appeal of divine love and to God's need of His other self, a response which is heard in the heavenly and spiritual sphere and which is re-echoed upon earth and in the natural world. The freedom of the Son of God has its source in itself and in Him. It is the freedom of absolute spirituality undetermined from without. But the whole generation of Adam is in the Son of God, and it finds in Him the inner source of its liberty which is, not only a freedom like God's, but freedom in relation to God and in its attitude towards Him. To receive the freedom of Christ is not only to receive the freedom of God but to receive also, by partaking of Christ's human nature, that freedom which enables man to turn to God. It is thus the power of becoming God's free sons and so making that loving response to God which He needs.

It is therefore not a question of either monism or dualism but rather of the divine-human mystery of the two natures of Christ, and also, consequently, of the two natures of man. The mystery of human freedom and the solution of its inherent tragedy must alike be sought for in the dogma of the divine-human nature of Christ. Monophysitism, to which our thinking naturally inclines, can only be banished by Christological thought. Christ is man in the absolute sense and not merely God, and it is for this reason that in Him also human freedom is a factor to be considered. In the work which He accomplished not only the divine but also human nature, that of the heavenly Adam, played its part.

The whole of mankind participated through Christ in the work of salvation and in the deliverance of the world. The whole human race offers in Christ a free response to God. We belong to the same race as Christ and through His humanity we are associated with His human freedom. Through Christ we have our part in the Second Hypostasis, in the divine mystery which transpires within the inmost depths of the Holy Trinity.

The spiritual man enjoys freedom because he belongs to the generation of the Son. In Him is revealed the source of human freedom which comes from Christ. The freedom of the Son is to be found in the unfathomed depths of the human Hypostasis in the Divine Being. The freedom of those who belong to the generation of the New Adam is associated with love, that is free love, or rather freedom in love, and the fatal effects of evil are overcome. To perceive the mystery of human freedom is to be victorious alike over monism and dualism, and to share in the mystery of the two natures, which is the mystery of Christianity.

God wills man's being. He does not will merely the existence of a divine nature but also of a human. God has not created human nature simply to destroy it. He longs for His other self, loving and beloved, for God is infinite Love, and Love cannot rest shut up within itself; it is always moving out to others. God finds in His Son His Friend, both loving and beloved. It is in the Son that the response of the Heavenly Man to the divine love takes place. But love can only be free and it is love of this kind that God wants. The activity of free love, welling up from unfathomable depths, is accomplished in the Son, and it is through the Christ that this experience transpires in all the children of the spiritual Adam. In the Son the unique spiritual man and the whole spiritual race of mankind are mysteriously united. Here individualist isolation is impossible. The absolute Heavenly Man is both the unique Man and the whole of *soborny* humanity. Not only is the lost and shattered freedom of the Old Adam re-established in Christ but the higher liberty of the New Adam is also revealed to us.

This freedom is quite different from the first kind of freedom for it is united to love and illuminated by it from within. The freedom of the spiritual Adam is sanctified by grace and it is through the Son that man receives it. This grace is not a constraint put upon the freedom of man, and it is not imposed upon him by exterior authority. In the grace which comes from the Son not only divine but also human energy is at work. Grace acts like a third and higher sort of liberty. The mystery of grace and its inner union with freedom is again the mystery of the union of the two natures. Grace proceeds not only from the divine nature of Christ, but also from the human, and from His heavenly humanity. Here we see the third kind of freedom, namely, that of man, in an active and illumined state. It is, in fact, freedom united to grace and love, and sanctified by grace. Moreover, that which occurs in time and on earth occurs also in heaven and in eternity. The humanization of God takes place exoterically on earth in the time process, but esoterically in heaven and in eternity. This is the mystery of the spirit in which the Son is eternally begotten of the Father.

Grace is the realm of the Third Hypostasis, that of the Holy Spirit. In this kingdom of the Holy Spirit the freedom of God is not opposed to that of man nor is freedom in antithesis to grace which itself acts from within the sphere of liberty. The divine, mystery of life is accomplished. God meets the beloved and the reciprocation of His love is infinitely free. The mystery of the unity between two persons finds its solution in the Trinity. No resolution of the relations between God and man is possible apart from the Third Person, that is, apart from the Spirit Who is Love realized. The kingdom of Love in freedom is the kingdom of the Trinity. The experience of freedom and its inherent tragedy bring us to the Trinity. It is only within Christianity that the fulness of human liberty exists, for nothing external can comprehend it. Abstract monotheism is always despotic, for it regards God as an absolute monarch and leaves no place for freedom. Only the religion of God in Three Persons succeeds in definitely getting past this monarchist or imperialist conception of God by revealing the life of God as a divine Trinity and thus vindicating liberty.

The mystery of the Cross is the mystery of freedom. God the Son, veiled beneath the form of a crucified slave, does not force recognition of Himself upon anyone. His divine power and glory are manifested in the activity of faith and of free love. The Crucified addresses Himself to the freedom of the human spirit for without a free and truly heroic act on the part of the spirit there can be no recognition of Him as God. A crucified God is hidden as well as revealed. The constraint exercised by the natural world wholly disappears in the process by which the divine is revealed, for everything turns on the existence of an inner freedom. The natural man, obsessed by the forces of the external world, sees nothing in the Crucified but a man suffering torture and humiliation, and the consequent defeat and annihilation of truth so far as this world is concerned. Divine truth seems to be powerless. Is it possible that God can appear here below not as power forcibly transfiguring and overcoming life, but as crucified and to all appearance impotent when confronted with the forces of this world?

It was here that the Jewish people were led astray by refusing to recognize in the figure of the Crucified the expected Messiah and Son of God. The true Messiah, according to them, must appear in power and glory, and by founding a powerful Kingdom of Israel end the existence of suffering and evil. The Cross of Calvary was a stumbling-block for the Jews and remains so to this day for most of the Aryan race as well, for they expect the manifestation of the truth in power and the victory of truth in the visible world. This temptation means nothing more nor less than a denial of all freedom of spirit, an inability and even a refusal to see, beyond material humiliation and defeat, the invisible spiritual triumph of divine truth. The coming of the Son of God and the Messiah in His power and glory as the King of the world and as a conqueror would have been the end of the freedom of the human spirit and the realization of the Kingdom of God by means of necessity and compulsion.

Atheistic Communism, which involves the superseding of

Christianity, has as its goal the realization upon earth of a realm of justice and a Kingdom of God here below, without a belief in God or in the Cross and in crucifixion. But the religion of truth crucified is the religion of the freedom of the spirit. Truth crucified possesses no logical nor juridical power of compulsion and it made its appearance in the world as infinite love, and love does not compel ; rather it makes man infinitely free. In the sphere of love everything becomes near to us in spirit ; in love we are freed from all that is strange and hostile and so attain the fulness of liberty. Freedom must bring us to love, love must make us free. The grace of Christ is just the mystery of freedom which loves and that of love which sets us free. On the Cross His grace was made manifest. In the suffering of the God-Man willingly endured, which sets men free, there lies hidden the mystery of Christian love.

VI

In the social, exoteric, and historical life of the Church authority plays a prominent part. The outward expressions of authoritarianism loom largely in the history of the Christian nations. But what is the explanation of authority in Christianity which is the religion of freedom ? From the point of view of the phenomenology of religious experience authority is a secondary and not a primitive phenomenon and always presupposes both faith and freedom.

The authority of Popes and Councils is not that of an external reality which can force us to recognize it. Material constraint in matters of faith has been a manifest betrayal of Christian principle. If we do not believe in Popes or Councils, and if we do not see in them spiritual realities, then they possess no sort of authority over us. We shall then regard their claims, so far as we are concerned, as an outward restraint imposed by the material and natural world, like a blow from a stick or the fall of a stone. In order that they may have authority over us, we must endow the Council or the Pope with the attributes of authority by an act of faith. If the Pope condemns a book or the opinions of a fervent Roman Catholic his action has a profound importance for the person concerned because it proceeds from recognized authority. But if the Pope condemns a book or the opinions of a man who does not believe in the Roman Catholic Church, then his action is quite meaningless and has no value for the man concerned.

It is absolutely impossible to conceive or to justify the naïvely realist idea by which authority is accorded a primacy over the freedom of the spirit. An authoritarian attitude of mind which rejects freedom always proves to be possessed by a naïve realism, and, so far as it is concerned, authority is an external and objective reality like others which exist in the natural world. It is, in fact, always an indication of religious materialism. For a mind of this type the authority of the Pope possesses a right to constrain analogous to that possessed by material objects. The spirit remains passive in the act of perceiving and accepting an authority of this sort. But the spirit does not remain passive except in the perception of objects belonging to the empirical and external world, for in order to conceive and recognize these objects the free action of the spirit is not essential. But the spirit is active when it is a question of perceiving or accepting the realities of the spiritual world. In this case naïve realism is quite impossible.

The Pope is not an empirical external reality and he cannot be accepted in his qualitative authority apart from the active occurrences of the spiritual life. His authority is invisible and like all invisible things can only be demonstrated by faith. His authority remains hidden and invisible for those who do not believe as Roman Catholics do. Conciliar authority is also something invisible which can be revealed only by faith, and it possesses no external or tangible proof of its authenticity. The only true Council which can claim authority is one in which the Holy Spirit is at work ; but the action of the Holy Spirit cannot be demonstrated by proof of a purely outward nature. A Council acquires recognition as true and authoritative through the *sobornost* of the Christian people. And even in Roman Catholicism, with all its extreme authoritarianism, the infallibility of the Pope had to be proclaimed by the Vatican

Council in spite of everything ; that is to say, it had to be recognized by the Roman Catholic world in order to enjoy authority. There is, in fact, in the very idea of authority and infallibility an inner contradiction which Roman Catholic thinkers have been unable to resolve. The freedom of the spirit is, inwardly and ideally speaking, prior to authority, though, of course, not always so from the social and psychological standpoint. Liberty is at once more original than authority, for the origin of the latter is in liberty. The seat of authority is not in the object but in the subject. Authority means one of two things ; it is either our free acceptance of a certain principle, or else the enslavement of the spirit.

Authority does not provide us with any outward demonstration of truth which is unshakable, tangible, or coercive in character ; it provides no escape from the burden of freedom. The outward signs and criteria of religious truth which are given to us as constituting authority, that is to say, that are naïvely displayed as empirical realities capable of bringing conviction, are always a snare and a delusion ; they reflect the inner occurrences of spiritual experience. There are no compelling and material proofs of religious truths, nor can there be any. The criterion is in ourselves, not outside. The authority of Œcumenical Councils which are the source of Orthodox truth also demand our individual sanction, our own acts of freedom and of faith, as well as our spiritual life and experience. An Œcumenical Council is not true for me unless it is an inward occurrence of my own spiritual world, that is, an experience lived out in me and in the inmost depths of my spirit. A Council, in so far as it is simply a projection upon the outward historical plane, has only a secondary and reflected significance. Nothing possesses authority for me save that which is recognized as truth in my own spiritual world, as a genuine contact with primary reality having its origin in the primordial freedom of my spirit.

Papalism only succeeds in making an illusory escape from these difficulties, which are indeed inseparably connected with the very conception of an external authority requiring tangible evidences of truth. Its sphere of activity is secondary and not primary. Even if we grant papal infallibility to be the unshakable criterion of all religious truth, the truth concerning this infallibility has itself no external and unshakable authority upon which to rest, for it is cradled in freedom and owes its very choice to freedom itself. By entering upon the domain of the criteria of authority we restrict ourselves to secondary activities. The truth of the supremacy of freedom over authority is not a truth of psychology, for psychological processes are diverse and complex, but it is a truth of the spirit, of the basic and original life in its initial phenomenon. The first and last criterion of truth is in the truth itself, just as the first and last criterion of the knowledge of God is in God Himself. The authoritarian mind seeks for criteria of God in the lower world of nature because it has no faith in those of the divine world. This means an assimilation of the spiritual to the natural world, of the Kingdom of God to the kingdom of Cæsar. The application of principles of this kind always means the subjection of the Church to the State, and presupposes a faith in the State as great as that in the Church.

In Orthodoxy the conception of authority has not achieved a more profound development, but its superiority to that of Roman Catholicism is due to its greater freedom of spirit. Khomiakov completely rejected authority in Orthodoxy and he made freedom the foundation of authority. The principle of freedom in Orthodoxy is not associated with individualism and with the affirmation of the right to freedom of each isolated individual, for freedom depends on *sobornost* ; it is freedom in love. Nevertheless in Orthodoxy the authority of custom and the union between the Church and the State which controlled it has been very strong. Authority rests with the whole Church, which is a mystical and spiritual organism whose authority is not external and material but inward, and part of the spiritual life in *sobornost.*

Authority of an inward and spiritual character presupposes freedom and rests upon it. The refusal to recognize the freedom of the spirit is one of the temptations of the devil which Christ repelled in the wilderness. Truth must correspond to my spiritual nature and life. It cannot be something external imposed upon me by force. In the spiritual world there is no despotism and compulsion is wholly out of the question. There must be a close and intimate kinship between myself and the mystery which is to be apprehended. The truth of the divine life cannot be imposed upon me because the very meaning of this truth presupposes my freedom. The slavery of the spirit, reflected in purely authoritarian embodiments of the religious consciousness, is only the result of a freedom which has been defeated from within by evil. Apart from freedom there is no spirit and apart from spirit there is no freedom. An authoritarian form of piety is merely the expression of a low level of spirituality and of " natural " religiosity. In the higher stages we pass beyond authoritarianism. But this does not mean that the authoritarian expressions of the religious life have lost their meaning in relation to the historical development of Christendom and that they must therefore be openly repudiated, for it is impossible to get the better of authoritarian forms of religion by external measures, nor can they be forcibly rejected. To rise above them is an inward and spiritual process. Freedom cannot be accepted from without. Freedom in science, art, society, and in love can only be achieved by a free spirit. Souls in bondage can create nothing free.

Whatever may be the level attained by man as a psycho-corporeal being he cannot lay claim to pure autonomy which requires man's spiritual estate for its manifestation. The claim to freedom in a general sense is a false one, for freedom has to be manifested in spiritual life and experience and is not the result of declamation. This is why the freedom demanded in revolutions habitually gives rise to new forms of tyranny and slavery. Freedom cannot be exacted by force, for one must first possess it in oneself and it must be discovered from within. The development from heteronomy to autonomy in religion can only be the result of spiritual growth. Christian experience is not exclusively personal and individual, it is also *soborny* and collective. The Christian world is an integral spiritual organism, and, like all organisms, it possesses a hierarchic structure. That which transpires upon the highest levels of the spiritual life has also an importance for the very lowest, and in some measure sustains every other part of the spiritual life.

Above all, heteronomy has a social and historical significance, and though it has no connection with truth itself it is related to its activity in history on the social side. While heteronomy must be regarded in the light of autonomy, just as necessity must be envisaged from the point of view of freedom, yet in practice the idea of autonomy itself is developed by a philosophy which is at the mercy of an evil individualism itself the product of division ; thus autonomy is affirmed as against heteronomy as if it were the revolt of the religious individual against religious society. The affirmation of religious freedom in Protestantism contains an undoubted truth, but from the Orthodox point of view this freedom has been affirmed by way of " protestation," that is, in a negative rather than in a positive fashion, and even the problem of freedom has not been sufficiently deeply understood. The Protestant mind inclines towards individualism. The life of the spirit is the life of the soul which looks towards the spiritual world and to which divisions and " extrinsicisms " are completely alien. The fault does not lie in the fact that Protestantism makes an exaggerated claim for the freedom of the human spirit, but that it does not make a sufficiently deep and radical affirmation of it. Protestantism inclines towards monophysitism, or the denial of man and of human freedom, and an extreme antithesis between freedom and grace. German idealism, which developed on the spiritual soil of Protestantism, has indeed rendered notable service in the struggle for the freedom of spirit and has stated and justified the idea of autonomy (Kant, Fichte, Hegel). But German idealism is also infected by monophysite heresy, for while recognizing the divine freedom it ignores that of man. The merit of the great German idealists lies in their doctrine of freedom as the result of a higher spirituality and not as an external claim preferred by those who are themselves spiritually enslaved.

At any rate we must recognize the fact that the whole controversy between the autonomous and the heteronomous belongs to the secondary rather than to the primary sphere of reality. Autonomy is a correlative of heteronomy. There is no formal autonomy in the inmost depths of spiritual freedom, for there is no distinction there between autonomy and " theonomy." A free theonomy transcends both autonomy and heteronomy. For autonomy itself is a completely formal conception of freedom, and in fact it affirms the latter on behalf of the natural Adam without any understanding of why it is necessary. Autonomy and heteronomy are juridical and not spiritual categories depending upon the requirements of a divided world in which coercion is a dominating principle. But freedom is a spiritual category belonging to a much more profound range of experience than the conflict between autonomy and heteronomy. A world in which autonomy is affirmed in opposition to heteronomy has already forfeited the freedom of the spirit. An autonomous consciousness is essentially formal and belongs to a stage in the spiritual life in which freedom is without a defined objective, in which a man wishes to be free from all arbitrary exterior restraint, to be self-determined according to his own will, and to live according to his own principles. Autonomy is thus not only opposed to heteronomy and rightly so, but it is also in conflict with theonomy ; and here it is at fault. A more profound and positive truth is to be found in the fact that none of us can live solely according to our individual principles, nor can our freedom remain negative, formal, and without an object, but it is, rather, essential to that response which God demands from us and to our conversion to the divine life. The freedom of the Old Adam, of the natural man, is purposeless and infantile, a mere desire to escape from our swaddling-clothes. The freedom of the New Adam, that is, of the spiritual man, is, on the other hand, a freedom which possesses a definite content ; it is inward and positive, a desire to live for God and in God. In fact both heteronomy and autonomy are characteristics of immature minds, which lack true spiritual freedom, and which have failed to grasp the fact that freedom is neither a claim nor a right, but rather a burden to be carried and a duty to be performed ; still less is it realized by such minds that

God needs human freedom in order to carry out the purpose which He has conceived for man. Freedom is a " concentration " not a " dissipation " of spirit ; it is austere and difficult. The free life is the most complex while the easy life is that which is subject to restraint and necessity. Freedom entails suffering and tragedy. The abandonment of freedom brings with it an apparent relief from the sufferings and tragedy of life. Heteronomy involves the conception of God as an Oriental despot demanding a slavish submission from His servants. It is the idea of God which is mirrored in the sin of natural humanity.

This idea of God has been deeply impressed upon the Christian world and continues to exercise an influence even to-day. Man is the slave of God, the subject of an autocratic potentate, who must carry out his Master's will whatever it may be. The Fall is a formal transgression of the will of the Lord, an act of disobedience to the law of the Master of life. A formal and juridical interpretation of the Fall means also a formal and juridical interpretation of Redemption. God, personified as an autocrat and a despot with limitless power, demands from man, not the performance of a truth and a righteousness which have a meaning for him and some correspondence with his spiritual nature, but the carrying out of His formal will and of His orders, even if they are devoid of meaning and completely transcendent so far as human nature is concerned. Man, so it is held, must carry out the will of God without even asking in what this will consists and what it means. But the fulfilling of the will of God does not enlighten us as to its nature, and in this case the question is still put in a juridical fashion. If God is infinite love one consents to do His will, however difficult it may be ; but if God is hate, one would refuse to do His will, even were it easier. In one's picture of God one cannot separate the idea of God from Intelligence, Love, Truth, Righteousness, and Beauty. Such a separation means slavery for the spirit, and God becomes simply an Asiatic despot.

The controversy bearing on this subject as to whether God is subject to truth and righteousness, as Plato thought, or whether He is absolutely free, and truth and righteousness are merely His desire, as Duns Scotus thought, is based upon a separation between that which cannot be separated. We cannot say that God is subject to truth and goodness as to principles which control Him, nor can we say, on the other hand, that truth and goodness are not what God desires. A dissociation of this kind is not applicable to the divine nature, and it is, moreover, quite as impossible to conceive of God from the point of view of human morality as it is to regard Him as a despot. It is quite impossible for God to will what is meaningless, not because He is limited by truth, goodness, and beauty, but because He is Truth, Goodness, and Beauty, and because freedom and the necessity of Truth, Goodness, and Beauty are identified in Him. God cannot will that which has no meaning because He is Meaning, and Meaning is the immanence of His idea. The Wisdom inherent in God cannot will bondage because that is an evil. God can only will freedom because it is His idea and His plan for the world. He cannot desire that man should carry out His will in a formal spirit of blind submission, because His will cannot be separated from the idea of God, of Meaning, of Truth, of Righteousness, and of Freedom, without which there is neither Meaning nor Righteousness. Above all God expects freedom from man.

Such then is, God's will, which is inseparable from the very idea of God and which must therefore be fulfilled. Moreover, in order that the will of God may be fulfilled, I have no right to regard myself as a slave, for I must be spiritually free in order to perform it. It is in the full liberty of the spirit and as a spiritual being that I must submit to the will of God. We are no longer slaves, but sons possessing freedom which has been bought for us at a great cost. In the Son the Father is revealed as infinite love. We can no longer regard God as a sovereign exacting obedience to His will and a formal submission to His power, since such a conception is due entirely to the oppression exercised by sin upon the natural man.

If freedom cannot be opposed to grace neither can it be opposed to humility, which is an inner spiritual phenomenon itself depending upon freedom. Without freedom there can be no humility, otherwise it would be valueless, save as throwing light upon the nature of humanity. Humility is the victory achieved through freedom over all the pride which arises from self-assertion and over all those hatreds which spring from the lower aspects of our nature. Humility is the way to rebirth and to the centring of life, not on that which is without, but on that which lies in the innermost depths. Humility is not the outward submission of our own will to the will of a stranger, and so far as religion is concerned, it bears no sort of resemblance, for example, to the submission of members of the Communist Party to the discipline of the central committee. For in submission of this kind human nature remains unchanged and the relationship between man and the force to which he submits is an entirely pagan one, while in the experience of true humility human nature is transformed and enlightened. Humility is an activity of man which is directed towards himself and it presupposes an intense freedom of the spirit. It means freedom from the influence of everything arbitrary, external, and alien to humanity. It is the way to freedom of spirit, to the rejection of everything that can enslave, and to that inner freedom which overcomes all the evils of life. A servile conception of humility distorts the true meaning of Christianity and the spiritual life.

Humility is both the source of spiritual peace and also a means of union with powers higher than our own, nor has it any connection with that slavish submission which comes from the absence of peace and unity and the experience of division and estrangement. To subdue our wills is to experience the greatest freedom and to liberate them from influences of a lower kind. Humility is one of the paths to freedom ; it does not involve heteronomy in any sense of the word and its manifestation in the life of the greatest saints and mystics is that of a completely autonomous species of religious experience. An act of humility is not the act of a will alien to my own, but that of my own will enlightened and transfigured by a higher spiritual nature. For example humility towards an elder in the shape of the submission of my will to his spiritual direction is an entirely voluntary act, an act of freedom and not one of forced submission. By egoistical self-assertion I destroy my own freedom and am virtually reduced to non-existence. Humility means the abandonment of self-centredness for God-centredness. The autonomy of ethics, science, art, law, and economics asserted by modern history is not the autonomy of man himself. In fact it means freedom for everything but man, who thus becomes the slave of autonomous ethics, science, law, and economics.

VII

Does Christianity recognize freedom of conscience and religious toleration ?

This is a question with a history written in blood and tragedy. The Christian world has gone astray. While fire and the sword, the most hideous of passions, and all the extremity of violence have found employment in the service of the religion of love and freedom, it has been left to men utterly indifferent to all religion to defend freedom of conscience and religious toleration.

For one who believes in nothing and is indifferent to truth it is easy to be tolerant towards every belief. But the real problem is how to reconcile an ardent faith and devotion to sovereign truth with a toleration for erroneous belief and a denial of that truth ? Is not religious toleration always a proof of indifference ? So at any rate those Christians think who deny liberty of conscience. The defence of the spirit of toleration has become the prerogative of liberalism and of a humanism which possesses no religious faith. Freedom of conscience is affirmed as a formal principle having no relation to any positive truth whatsoever. Religious men believing in a positive truth free from all error have only defended freedom of conscience when their own faith was persecuted and oppressed. The Roman Catholics, who are the least inclined to recognize the principle of freedom of conscience, appealed in Russia to that principle when the Roman Catholic faith was oppressed and its rights restricted. Christianity in the person of the apologists and doctors of the Church during the period of the persecutions before Constantine the Great maintained the cause of freedom of conscience in matters of religion. But when Christianity became the dominant religion we hear no more of these arguments in favour of religious freedom, and, on the contrary, we find appeals to force against heretics and dissenters and to the intervention of the sword of the State in questions of faith. This, then, is how the question arises historically and it has been a fruitful source of lying hypocrisy and a gross utilitarianism.

But how are we to put this question of religious freedom from the Christian point of view? How can it be stated in its inner essence and free from all human interests and from all the positivism and utilitarianism which are historically interwoven with Christianity? Christianity is exclusive and cannot tolerate any approach to error. It cannot be indifferent as to whether men prefer a lie to the truth, because it cannot recognize them as being of equal value. A formal liberalism which is indifferent to truth is alien to Christianity, which cannot therefore defend freedom of conscience by recourse to its arguments. Christian liberty is not the formal and meaningless liberty of the natural man; it is not a right as in humanistic liberalism; it is an obligation and a duty to God, and if Christians have to maintain the cause of freedom of conscience it certainly cannot be by appealing to liberalism, and to the formal and juridical arguments which are employed by a world which is indifferent to faith and truth of every kind, and which clings to the freedom of untruth and evil. Those who deny the very existence of the religious consciousness cannot defend the liberty of religious thought except in a purely external fashion, for it is only useful from their point of view as a protection for their own right to atheism and untruth and to preserve their tranquil enjoyment of error. But is is only in Christianity that freedom of conscience has any inner meaning or religious justification. Christianity demands toleration for the inner experience and spiritual development of the human soul, because freedom is part of the Christian faith, and because Christianity is the religion of freedom. God Himself is

152

infinitely tolerant towards the evil of the world. He bears with the greatest of wrong-doers for the sake of freedom. Christianity asserts freedom of conscience materially and in no formal sense, and it does this, not because it is indifferent to truth nor because it is tolerant of untruth, but rather because it believes in truth which is the revelation of the freedom of the human spirit. Christ opened up for us a freedom of the spirit which knows no limits and sealed it with His blood for all eternity. Faith in Calvary is faith in freedom.

The demand for freedom of religious thought in Christianity is far more profound than it is in liberal, humanist, and non-religious circles. Every form of coercion of the human soul in matters of faith is a betrayal of Christ, a denial of the very meaning of the Christian religion and of the nature of faith itself. Man has to be tested through freedom in order that he may know how to win the victory freely over the things which try him. Man must seek diligently for the truth. The denial of religious freedom, fanatical intolerance, and coercion in things spiritual all spring from the idea of salvation by compulsion, an idea opposed to the whole meaning of Christianity. God Himself could have saved the whole human race by force had He wanted to, and in a far more radical fashion than the hierarchy or the State could ever do. But God does not wish to impose salvation upon anyone, for it is quite contrary to His plan for man and for the world. God awaits man's free response to His call, He wants the unforced love of His other self. God might say as man does, " You cannot love to order." Force cannot open the way to Paradise.

The idea of salvation by compulsion, which has had such fatal consequences in history, is due to a false identification of the Kingdom of God with the kingdom of Cæsar, by which the spiritual world is degraded to the level of the natural. In the kingdom of Cæsar coercion and slavery are everywhere in evidence, whereas the spiritual world, the Kingdom of God, is an order of liberty. Nobody can be saved by coercion because salvation presupposes an act of freedom and because it is the inner illumination of freedom.

The history of Christianity is full of acts of violence, but these form no part of the spiritual order of things, nor have they any connection with the inner history of Christianity ; they belong rather to the social activity of mankind and are determined by the prevailing condition of the natural man. Though mediæval Christianity witnessed only too many acts of violence and bloodshed, Christianity itself is not responsible for these things but rather human nature, which was only being Christianized with some difficulty. The things for which the Catholic Church has been commonly blamed should rather be laid at the door of the cruelty of human nature. But the question of religious freedom is not a historical problem, it is the question of the very essence of the Christian faith. From this point of view religious toleration is not the tolerance of the erroneous opinions of man, but a feeling of love and solicitude for every human soul.

Man comes to God by many arduous ways and through much suffering, through the experience of life's tragedy, and through spiritual struggle. Trials beset his path in those personal experiences which belong to each individual alone. None of us can claim to possess truth in its fulness while regarding our neighbours as completely in error. Fulness and completeness are to be found in God alone, and all we can grasp is but a fragment of the truth, for only a few stray beams of its light become visible to us. The restriction and denial of freedom of conscience means the mechanization and the materialization of the religious life and the denial of the spirit and spiritual life which are essentially free. The present-day revolt of man against coercion in matters of faith and religion is completely justifiable. This revolt can and does bring in its train certain fatal consequences and may mean a loss of faith, yet it contains an inner moment of truth, namely the truth of freedom.

It is impossible to build the Kingdom of God by force ; it can only be created in freedom. It was the use of force which brought to an end the various historic theocracies and their fall was providential. Without man and without human freedom God cannot and will not establish His Kingdom, which is of necessity human as well as divine in character ; and here we have a truth which man must pursue to the very end. Nothing in this world can arrest its progress because God Himself wills that man should completely fulfil his freedom and come through liberty into the divine fulness. Man must pass through the tragedy of freedom in order to reach its final issue in the freedom of Christ, that is, in the third kind of freedom. Freedom is man's fate and destiny, however paradoxical that may appear. The fanaticism which inspires to violence is only a form of madness which proceeds from the incapacity of the natural man for receiving into himself the truth of the spirit and of Christianity in all its divine fulness. Fanaticism means the imprisoning of the spirit within the passions of the soul and the body, the stifling of the spiritual man by the natural, and it is in continual conflict with even the most elementary laws of spiritual hygiene. For when man nourishes hatred in the name of love, when he has recourse to violence on behalf of freedom, he is quite clearly mad, and has lost his " psychical " equilibrium as a result of his powerlessness to receive within himself the truth of Christianity. Nothing is more difficult for man than to accept the freedom of truth within himself and to remain faithful to it. His ideas become confused and his heart burns within him. The evil which he compasses appears to him to possess a good motive. Now it is true that the Greek world was certainly more balanced and less prone to violence than is the Christian world, but that was because it did not have to accept for itself the supreme truth of freedom. It is this truth which has proved to be too heavy a burden for humanity, and having remained for long unapprehended it has been the origin of hitherto unprecedented violence.

It is through the tragedy of freedom that Christian renaissance on a world scale will take place. The Christianity of the future will be a Christianity of the freedom of the spirit which has success-fully passed through the trials of freedom by overcoming the temptation to refuse them. Christianity can be renewed not through opposition to that which is eternal, but through the birth of a new soul able to apprehend its immutable truth. This new soul can only accept a Christianity of the freedom of the spirit, for the bondage of the spirit and the tyranny and coercion from which it suffers is part of the kingdom of Antichrist. The freedom of the spirit has been the fundamental theme of Russian religious thought. Slavophiles maintained the freedom of Christianity, and the greatest apostle of it was Dostoievsky himself.

The problem of the freedom of the spirit lies at the very centre of the Christian consciousness, and the problems of evil and of redemption, and that of man and his creative powers, are closely connected with it. Creation is impossible under the dominant influence of an authoritarian mentality. Creative life cannot simply consist in obedience and submission to authority. It always presupposes the freedom of the spirit and is indeed the manifestation of this freedom. In creation something else besides humility always has its part to play, for, though humility is an indispensable moment of the spiritual life, it does not mean that there is no place at all for the daring of freedom. The denial of freedom means a curtailing of human individuality and the extinction of the spiritual life of man. Individuality revolts against transformation into an automaton. The idea of Christian freedom, considered funda-mentally with all its consequences, presupposes the affirmation of freedom in all spheres of human creativity, in science, philosophy, and art, in social relationships, and in love. Coercion in these matters has no value whatever from the Christian point of view. In all spheres of creation the truth of Christ must be revealed in the very depths of liberty. Science, art, society, like the free love between man and woman, must serve the truth of Christ and must turn their creative forces towards God as the manifestation of a free love towards God. No outward limitations can be imposed on freedom of thought and feeling. The life of Christ must be born within them ; the void and non-being of evil and the nothingness of all forms of atheism must be clearly revealed. This is the line of development, through immanence, the only one which humanity can follow, which has brought it to the very climax of the trials and contradictions of culture. The final separation of the two kingdoms will take place along this line of freedom which will lead definitively either to God or to the devil.

And the time is coming, indeed it has already come, when freedom will be found only in Christianity, when the Church of Christ will defend the freedom of man against the violence of the kingdom of this world, that kingdom of Cæsar which has now become definitely irreligious in character. This has already happened in Communism, which has destroyed the freedom of the spirit and denies personality. The denial of the freedom of the spirit is precisely the spirit of Antichrist whose coming will be marked by extreme tyranny and by the absolute autocracy of the powers of this world. Only in Christ's Church will deliverance from this destructive tyranny, this very incarnation of the spirit of the Grand Inquisitor, be found. In the kingdom of Christ all power and all autocracy, whether individual or collective, are limited, for there only the power of truth and justice are recognized. The Christian spirit of freedom is directed against all tyranny, whether proceeding from " the left," " the right," or " the centre," whether it be monarchist, aristocratic, democratic, socialist, or anarchist in character. It is not the same thing as the spirit of liberalism, which is always indifferent to truth, but it is that of sanctified freedom and the freedom of love. The search for the Kingdom of God is the manifestation of the freedom of the spirit. The Kingdom of God, which is above all the object of our search, is the kingdom of the spirit. In the spiritual world external tyranny and compulsion of every kind, besides that which results from division, are no more. To attain to the Kingdom of God is to pass into a spiritual world where everything differs from that which we find in this natural world. God will be all in all and freedom will triumph over force. To enter into the spiritual world man must make an act of freedom and heroism, and this must not be something which he accepts from without but rather that which he must discover in himself.

CHAPTER FIVE

Redemption and Evil

I

THE problem of evil lies at the heart not only of Christian thought and experience but of religion of every kind. The longing for deliverance from the evil of existence and the suffering involved in being itself is the origin of religion. In a word all religions, and not only those of redemption in the strictest sense of the word, promise freedom from evil and the suffering which comes from it. In religion man seeks to escape from the state of isolation and solitude in which he finds himself in the midst of a strange and hostile world ; he seeks to return to the true native land of the spirit. Even totem worship meant a search for a protector and deliverer from the evil powers of the surrounding world.

The rationalistic mind of modern man considers the existence of evil and suffering as the principal obstacle to his faith in God and as the most important argument in favour of atheism. It seems difficult to reconcile the existence of God, as an All-merciful and All-powerful Disposer with that of evil which is such a formidable and powerful element in our world. This argument (and it is the only serious one) has become classic. Men lose faith in God and in the divine meaning of the world because they find evil victorious and because of their experience of the meaningless sufferings of which evil is the cause.

But in the historical development of the human consciousness faith in the divine arose just because men experienced great sufferings and felt the need of freeing themselves from the power of evil. If this evil which confounds our world had not existed man would have been content with this world here below, and the latter, free of all evil and pain, would have become his only god. Deliverance would not have been indispensable. The sufferings of life which attest the existence of evil are a great school of religion through which mankind has to pass. A life knowing nothing of evil in any shape or form would in this world have meant a self-satisfied existence. The existence of evil is not the only obstacle to our faith in God, for it is equally a proof of the existence of God and the proof that this world is not the only nor ultimate one. The experience of evil directs man's attention towards another world by arousing in him a discontent with this. It is pessimism and not optimism which lies at the bottom of religious experience and the religious consciousness. All religions of deliverance are pessimistic with regard to life generally and the natural world, and here Orphism and Buddhism are one with Christianity. The positive meaning of being belongs to another order and to the spiritual world. Our natural world is apparently in the victorious grip of the inane for it is dominated by corruptibility and death, animosity and hatred, egoism and discord. Man is overwhelmed by the meaningless evil of the whole of life. In religion and in faith he turns towards the world of meaning and receives strength from that world where love triumphs over hatred, union over division, and eternal life over death.

The existence of evil is a problem for theodicy, for the justification of God. Why does God allow this terrible evil to exist, and why does He suffer it to triumph? The whole world is full of discord and bloodshed. Satan and not God seems to be its master. Where then is the activity of divine providence? We may remember the argument of Ivan Karamazov about a child's tears which ended in his refusal to accept a passport to universal harmony.[1] The Euclidean spirit which refuses to grasp the irrational mystery of life claims to make a better world than that which has been created by God, a purely rational world in which there would be neither evil nor suffering. The man who is possessed by

---

[1] Dostoievsky, *The Brothers Karamazov*, vol. i, chap. 3.

this Euclidean spirit cannot conceive why God did not create a happy world without sin and incapable of evil. But the " good " human world of the Euclidean spirit is distinguished from the " bad " divine world by the complete absence of freedom which does not form part of its original design, and man in this case would be nothing but a good automaton. The absence of freedom would have made evil and suffering impossible, and man is ready to give up his liberty in order to be finally delivered from his pain. In the Euclidean world there would be no more free trial or unfettered search. The world that God has created is full of evil, it is true, but at its heart there lies the greatest of all goods, namely the freedom of the spirit which shows that man bears the divine image. Freedom is the only answer to the problem of justifying God. The problem of evil is the problem of liberty. Without an understanding of liberty we cannot grasp the irrational fact of the existence of evil in a divine world. There is in the very origin of the world an irrational freedom which is grounded in the void, in that abyss from which the dark stream of life issues forth and in which every sort of possibility is latent. These unfathomable depths of being which are prior both to good and evil are incapable of final rationalization, for there is always within them the possibility of an influx of new and obscure forces. While it is true that the Logos brings light in place of darkness and that the harmony of the cosmos replaces chaos, yet apart from the dark abyss of chaos there would be neither life nor liberty, nor indeed any meaning in the process of evolution. The dwelling-place of freedom is the abyss of darkness and nothingness, and yet apart from freedom everything is without meaning. It is the source of evil as well as of good. Thus the fact of evil does not imply that all is meaningless ; on the contrary, it actually establishes the existence of meaning. Freedom is not created because it is not a part of nature ; it is prior to the world and has its origin in the primal void. God is All-powerful in relation to being but not in relation to nothingness and to freedom ; and that is why evil exists.

Every serious conception of life implies the vision of evil and the admission of its existence. To ignore it or not to see it makes a man irresponsible and superficial, cutting him off in some measure from the deeper and more profound elements of life. To deny evil is to lose the freedom of the spirit and to escape the burden of freedom. Our present age has witnessed a terrible increase of evil coupled with the denial of its existence. But man is powerless to resist evil if he fails to recognize it as such. Human personality deceives itself when, having made a distinction between good and evil, it thinks itself competent to delimit evil. When we abolish such limits and when man finds himself in a state of confusion and indifference, his personality begins to disintegrate, for the power of conscience is inseparably connected with the denunciation of evil. In the confusion and state of indifference resulting from the loss of the perception of evil man loses his freedom of spirit and begins to reach out after a good which is guaranteed to him by necessity, and thus his centre of gravity ceases to be within himself but passes into the external and outward, and he ceases to be determined from within. Rationalism denies the irrational mystery of evil because it denies that of freedom. It is more difficult for a rationalist to believe in the devil than to believe in God, and people with this mentality elaborate a variety of theories which deny the existence of evil and by means of which evil is transformed into a mere insufficiency of goodness or else a stage in its development. Evil is denied alike by evolutionists, humanitarians, anarchists, and theosophists.

II

The inner dialectic of freedom produces evil from within itself. The source of evil as well as the source of life is to be found in primal irrational freedom and infinite potentiality. Initial freedom was the origin of evil at the highest levels of being. The spirit which belonged to the highest degree of existence was the first to separate himself from God by his own free act, and his self-assertion and spiritual pride exercised a corrupting influence upon the whole ordered hierarchy of being. It was in the highest ranges of the spiritual and not in the shallows of the material world that evil first showed itself. Evil in its origin is spiritual by nature and belongs to the spiritual world. The evil which we know here below and which binds us to the material world is only the result of evil in the spiritual sphere. That spirit who once in the heavenly places believed in God fell through pride and rebellion to the lower regions of existence. The world is an organic hierarchy in which every part is linked to another and in which everything that takes place in the upper regions also affects the lower. The separation from God of one part involved the separation of the whole soul of the world with it, including all humanity and indeed all creation. The myth of Satan is a symbolic reflection of an event belonging to the highest levels of the spiritual world. It was there that the clouds first gathered and that for the first time freedom gave a negative response to the appeal of God and to God's need to experience the love of His other self. It is at this point that creation by a process of self-affirmation began to enter upon the path of isolation, division, and hatred. Man, together with all creation and the whole hierarchy of the universe, became separated from God, and it was spiritual forces that were responsible for leading him astray. Pride is the temptation of a higher order of spirit which seeks to put itself in the place of God.

It is thus that in our own experience of life evil comes to us in the first instance through higher spiritual forces, and it is only later that it finds expression in our subjection to lower elements and to carnal passions. The divine appeal is above all addressed to a spirit of a higher order and to the freedom which such a spirit possesses, and it is from this that the initial response proceeds. The materializing of man and his subjection to lower natural elements is only the result of an event which has already taken place in the spiritual world. Spiritual presumption so far from raising man to the level of divinity only leads to his precipitation in the abyss of materiality.

The myth of the Fall is a symbolic account of events in the spiritual world which through analogy with our natural world represents Satan and man to us as being realities of an external nature.

But in the spiritual world there is no such extrinsicism ; the interior hierarchy of being has an entirely different structure from that of the natural world, for within it everything is inward in character, and all is in all. That is why in the spiritual world Satan, in so far as the higher degrees of the spiritual hierarchy are concerned, and man, as king of creation, are inwardly related to one another and mutually incorporated. Satan is also an inner reality of the spiritual world of man, and he only appears to be something external through analogy with the natural world. He is a reality of a spiritual order and cannot be conceived in a naïve realist sense. He is not the autonomous source of evil in his original being but only the manifestation of irrational freedom at the highest spiritual levels.

The difficulty which thought experiences in explaining the origin of evil lies in the fact that neither monism nor dualism, to which reason naturally inclines, is able to comprehend this phenomenon. The source of evil cannot be in God, yet apart from God there is no source of being or of life. Evil does not proceed from God, but yet there is no other being who, if such existed side by side with God, could provide us with an explanation of the origin of evil. Evil being absolutely irrational, it is therefore incapable of being grasped by reason and remains inexplicable. It has not, nor can it have, any basis in reason, and possesses no positive source. It takes its origin from the fathomless abyss, from that void to which we cannot give the name of existence, and, just because reason is forced to discover the meaning of things, evil represents the absolute limit of irrationality.[1] Evil is non-being and has its roots in non-existence. But non-being can have no meaning, for meaning is always ontological. Therefore that evil to which a meaning can be assigned is thereby transformed into a good.

Pure monism is obliged to consider evil as a moment within the good, as good which we fail to understand or which is insufficiently revealed. The Divine Being is unique, everything is in Him and everything proceeds from Him. Evil has its source in the Divine Being, but it only appears as evil because we see it in part and not as

---

[1] Schelling has given us a deeper philosophy of evil.

a whole ; when all is seen and understood evil disappears and is transformed into the good. Thus monism (or pantheism) must end in the denial of the existence of evil ; being incapable of discovering its source, such a philosophy seeks to explain it by appealing to our ignorance of being as a complete whole. And as an antithesis to pure monism we have pure idealism.

Dualism regards the origin of evil as residing in another being existing side by side with the divine. A logical dualism has to admit the existence of an evil deity corresponding to that of the good God, examples of which may be found in Persian dualism, Manicheism, and ancient Gnosticism. According to these theories evil has an independent, positive, and ontological source. Side by side with the good being of the spiritual world there is an evil being, a lower material world possessing independent reality. By presupposing the existence of some sort of lower being apart from God and opposed to Him and in thus attempting to determine the origin of evil, dualism limits the Divine Being. Satan is transformed into an independent evil deity. Now the idea of Satan in Christianity has its source in Persian religious thought. On such a theory matter is the creation of a god of evil and possesses independent reality and dominates the spirit. Pure monism and pure dualism do not understand and therefore reject the mystery of freedom ; they regard evil from an exterior point of view without grasping its inward origin. Either evil finally disappears or it appears as a force completely outside and apart from the human spirit. But if evil cannot be regarded as having its source in God, and if outside God there is no other source of being, how can the phenomenon of evil be explained ? How can this dilemma be resolved ?

To the Christian way of thinking neither monism nor dualism is right, and it has its own peculiar solution of the problem of the origin of evil. For Christianity this question is connected with that of freedom and cannot be solved apart from it. Indeed monism and dualism both involve the denial of freedom, and are thereby incapable of comprehending the phenomenon of evil. The interpretation of the mystery of evil through that of freedom is a supra-rational interpretation and presents reason with an antinomy. The source of evil is not in God, nor in a being existing positively side by side with Him, but in the unfathomable irrationality of freedom, in pure possibility, in the forces concealed within that dark void which precedes all positive determination of being. Thus evil has no basis in anything ; it is determined by no possible being and has no ontological origin. The possibility of evil is latent in that mysterious principle of being in which every sort of possibility lies concealed. The void (the *Ungrund* of Boehme) is not evil, it is the source of every kind of life and every actualization of being. It conceals within itself the possibility both of evil and of good. An initial, irrational, and mysterious void lies at the heart of the whole life of the universe, but it is a mystery beyond the reach of logic.

This mysterious and irrational world-principle has received brilliant exposition at the hands of the German mystics Eckhart and J. Boehme, and also of early nineteenth-century German philosophers. According to the remarkable theory of Schelling on the subject of freedom, evil is a return to the state of pure power. In the beginning was the Logos, the Word, the Meaning, and the Light. But this eternal truth of religious revelation only means that the kingdom of light and of meaning has been realized initially in being and that the Logos triumphed from the beginning over darkness of every kind. Divine life is a tragedy. Even at the beginning, before the formation of the world, there was the irrational void of freedom which had to be illuminated by the Logos. This freedom is not a form of being which existed side by side with the Divine Being, the Logos, or Mind. It is rather that principle without which being could have no meaning for God, and which alone justifies the divine plan of the world. God created the world out of nothing, but it would be equally true to say that He created it out of freedom. Creation must be grounded upon that limitless freedom which existed in the void before the world appeared. Without freedom creation has no value for God.

In the beginning was the Word, but in the beginning also there was freedom. This latter is not opposed to the Word, for without it the Meaning of the world does not exist. Without darkness there is no light. Good is revealed and triumphs through the ordeal of evil. Freedom makes both good and evil possible. The evil to which it gives rise has no independent existence, it is that non-being which must be distinguished from the original void. But non-being exists and may be possessed of considerable power, namely the power of untruth. Evil is a caricature, at once a malady and a malformation of being. It means a transgression of the hier-archy of being which has its origin in non-being, and which involves separation from the hierarchic centre, the debasement of the higher elements and the elevation of the lower. It constitutes a definite breach with that original centre and source of being from which everything with its determinations emanates.

Above all, evil is a lie ; it is always pretending to be that which it is not, and its seductive power lies in deception. The Devil is an impostor, having no source of life or being of his own. Every-thing he has he takes from God and then caricatures it ; his power is fictitious, illusory, and deceptive. There is no such thing as a kingdom of evil in the sense of something positive existing side by side with the Kingdom of God and the Divine Being. Evil has always a negative character for it destroys life and being, in fact it destroys itself, and there is nothing positive about it. Many doctors of the Church have taught that evil is non-being ; the negative non-ontological character of evil reveals itself also in our own ex-perience of life.

All that we regard as indisputably evil has a negative character and contains nothing positive. Animosity, hatred, envy, vengeance, depravity, egoism, cupidity, jealousy, suspicion, avarice, vanity—all these destroy life and sap the strength of those who come under their sway. Evil passions of whatever kind destroy themselves in the end and involve death both for man and for the world, and this is what we mean by a " bad infinity ". Man is precipitated by evil into a life which is illusory, false, and non-ontological. Murder and death are latent in the elements of evil and in all evil passions.

Animosity and hatred are akin to murder, death, and the destruction of being, while love is the affirmation of life and being in everything and everybody.

Positive being can only mean a kingdom of love. In love the image of every human being and every divine creature is affirmed. The loving subject desires eternal life for the loved object, while those who hate desire death and the end of life. The degree in which being is affirmed or denied depends upon the degree in which men love or hate. That is why deliverance from evil and death can only take shape as infinite love. The promises which evil holds out to us can never be fulfilled. Evil cannot create a kingdom of life since, in the very act of seducing the good, it creates a breach with the source of life itself. Marx, for example, regarded the end he had in view as a good one, but to attain it he sanctioned the use of evil means. It was by evil, by hatred and animosity, by covetousness and revenge, by disunion and violent destruction that he claimed to bring men to a kingdom of peace and unity, and to the brotherhood of mankind. But the evil methods thus employed tend to become the sole content of life and in the end they triumph. Hatred can never lead to love, neither can division lead to union, murder to life, nor violence to liberty. No good objective can be achieved by evil means, for it is always the evil that triumphs. When hatred has infected and possessed the human heart it can only achieve the works of destruction. When we feel animosity towards those who commit evil we are powerless to overcome it and are ourselves its tools. Even the struggle against evil can itself easily degenerate into evil. The victory of the good is always positive ; it does not deny life, it affirms it. We must begin by struggling against the evil in ourselves and not against that which we see in others, for too often feelings of hatred towards evil-doers are merely a form of self-affirmation.

The cause of evil lies in a false and illusory self-affirmation and in spiritual pride which places the source of life not in God but in self, to the annihilation of human personality in so far as it bears the divine image ; it constitutes a return to the void from which the world came into being. Pride and egoism lead to the abyss, to non-being, and to death. By isolating himself in himself, and by taking as the centre of his life not being but his own self, man is not only separated from God and from the sphere of the divine, but is also deprived of all true riches of his being. Being is a hierarchy, and is only affirmed through the preservation of harmony, which is itself the inevitable result of a true hierarchy.

Self-affirmation and egoism destroy this harmony, and by so doing destroy human personality by separating it from the source of life. Man no longer finds his place in the divine sphere and must therefore seek it elsewhere and outside himself. But outside God and the divine sphere there is only non-being, the realm of illusions and lies. To base life on pride and egoism, as Max Stirner tried to do, is to build on the void. When man pursues this path he leaves the realm of being and enters that of non-being.

There is no one who does not know from his own experience that egoism and self-affirmation involve the sapping of our vital forces and in the long run the very destruction of life itself. While that " bad infinity " which is constituted by the aching void of desire and concupiscence is but yet half-disclosed, life itself disappears. Egoism, selfishness, and lust invariably indicate that contact with the real source and origin of life has been lost. Evil is the denial of love which is itself simply the affirmation of all life in God. Evil is a meaningless desire for a life apart from reality and apart from God which seeks to invest non-being with the character of being. It has its origin in that unenlightened freedom which is its chief attraction, but it always means the end of the freedom of the spirit and the establishing of the tyranny of necessity. The consequences of evil are always the same, namely loss of unity and disintegration of being, followed by violent conflict between the elements thus separated. The world breaks up into isolated individual units unknown to one another and therefore hostile.

Being is only free when it is united in that love through which it is allied to God. It is only in and through God that everything is linked up and brought into unity. Apart from God everything is alien and remote and is held together simply by force. Satan by dint of his superior spiritual powers has succeeded in leading men astray by suggesting to them that they will become as gods. But by the pursuit of evil and by the substitution of himself for God, man, so far from becoming the God-like being of his dreams, becomes the slave of his lower nature, and, at the same time, by losing his higher nature becomes subject to natural necessity and ceases to be spiritually determined from within. He is deprived of his freedom. Thus evil involves that displacement of the true centre of being and that complete revolution of the hierarchy of the universe which involves, not only the spirit's being possessed in its pride by the material principle, but the actual substitution of the material for the spiritual. The hard and resistant appearance of the material world is simply the result of its having lost its true centre in the spiritual world. The spirit, in all its pride and egoism, is driven forth into that material sphere which is itself nothing but the result of the disintegration of the world by the forces of hatred and animosity. A covetousness which knows no limits and passions which remain insatiable take possession of those who are thus cast forth into a world of hatred and disunion. But man, having no source of life in himself, must perforce seek it in a being either higher or lower than himself. Now Satan has no independent source of life of his own and can therefore only compel man to derive his life from the lower elements of nature.

This lower nature, when it occupies its proper place in the hierarchy of the universe, is not in itself evil for it belongs to the divine world. It is only when it usurps the place of something higher that it becomes untrue to itself and an evil. Animal nature certainly has its place in the scale of values and an eternal destiny ; but when it takes possession of man, when man submits his spirit to the control of a lower element, then it does indeed become an evil thing. For evil is a question of the direction pursued by the spirit, not of the constitution of nature itself. Temptations to evil are always brought to an end by death, which is the void, the tedium of non-existence. Evil always produces a surfeit, but without the sense of gratification which it is incapable of effecting, and therein lies the mystery of it. But it is difficult for man to discern when he is deceived. He cannot explain to himself why he remains in bondage to the " bad infinity " of life, and why he is unable to win life itself. Evil passions enslave him ; he is possessed by them. As long as man is in their grip he can never know what self-determination in freedom really means, and when he imagines himself to be free in the enjoyment of his passions he is simply living in a world of false appearances and is the victim of a terrible illusion. What he takes for freedom is in reality the most terrible form of bondage, for a bad life is a life without truth, a life of appearances and not of reality, to which one is forced to submit. Evil has its abode in the very depths of human nature and in the spirit. But when once the human spirit has chosen that which is evil it is no longer able to determine its life freely on its own account. Henceforth it is at the mercy of invisible forces, obedient to a master whom it does not know. Nor can man free himself from the control of this master by the exertion of his own natural powers, though we are not to conclude from this that positive and creative spiritual forces no longer exist within him. The spiritual nature of man is corrupted and contaminated, but though much shattered it is still preserved and is not completely destroyed. In human nature the divine idea and image have been obscured in the primal void of initial non-being, from which God called man to life by the act of creation. But human nature remains capable of enlightenment and there remains within it an ardent longing for the divine which makes both revelation and salvation possible. Evil has not finally possessed man's nature for it is a dual nature belonging to two worlds, and even after the Fall man did not completely break with God, Who continues to have dealings with him and to impart to him His regenerative powers. Man does not belong exclusively to the realm of non-being ; he maintains a link with the Being whose activity is still directed towards him. God and the Devil are at war within the human heart, and fallen man preserves the divine image

in spite of everything, for he has passed through the experience of
evil as a being of a definitely higher order.

The negative results of evil in man indicate precisely his predestination to a higher life. Even before the coming of Christ a high
type of spiritual life and a considerable creative power were possible
in the pagan world, of which the culture of Greece is indeed the
practical and incontestable proof. The higher spiritual nature of
man was at work in Plato. In him man's desire for God and the
divine life are evident. Human nature preserves its independence
which is necessary to the divine task in the world. But the final
victory over evil cannot be achieved by the natural powers of man
in separation from God.

III

Christianity is the religion of Redemption and therefore presupposes the existence of evil and suffering. It is therefore idle to
invoke them as evidence against the Christian faith. The very
reason why Christ came into the world is because of its sin, and
Christianity teaches us that the world and man must bear the Cross.
If suffering is the result of evil it is also the path by which we are
to be freed from it. For Christian thought suffering is not necessarily an evil, for God Himself, that is God the Son, suffers. The
whole creation groaneth and travaileth together waiting for its
deliverance. But the opponents of Christianity constantly base
their attacks upon the fact that the coming of the Saviour has
not delivered the world from suffering and evil. Almost two
thousand years have passed since the coming of the Redeemer and
the world is still full of bloodshed, while humanity is racked with
pain and the amount of evil and suffering has actually increased.
The old Jewish argument seems to have won the day. The true
Messiah will be he who will finally deliver humanity from evil
and suffering here below.

But we forget that Christianity recognizes the positive value of
the sufferings which mankind endures on earth, and that it has never

promised us happiness or blessedness here. Besides which Christian prophecy as to the fate of humanity has been fairly pessimistic in character. Christianity has never upheld the view that universal peace and the Kingdom of God upon earth would be achieved by the intervention of some overwhelming power. On the contrary it recognizes the freedom of the human spirit in a very high degree, and it regards the realization of the Kingdom of God without its participation as an impossibility. If the justice of Christ is not realized in the world, that is due rather to human injustice. The religion of love is not responsible for the fact that hate predominates in our natural world. It is impossible to refute Christianity by appealing to the fact of the existence of tremendous evils and sufferings in life. Christianity is the religion of freedom and that is why it cannot admit that evil and suffering are to be removed by employing compulsion and violence. Christianity gives both meaning to suffering and deliverance from evil. But deliverance certainly implies in itself the participation of human freedom in the process.

It is impossible for us to conceive the mystery of Redemption rationally any more than any other mystery of the divine life. The juridical theory of redemption, which from the days of St. Anselm of Canterbury has played such a big part in Catholic theology and from which Orthodox theology is not entirely free, is a rationalization of this mystery, which is thus interpreted according to a scheme of relationships existing in the natural world. This juridical conception was simply an attempt to adapt celestial truth to the level of the natural man. It is not a spiritual conception at all. To regard the universal tragedy as a judicial process initiated by an angry Deity against offending man is quite unworthy. To think in this fashion is to adapt the divine life which is always mysterious and unfathomable to pagan conceptions and the spirit of tribal vengeance. God, according to pagan-Jewish thought, is regarded as a fearful tyrant Who punishes and takes vengeance for every act of disobedience, Who demands a ransom, a propitiatory victim, and the shedding of blood. God is represented in the guise of human nature as it existed in ancient times, in which such ideas as wrath, vengeance, " repurchase," and cruel punishment are all to be found. Upon the juridical theory of redemption the stamp of Roman and feudal conceptions regarding the rehabilitation of man was irrevocably set.[1] The transgression of the Divine Will leads to a judicial process and God demands repayment ; He must receive compensation in order to pacify His wrath. No human sacrifice will satisfy Him or make Him yield. Only the sacrifice of the Son is proportionate to the crime committed and the offence it has caused.

All these conceptions are merely pagan theories transported into Christianity, and such attempts to understand the mystery of Redemption have an obviously exoteric character. The pagan world was attracted to the Redemption revealed in Christianity. But though it was full of a great hope its ideas of Redemption were naturalistic and not spiritual ; its expectations suffered from the limitations inherent in the natural world. Paganism already had the conception of the expiatory character of blood-sacrifices which were at once the food of the gods and the means by which they were appeased. The divine nature in some way demanded human suffering and human blood, and in such ideas we see at once the whole limitation of naturalistic religions. God, perceived through nature, was thus invested with those relationships and properties which belong to the natural world. But by means of His Son Who acted as an intermediary the heavenly Father reveals Himself not as sovereign, or as judge, but as infinite love. " God sent not His Son into the world to condemn the world, but that the world through Him might be saved." " I came not to condemn the world, but to save the world."

The Redemption achieved by the Son of God is not a judicial verdict, but a means of salvation ; it is not a judgment, but a trans-

[1] The Metropolitan Anthony, the most irreconcilable opponent of the juridical theory, particularly insists upon this point. See his *Dogma of Redemption*. There is a certain element of truth in his criticism, but his rationalist denials lack mystical penetration into the idea of sacrifice.

figuration and illumination of nature—in a word, its sanctification. Salvation is not justification, but the acquiring of perfection. The conception of God as judge is that of the natural man and not the spiritual, to whom a quite different aspect of the divine nature is revealed. It is impossible to attribute to God the kind of sentiments which even men themselves regard as blameworthy, as, for instance, pride, egoism, rancour, vengeance, and cruelty. The natural man has given to the world a monstrous idea of God. According to the juridical conception of Redemption the religion of Christ is still a legal religion in which grace is not conceived ontologically.

In Christianity Redemption is the work of love and not that of justice, the sacrifice of a divine and infinite love, not a propitiatory sacrifice, nor the settlement of accounts. " For God so loved the world that He gave His only-begotten Son that whosoever believeth in Him should not perish, but have everlasting life." Bukharev, on the theory that the Lamb was slain from the foundation of the world, puts forward the remarkable idea that the voluntary sacrifice of the Son of God was part of the initial plan of creation.[1] God Himself longs to suffer with the world. The juridical interpretation of the evolution of the universe transforms Redemption into a judicial process.

God requires that justice should be done and demands compensation for the loss He has sustained. In a conception of this sort the old pagan idea of sacrifice still persists. The human mind has found it difficult to grasp the sacrifice of Christ and the mystery of the Redemption. The Cross, which is a stumbling-block to the Jews and foolishness to the pagans, continues to be a source of trouble to the Christian world, and the interpretation commonly given to it shows that men still distort its meaning by thinking of it in Jewish-pagan terms. Catholic theology in particular still bears the marks of Roman paganism with all its juridical formalism.[2] The legalistic spirit in Christianity is far from easy to overcome.

[1] Cf. Bukharev, *Contemporary Spiritual Needs in Thought and Life*.

[2] *Dogmatic Theology*, by the Orthodox Metropolitan Macarius, is imbued with the same spirit.

Man requires law and is therefore naturally inclined to see law at work everywhere. Christ does not indeed reject law, but He reveals to us a spiritual world where love and freedom enlightened by grace effectively triumph over law. Freedom of the lower kind, however, which has not been born again by grace, cannot deny law, for it is subject to its action. Christianity is not the religion of law, but that does not mean that we have to become antinomians. The law of the Old Covenant and the grace of the New have totally different spheres of activity, and that is exactly why it is impossible to conceive the latter in juridical terms. Law and justice are unable to explain the mystery of the relations between God and man.

The New Testament shows that God expects not a formal obedience to the law, but the free love of man. Law is the accusation of sin, a vision of the Divine Will distorted by sinful nature and not an original expression of God's feelings towards man. This mystery is revealed in Redemption.

The juridical conception of Redemption supposes that man's sin can be forgiven and the divine wrath appeased when the sacrifice of the Son has been offered. On such a view the relations between God and man are of a purely external character and nothing essential can be, nor should be, forgiven. It is not God who is unable to pardon man, but man who cannot pardon himself, any more than he can absolve himself from his apostasy from God and from the divine plan.[1] Anger in every shape and form is foreign to God, Whose mercy is infinite. But man preserves his higher spiritual nature which has been created in the image of God and it is that which cannot be reconciled with the degradation of the Fall ; it is injured by this infidelity to God, by this treachery of the Old Man, by this choice of darkness and nothingness in preference to the divine light. Man longs to redeem his sin but he feels his powerlessness and waits for the Redeemer and Saviour who will bring him back to God.

The spiritual nature of man does not merely demand pardon for

[1] This idea is developed in a remarkable way in the second volume of Nesmelov's book, *The Science of Man*.

sin, but rather its final defeat and extermination, that is to say, the transfiguration of human nature.

The meaning of Redemption lies in the coming of the Second Adam, the new spiritual man, in the coming of that love of which the Old Adam was ignorant, in the transformation of the lower nature into the higher. It certainly does not lie in the mere regulation of the external relationships between the Old Adam and God, nor in the pardon and satisfaction granted to one party by the other. The meaning of the coming of Christ into the world lies in a real transfiguration of human nature, in the formation of a new type of spiritual man, and not in the institution of laws, by the carrying out of which the spiritual life may be acquired. Thanks to the coming of Christ the spiritual life can really be attained. Here there can be no question of external relationships because the whole matter must be regarded spiritually from the point of view of immanence. Man hungers for a new and higher kind of life which is in accordance with his dignity and is eternal. It is this which really constitutes the revelation of the New Covenant. In Christianity the central idea is that of transfiguration, not justification. The latter has occupied too prominent a place in Western Christianity. In Eastern Christianity and in the Greek Fathers, on the other hand, the idea is modified in human nature. But the idea of transfiguration and of divinization was fundamental.

The coming of Christ and Redemption can be spiritually understood only as a continuation of the creation of the world, as the eighth day of this creation, that is to say, as a cosmogonic and anthropogonic process, as a manifestation of divine love in creation, as a new stage in the freedom of man. The advent of the new spiritual man cannot merely be the result of the evolution of human nature. On the contrary it presupposes an entry of the eternal and spiritual into this natural time-world of ours. The natural evolution of humanity leaves us shut up within the restraints and limits of natural reality. Original sin, the evil which lies at the root of this world, continues to isolate the terrestial world and hold it in bondage. Deliverance can only come from above. The power of the spiritual and divine world has to come into our fallen natural reality, and by transfiguring our nature, break down the barriers dividing the two worlds. Thus the history of Heaven becomes that of earth. The human race which is that of the Old Adam had to be prepared historically to receive the new spiritual man who comes from another world ; a preparatory spiritual development had to take place first. Within the sphere of humanity and in the natural world there had to be a pure and spotless being capable of receiving the divine element, a feminine principle enlightened by grace. The Virgin Mary, the Mother of God, was simply the manifestation of this principle, through which the human race was to receive the Son of God and the Son of Man. In Christ, the God-Man, the infinite divine love met the answering love of man. The mystery of Redemption is that of love and liberty. If Christ is not only God but also man (which is what the dogma of the Two Natures teaches us) then in Redemption not only the divine Nature played its part but also human nature, that is, the heavenly spiritual nature of mankind. Christ as God-Man reveals the fact not only that we belong to an earthly race but that the spiritual man, thanks to Him, abides in the very depths of divine reality.

In Christ, as Man in the absolute sense, summing up in Himself the whole of spiritual humanity, man makes a heroic effort to overcome by sacrifice and suffering both sin and death, which is the consequence of sin. And this he does in order to respond to the love of God. In Christ human nature co-operates with the work of Redemption. Sacrifice is the law of spiritual ascent and with the birth of Christ a new era in the life of creation begins. Adam underwent the trial of his freedom and failed to respond to the divine call by an expression of free and creative love. Christ, the New Adam, makes this response to the love of God and thereby points out the way to this response to all who are spiritually His.

Redemption is a dual process in which both God and man share ; yet it is but one process, not two. Without human nature and the exercise of human freedom it would be impossible. Here, as everywhere else in Christianity, the mystery of the theandric humanity of Christ is the key to any true understanding. There is no final solution to this mystery except in the Trinity, for it is in the Spirit that the relations between the Father and the Son are resolved. Evil cannot be overcome except by the participation of human freedom in the process. But evil undermines and alters the character of this freedom which alone permits of its defeat.

Here we have the fundamental antinomy which finds its solution in the dual mystery of Christ's nature. The Son of God, the Second Hypostasis of the Divine Trinity, overcomes the opposition between human freedom and divine necessity by the suffering of the Cross. In the passion of the Son of God and the Son of Man on Calvary freedom becomes the power of divine love, which enlightens and transfigures human freedom in the saving of the world. Truth in the guise of suffering and love makes us free without constraint ; in fact it creates a new and higher kind of freedom. The freedom which the truth of Christ gives us is not the result of necessity. Redemption cannot be understood as a return of human nature to its primitive state before the fall of Adam. Such a conception would indeed make nonsense of the whole process of the universe. But the new spiritual man is superior not only to fallen Adam, but to Adam before the Fall, and his advent marks a new stage in the creation of the world. The Old Adam gives us no clue to the mystery of infinite love and the new type of freedom, for that mystery is only revealed in Christ.

The coming of Christ cannot be subordinated to such an exclusively negative source as the existence of sin and evil ; it is the positive revelation of the supreme stage of creation. Redemption is not the return to the condition of Paradise but the passage to a higher state of existence, to the manifestation of the spiritual nature of man and of a creative freedom and love hitherto unknown. Redemption is then a new moment of creation. Creation was not finished in seven days ; these were but one epoch in its destiny. The world is dynamic and not static. It is always possible to reach fresh heights. The description of the creation of the world in the Old Testament fails to disclose the creative activity of God in its fulness ; and in the

178

interpretation of creation the mind of the New Covenant is not to be limited by the Old. The creation of the world continues and the world enters upon fresh periods of development.

The appearance of Christ marks a new era in the destiny of the world, a new moment in the creation both of the world and of man. Not only human nature but the whole universe and the whole of cosmic life was transformed after the coming of Christ. When the Blood of Christ shed upon Calvary touched the earth, earth became a new thing, and it is only the limitation of our receptive faculties which prevent us from seeing it with our very eyes.

The whole life of man and of the universe is already different since Christ came and constitutes in fact a new creation. But only a theology free from the spirit of the Old Covenant can comprehend this truth. Redemption is precisely the only possible theodicy, the justification of God and His creation. Without freedom which is both the void and infinite power there would be no possibility of universal evolution nor of anything new.

IV

By a spiritual understanding of Redemption we get definitely beyond what might well be called the " vampire " idea of God. The whole pagan world was feeling its way towards this mystery and had a foretaste of the coming of the Redeemer. Even as early as totemism we find a naturalistic Eucharist. But the redemption which was thus hoped for and anticipated was reflected in a very imperfect fashion in these natural elements and was connected with the idea of blood-sacrifices. While the pagan deities thirsted for blood, man on his part devoured his gods. Paganism had its suffering redeemer-gods, of which Dionysos, who was torn in pieces by the Maenads, is an example. But in Christianity, where Redemption is actually accomplished, the Eucharistic Sacrifice has an essentially different character. Christ is the Lamb sacrificed as a whole burnt-offering for the sins of the world. But it was the wicked men of this world who crucified Christ and shed His Blood, whereas Christians offer a bloodless sacrifice of love. The communion of the Body and Blood of Christ has nothing in common with the "vampirism" of natural religions. In Redemption and the Eucharist the spirit rises above the welter of nature. In the Redemption which Christ achieved the forces at work are supernatural and belong to another world which enters into ours and transfigures it.

But Christian thought is still obsessed by the idea of natural necessity and the pagan conception of blood-sacrifice still needs to be transcended. J. de Maistre, for example, makes such a close connection between the Eucharistic Sacrifice of Christ and the blood-sacrifices of paganism that he virtually identifies them. The blood of the innocent victim purchases redemption for the sins of the guilty. Man must be acquitted in the sight of God in respect of all the wrong that he has committed. This is a conception particularly associated with Catholicism, in which an element of "vampirism" still persists (e.g. in relation to the blood of innocent victims). But this blood is the great sacrifice of love in which we are all called to co-operate and which is spiritual in character. We have inner mystical communion with Christ and participate in the work which He has accomplished. The spirit of Christ was already at work in the ancient world in the higher elements of pagan religion, in the victories of the spirit over nature, in Orphism, and in Plato ; but it is only in Christianity that it was finally manifested in the flesh.

There are in Christianity two spiritual types which have left their mark on the attempts made to understand the mysteries of the Christian faith. The former lives above all in fear of perdition, and feeling itself to be under the condemnation of justice seeks salvation and deliverance for itself. The latter seeks above all for the higher life, the divine truth and beauty, the transfiguration of all creation, the appearance of a new creation and the new spiritual man. The former is connected with the Old Covenant and tends to regard Redemption from a juridical standpoint. The latter is inspired by the New Covenant and tends towards an ontological view of Redemption which regards it as a new moment in creation, the coming of a new spiritual man.[1] These two different spiritual orientations are in conflict within Christianity. Thus we find that Clement of Alexandria, whose spirit is Hellenistic, aspired to contemplation and union with God rather than the pardon of his sins, while St. Augustine, on the other hand, desired above all things pardon and justification.[2]

V

Evil must be unmasked if it is to be defeated, for ignorance or denial of evil weakens our resistance to it. Man must learn how to " try the spirits ", for he is often in the grip of devils who appear as angels of light. But there is also another danger, that of a too exclusive concentration upon evil, which consists in seeing it everywhere, and which by an exaggeration of its power and attraction amounts to a continuous obsession with it. Man is thus plunged into an atmosphere of suspicion and distrust. He has more faith in the power of Satan than in that of God ; he believes more in Antichrist than in Christ Himself. Thus a most pernicious spiritual tendency is set in motion which spells destruction for all positive and creative life. Evil has its effect upon man not only when he denies its existence, but also when he exaggerates its significance. It is a dangerous proceeding to invest evil with a virtual halo. In the struggle against evil man is often contaminated by it, for in some measure he tends to imitate his opponent. Distrust and hatred of evil degenerate into a new form of evil. The struggle easily gives rise to new evils because of the sinful state of human nature. The history of nations is full of examples of evil provoked by the struggle against evil, whether it be a conservative or a revolutionary struggle.

[1] In that remarkable Russian book, *The Way of a Pilgrim* (translated by the Rev. R. M. French), we read, " The fear of suffering is a mercenary motive. God wants us to come to Him by the path of sonship."

[2] Cf. the excellent book of E. de Faye on the subject of Clement of Alexandria.

Our attitude towards evil must be free from hatred and has itself need to be enlightened in character. (We have to be gentlemen even in our dealings with the devil.) Satan rejoices when he succeeds in inspiring us with diabolical feelings with regard to himself. It is he who wins when his own methods are turned against himself. It is he who inspires men with the fallacious notion that evil can be used to fight evil. Man who fights evil often finds himself caught in his own trap, which in the end holds him a prisoner. Imperceptibly the means by which the struggle is prosecuted become ends. What man believes to be the struggle against evil becomes itself a good. The State is appealed to in order to restrict the manifestation of evil in the world, but the methods it uses for this purpose easily become evil themselves.

Even morality itself shows a tendency to degenerate into its opposite by stifling the creative life of the spirit. Law, custom, and ecclesiastical law may debase life. An obsession with evil and the need to struggle against it by the use of constraint and violence enslave men to sin and hinder their deliverance from it. True spiritual health does not consist in being absorbed in the sphere of evil, but in concentrating upon what is good, upon the divine world, and the vision of light.

When men become haunted by such ideas as that of a world-wide conspiracy of Jews or Freemasons and think they can see everywhere the agents of such plots, they are simply committing spiritual suicide, and by shutting their eyes to the light become a mass of hate, suspicion, and revenge. Here we have a purely sterile and destructive spiritual tendency. We must not imagine we can see Satan everywhere and hand over the world to him. A continual denunciation of evil and its agents merely encourages its growth in the world—a truth sufficiently revealed in the Gospels but to which we remain persistently blind. Our first need is to discover the bad in ourselves and not in others. True spirituality consists in believing in the power of good rather than that of ill, in God rather than Satan. Good thoughts and feelings develop the power of goodness in the world, while those which are bad augment evil. But this elementary law of spiritual health is not recognized by people. Hatred of evil destroys the spiritual world of man just as much as hatred of the good, which does not mean to say that our attitude towards evil must not be ruthless nor that there can be any question of a truce with it. The error arises in the consolidation of the powers of evil in the interests of a struggle waged on behalf of the good. Evil cannot be fought simply by exterminating it ; it must be overcome, and conquered.

Now the most complete victory over evil comes through the conviction of its emptiness and vanity—in a word, of its non-being. The exaggeration of the power of temptation can hardly be a positive means of overcoming it. Evil entices a man but it is not in itself enticing. The attraction of evil is a lie and an illusion, which must be dispelled by all the spiritual energy in our possession. The devil is not conspicuous for his talents ; in fact he is a bore. Evil is non-being but non-existence is the last extremity of boredom, emptiness, and impotence ; which is, moreover, exactly what we always find when we finally come to the end of any experience of evil. As long as in our struggle against evil we regard it as something strong and enticing and at the same time both awe-inspiring and forbidden, we are not going to achieve any radical or final victory over it. The evil which is regarded as powerful and enticing is an evil yet unconquered which will remain invincible as long as it is so regarded. Only the knowledge of its absolute emptiness and tedium can give us the victory over it and destroy it at its very roots.

No evil passion pursued to the end has any positive content. All evil consumes itself. Its nothingness is laid bare by its own inner course of development. Evil is the sphere of phantasy (an idea admirably developed by St. Athanasius the Great). Evil is evil not because it is forbidden but because it is non-being. The Old Testament regarded evil as above all a transgression of the divine law, but failed to explain why evil is evil and what was the basis of its opposition to good. The normal conception of good and evil is not a profound one, for they must be understood ontologically.

It is only by an inner proof of its non-being that we can really know evil and understand the meaning of the opposition existing between it and the good. Evil is knowable only in the experience of the knowledge of it, that is, in the inner victory achieved over it, for it is only in this experience that we realize what an aching void it is. When man picks the fruit of the tree of the knowledge of good and evil he sets out upon the path of evil and formally transgresses the divine Will. But on this path he learns to know the vanity and emptiness of evil and understands through his own experience why it is forbidden.

But can there be a " Gnosis " or knowledge of evil ? The Old Testament, in which law predominated, answered this question in the negative. Evil is a barrier and therefore can only be a species of prohibition. But man already embarked upon the way of knowledge cannot return to the state of original ignorance. Also the void of evil must be experienced and we must be convinced of its non-being. Herein lies the fundamental antinomy with which it is associated.

Evil is evil and must be consumed in the flames of Hell, for there can be no reconciliation with it. So the former of these two theses runs. The latter is the entire opposite of this. Evil is the path by which we reach good, the experience of the freedom of the spirit, and an inner victory over the temptations of non-being. The former thesis is perfectly clear and conceals no hidden dangers of any kind. The latter is dangerous and may become a source of difficulty. Does not the knowledge of evil lead to its justification ?

If we consider evil as an indispensable necessity and possessing a meaning of its own, is not this a justification of it ? If, on the other hand, it is absolutely meaningless and is incapable of explanation it it unknowable and can be given no meaning. But how are we to escape from this difficulty ? Here is a fresh antinomy. Christ has come into the world because it was in the power of sin. Redemption, that is to say the greatest event in world history which was the determining factor in the creation of a new race of spiritual men, is the result of the existence of evil, for if it had not existed there would have been no Deliverer, the coming of Christ would not have taken place, and the love of Heaven would not have been revealed.

Evil is thus the motive force behind the life of the universe. Without it the primitive condition in which Adam was created would have persisted through the centuries, all the possibilities of being would still have remained latent, and the New Adam would not have made his appearance. The good which has triumphed over evil is superior to the good which preceded it.

This difficult problem is one which theology has never been able to solve, for it is afraid to get to grips with it. To find a solution of this difficulty we must begin by admitting the existence of the difficulty, that is to say, by admitting the antinomy which evil presents to our religious thinking. This difficulty cannot be resolved by rational thought and concepts ; it is bound up with the mystery of freedom. The antinomy of evil can be resolved only in spiritual experience. Dostoievsky had a remarkable understanding of it. The experience of evil, the denunciation of its nothingness, can bring us to the highest good. Having lived out the experience of evil we can comprehend the fulness of truth and goodness. It is indeed true to say that whole peoples and in fact all mankind pursue this path and, having tried evil, gain the knowledge of the power or goodness and the profundity of truth. Man learns the nothingness of evil and the grandeur of goodness not through the operation of a formal law nor by means of prohibitions, but by his living experience of the road of life. For the rest, the experimental spiritual path is the only way of knowledge. But what deduction can we draw from this for our spiritual lives ? Can we say that we will embark on evil courses in order to enrich our knowledge and arrive at a higher good ?

From the very moment we begin to regard evil as a means of achieving good and as a positive method of knowing the truth, we are lost, and are no longer able to demonstrate its untruth and vanity. The experience of evil can bring us to the good only on condition that we know and reveal its untruth and its non-being ;

it can enrich us only as we denounce it and deny it in the most absolute fashion as a vehicle for the enrichment of our spirits. So the antinomy of evil finds its solution in spiritual experience. It is not evil itself which enriches life, for non-being can confer no enrichment ; *that* springs from the inner denunciation of evil, from the suffering in which it is destroyed, from the tragedy which has been endured, and from the light seen in the darkness. All satisfaction with evil, all attempts to envisage evil as an approach to something higher, mean loss, a movement in the direction of non-being which deprives man of the experience which could bring him enrichment. To know evil is to know its non-being, not to justify it. Only its ruthless denunciation and destruction in oneself can make it an approach to the good.

Thus without being afraid of the paradox we are forced to recognize that evil possesses a positive meaning, but this meaning is closely connected with freedom, without which all theodicy would be impossible. We should find ourselves obliged to say that the divine creation has failed. The innocence imposed in Paradise could not be maintained ; it had no value and we cannot return to it. Man and the world are undergoing a voluntary testing and the experience of freedom of knowledge, and they turn freely to God and to His Kingdom.

Christianity teaches us above all to be ruthless with regard to the evil within us, but in the process of extermination we must be indulgent towards our neighbours. We can be maximalists only in relation to ourselves and not to others. We must first realize the power and beauty of goodness in ourselves and not impose on others what we have been unable to compel ourselves to realize. The lie *East Europe* in the soul which is common to political and social revolution consists in the desire to eliminate external evils while allowing them to flourish within. Revolutionaries (and counter-revolutionaries too) never begin by overcoming and getting rid of the evil in themselves ; they prefer to exterminate it in others in its secondary and outward manifestations. A revolutionary attitude towards life is a superficial one and lacks depth. There is nothing radical about revolutions ; they are to a big extent simply masquerades in which nothing is changed but the outward dress of the performers. Revolutions do not so much overcome evil as give new birth to it by provoking fresh evil.

It is true that revolutions have certain positive results besides and that they determine new epochs in history, but the good which they do is the result not of revolutionary but of post-revolutionary activity. It is due to the understanding of what has been lived through. Evil can be overcome only inwardly and spiritually. Victory over it is linked up with the mystery of Redemption and can only be achieved in and through Christ. We triumph over evil only in communion with Christ and in co-operation with His work, through the bearing of His Cross. For those who employ force the conquest of evil is impossible.

Tolstoi's theory of non-resistance to evil is a false one because it confuses two quite distinct issues, namely that of the inner victory over evil and that of the external limitations which have to be imposed on it. Externally we can, indeed we must, limit its manifestations, for we cannot, for example, permit one man to kill another ; but we do not thereby destroy the inner source from which such evil springs, and the desire to murder and to commit violence is not overcome. In the history of Christianity there has been a good deal of abuse of the principle of resisting evil by force and it was believed to be possible to overcome it by the sword. This was the result of confusing the Kingdom of God with the kingdom of Caesar and of the violation of the frontiers between Church and State. Evil cannot be defeated by the State, which itself belongs to the natural world, which exists because evil exists, and is often itself a source of evil. The problem of evil brings us to a final antinomy. Evil is death and death is the consequence of evil. To destroy evil at its very root is to take the sting out of death. Christ has conquered death and we must freely accept death as the path to life and as an interior moment of it. We must die in order to be reborn. Death is an evil imposed upon us by the lower and external world to which we are subjected through sin and through our separation from the higher sources of life ; but by accepting it freely and without revolt as the inevitable consequence of sin, we are able to overcome it spiritually. It thus becomes for us a moment of the interior mystery of the spirit. Death regarded from an inward and spiritual point of view is something quite different from death considered externally as a fact of the natural world. Christ Who knew no sin freely accepted Calvary and death, and we must follow in His footsteps, for by co-operating with the life and death of Christ we are victorious over death. From an inner, spiritual, and mystical point of view death does not exist ; it is for us the way leading to life, in which the life of sin is crucified and the path to eternity opened up. In communion with the initial sources of life we triumph over the destructive consequences of death. Death is not simply and solely an evil for Christian thought, it is also a good. A life in the flesh in this sinful and wicked world if it had no end would be too terrible to contemplate, for such an existence would be nothing more nor less than spiritual death.

The transfiguration of our nature and resurrection to eternal life in God is the final goal to which a will directed towards goodness, truth, and beauty aspires. The transfiguration of the life of the world into eternal life is the supreme end of everything. The way which leads to it involves the free acceptance of the cross, suffering, and death. Christ is crucified above that dark abyss in which being and non-being blend one with the other. The light which shines from the Crucified is a light shining in the darkness. It is this light which both illuminates the obscurity of being and overcomes the darkness of non-being.

CHAPTER SIX

God, Man, and the God-Man

I

BOTH philosophy and theology should start neither with God nor with man (for there is no bridge between these two principles), but rather with the God-Man. The basic and original phenomenon of religious life is the meeting and mutual interaction between God and man, the movement of God towards man and of man towards God. This fact finds its most concrete and fullest expression in Christianity, in which the humanity of God is revealed. The humanization of God is the fundamental process of the inner consciousness of humanity. In the earlier stages of this evolution God was confused with the forces of nature, animals, and plants. Totemism, for instance, was the revelation of the God-animal. The type of thought which made God in the image of man was the counterpart of that which made man in the image of God. God without man, an " inhuman " God, would be Satan, not God-in-Trinity.

The fundamental myth of Christianity is the drama of love and freedom between God and man, the birth of God in man and the birth of man in God. The coming of Christ, the God-Man, is a perfect union of these two movements, the realization of unity in duality and of the divine-human mystery. The mystery of religious life remains inexplicable without the co-existence of unity in duality, without the meeting of the two natures and their fusion without loss of distinction.

The initial phenomenon of religion, that is to say, this religious drama of separation and of meeting, this mystery of transfiguration

189

and of union, can be explained neither by monism nor by monophysitism nor yet by dualism. For the former everything is included in an abstract initial unity, for the latter everything is hopelessly divided against itself and incapable of achieving unity ; everything is externally opposed. The powerlessness of monism and dualism to conceive the divine-human mystery is precisely the powerlessness of rational thought. According to the rational conception of divinity there is nothing but an abstract Absolute, without any concrete inner life, and without the tragedy of those relations between God and His other self which attain their perfection in the Third Hypostasis. The living God and the drama of the divine life only exist for the symbolic and mythological consciousness. It is only for thought of this kind that God and man appear face to face with one another as living personalities whose relationships constitute a concrete form of life with the tragedy always inherent in it.

Abstract theism, which has been the form taken by abstract monotheism, conceives the life of God in terms of a celestial monarchy or empire, investing God with the attributes of autocracy and self-sufficiency. But such a celestial monarchy is completely out of harmony with the Christian doctrine of the Trinity and the love which fills Its inner life. The organization of earthly life in conformity with the pattern of this heavenly monarchy is the affirmation not of the Trinity and of the Unity in love, but rather of arbitrary power and despotism. Traditional affirmative theology has been closely confined within rational concepts and that is why it has been unable to grasp that inner life of the Divine Being, in which alone the creation of the world and man (that is to say, the attitude of God towards His other self) can be understood. The creation of the world and of man has been regarded exoterically, from the outside. Rationalistic and exoteric religious thought is obliged to maintain the cruel idea that God created the world capriciously, without necessity, and entirely unmoved from within.

According to such a conception creation is without significance, not divine, and for the most part condemned to perish. Theological teaching falls into a rationalistic dualism which is at the opposite pole to rationalistic monism. Only mystical and symbolic theology can rise to an esoteric conception of the mystery of creation as the interior life of the Divine. This mystery is the need which God feels for His other self, of one who loves and is beloved, of the love which is realizable within the Trinity in Unity, which exists both above, and below, in heaven, and on earth.

The theological and metaphysical doctrine of the absolute immobility of the Divine is exoteric and rationalistic, and illustrates the limits of all logical concepts in relation to Divinity. The idea of God as *coincidentia oppositorum* is more profound and was that favoured by St. Augustine and the mystics. In God absolute rest is inseparably connected with absolute motion. It is only in our rational consciousness and in our natural world that rest excludes motion, and that motion is incompatible with rest. The absolute perfection of Divinity contains within itself absolute rest and absolute motion. For rationalist thought motion in God appears to be opposed to His perfection and seems to imply a certain insufficiency in Him. But the idea of God that we make for ourselves cannot be anything else but contradictory, for opposites are naturally identified in Him. The fact that God longs for His other self, for the free response to His love, shows not that there is any insufficiency or absence of fulness in the Divine Being, but precisely the superabundance of His plenitude and perfection. We cannot regard absolute fulness and perfection from the static and abstract point of view, for they can only be thought of in terms of a concrete dynamism, as life and not as substance.

Theology of the mystical and negative type favours such a conception of God and in some degree prepares the ground for it. It is true that this kind of theology may appear to lead us in respect of our knowledge of God to extreme forms of abstraction from all concreteness such as is found, for instance, in Plotinus' doctrine of God. But for Christian thinking this knowledge of God is capable of being simply a purification and a preparation for a positive symbolical and mythological comprehension of the concrete life in

God. The theological and metaphysical doctrine of the absolute immobility of the Divine Being, which is the one traditionally and officially recognized, is in striking contradiction to the essential mystery of Christianity. A really profound Christianity does not order the relations between God and man and between God and creation upon a basis of static categories. So far as it is concerned these relations are a mystery inaccessible to absolute thought and incapable of being reduced to categories of a rigid type.

At the heart of the mystery of Christianity stands the Cross of Calvary with the sufferings and death of the Son of God, the Saviour of the World. The theory of the absolute immobility of the Divine is in opposition to the mystical fact of the sufferings of our Lord. Christianity is the religion of the suffering God. It is not God the Father Who suffers, as the Patripassians used to hold, but the suffering of the Son is a measure of suffering within the inner life of the Trinity. The doctrine of the absolute immobility of God is a form of abstract monotheism which contradicts Christian teaching as to the Trinitarian nature of the Divine and Its interior life. This doctrine betrays the influence of Parmenides and the philosophic school of Elis.

The perception of God as a Trinity is the perception of the inner esoteric movement within God which has quite clearly no analogy with that which transpires in our natural world. The internal relationships between the Hypostases of the Trinity are dynamic and not static and are revealed as concrete life. Similarly the mystery of the creation of the world cannot be understood intimately and esoterically except through the inner life of the divine Trinity, the inner movement within the Divinity, the divine dynamic. When we approach this mystery we find ourselves on a razor edge and it is very easy to fall from it in either direction ; a fall which the Church calls heresy. Official theological teaching which forbade in a measure those paths of knowledge in which it is easy to go astray constituted a preventive force not without pedagogic significance. But all forms of heretical deviation are indications of a rationalistic approach to the divine mysteries, and an incapability of conceiving the antinomy inevitable in all our thinking about God. Heretical doctrines are always rationalizations of spiritual experience because they regard as the whole truth what is only partially true. The mystics of Christianity do not make this mistake. They put forward the most daring ideas which alarm the minds of average people and appear sometimes even more extravagant and more contrary to our accustomed faith than the teaching of heretics. But the true mystics describe the very depths of spiritual experience, the initial mystery of life ; they do not attempt to elaborate concepts nor abolish the antinomy of the spiritual life. Therein lies the whole importance of mysticism and the whole difficulty that our mind experiences in assimilating it.

St. Simon the New Theologian said, " Come Thou, Who remainest unmoved yet Who ever moveth and dost direct Thyself towards us." In these mysterious words which official theology conceives with difficulty, he expresses the truth of spiritual experience, namely, the coincidence of motion and rest in God. Here we have no metaphysic based upon concepts, but rather the original experience of the spiritual life directly expressed. Thomism denies potentiality in God and with it the possibility of movement, and elaborates a rationalist doctrine of God which is based upon Aristotelian philosophy. But if God is *actus purus*, then the creation of the world, that is creative activity in God, remains unintelligible.[1] The restricted nature of theological doctrines is due to the fact that affirmation has concealed negation. When Christianity professes the doctrines of the Trinitarian nature of God and the expiatory sacrifice of the Son it thereby acknowledges the existence of a process in God, a divine tragedy. But the divine process cannot be assimilated to that which takes place in our time-series with its divisions. This divine process in eternity is not opposed to divine rest. The divine life is a mystery which is accomplished in eternity. It is revealed to us in spiritual experience, for everything that takes place above has its reflection below. Similarly the process of divine

---

[1] Laberthonnière treats this problem very well in his *Christian Realism and Greek Idealism.*

birth which transpires in heaven takes place also in us, in the very depths of our being.

The great German mystics made a distinction between God (*Gott*) and Divinity or Godhead (*Gottheit*). Such for instance was the teaching of Eckhart. Boehme maintained the doctrine of the *Ungrund* which was at a deeper level than God Himself. The meaning of this distinction between God and Divinity is not expressible in metaphysics or ontology. This truth can only express itself in terms of spiritual life and experience and not in the categories of a rigid ontology. As rigid ontology this truth can easily degenerate into a heresy. Eckhart describes the relationships between God and man which are revealed in mystical experience. God exists if man exists. When man disappears, God will also disappear. " Before the creature existed God was not God." God became God only in relation to creation. In the primal void of the divine Nothingness, God and creation, God and man disappear, and even the very antithesis between them vanishes. " Non-existent being is beyond God and beyond differentiation." The distinction between the Creator and creation is not the deepest that exists, for it is eliminated altogether in the divine Nothingness which is no longer God. Negative mystical theology penetrates beyond the Creator in His relationship to creation and beyond God in His intercourse with man. The Creator is manifested at the same time as creation, God and man appear simultaneously. It is a theogonic process of the divine Unfathomable which is the counterpart of the anthropogonic process.

Angelus Silesius says, " I know that without me God could not endure for a moment. Were I brought to naught He would yield up the Ghost for lack (of me)." He also says " I am as great as God, and He is as little as me." These bold words, coming as they do from a man who was a mystic and a poet and at the same time an orthodox Catholic, may well disturb and even alarm us. But we must try to grasp their real meaning. It is not an easy task to understand the mystics; they have a peculiar language of their own and this language, while it is universal, is impossible to translate into metaphysical and theological terms. Angelus Silesius does not attempt to build up a system either of ontology or theology, and contents himself with describing mystical experience. He speaks of the infinite love between God and man. The loving subject cannot exist a moment without the loved object, and perishes with it. The extraordinary phraseology of Angelus Silesius depicts the mystical drama of love, and the infinite intensity of the relations between God and man. Mysticism can be expressed only in terms of experience. Thus it is always a mistake which shows a want or proper understanding to interpret the mystics from the point of view of metaphysics or theology, and to relate them to this or that doctrinal tendency.

All the great Christian mystics, whatever confession they belonged to, have taught that in eternity, in the depths of the spiritual world, a divine process takes place in which is revealed the relationship between God and man, and the birth of God in man and of man in God, where lover and beloved meet. These are truths of spiritual experience, living truths, not metaphysical categories nor ontological substances. The movement in God, however it is unfolded in spiritual experience, is not a process in time which transpires in successive order. It is the ideal achievement, the divine mystery of life taking place in eternity. Only a symbolic and mythological approach to the relationship between God and man can bring us closer to this divine mystery ; metaphysical conceptions only mask the inner life. Personalism is, so to speak, incomprehensible by means of abstract metaphysics. God and man are living personalities whose relationship is intimate to the highest degree and constitutes the concrete drama of love and freedom. Such a living personalism is always mythological. The meeting of God and man is a mythological representation and not a philosophical proposition. This meeting has found its most intense expression in the prophets of the Bible and not in the Greek philosophers. Our thinking is irresistibly attracted towards an abstract monism for which the living personality of God and man and the tragedy of the religious life does not even exist.

Prophets and mystics, apostles and saints, revealed to the world the mysteries of life in its basic and original form. They spoke to it of their spiritual experiences and their intercourse with God, which are the fundamental verities of the religious life. The theological and metaphysical elaboration of this original experience is secondary, and categories and concepts which rationalize living religious experience enter into the composition of theological doctrines. They are a deviation in the direction of abstract monism and dualism. Theological theism, dominated by concepts, which regards the extrincism and non-divinity of creation as absolute, is a rationalization of the divine mysteries of the divine just as much as the pantheism which identifies the Creator and creation. Detachment from the sensible and concrete world, and all multiplicity and mobility in nature, combined with an orientation towards the unchanging world of ideas, is not the highest degree of spiritual experience and contemplation. Plato and Plotinus failed to penetrate to the divine mystery of life. Life in its basic and original form is both higher and deeper. In the history of the Christian consciousness and Christian theology two moments are united, namely, that detachment of thought which seeks the world of ideas, and the spiritual sense of the concrete and of the mystery of life. The heritage bequeathed by the Greek spirit has dominated Christianity too much with its detached thinking and lack of concrete life ; it gives precedence to metaphysics over mythology. But it is mythological thought, nevertheless, which lies at the root of Christianity.

II

In spiritual experience we see man's hunger for God. The human soul searches for a higher being, a return to the source of life and to the native land of the spirit. Human life becomes truly terrible when there ceases to be anything above man and when there is no place for the mystery of the divine and infinite. It is then that the tedium of non-being becomes apparent. The image of man is defaced when the image of God is obliterated from the human soul. Man in seeking for God seeks for himself and for his own humanity. The human soul suffers the pangs of God's birth within it. This birth of God in the human soul is the true birth of man. It is nothing else than the movement of God towards him and an answer to his own hunger for God. But it is only one of the aspects of this original religious phenomenon, to which there is another side and in which another movement is involved.

Spiritual experience also shows us that God longs for man and that He yearns for the birth of man who shall reflect His image. The great mystics in describing the spiritual life have spoken of this longing of the Divine for the human, for it is in mysticism rather than theology that this mystery is expressed. The primordial idea in man is the idea of God which is the theme of humanity, just as man is the theme of God. Infinite love cannot exist without a loving subject and a loved object. The birth of man in God is the answer to divine aspiration, the movement from man towards God.

The whole complexity of the religious life and the inter-relation of God and man springs from the existence of these two movements. If the religious life was simply the result of one movement, namely, that of God to man, having its origin solely in the will of God and His revelation, it would be a simple matter and the achievement of the goal of life would be possible, the Kingdom of God would be easily realizable. In a word the tragedy of the world would not exist. But the birth of man in God, his response in other words, could not be solely the work of God, for it is equally the work of man and his freedom. Because of the very nature of God Himself who is infinite love and the cause of the divine plan of creation itself, the Kingdom of God can be realized only through man's co-operation and the participation of creation itself. Despotism is as untrue in heaven as it is on earth. The Kingdom of God is that of God-humanity, in which God is finally in man and man in God, and this is realized in the Spirit. With this process is connected the fundamental myth of Christianity, a realist myth in the deepest sense of the word, which expresses the initial principle of being, the basic and original phenomenon and the mystery of life. This is the myth of the dual nature and movement of the God-Man.

It is the Son, born from all eternity, equal in dignity to the Father, Who responds to the divine aspiration of the loving subject and the loved object. It is the divine, absolute, Man, the God-Man and that, not only on earth in our natural historic world, but also in heaven in the divine reality of the Trinity. It is thus that nature, not indeed our sinful fallen nature, but spiritual human nature (which is pure and heavenly) succeeds in reaching the very heart of the divine Trinity. In the Son, in the divine Man, in the God-Man is comprised the whole human race, mankind in all its multiplicity and in every shape and form. In Him the antithesis between the one and the many is mysteriously resolved. The human species belongs under one of its aspects only to the generation of the Old Adam, the sinful and fallen race of our natural world. Under its other aspect it is heavenly and belongs to the generation of the Spiritual Adam, to that of Christ. Through the birth of the Son in eternity the whole spiritual race and the whole universe comprised in man, in fact the whole cosmos, responds to the appeal of divine love. The creation of the world could not have taken place in our fallen time-series which is the offspring of sin. Creation took place in eternity as an interior act of the divine mystery of life. The biblical conception of creation is only the reflection of this interior act in the consciousness of primitive man. Man after falling into a lower natural sphere is cast forth from divine Reality, but the Christian revelation re-establishes man at its heart. Through the Son we return to the bosom of the Father. With Him a new race of human beings begins, the race of Christ, born and regenerated in the Spirit. Christ is in man and man is in Christ. He is the Vine and we are the branches. The whole regenerated human race dwells in Christ the God-Man. In the spiritual man is included the cosmos and all creation. But the cosmos was violently separated from fallen man so that it became something external to him to which he was enslaved. Nevertheless the cosmos returns to regenerate man. In the spiritual world the cosmos dwells in man as man dwells in God.

Man is a microcosm by nature and in him are comprised all the spheres of cosmic reality and all its powers. Through sin and through the Fall man lost the idea of himself as a microcosm and became individualistic in his consciousness. The cosmos appears to the natural man simply as external nature, the inner life of which remains beyond his comprehension. It is only to the man who himself possesses an inner life that the inner life of the cosmos is revealed as a spiritual reality. Thus man attains a knowledge of the cosmos by the same means that he attains self-knowledge. Through Christ, the Logos, not only the human race but the whole universe turns to God and responds to the divine appeal and to the divine need of love. In man the mystery of the Bible, the mystery of Genesis, is revealed.[1]

The divine mystery, however, is not fulfilled in Duality for it pre-supposes the existence of three Persons. The relations between God and the Other Person are fulfilled in a Third. The loving Subject and the loved Object find the fulness of their life in the kingdom of love which is the Third Person. The kingdom of God (the kingdom of an enlightened humanity and an enlightened cosmos) is only realized through the Holy Spirit in Whom the drama is completed and the circle closed. It is only in this " Trinality " that the divine life is given to us in perfection, that the loving subject and the loved object create their kingdom and find the final content and fulness of their life. The Trinity is a sacred and divine number which signifies fulness and the victory over strife and division ; it is *sobornost,* the perfect society in which there is no opposition between personalities, hypostases, and the one Being. The mystery of Christianity is the mystery of unity in duality finding its solution in trinity-in-unity. This is why Christianity is based both upon the Christological dogma of the divine-human nature of the Son and upon the dogma of the Trinity. The affirma-

---

[1] St. Martin said, " The best possible translation of the Bible that can ever exist is man himself".

tion of being is the life of the Holy Spirit and in the Holy Spirit. In the Spirit man and the world are transfigured and deified. The Spirit constitutes Life itself in its basic and original form. The divine mystery of Life is just the mystery of the three Persons, which belongs both to heaven and earth. Wherever there is life there is the mystery of the three Persons, there is the distinction of the three Hypostases and their absolute unity. This mystery is reflected and symbolized everywhere in the life of man and of the world.

Life is in principle both the differentiation and the unity of personalities. The fulness of life is *sobornost* in which personality finds its final realization and integration. The meeting of one person with another always finds its fulfilment in a third. Two become a unity not through duality but through trinality in which they achieve their common entity. Being, were it single in character, would have remained in the embryonic stage, that is, in a state of indifference. Had it been a duality and nothing more it would have been hopelessly disunited and divided. That it can reveal its content and manifest differences while still remaining a unity is due entirely to its triune nature. Such is the nature of being, the basic and original fact of its life. The life of man and of the world is an interior moment of the mystery of the Trinity.

III

The interior life of God is realized by man and by the world. The interior life of man and of the world is realized by God. Man who is at the centre of being and called to play the most important rôle in the life of the universe, can have no positive life-content without God and without the world, that is to say, without that which is above and below him. He cannot remain solitary for he has no source of life in himself alone upon which to draw. When man stands alone before the void of non-being he is attracted towards it, and feels that it is a part of himself. If nothing exists but man in his solitariness then there is neither man nor anything else at all. An exclusive psychologism involves the affirmation of non-being and the destruction of man's very core. Human beings cannot build up their lives on themselves. The creation of life always pre-supposes for man the existence of another. If this Other Being Who is divine does not exist for him, he determines his life in reference to another which is of a lower nature. In separating himself from God and the higher world man submits himself to the lower world and becomes enslaved by it.

The submission of man to the elements of the natural world means the destruction of the ordered hierarchy of the universe. The relative position of the higher and lower elements in it is reversed, and everything is thrown out of place. Man, the king of the universe, becomes the slave of nature and necessity. Man is separated from God and the world from man, so that the world becomes something external to man which forces him to submit to its own laws. Man loses his spiritual independence. He begins to be determined from without and not from within. The sun ceases to shine upon him and to be the light of the world as before. It now becomes part of the nature which is external to man, the life of which depends entirely on illumination from without. The whole universe being separated from God ceases to have an inner radiance ; it needs a source of light exterior to itself. The principal result of the Fall is just this loss of inner illumination and the sub-ordination of everything to an external source. When man dwells in God then the cosmos is in man ; he has the sun within himself. When God and man are separated the cosmos and man are separated too. Necessity reigns in the cosmos and it is no longer subject to man's command.

St. Simon the New Theologian said, " When Adam was driven out of Paradise, the whole creation refused to submit to him any longer. Neither the moon nor any of the stars would appear ; the springs refused to send forth their waters and the rivers stopped in their courses ; the air was minded to keep so still that sinful Adam might not even be able to breathe. When the beasts and all the terrestrial animals saw that he had lost the garment of his first glory they began to despise him ; the heavens were ready to fall upon him and the earth desired to support him no longer. But what did God do, He Who is the Creator of man and of all things ? By His creative power He restrained them and in His mercy and goodness He did not suffer the elements forthwith to loose themselves upon man. He ordained that creation should continue subject to Adam and that having become ready to perish it should serve man who was in a like case and for whom it had been created. Nevertheless when man is born again and becomes spiritual, incorruptible, and immortal, creation, which has been subjected to man by God, will be freed from this task and will likewise be born again, becoming incorruptible, and in a measure, spiritual." Thus does a great mystic describe the day in which man lost his central position in the cosmos, and the bond which now fetters him to it.

Once separated from God and the spiritual world man loses his independence and his spiritual individuality ; he is subject to the laws of the animal world, becomes the instrument of the racial principle, and is condemned to live dominated by tradition in families and states in which this principle is a preponderating factor. Man is born and perpetuates the race of fallen Adam, which is subject to an indefinite process of birth and death, to that bad infinity of endless generations born only to die. The hopes of personality for eternal life are destroyed by this racial principle or element. Instead of eternal life and that fulness which personality demands there is nothing but the endless dissolution of generations which rise and then disappear. The link which binds birth and death cannot be broken by the racial element. Birth carries within it the seed of death, the breaking-up of individuality, and the loss of its hopes. He who begets is himself condemned to die and condemns to death those who in their turn come to birth. In the racial element on which the sinful life of natural humanity is based there is no victory over death and no achievement of the life incorruptible.

Sex with its generative function, which subjects man to natural law and links him with the natural world, is the result of sin and separation from God. Through birth man bears the consequences of sin but, even though he redeems it, he is unable to overcome corruptible nature and to attain eternal and immortal life. The new spiritual race of Christ is not a race born on earth according to the laws of the animal world and so prone at all times to the temptations of a lower element. Separation from God meant for man precisely the loss of his integrity, chastity, and virginity ; in other words, of the " male-female " image of the Divine Being.

According to the ingenious doctrine of Boehme man lost the eternal Virgin (Sophia) who departed from him and took refuge in heaven. This separation of the feminine element from " male-female " humanity meant that femininity became something apart from man, and the object of a tormenting attraction from which there was no escape. But while in his integrity and chastity man dwelt in God he had been able to comprehend femininity in Him. And it is here that we rediscover all that concerned man and the cosmos, for sin is above all the loss of integrity and chastity, which involves division and dissension. A virtuous integrality is precisely a synthesis of chastity or virginity, that is to say, the union in man of the masculine and the feminine. Sensuality and depravity are the result of this loss of integrality, an inevitable consequence of the division that has taken place within man. Everything has become, as it were, externalized and mutually exclusive. It is the same with regard to masculinity and femininity. The feminine element is an external, attractive, and seductive element without which the masculine cannot exist. Man cannot remain in a state of division, a mere incomplete half of his true self. This is why the human race suffers, for it has a desperate longing for this reunion and redintegration, and the full realization of its complete " male-female " being. But in the racial element which bears the marks of this division integrality is never acquired, the " male-female " image is never restored, man's ardent longing for eternity and for his virgin remain unfulfilled. Each individual man or woman is in different degrees bi-sexual and it is just this fact which makes the whole of life so complex.

*[margin note: * See the Symposium]*

The teaching of Boehme about Sophia is precisely that of the Virgin and the " male-female " image of man. " Through lust Adam was parted from the Virgin, and through lust he gained his wife ; but the Virgin is always waiting for him and if he only desires to be born again she will receive him and crown him with glory." [1] " The Divine Wisdom is the eternal Virgin and not woman, she is unsullied purity and chastity and she appears as the image of God and the image of the Trinity." [2] " The Virgin is from all eternity, she is uncreate and unbegotten ; she is the Divine Wisdom and the image of Divinity." [3] " The image of God is the masculine virgin and not woman or man." [4] " Christ on the cross delivered our virginal image of masculinity and femininity and in His divine love He dyed it crimson with His heavenly Blood." [5] " Christ was born of the Virgin in order to hallow afresh the *Tincture* of femininity and to unite it to the masculine principle so that man and woman might become alike ' male-female ' as was Christ." [6]

Wisdom is eternal virginity and not eternal femininity, for the wisdom-cult is that of the Virgin and not that of the feminine principle which is the result of division and the Fall. That is why the cult of Wisdom is almost identical with that of the Virgin Mary, the Mother of God. In her, nature became virginal and she conceived by the Spirit. Thus there arose that new humanity, the seed of Christ, which is immortal and triumphs over the bad infinity of birth and death. The integrality of man's image is restored through the Virgin Mary and her conception of Him Who is both Son of God and Son of Man. It is the way of chastity, purity, virginity, the way of mystical love.

The doctrine and cult of virginity have always had a more profound significance for Christianity than the doctrine of marriage

---

[1] Cf. Boehme's " Sämmtliche Werke ", Herausg. von K. W. Schiebler, 1841, vol. iii, *Die drei Principien göttlichen Wesen.*

[2] See vol. iv, *Vom dreifachen Leben des Menschen.*

[3] *Idem.*   [4] See vol. v, *Mysterium magnum.*

[5] *Idem.*   [6] *Idem.*

and the sanctification of procreation, which have alike received insufficient emphasis. The revelation of the mystical and positive meaning of the love between man and woman (*eros* not *agape*) is part of Christian problematics. The mystical significance of love has not received dogmatic elucidation, and what the Fathers of the Church have to say on this subject is poor and inadequate.[1] The Christianity of the Fathers teaches us to acquire virginity by means of asceticism but reveals nothing of the mystical significance of love as the way to virginity, the re-establishment of man's image in its integrity, and eternal life. Christianity has been right in justifying and sanctifying marriage and the family for sinful humanity, for in this way it preserves and spiritualizes fallen sex-life, but it says nothing about transfiguration or the coming of a new sex. This form of transfiguration has, like many other things, failed to receive its proper emphasis in Christianity. The sanctity of motherhood possesses cosmic significance, though to say that does not solve the question. The gulf which separates racial love (the love that begets) and the mystical love whose goal is eternity creates an antinomy for Christian thinking. The Church teaches that sex which is fallen and divided against itself is transformed in the Virgin Mary into an illumined virginity and motherhood, and receives into itself the Logos of the world Who is born of the Spirit. But it seems that no deduction has been drawn from this with regard to the positive methods by which the old racial element, that is the sexual element, can be illuminated and transfigured. The positive religious significance of love, the link which unites it to the very idea of man as an integral being, is not revealed. This is due to the insufficient attention paid to anthropology within Christianity. Love, like so many other things in the creative life of man, remains unexplained and unsanctified, outside the pale, as it were, condemned to a tragic destiny in the world. The Christian doctrine of marriage and of the family, like that of government and of the

---

[1] In patristic literature the only work worth noticing is *The Feast of the Ten Virgins or of Virginity*, by St. Methodius Pojarski. But there is nothing at all profound here except his doctrine of virginity.

state, has a profound meaning for the natural and sinful world, and for the racial element in which man undergoes the consequences of sin. But the problem of the meaning of that love which is the result neither of physical attraction nor of childbearing nor yet of the social organization of the human race is not even broached. Love by its nature occupies the same place as mysticism. It too is aristocratic and spiritual, and incapable of being assimilated to the democratic "psychical" and corporeal organization of human life. Love is bound up with the initial idea of man. We have no vision of the religious meaning of love except in the symbolism of the relations between Christ and His Church.[1]

IV

Christianity is the religion of the divine Trinity and God-humanity. It pre-supposes faith in man as well as in God, for humanity is a part of God-humanity. An "inhuman" God could not be the God of Christianity. Christianity is essentially anthropological and anthropocentric and exalts man to an unprecedented height of sublimity. The second Face of Divinity is manifested as the human face, and by this very fact man finds himself at the centre of being ; in him the meaning and the goal of creation is revealed. Man is called to participate in the work of God, which is the work of the creation and organization of the world. Christian mystics have had a bold conception of the central and supreme plane occupied by man in the universe.

In the loftiest ranges of the Christian consciousness we discover that man is not only a creature but infinitely more, since through Christ, the Second Hypostasis of the Trinity, he is incorporated into the divine life. Only Christian thought has recognized man's

[1] *The Meaning of Love*, by Solovyov, is the most remarkable book about love. See also that ingenious but little appreciated book of Bakhophen, *Das Mutterrecht*, which analyses the masculine and feminine principles in primitive religion.

eternity which he inherits in the divine life ; he cannot evolve by any conceivable process from one order to another or become either a devil or an angel. The eternal face of man abides in the very heart of the Divine Trinity Itself. The Second Hypostasis of Divinity is divine humanity. Christianity overcomes heterogeneity and establishes an absolute kinship between man and God. The transcendent becomes immanent. In Christ, the God-Man, the free activity not only of God but also of man is revealed. That is why all monophysitism which diminishes or denies the value of human nature is a denial also of the mystery of Christ, of the divine-human mystery of unity in duality. All the weaknesses and failures of Christianity in history spring from the difficulty experienced even by Christians themselves in grasping the divine-human mystery of a nature which is both single and dual. In addition to this the tendency towards a practical monophysitism is another cause of such failure. Even in the Christian era of universal life the human mind is still equally subject to monistic influences, and thought naturally tends in that direction. Thus German idealism at the beginning of the nineteenth century, though one of the most powerful manifestations of the philosophical genius of humanity, succumbed to the heresy of monophysitism and turned its attention to monism, which denies the independent existence of human nature and places considerable limitations upon it.

Fichte and Hegel only recognized the divine nature and denied the human, which in their view is only a function of divinity. It is not men but Divinity alone which knows. In the " I " of Fichte and in the " Spirit " of Hegel man as something concrete disappears. But the idealistic monism which results from such theories is forced to deny both man and God, for it can only recognize the divine as impersonal and abstract. Monism refuses to admit the nuptial mystery of the religious life and contradicts the original phenomenon of spiritual experience. This monophysitism of German idealism may be discovered in a latent condition as early as Luther, who rejected the freedom of the human spirit, the activity of man in the religious life, and finally the whole independent existence of human nature.[1] Already in St. Augustine there are certain tendencies and lines of argument which were later appealed to in order to lessen the importance of human nature. By making a distinction between the Creator and creation, as between that which is immutable and that which is not, every modification becomes an imperfection and a regression. The Divine Being is immutable and therefore perfect. Human beings are subject to change, but these changes are regressive and not progressive. The Fall is just an example of this. Man can only perfect himself through the action of grace. Thus St. Augustine denies to man both a creative nature and creative freedom. By this doctrine, elaborated under the influence of the struggle with Pelagianism, man suffers a signal diminution of his importance.

Catholic anthropology also reduced man's significance but in a different way. According to this view man was created a natural being and it is only later through the action of grace that he received spiritual and supernatural gifts. After the Fall man lost these gifts and became once more a natural being for whom the spiritual in all its forms was external. The deduction from this was that man was not created a spiritual being in the image of God. Nevertheless the truth is that man *is* a spiritual being.

V

The relations between God and man may be conceived under three different aspects. Firstly there is the transcendent dualism which subjects the human will to the divine in a purely external fashion. Thus the two natures remain divided, mutually estranged, and externally opposed to each other. Secondly there is immanentist monism which makes a metaphysical identification between the human and the divine wills and rejects altogether the independent existence of human nature. It sees in man only a manifestation of the divine life, a transitory moment in the development of divinity.

[1] See Luther's book, *De Servo Arbitrio.*

Thirdly there is what may be called "theandric anthropomorphism", a creative and Christian standpoint which recognizes the independent existence of the two natures and the reciprocal action of divine grace and human freedom. Man, "the other divine", makes a free response to the call of God which reveals his creative nature. In Christianity itself these three different conceptions can all be found in a greater or a lesser degree. The third presents the greatest antinomy for rational thought while it is also the cause of considerable complication in the Christian doctrine of Redemption and in our understanding of the work of universal salvation and deliverance.

Here we may distinguish two lines of approach both of which are rarely met in pure isolation. God, through the organized action of grace, helps man, who has lost his freedom through the Fall, to save himself and to overcome sin. This conception in its most extreme forms amounts to a justification of the use of forcible methods to secure the salvation of others. But there is another way in which we can understand the meaning of life. God expects from man a free response to His appeal, an answering love and creative co-operation in overcoming the night of non-being. Man has to manifest all the activity of his spirit, all the intensity of his freedom, in order to accomplish what God expects of him. This conception furnishes a religious justification for man's creative powers. In Christianity these two conceptions are closely bound up with one another and cannot be separated. Through Christ, the God-Man, the Redeemer and Saviour of the world, the two movements proceeding from God and from man, from grace and from freedom, are united. God through the power of grace aids man in the conquest of sin, and so re-establishes the shattered forces of man's freedom. Man out of the depths of this freedom then makes his response to God, begins to open up to Him, and thus continues the work of creation. Man is not a slave, still less a mere nothing, and he co-operates with the divine task of achieving a creative victory over nothingness. Man is necessary to God, and God suffers when man fails to be conscious of his own usefulness. God helps man,

o   209

but man must also help God, and it is just at this point that we begin to touch upon the esoteric element in Christianity.

When we assert the doctrine of man's deification and the fusion of his being with that of God, the danger to be feared is that of pantheism in which man's independence disappears ; but when we assert the freedom and independence of man, as distinct from God, pride and dualism are the enemies against which we have to guard ourselves.

In the depths of spiritual experience there is revealed not only man's need of God but also God's need of man. But clearly the word " need " here is an inexact expression, as indeed are all human terms when applied to God. We use the language of symbols, we translate ineffable mystery into the language of our own experience. Can we dare to investigate the psychology of God and of His inner life, or must we always limit ourselves to the attempt to understand the external relations of God with the world and with mankind ?

Holy Scripture, which in this respect is to be distinguished from doctrinal theology, presents us with a psychology of the Divine and speaks to us of the affective and emotional life of God. In the Bible the relations between God and man are described in terms of a drama of love between the loving subject and the loved object, in which not only man, but God Himself is subject to passions, and experiences anger, sorrow, and joy. The God of Abraham, Isaac, and Jacob is not to be confused with the Absolute of philosophy nor with the God of theology. He is rather a God Who resembles man, a God Who is not inert but Who is capable of movement. " The Song of Songs ", which was a source of inspiration to the mystics, is indeed a picture of the emotional life of the Divine. This inner life of God was revealed to the Christian mystics and they found words to express the emotions experienced by God. In the great Catholic mystics, in St. John of the Cross for example, we find a more intimate vision of the relations between God and man. For him, God is not the inert and impassive Absolute. In Greek philosophy Heraclitus with his doctrine of a " fiery motion " was nearer to the Christian God than Parmenides, Plato, Aristotle, or Plotinus, whose influence has preponderated in all the theological systems of Christianity.

Léon Bloy tells us that God is suffering alone, and not understood ; he admits tragedy in God. The love of God has indeed made him use daring language, " God ", he says, " suffers and bleeds when He fails to find in man an answer to His love, when human freedom does not play its part in His work, and when man does not place his creative forces at His disposal." Human responsibility is indeed increased and ennobled by such a conception ! Man must not think only about himself and his own salvation and well-being ; he must also think of God and His interior life ; he must bring to God the disinterested gift of his love, he must quench the divine thirst. It is his debt of honour. The mystics have been ← able to rise to this level of disinterestedness, they consented to be no longer pre-occupied with their own salvation, they were even ready to renounce it, to suffer the torments of Hell if love for God were to demand it.

And here we come across a strange contradiction. On the one hand, theology fears to recognize movement, " nostalgia ", and tragedy in God since it upholds the doctrine of His immutability and immobility ; on the other hand, this very same theology elaborates a juridical theory of redemption, according to which the sacrifice of Christ is a propitiation for the divine wrath, a satisfaction afforded to an offended God. But is not the wrath of God which feels the offence itself part of the affective life of God and a movement within the heart of the Divine ? Why is it less humiliating to admit the existence of a feeling of offence in God than to admit divine languor ?

We have here a manifest contradiction in the doctrines of theology which is to be explained not by the desire to magnify God, but by the desire to humiliate man and to keep him in a state of distress. God expects infinitely more from man than what the ordinary teaching about Redemption and obedience to the divine Will suggests. Does not God expect man to reveal in freedom his creative nature ? Has not God hidden within Himself that which man will manifest in his response to the divine appeal ? God never constrains man, and sets no bounds to his freedom. The plan which God has conceived is that man should surrender his powers freely and in love, thus fulfilling a creative task in His Name. God expects from man his participation in the work of creation and in the victory of being over non-being, He expects from him an activity which is both heroic and creative. Those who rebel against this idea by maintaining that man's task consists only in his submission to the Will of God and in carrying it out become involved in a merely futile formalism. It is evident, of course, that man must submit his will to that of God and that he must overcome self-centredness for the sake of God-centredness and that he must carry out to the end the divine Will ; but does not the Will of God demand also that man, endowed with that creative liberty which bears the mark of the divine image, should participate in the work of creation in its eighth day ? Does not God expect free creative activity from man and the release of all the forces at his disposal ? Certainly the Will of God does seem to be of such a nature and man must submit to it.

It is the old question in the Gospel of the talents which must not be buried in the earth but put to profitable use. St. Paul also teaches us that the gifts of men are diverse and that men must be free in spirit and creative, not for themselves but for God, and for the sake of His Will. But the mystery itself of creative genius and of the nature of creativity is unknown and is not revealed in Holy Scripture. If this mystery were there revealed the freedom of creative action and all that we call heroism would no longer exist, and what God expects from man would be impossible. The creative mission of man in the world demands that man should become conscious of himself in freedom, and from this act there must result an absolute advantage for being.

Man's creative action, which is a continuation of the creation of the universe, is not arbitrary in character nor is it a revolt ; rather it is the submission and surrender to God of all the forces of his spirit. Man in his creative love for God does not only invoke Him on behalf of his human needs, expecting salvation from Him : he also offers Him all the superabundance of his forces and all his fathomless liberty with absolute disinterestedness. If man does not bring his creative gift to God, if he does not participate actively in building the Kingdom of God, if he shows himself to be a slave, if he buries his talents in the earth, then the creation of the world will receive a check and the fulness of the divine-human life conceived by God will not be realized ; God will suffer and will remain unsatisfied in His relations with His other self. Man must be more disinterested in his religious life and more free from tendencies to celestial eudaemonism. When man thinks only of himself, his needs, his well-being, and human salvation, he restricts God's conception of what man should be and denies his own creative nature. But when he thinks of God, and of God's longing for love, and of what God expects from him, he raises himself to a higher plane by realizing God's idea of him, by affirming his creative nature.

It is here that we find the paradox which exists in the relations between God and man. Personality is precisely the divine idea, the divine image and resemblance in man, in contrast with individuality, which is a naturalistic and biological conception. Thus in order to understand himself man must address himself to God, he must fathom the divine idea concerning himself, and direct all his forces to the realization of it. God wills that man should be, for God does not intend that He should be alone. The meaning of being lies in the triumph over solitude and the acquiring of kinship. Such is the very essence of religious experience. Man is called not only to seek for divine assistance and salvation, but to help God in the realization of His plan for the world. The natural man is too weak to accomplish his creative mission ; his powers are shattered by sin and his freedom is devitalized. In the generation of the New Adam, in spiritual humanity, the creative power and freedom of mankind are re-established through redemption. This creative force which is capable of satisfying the divine demand is only finally and perfectly acquired by means of a new, spiritual, birth ; it is obtained only in Christ. The creative energies of man never reach the height contemplated by God. The only man capable of discovering such a height and of turning towards God is the man who has been restored to his integrity, his virginity, and to the lost " male-female " image. It is then only that the disharmony between man and the cosmos and between the masculine and feminine elements can be overcome. In natural fallen man the potentialities of creation are enfeebled ; nevertheless in every creative act the divine Will is accomplished and man himself reveals the divine idea of man.

Nevertheless there is a form of creation which increasingly debases man's image. For authentic creative action supposes asceticism, purification, and sacrifice ; whereas fallen man in his state of self-satisfaction often creates not in God's Name but in his own ; he gives birth to a false and illusory being, to non-being. But creation in the name of self can never continue for long in the intermediate sphere of humanity ; sooner or later it is inevitably transformed into creation in the name of another, to wit, Satan. It is for this reason that the religious justification of the creative act is not necessarily the justification of all creation whatsoever, for creation may possess a fatal character.

Thus we come to consider the problem of the religious justification of creation in culture and in human action in history. That which takes place in the highest regions of the spiritual world takes place also on the plane of our historic reality.

VI

Patristic anthropology failed to discover the whole truth about man ; it did not deduce from Christological dogma all those conclusions about human nature which are capable of being drawn from it. Juridical conceptions of Christianity distorted its view of ontological and anthropological questions, whereas in fact a true anthropology is contained in Christology. Christological and anthropological science are in all points similar to one another. Upon one's conception of Christ will depend one's conception of man. Human personality in the true sense of the word only exists in Christ and by Christ ; it only exists because Christ, the God-Man, exists. The ontological " depth " of man is bound up with the fact that Christ is not only God but also Man. That is why human nature participates in the life of the divine Trinity. The positive doctrine of man can only be deduced from the dogma of the divine-human nature of Christ and the consubstantiality of the Son with the Father. A really profound Christological anthropology will be a Christology of man.

The generation of Christ, the race of spiritual humanity, must also have its anthropological science rooted in the science of Christology. The Fathers and Doctors of the Church, whose attention was wholly occupied by the highest things and by the thought of God Himself, were absorbed in a heroic struggle against sinful human nature ; it was possible for them with their spiritual temperament to formulate the doctrine of the Person of Christ and of the Holy Trinity, but they were unable to develop a theory of man to correspond to it. Instead they elaborated a negative anthropology which dealt with the sinful nature of the Old Adam, and they sought for means by which they might prosecute their struggle against the passions of men.

Thus in the history of Gnostic mysticism there is no exoteric doctrine about man except in the Cabala, in Boehme, and Francis Baader, and in the mysticism which owed something to Semitic sources. Teaching of this kind can scarcely be found in the mysticism of Plotinus, Eckhart, and the Quietists. The positive teaching of the Fathers had already reached supreme perfection ; it was concerned with such questions as the obtaining of the grace of the Holy Spirit, the illumination of the creature, and the deification of man. But man's creative nature, which lies between these two opposite poles, was given no religious sanctification and was relegated to the secular sphere. Man's creativity thus affirmed and expressed itself apart from religious sanctification and interpretation, it went its own way, and manifested itself in a reaction against the mediaeval oppression of human freedom.

In the Middle Ages the spiritual nature of man was at once more robust and on a higher level than it has been in the modern period. It was then that its creative forces were husbanded. But human freedom had not yet been sufficiently tested nor had it consented to realize the Kingdom of God. The creative powers of man had not yet found their definitive expression. Humanism arose in the midst of the Christian world because Christianity had obscured the truth about man, because there was a mystery in it, and because it was given neither expression nor sanctification. The advent of humanism into the Christian world is a paradox and can never be anything else. But humanism in modern history is to be clearly distinguished from ancient humanism since it could only arise in a Christian period of history. It is connected in some way with a Christian problem which is both harassing and insoluble. Christian humanity cannot abandon that human image which had its realization in Greek culture, tragedy, and philosophy. Humanism is a false mentality developed in isolation from God and there lies hidden within it that which may annihilate man. Nevertheless humanism is the pathway to the freedom of man in which his creative forces are tested and human nature discovers itself.

Man could not remain satisfied with the anthropology of the patristic and scholastic periods ; he began to discover and to sanctify the creative nature in himself. Society could not go on living under a theocracy imposed from without. Human nature remained pagan, unilluminated, and untransfigured; theocracy and the Kingdom of God were not really achieved, and men were content with certain outward conventionalities. It was inevitable that the authentic realities of humanity would be manifested sooner or later. The secularization which characterizes the humanistic period is not in itself the origin of the evil, nor is it to blame for the separation between all forms of culture and society and God. All that it did was to expose the realities of the situation. Mediaeval theocracy, in spite of its high spirituality, did not reveal the truth about man, and so it had to decay. The new humanity pursued a course which was bound to make it experience to the full the fatal consequences of its self-centred isolation. Man had to discover all the possibilities of his earthly life in order to know and impeach everything by personal experience. Humanism contains within itself a fatal dialectic which must bring it to its final doom. Man in his solitude, detachment, and egocentricity cannot find the infinite sources of life, and the forms necessary to safeguard and affirm his own image.

Humanism sees exclusively in man the child of the natural world, for humanist anthropology is naturalistic. It no longer sees in man a being who belongs to two worlds and to two orders, the point of intersection between the spiritual and natural spheres. For humanism man ceases to be a mystery or an enigma, and he is no longer the experimental refutation of the claim of this world to be sufficient unto itself. Original sin is denied and consequently there is no explanation even of how the natural world began. Humanist thought places man finally in this world and on the surface of the earth. If patristic anthropology deviated, in fact if not in principle, towards a certain monophysitism, humanistic anthropology is equally monophysite, though at the opposite pole.

The full divine-human truth of Christianity in all its completeness could not be assimilated by mankind, and has suffered from being divided. Sometimes, in obedience to the command to love God, man has been neglected and so the love of God has been itself distorted ; sometimes men could see nothing but the love of man and that also suffered in consequence. From the monophysite and monist point of view the nature of man, at once two-fold and single, earthly and heavenly, bearing the image both of the beast and of God Himself, is an unsolved riddle. When man denies and effaces the divine image in himself, he cannot long preserve the human image, and the animal then predominates in him. By losing the support of God he submits himself to the unstable elements of this world which must sooner or later submerge and engulf him.

The very idea of man can only be constituted by the idea of God,[1] for man is precisely this idea and he only exists ontologically

[1] There are some very interesting ideas on this subject in Max Scheeler's *Vom Umsturz der Werte*. I. Band, *Zur Idee des Menschen* and *Vom Ewigen im Menschen*.

through it. Man cannot be simply and solely a human idea or an idea of the natural world, for he would then lose all ontological basis and disappear. This is why the spiritual pride of man constitutes the original source of sin and evil and leads to the annihilation of his being. The natural man cannot preserve his qualitative originality, his unique place in the hierarchy of being, when he finally denies the spiritual man and loses the basis of support which he possesses in the other world.

There was in humanism a period of expansion of the purely human domain. It was its most creative period, in which the forces of mankind which had been built up during the Middle Ages were manifested. French humanism of the sixteenth and seventeenth centuries was Christian, and St. Francis de Sales [1] may be included among the humanists of that time. At the time of the Renaissance man had not finally broken with the higher world and still bore the divine image. In the transitional period in the development of man's consciousness, which was a period of expansion for humanism, its positive sides were revealed, the soaring of man's creative genius, the overcoming of the cruelty inherited from the ages of barbarism, and the resurgence of the " human ", only possible in a Christian world. There is in humanism an unconscious positive truth, the truth, namely, of compassion, but in humanism it is infected with untruth and error. Humanism is nevertheless superior to bestialism and its untruth cannot be purged by a return to the latter.

The superseding of humanism means the attainment of the full divine-human truth of Christianity, the achievement of something higher and not the return to a Christianity distorted by barbarous elements. Humanism is two-fold by nature and in its results. On the one hand it is the revelation of positive human forces which are unconsciously a part of Christianity, and on the other of negative principles which lead to a final rupture with the divine world and threaten man with annihilation. It is thanks to humanity-

[1] Brémond speaks of a devout Humanism ; see his *Literary History of the Religious Sentiment in France*, vol. i.

ism that a free science has been able to develop. But having reached in the nineteenth and twentieth centuries the summit of its negative development, humanism is degenerating into its opposite and is tantamount to a denial of man and the destruction of all that can be considered humanitarian.[1] Communism is an example of this transformation which humanism undergoes when pushed to the extreme, but we can trace it also in all the current tendencies which are characteristic of to-day, in contemporary science, philosophy, and morality, in the general manners and customs of the time and in modern technical development. At the end of the humanistic period, in our mechanized civilization, man's personality is rudely shattered. Danger threatens us and only a Christian renaissance by means of the divine-human truth of Christianity can save man and preserve his image.

Modern history has produced no Christian heresy, and we may ask whether the religious indifference of this period does not make the rise of heresies impossible. But that is to adopt a superficial standpoint. Since the coming of Christ the whole life of the universe is lived beneath the sign of Christianity and nothing can any longer be indifferent in relation to it. Modern history created the great heresy of humanism, which could only arise in a Christian atmosphere and is an answer to the religious question about man. It is an anthropological heresy which has entered the world with religious pretensions. Besides, heresies have at all times brought forward vital questions, to which the mind of the Church had given no sufficiently clear and explicit answer. Heresies have had considerable importance, for they have stimulated positive development and dogmatic creation in the Church. They always contained some truth, to which was sometimes added both exaggeration and falsehood. Heresy upsets the balance of things and is incapable of comprehending the fulness of truth ; it takes a part to be the whole and rationalizes the theme which spiritual experiences puts to it. The mind of the Church in answering heresy draws up formulas

[1] This idea is developed in detail in the author's work, *The Meaning of History.*

which contain the fulness of supra-rational truth and points out the sane and right lines of development for the spiritual life. But the Church has yet to give a positive answer to the heresy of humanism, and has not developed all the possibilities which are contained within Christianity which could furnish a solution of the religious problem of man. Nevertheless there is no reason to suppose that the Church will not respond sooner or later by a clear dogmatic statement with regard to the true nature of a Christian anthropology.

The whole point of the question lies in the following ; does humanism really put to us a grave and deep problem for solution ? Too few of those who are attached to the traditions of the Church grasp its depth and importance. The world remains divided into two camps ; on one side there is the mind of the Church and on the other humanism. These two have not yet met face to face in order to state and solve the religious problem of man. It is only among certain isolated geniuses that this problem reaches an extreme degree of intensity in which Christianity and humanism are both brought into the picture. Such men of genius were Dostoievsky and Nietzsche. While totally different from one another they both did service to the religious knowledge of man and both force us to leave that neutral ground which is equidistant from Heaven and Hell, and from God and Satan.

It is in overcoming the antagonism between the God-Man and the man-god that the religious question about man will be put clearly and fully. But the answer that the mind of the Church will give to humanism will be essentially different from all its previous answers to heresy, for the truth about man's creative nature will have to be revealed in that answer. In this revelation it is inevitable that an exceptional activity will possess man. It is also natural to suppose that man through his creative energy is already preparing the answer to this problem, but that the Church in the external sense has not yet recognized this task as its own and has not admitted that it is an organic part of its divine-human function. The Church is God-humanity, and that is why in its approach towards fulness and completeness the creative activity of man must play a preponderating part. The Church cannot realize itself without the human element, God Himself cannot do without it. But man can put his free creative activity at the service of God as he can at that of Satan, the spirit of non-being. This activity of man during the humanist period has a two-fold character and is directed towards two opposing kingdoms. That is the tragedy of the historical process.

There is in humanism a Christian truth which belongs to the Church itself, but there may also spring from it the religion of Antichrist which is opposed to Christianity, 'and within which God and man are alike annihilated. The whole of man's suffering arises from the necessity of distinguishing between these two opposed principles. For the solution of this terrible problem much depends on man himself and his freedom of choice. The gifts of religious knowledge and of Gnosis belong neither to the ecclesiastical nor the angelic hierarchy but to man and his creative genius. Moreover these gifts are by no means proportionate to his saintliness, as the spiritual history of mankind only too clearly shows.

VII

The consciousness of man and the development of his spiritual forces are not only determined by his relations with God but also by his relations with nature ; and man in the course of his historic destiny has taken up different attitudes towards nature. Three periods may be distinguished which correspond to these different relations. Firstly, there was the stage of man's primitive absorption in nature, a primitive cosmic consciousness of life in general bound up with the life of nature. Secondly, there was a period of detachment from nature when man opposed nature and engaged in a spiritual conflict with it. Thirdly, there was a period when man turned to nature with the idea of mastering it, a period of struggle against it of a material order.

To these three periods there correspond three different conceptions of nature. In the first nature is regarded as animate and peopled with bad and good spirits. The Great Pan is still in existence. Primitive magic is at once the science of this period and its technical application. Man struggles with the forces of nature in order to live, but in his struggles he is associated with the spirits of nature. In totemism, the primitive form of the religious life of humanity, men worship animals, which they regard as the protectors of their social groups and clans. In sculpture there is no distinction between the image of men and of animals, the images are confused. It is precisely to this period that paganism, polytheism, and the dissolving of the divine image in the multiplicity of nature belong. The gods of nature are revealed and man's life subordinated to them.

But already in the pagan world there is discernible the hope and desire of man to rise superior to nature and to free himself from the power of the demons. It is the beginning of this second period which finds its definitive expression in Christianity. Man in the process of achieving his liberty, as he ascends in the scale, frees himself from the soul of nature with the object of acquiring spiritual independence and of finding some support and foundation for his life, not in the natural external world but in the inner and spiritual sphere.

The Redemption wrought by Christ reveals to us quite a different attitude, for it is only through that that man can acquire that spiritual independence which is able to overcome the powers of nature. The gods die, the Great Pan disappears into the depths of nature and remains imprisoned there. Men had to break free from nature and conquer paganism in themselves. There had to be freedom from the worship and the power of the demons who had bewitched and terrorized the ancient world. There was in paganism, besides the happy life in the bosom of a divine nature, the anguish and fear which were the result of mysterious forces. Magicians endeavoured to master these demoniacal powers and the cults of the ancients attempted to placate the gods. But in the pagan world real spiritual freedom could not be obtained. In order to fortify the spiritual man and to give him another foundation for his life the Christian Church set man in conflict with natural demonism and forbade him all relations with spirits. At all costs man had to be protected from the overwhelming forces of cosmic infinity.

The second result of this attitude towards nature was expressed through its mechanization. A pagan attitude of dependence upon it made it impossible to know nature scientifically and so to master it technically. That was only possible in a Christian world. Paradoxical as it may appear it is precisely Christianity which favoured the development of the natural and technical sciences, for they were born of the freedom of the human spirit from the powers of nature and of demonolatry. It was impossible to have any knowledge of the demons of nature through science or to overcome them through mechanical inventions. They could only be imprisoned with the aid of magic or appeased through blood-sacrifices. Animism authorizes science and mechanical invention only in the form of magic. The existence of the cosmic order was still admitted in the Middle Ages, but the mediaeval mind was impregnated with a religious and moral dualism. Man waged a spiritual warfare with nature both within him and about. He underwent an austere asceticism in which he developed and concentrated his inner spiritual forces, and in this way his personality was forged. But in the first as in the second period the cosmos subsists for man.

The third period begins with the Renaissance. Man once more turns towards nature and thirsts to know its mysteries. In humanism he feels himself once more a natural being, but one who aspires to master nature. In this way technical advance becomes possible through the encouragement given by the Renaissance to the natural sciences. Nature becomes external and quite alien to man ; he is no longer aware of its soul which ceases to be the cosmos, and he himself becomes an object of natural science and mathematics. It is no longer demonism nor its spirits that modern man fears, but rather his own inanimate mechanism. The mechanical conception of the world, due to the spiritual victory of Christianity over nature, becomes a force hostile to this faith.

But Christianity nurses the hope of a fourth period in man's attitude towards nature. This will begin when man turns once more towards the inner life, when he will see once more the divine cosmos but will unite this faith to a spiritual power over the elements, thus affirming his sovereignty in the world.

In our modern period, culture, the foundation of which is always religious, whose nature is always symbolic, whose very existence presupposes disinterested contemplation and creation, is beginning to be transformed into a civilization which is secularized in every direction, absorbed in the cult of power and well-being, and dominated by a naïve realism. This civilization constitutes the extreme limit of the mechanization of human life and nature. Everything organic in it is dead. The mechanical inventions which the power of human science has created enslave not only nature but man himself. The latter is no longer the slave of nature, but, while free from its organic forces, he has become the slave of the machine, and a prisoner in the social environment which it has created. In the civilization which is the final result of humanism the human image begins to vanish. Culture is powerless to fight against the increasing power of civilization. There is indeed a will to modify and transfigure life ; but culture does not transfigure life, it only succeeds in furnishing great creative values, such as philosophy, art, and the institutions of the law and of the State. The aspiration towards real life and its transfiguration has two goals. Firstly there is the social and technical transfiguration of an atheistical civilization, and secondly there is its religious transfiguration, the spiritual illumination of man and of the universe. These two purposes are confronting one another in the world. . . . Such, then, is the scheme of relations between man and nature.

Man is the creation of God and, metaphysically speaking, he precedes the natural world and its historic destiny. The phenomenon of humanity cannot be deduced from the development of the natural world. On the contrary man possesses in the natural world an evolution of his own. Fallen man only rises in the scale and gains possession of his image by a process of progressive development, and herein lies the truth of evolutionism. Man has become entangled with a nature lower than his own and has lost his image. He begins his natural life on the lowest levels of animal existence. Human personality does not awaken from the state of unconsciousness produced by the Fall and separation from God except by a long and very painful struggle and growth.

In ancient Greece, where for a moment the lost vision of Eden was recaptured, man was exalted for the first time in the pagan world and his image found expression in plastic forms of undoubted magnificence. For a long time the limits of human nature were not clear. The image of man was still confused and was not separated from the image of the gods and that of animal nature. There is yet no precise differentiation between man the hero, and the god. The hero is not simply a man, he is a demi-god. An anthropogonic process took place in ancient Greece through the creation of gods and heroes. In order to rise above the state in which the human and the animal image were confused, man had to receive in himself the image of the god and the demi-god, a principle regarded as superhuman.[1]

If in the last days of the humanist history of Europe, Nietzsche hoped to raise man to the level of superman by trying once more to confuse the image of man with that of the god or the hero, we must remember on the other hand that in the dawn of Greek humanism man arose out of super-man. In Greek sculpture the revelation of the human image was given to us in beauty, and man escaped from that state of confusion with the animal which he had inherited from the East.

The culture of the West had its birth in Greece, and at its heart lies the Aryan myth of Prometheus which is very different from that of the Bible. The myth of the Fall of the first man is deeper and more fundamental than that of Prometheus. The Fall of Adam determines even the existence of the natural world and its whole

[1] See E. Rode, *Psyche, Seelenknet, und Unsterblichkeitsglaube der Greichen*, in which the author shows us how the soul and its immortality were revealed.

destiny. The myth of Prometheus reveals to us a spiritual phenomenon (which has already occurred in the natural fallen world)
as an important and a determining moment in the destiny of
humanity. This myth is not a metaphysic, it deals with the origin
of human culture. It tells us that the super-man, the hero, struggles
on behalf of man and his culture with gods and demons, with the
spirits of nature, and with the elements. Man and culture do not
begin to exist in this natural until the fire of heaven has been stolen
which belongs only to the gods, until that moment when man
appropriates to himself that supreme principle which only the
violent can take by force. Prometheus frees man not from God,
Who was veiled from his eyes, but from the gods of nature and
from the power of the elements. He is the father of human culture.
The titanic struggle with the gods was not a struggle with God
Himself. Thus the myth of Prometheus cannot be opposed to the
biblical myth on which Christianity rests, for they belong to quite
different planes.

The Promethean principle is the eternal principle without which
man could not exist. In his separation from God man was obliged
to exalt himself by the affirmation of the Promethean principle,
without which he would have remained in a state of confusion, and
could not even have been revealed. Man had to free himself from
this submission to the gods of nature. It was his way of approach
towards Christianity and the coming of the New Adam. The
image of man could only be manifested through the medium of
this heroic and titanic principle of rebellion against the gods. It is
the cosmic struggle in the sufferings of which man is born. The
Promethean myth is the great anthropological and anthropogonic
myth. Without Prometheus there would be no culture in the
world and the creative genius of man would not exist. It is a myth
which must receive sanctification in Christianity.[1]

The myth of the Fall is concerned with man's attitude towards
God while that of Prometheus deals with his attitude towards

[1] Certain doctors of the Western Church saw in the myth of Prometheus
a pagan corruption of the idea of the creation of the world by the true God.

nature. Man when separated from God was necessarily in a situation analogous to that of Prometheus with regard both to nature and the powers which dominated it, and it was in this way that man's destiny was portrayed in Greek mythology.

In ancient tragedy, too, that splendid manifestation of the universal spirit, man is confronted with destiny. Here we see the submission of fallen man to an inexorable fate and his struggle against it. Through the Dionysian tragedy and the sufferings of the hero man seeks to free himself from this fatal subordination to nature. A tragic ending awaits the hero which he is powerless to escape. Yet through this there comes a certain purification and a redemption. It is through tragedy that man finds his way to Christianity in which tragedy is finally resolved.

Greek tragedy revealed to the world the great drama of life and human destiny. For the ancients it was a revelation which freed them from their limitations and turned their attention towards another world. In Greek culture humanity revealed itself in different ways ; the humanism of the ancient world was affirmed, and man was prepared for the truth of Christianity, the truth of the God-Man. The ancient legends of titans and heroes were no solution of the problem of human destiny ; all they could do was to state it. For the solution of it we have to wait for the religion of the God-Man. The Christian ascetic and saint do achieve this final victory over " the world ", the elements of nature, and fate, which was so tragically beyond the powers of heroes and titans. The goal of the hero of tragedy is death, that of the Christian is Resurrection.

The image of man was manifested in ancient culture in the interaction and struggle between the Dionysian and Apollonian principles. The Dionysian principle is that original element without which man has no source of life. It is the superabundance of this Dionysian force which gives rise to tragedy through the disruption of individuality. The cult of Dionysos is orgiastic. Man seeks in it deliverance from the evil and torments of life by the dislocation of individuality, and by the loss of personality, by losing himself, in fact, in the primal natural element. The religion of Dionysos is the religion of impersonal salvation. The Dionysian principle by itself can neither fashion man, nor affirm and preserve the human image. Moreover the predominance of Dionysian cults meant for man a return, in some measure, to the East and to the oriental principle of " non-differentiation ".

Personality was forged by the religion of Apollo, the god of form and measure ; indeed, it took its rise thence. The Apollonian principle is *par excellence* the principle of individuality and aristocracy. The Greek genius for form sprang from the cult of Apollo. But an exclusive predominance of this principle means a complete breach with that of Dionysos. The genius of Greece refused to submit to oriental influence and would not allow itself to suffer disintegration at the hands of the Dionysian element. It submitted to the restrictions which Apollonian " form " imposed upon it. The Dionysian principle in itself is an ugly one.[1] The cosmos is beautiful because it is an alliance between the Dionysian element and Apollonian " form ". Man possesses beauty, the divine image and resemblance, because in him also these two principles are reconciled. A balance between these two principles is the ideal to be aimed at, and the Greek world knew how to attain it. But this balance was capable of being disturbed by either one of these two principles.

If, on the one hand, the exclusive triumph of the Dionysian element threatens the loss of man's personality, on the other hand, the exclusive triumph of the Apollonian element involves an outward formalism, a purely formal culture, an Alexandrianism, a certain antique positivism. The Apollonian principle is that of measure and excludes the infinite, while the Dionysian principle links man to infinity without giving him the ability to distinguish its higher and lower elements. The ancient world was never able to free itself from the antagonism between these two principles and could not save man from the danger which awaited him.

[1] W. Ivanov, a Dionysian poet who knows the religion of Dionysos very well, assures us that this is so.

VIII

A definitive revelation and affirmation of human personality is only possible in Christianity, for it is Christianity which recognizes the importance and eternal value of the individual human soul and its destiny. The human soul has more value than all the kingdoms of the world for it enshrines the infinite. Christianity appeared in the world primarily as the religion of the salvation of man and this very fact shows its concern for the human soul and personality. It never looks upon man as an instrument or means to any other end whatever, or as a fleeting moment in the cosmic or social process. This attitude towards man is inherent in it. The Christian consciousness has as its foundation the recognition of the eternal value of that which is unique and cannot be repeated. It is only in Christianity that the eternal value of the individual is revealed. The unique and inimitable countenance of each human being only exists because of the unique and inimitable Countenance of Christ the God-Man. In Christ and through Christ the eternal countenance of every man and woman is revealed. In the natural world it suffers division and becomes simply a medium at the service of the natural race. A true anthropologism belongs to the Christian consciousness alone, and the goal towards which the ancient world was moving is only realized in Christianity.

But the way of Redemption, which delivers the human soul from the bondage of sin and from the influence of baser elements, for some time obscured the creative mission of man. The Fathers were preoccupied with the salvation of the soul rather than with creation. The Church gave religious sanction to that state of the human soul which we call holiness, but refused it to that condition of human nature which we call genius. Holiness is " anthropological " for it is the supreme acquisition of human nature, its illumination and its deification. In this it is distinguished from priesthood which is not a human but an angelic principle. Nevertheless, is the way of holiness and its acquisition unique ? Can it be said that all man's creative life, which is not based upon holiness, is only permitted because of the sinfulness of human nature, and that it possesses no positive religious justification ?

This is a very difficult question for Christian thought, and the impossibility of answering it means that human nature remains disunited and for the most part unsanctified. The way of creative inspiration continues to be terrestrial, secular, and unholy. The religious significance of genius as a supreme manifestation of human creation fails to be disclosed. What meaning, parallel to that given to the existence of saints and ascetics seeking the salvation of their own souls, can Christian thought give to the life of geniuses, poets, artists, philosophers, savants, reformers, inventors, to those, in a word, whose major function is to create ? We cannot escape this question by suggesting that Christianity does not in any way deny the manifestations of creative genius. The problem is infinitely more complex and affects the most profound metaphysics of Christianity as well as its dogmatic consciousness. Is creative inspiration a spiritual experience, the manifestation of the positive mission of man ? Does God in fact expect creative heroism from man ? Creation cannot be merely permitted or excused ; it must be capable of positive justification at the bar of religion. If man becomes a poet or a philosopher merely because his sinfulness and weakness prohibit his following the only true path (the path of asceticism and holiness), then the poet and philosopher are condemned by the Christian consciousness, and their creative work must be rejected as vanity and dust.

Obviously man must follow the path of purification, asceticism, and sacrifice, and must struggle against his lower nature. All creative work, all knowledge, all art, the making of all that is new, is impossible without some self-limitation and a transcending of one's lower nature. Only the man who places the object of his creation above himself and who prefers truth to self is capable of creating anything in life. That is a spiritual axiom. The poet may be a great sinner and fall very low, but at the moment of poetic inspiration and in the kindling of the creative spark he rises above himself and the level to which he has fallen. This thought is expressed in the famous verse of Pushkin. " When not called by Apollo to perform the holy sacrifice the poet is perhaps the most miserable of all the miserable children of this world."

The creative life possesses its own holiness without which all creation is corrupted, as well as a certain piety without which the creator loses his power. But the whole crux of the religious problem of creation lies in the following question : is humility the only true foundation of the spiritual life, or is there another on which creative energy may base itself? When one makes a phenomenological and psychological description of creation one is forced to recognize that the latter, in whatever sphere of life it may be, does not depend exclusively upon the spiritual phenomenon of humility. Humility lies at the root of the spiritual life of the Christian, and it is thanks to it that sinful human nature is transfigured and self-centredness overcome. This spiritual process also takes place within every man who creates, for he must transfigure his own nature and free himself from the burden of sin by humility, detachment, and the sacrifice of his self-centredness. We must get beyond self-satisfaction if the need to create is to arise at all. But creation itself, the outburst of creative energy, indicates a different moment in spiritual life and experience.

Man at the moment of creation does not think of victory over sin for he already feels free from its weight. Creation itself is no longer either humility or asceticism but inspiration and ecstasy, the striving of the whole being, in which positive spiritual energy is both manifested and released. The problem of the justification of creation is that of creative inspiration as a spiritual experience. Creation may acquire a religious meaning and justification, if, in the phenomenon of inspiration, man is responding to a divine call to co-operate with divine creation. But if the call to create is answered by an appeal to humility the problem has clearly been misapprehended and discussion can be carried no further.

The savant has never yet made discoveries, neither has the philosopher penetrated the mystery of the world, nor has the poet given us poems, the painter pictures, nor the inventor inventions, nor yet again has the social reformer created for us new forms of life, by taking humility as a starting-point and by deploring the frailty, sin, incapacity, and apparent nothingness which possessed them. The act of creation presupposes an entirely different spiritual condition, namely, a superabundance of creative energy which has free scope and in which the whole man feels that he is involved.

At the same period of his life, however, the man who creates may pray with humility, confess his sins, submit his will to that of God, experience inspiration, as well as be conscious of his creative powers. For in creative inspiration and in ecstasy there is an extraordinary detachment, a victory over the " necessity " of sin, and an interior unification and forgetfulness of self. Indeed there is perhaps in these things more detachment than there is in humility because one is thinking more of God and less of oneself. In the salvation of the soul and in redemption man is still thinking of himself. Creation is in a profound sense the contemplation of God, truth, and beauty, of the supreme life of the spirit. God is not content that man should seek salvation, for He wants man to reveal his creative love for Himself in the positive revelation of his nature. But God does not desire man's abasement. True creation can never be creation simply and solely in the name of man ; it must be in the name of what is higher than man, that is of God Himself, even if this name only represents truth, beauty, of goodness so far as the human consciousness is concerned.

Creation is by its very nature a sacrifice, and the destiny of creative genius is a tragic one. The creation of man, like everything which becomes incarnate in this world, like the very organization of the Christian Church itself, can easily be defiled, and lose its true nature through degeneration. As soon as man begins to create in his own name, and to affirm himself in his creation by refusing the path of sacrifice and asceticism, his work is threatened by eventual sterility. Vanity lies in wait for the creator and even his creative nature becomes warped.

In the spiritually fallen world of to-day there is a truly fearful emptiness and " non-being " in our literature, art, and philosophy, as well as in the new modes of living which are being evolved, and in our new social structures ; for the absence of true objective realities in creation is a very terrible thing. Contemporary aestheticism such as is manifested in scientific thought, in art, in law, in political life, and in the sphere of technology, is the expression of a hopeless separation between the creative process and real Being, that is, God. It is the expression of an indifference to everything which exists or does not exist ontologically. There is in all this a decadence which hides from the modern consciousness the religious significance of creation. Contemporary creation is for the most part devoid of religious meaning and objective reality and constitutes a temptation from the Christian standpoint. It is provoking a religious reaction against itself in our modern civilization.

IX

In the Christian world there are always two conflicting tendencies ; there is the manifestation of the creative spirit of man and the monophysite reaction against it. This monophysite tendency certainly exists to-day. It fails to see the religious problem of man and finds itself powerless to overcome humanism, for humanism can only be defeated by the positive discovery of the truth about man and his creative mission. Monophysite negations inevitably provoke a humanist reaction.

Monastic and ascetic Christianity based upon patristic anthropology, or, to put it accurately, upon a mere fragment of its doctrines, which considers asceticism as the only line of spiritual development and censures all those other ways which lead to human creation, cannot free humanism from that universal crisis which is only the counterpart of that which Christianity itself is undergoing. The mystical-ascetical conception of the world is often simply a veiled form of Manicheism.

To-day no thinking Christian with any sense of responsibility can possibly pretend that nothing particular has happened in the world and in human history since the conciliar period and its many doctrinal conflicts, or that there are no new problems for religious thought to face, that nothing has changed, and that there is simply the old question of human sin which continues to ruin everything as it has done in the past. Man is travelling by a long and difficult road and has lived through a tragedy that earlier and more simple ages have not known, with the result that the extent of his experience has been infinitely extended, his psychological make-up has been modified, and entirely new problems are now confronting him.

The fresh demands which the soul of man is now making cannot be satisfied by the methods which were once employed by the Fathers of the Church in a period entirely different from ours. The human element in the Church changes and develops. We must continue to-day under new forms the creative work of the ancient Doctors of the Church, but not adopt their answers to questions which are now out of date. Christianity will not be able to continue if it remains in a state of decadence and wedded to the past, if it persists in living on its capital instead of looking for fresh riches. The gates of hell will not prevail against it because it contains an eternal and inexhaustible spring of creative energy. But Christian humanity may undergo a period of decadence. The monophysite reaction was a period of this kind. Nietzsche was a victim of this decadent monophysitism which appeared within Christianity, and which involves the denial of man. He was afflicted with a thirst to create for which he could find no religious justification. He rebelled against God, Who, according to him, forbade all creation.

The Church, whose consciousness was superficial, failed to observe (if we may so put it) how long the road was upon which man was travelling, nor was it sufficiently attentive to the changes which took place in the human soul. The Church, in the differential not the integral meaning of the word, did not recognize as its own the positive creative work of man. It was as though it had forgotten its proper divine-human nature. Man has been profoundly changed, he has been defiled by new sins and suffers fresh torments ; moreover he desires to love God with a new creative love. But those who represent the mind of the Church as it existed in bygone days believe that it is always the same unchanging soul with which they have to deal, with the same sins, and the same problems. But man has passed through successively the experience of a Hamlet or a Faust, a Nietzsche, and a Dostoievsky, through humanism, romanticism, and a taste for revolution, through modern philosophy, and through science ; it is impossible to obliterate a past of this kind.

When the experience which has been lived through is superseded by one of a higher kind it is henceforth a part of it. That is one of the laws of life. The soul changes and is infinitely more sensitive ; side by side with new sins and temptations there has arisen within it a new compassion for all that is alive unknown to ruder generations which have gone before. This new sensitiveness has extended to the sphere of human relationships, and has produced a double process in the world which is at one and the same time a democratization and an ennobling of the soul.

A positive Christian answer will have to be given sooner or later to man's longing to create for the fate of Christianity in the world depends upon it. Christianity itself has made man's *psyche* infinitely more complex than it was, but it has so far failed to provide it with sufficient illumination. We must always distinguish between the deep underground activity of Christianity in history, and its external surface action which is part of the consciousness of the Church. The coming of Christ into the world brings with it the Christianization of the whole cosmos and not only the setting up of visible Churches. We see this double action of the forces of Christ everywhere. Thus it was Christianity which introduced into the world the love of man and woman, the new romantic love unknown to the pre-Christian world. But the consciousness of the Church has not solved the problem of the religious significance of love. Christianity has forged human personality and made possible the birth of that particular individuation which has become more and more refined in modern times. But the consciousness of the

Church persists in ignoring the development of individuality and its tragic destiny in the world. On the other hand our modern age develops and intensifies the feeling of individuality while at the same time oppressing the individual by reducing him to the common level and subordinating him to the masses.

We live in the midst of these contradictions and suffer from them. Man, in the course of a process of development which appears to be quite natural, breaks free from custom and mass consciousness, and attains to personal consciousness and individual forms of creation in life. This is the origin of certain great changes in the " style " of Christianity, which is now in a stage of transition, having lost its former austerity and integrality. It can no longer be a Christianity of mere habit and custom. The old order and the old racial consciousness have broken down.

The new race created by Communism bears the image of Antichrist. Human individuality is crushed out of existence between what remains of the old generation and the beginnings of the new. There can be no question in these circumstances of a return to the state of affairs in which Christianity and the traditional organization of life were unified. An attempt of this sort is merely the reaction of impotence. Christianity must achieve a new " style " for itself more in accordance with the new stage of development in human society, although, since the present is a period of historical and psychological transition, such a new " style " cannot be regarded as of absolute or eternal validity. The finite must not be allowed to dominate the infinite ; the spiritual must not be subjected to natural forms of purely temporary significance. A false conservatism is always engaged in binding the infinite spirit to finite forms and in substituting the latter for the divine essence of things. Romanticism with its longing for the infinite is right in rebelling against this false classicism and in refusing to come to terms with the finite.

We are living in an age when the static, classic, " style " of Christianity is impossible, and when the tyranny of custom is an obstacle to the infinite expression of being. In fact the Christianity of our time has already undergone a change and there is at once something fresh yet something eternal about it. It is neither classic nor static. It points the way to a spiritual movement of intense dynamic quality which has yet to find its symbolic expression.

The Christianity which dominates our present era is inevitably a Christianity which has lived through a period of decadence, the collapse of humanism, the storms of revolution, a fierce division in the world of thought of unprecedented intensity, and much striving after liberty and human creation. The old forms of culture do not correspond to the present epoch of catastrophe. Eternal being cannot be discovered among our vanishing customs. Christ came for the whole of the universe and for all men at every period. Christianity exists not merely for simple souls, but also for the more complex ones. We need to remember this. For a long time the predominant " style " of Orthodoxy has been adapted to the requirements of the rude and simple, yet in fact the human soul has become more complex and more refined. What is to be done about this question ? Is it conceivable that Christ did not come for the more complex type, and that the truth of Christianity does not exist for such ?

Christian truth exists for everybody and everything, but the static forms of the Christianity of any particular period can only be adapted to souls of a given kind. Russian " starchestvo ", for example, elaborated a form of Christianity which had its special " types " of soul. It is undeniable that even such an important manifestation of Christianity as this was powerless to meet the needs of man's creative desires. It could, for instance, never really grip the soul of Dostoievsky.

The hierarchy and the sacerdotal principle in the Church will never be able to solve the religious problem of creation which is the manifestation of the human principle and human nature. Only man himself can find its solution ; no authority of any kind whatever and no hierarchy which is not human can give an answer to this question. The solution of the religious problem of creation will be a human solution. The problem consists precisely in this, that its solution *must* be human, coming from man to God, and not from God to man.

Mankind in the Christian era has been torn by the following contradictions ; Christianity without human creation, and human creation without Christianity ; God without man, and man without God. The love of God has often been transformed into a hatred of man. When Christianity has reached its full development this antithesis will be resolved and there will be a positive revelation of God-humanity, the union of the two movements, the uniting of Christianity and creation.

The hour is at hand when it becomes more and more clear that it is only in and through Christianity that the image of man can be preserved, for the elements of this world are destroying it. The creation of man is possible and receives its justification when it is at the service of God and not of itself, and when it is associated with the divine creation. This problem is bound up with that of the divine consciousness, and with the final defeat of the last remnants of Manichean metaphysical dualism with its sharp antithesis between God and creation, and between the Church and the world. All authentic being is rooted in God ; apart from God nature does not exist, and there is only evil, sin, and non-being.

CHAPTER SEVEN

Mysticism and the Way of the Spirit

I

IF the word " mysticism " is derived from the word " mystery " then it must be regarded as the foundation and the source of its creative movement. Religious experience has its source in vital and immediate contact with the ultimate mystery. In the religious life we are stirred into activity and receive the new birth through a return to the final mystery of being, that is to say, to mysticism. In mysticism religion still burns and shines brightly. All the great pioneers and creative geniuses of the religious life were acquainted with this initial experience, those mystical encounters which brought them face to face with God and the divine. It was in the ardours of mystical experience that St. Paul received the revelation of the essential nature of Christianity. Mysticism is the soil on which religion flourishes and without which it withers and decays.

But in history the actual relations between mysticism and religion have been delicate and somewhat confused. Religion has been afraid of mysticism and often regarded it as a source of heresy, for mysticism was in some way a hindrance to its organizing functions and threatened to upset its recognized standards. But religion, nevertheless, needed mysticism and sanctioned its own particular form of it, as the very crown of its own life. There is an approved orthodox mysticism of Christianity just as there is a mystical system in other religions. Religious confessions have always endeavoured to subject to their own standards the mystical element, which was often violent and obstinate. There is, then, some difficulty in the relation between mysticism and religion.

239

This difficulty is even greater in our own days because mysticism is now in fashion and it is a word often used in an obscure and indeterminate sense. The introduction of mysticism into contemporary literature has had fatal consequences, because it was done with the intention of making it an attribute of refined culture. But such a proceeding distorts its eternal significance. Mysticism is not a refined psychologism, nor is it an irrational passion of the soul, nor yet simply the music of the soul. There is therefore a good reason for Christianity being opposed to the meaning which some would give to mysticism. The psychologism of the end of the nineteenth century and the beginning of the twentieth is in conflict with the real significance of mysticism, as it is for that matter with the Logos. But if we consider not contemporary literature but rather those classical examples of mysticism which are for all time, we shall be forced to recognize above all that mysticism belongs to the sphere of the spirit and not to that of the soul, that it is, in a word, " spiritual " rather than " psychological."

In mystical experience man always escapes from the isolated sphere of the soul and comes into contact with the spiritual source of being and divine reality. Our answer to a certain type of Protestant who gladly invests mysticism with the character of religious individualism is that mysticism is in fact an escape from individualism which it succeeds in overcoming. Mysticism is the depth and height of the spiritual life ; it is one of its qualities. It is intimate and hidden from the common view, but it is not individualistic. Windelband expressed in the following fashion the contradiction which according to him exists in German mysticism ; " while proceeding from the individual," he says, " it regards individuality as a sin". But there is a contradiction here on the plane of the soul which ceases to exist on that of the spirit. It must be continually repeated that mysticism is not a state of romantic subjectivism, for it is above the antithesis between the subjective and the objective. Nor is it a dreamy condition of the soul. It is essentially realistic and sober in the discerning and discovery of realities. The only true mystic is one who sees realities and knows how to distinguish them from phantasies.

Above all we must make a radical distinction between mysticism and magic. These spheres are totally different but are easily confused, for while the nature of mysticism is spiritual that of magic is naturalistic. Mysticism is union with God, magic with the spirits of nature and its elemental forces. Mysticism is the sphere of liberty, magic of necessity. Mysticism is detached and contemplative, magic is active and militant ; it reveals the secret forces of humanity and of the world without being able to reach the depths of their divine origin. Mystical experience constitutes precisely a spiritual deliverance from the magic of the natural world, for we are fettered to this magic without always recognizing it. Applied science possesses a magical nature and origin, for it is nourished by a desire to master the forces of nature. Magic is in essence distinct from religion and often opposed to it, yet the latter can, in spite of everything, comprehend within itself certain elements of magic.[1] A more profound understanding of nature is always magical. Magical forces operate everywhere in the world. Mysticism is compared to magic because of the existence of a pseudo-mysticism. There are two types of such false mysticism, one naturalistic and the other psychological. But neither of them are effective means of reaching the real depths of mystical experience for they exist in the isolation of the world of nature and of the soul. The only true mysticism is that of the spirit, in which a false magic and a false psychologism are both avoided. It is only in the depths of spiritual experience that man attains to God and passes beyond the limits of the natural and " psychical " world. But mysticism cannot simply be identified with the spiritual life which is itself an infinitely broader thing. Only the depths and heights of the spiritual life deserve the name of mysticism, for it is there that man penetrates to the ultimate mystery.

Mysticism presupposes mystery, that is to say, the inexhaustible and ineffable. But it equally supposes the possibility of vital contact

[1] Frazer particularly insists on this point, that magic precedes religion.

with this mystery and of a life in it and with it. To recognize the existence of mystery while repudiating a vital experience of it is virtually a denial of mysticism. Spencer recognizes that at the origin of being there is an unknowable, that is to say, a mystery. But Spencer being a positivist and not a mystic, the unknowable was for him merely the negative limit of knowledge. The enigma of mysticism is not the unknowable and does not imply agnosticism. Man, moreover, does not reach the deepest mystical levels of life through gnoseology, where he comes sooner or later into contact with the unknowable ; he reaches them rather in life itself and in the experience of union with it.

Mystery is not a negative category, but the positive fulness of life's infinite depths. Where there is no mystery everything is superficial and limited. There is an absence of the profound. Man is attracted by mystery, by the possibility of living in union with it. The Divine Countenance in its manward aspect is a mystery and we can only see it as such.

The very foundation of mysticism is an inner kinship or union between the human spirit and the divine, between creation and the Creator. It implies the overcoming of transcendence, and that sense of God and man being external to one another. Thus mysticism is always concerned with the immanence rather than the transcendence of God, an immanence, moreover, which is actually experienced. This is why mysticism always employs terms which differ from those of theology, and why in theological circles mysticism is always suspected of heretical tendencies. But mysticism is of such a profound nature that we cannot apply to it the more superficial criteria of heresy. Mystics are always suspected of pantheistic leanings and indeed, when an attempt is made to understand them rationally and to translate their experience into the terms of theology or metaphysics, they certainly come very near to pantheism. Yet while pantheism is in reality a highly rationalistic doctrine, mysticism uses paradoxical and apparently contradictory expressions, because for the mystics both the identity between the creature and the Creator and the gulf which separates them are both

242

equally facts of existence. Mysticism cannot be expressed either in terms of pantheistic monism or of theistic dualism.

The theology and metaphysics of the official Church, and in particular of the Roman Catholic Church, maintain an ontological dualism between the Creator and the creature, and between the supernatural and the natural. Everything is put into its appropriate place and no confusion is allowed. St. Thomas Aquinas, it is true, puts mysticism on a level with natural philosophy and theology, and here we can detect the influence of the pseudo-Dionysius.[1] But Thomist metaphysics and theology are not favourable to mysticism and they insist upon antitheses which the latter seeks to overcome ; they give to mysticism a special sphere of its own, but Christianity itself is not mystical so far as they are concerned.

In what, then, does the essence of mysticism consist ? *Mysticism is the overcoming of creatureliness* (*Kreaturlichkeit*). That is the deepest and most intrinsic definition of its nature. In mystical experience there is no longer any insurmountable dualism between the supernatural and the natural, the divine and the created, for in it the natural becomes supernatural and the creature is deified. But perfect union with God does not mean the disappearance of man altogether, nor the obliterating of the distinctions between the two different natures. It is only created nothingness which is superseded. Mysticism is the way of deification both for man and the world. On this point the mystics of all ages and creeds are at one.

Religion upholds the transcendental and dualistic opposition between God and man, and between the Creator and creation. Religious devotion is indeed based upon this sense of our insignificance as creatures.[2] Mysticism, on the other hand, shows us that the transcendental opposition between God and man, man's consciousness of his infinite smallness, and the isolation of the

[1] See the very interesting work by the Thomist Garrigou-Lagrange, *Christian Perfection and Contemplation according to St. Thomas Aquinas and St. John of the Cross* (2 volumes).

[2] Compare the *Mysterium tremendum* of R. Otto.

natural world, are not final truths, nor the definitive expressions of the mystery of life and being. Immanentism is present in all mysticism, but it is an immanentism of a special kind and differs completely from that which is gnoseological in origin. It is the immanence of the Holy Spirit in the created world.

Mysticism also by its very nature overrides the barriers which divide Christians, although it is true that there are types of mysticism belonging to particular Christian confessions which possess a technique of their own, which should, however, permit of the transcending of confessional limitations. Orphism and Plotinus, Hindu mysticism and Sufism, St. Simon the New Theologian, and St. John of the Cross, Eckhart and Jacob Boehme, are all in some measure in agreement. They speak to one another, each from his own world, and their language is often the same. This is a fact which it is impossible to deny, however unpleasant it may appear to the fanatical supporters of confessional mysticism.

We find this transcending of creatureliness among the best and truest mystics both of Orthodoxy and Catholicism. The great Eastern mystic, St. Simon the New Theologian, said, " I thank Thee O God that Thou, Who reignest over all, art now in very truth and unchangeably one spirit with me." And this is how he describes the light which he saw in moments of profound spiritual experience, " This light is not of this world, nor is it created, for it is uncreated and remains apart from creatures, as a thing not made among the things which are made." He describes mystical union and also the complete identification of the soul with God in the following terms, " But when He and I are one, what am I to call God, Who, though possessing a dual nature, is a single Hypostasis ? Having created me with a dual nature He has given me, as you see, a dual name. Here is the distinction. I am man by name, and God by grace." " Suddenly He came and united Himself to me in a manner quite ineffable ; without any ' confusion of persons ' He entered into every part of my being, as fire penetrates iron, or light streams through glass." " How else could the divine fire come down into your heart and burn within it, kindling the affections and uniting it to

244

God, thus welding into an indivisible unit the creature and its Creator ! " The path of mysticism leads to the transfiguration and illumination of the creature. " I rejoice in His love, and in His beauty, and I feel myself overwhelmed with divine happiness and sweetness." " I am filled with light and glory ; my face shines like that of my Beloved and all my members glow with heavenly light. Then am I lovelier than the loveliest, richer than the richest, stronger than the strongest, greater than the rulers of this world, more honourable than anything visible, and not only more honourable than the earth and all that is in it, but also than heaven itself and everything that it holds." " For the mind as it enters into Thy Light is itself illuminated, and becomes also a burning light like unto Thy glory, and it is called Thy mind ; for that which is counted worthy of such a state is also worthy to possess Thy mind and to be united inseparably with Thee." " He (the Creator) will make thy whole body incorruptible, and by grace will make thee God, and like unto the first Principle of all things."

" My hands are the hands of a poor wretch, but my feet are the feet of Christ. Unworthy though I be, I am the hand and foot of Christ. I move my hand and my hand is wholly Christ's, for God's divinity is united inseparably to me. As I move my foot it glows with the light of God Himself."

In speaking of a certain ascetic, St. Simon said, " For he possessed Christ wholly and was himself like Christ ; he had, as it were, not only his own limbs or members, but those of every other human being as well, having both one and yet many bodies. He meditated at all times like Christ Himself, remaining motionless and, as it seemed, impassible and invulnerable. He was, in fact, entirely Christ. Thus it was that he saw the Saviour in all those who by baptism have wholly put on Christ."

In the ecstatic mysticism of St. Simon we have portrayed for us those spiritual heights where the creature finds itself transcended, illumined with heavenly light, and deified. Analogous states are also described in the famous conversation of Motilov with St. Seraphim of Sarov, when both of them were " in the spirit "

245

Motilov saw the whole body of St. Seraphim filled with a light which shone all around him. Moreover, although it is true that Catholic mysticism differs from that of Orthodoxy, yet that great Catholic mystic St. John of the Cross also speaks of the transcending of creaturehood and of union with God.

" This venture has overwhelmed me with happiness ; for I was immediately transported into a divine and heavenly state where I held most familiar converse with God, that is to say, my understanding passed from a purely human state to one which was divine. For, in uniting myself to God through this inward purification, I have no longer a poor, limited, understanding as before. I know now by means of the divine wisdom to which I am united. My will also has surpassed itself and become in a measure divine, for being united to the love of God, it loves no longer in its own strength but in that of the divine Spirit Itself." [1]

" The state of union with the divine consists in the complete transformation of the will of the soul into that of God, in such a way that the Will of God becomes the only principle and motive underlying all action, as though the Will of God and the will of the soul were but one."

The state of union with the divine described by St. John of the Cross and all the Catholic mystics is that of a triumph over creatureliness, and has its classic expression in Eckhart. The Dominican Denifle has shown that Eckhart was an orthodox Catholic to a much greater extent than had hitherto been suspected and that in his recently discovered Latin theological treatises he was completely Thomist.

Here, then, is what Eckhart teaches. " God expects only one thing from you, and that is that you should come out of yourself in so far as you are a created being, and let God be God within you." " For the love of God come out of yourself, so that for love of you He may do the same. When both have done this what remains will be a measure unique in its simplicity." [2]

[1] Cf. *The Spiritual Works of St. John of the Cross.* 1864.
[2] Eckhart : *Spiritual Sermons and Reflections.*

Mysticism and the Way of the Spirit

The mysticism of Eckhart admits that the distinction between the Creator and creation, between God and man, may be definitely transcended in mystical Gnosis at its highest. " Non-being is beyond God and beyond differentiation. Here only I have been myself, willed, and lived myself, as being that which has created me. In this I am the first cause of both my temporal and my eternal being. It is only in this that I am born. . . . By virtue of the eternal principle of my birth I belong to every age, I am, and I shall remain, in eternity. . . . In my birth everything was born ; I was my own first cause and that of all other things. I desire that neither I myself nor they should be non-existent. But if I did not exist neither would God."

We find the same spirit in the great German mystic Angelus Silesius. " I must be the Word in the Word, God in God." " I am as great as God, He as small as I." " Every Christian must be Christ Himself." " He who wants God must become God." " God can only receive gods." All these extracts from different mystics (which could be indefinitely added to) are written in a peculiar language which is untranslatable in terms of metaphysics or theology. It is the description of mystical experience, and the methods employed in connection with it. Admittedly rational theology and metaphysics are right in insisting on the transcendent gulf between the Creator and creation, the supernatural and the natural world. But supra-rational mysticism is not less true when it envisages the possibility of bridging this gulf. One truth does not contradict the other. They both express different moments and states of experience. Mysticism does not mean the end of dogma, but it does penetrate to a deeper level than that reached by dogmatic formulas. Mysticism is deeper and more fundamental than theology though it obviously has its dangers.

In mysticism everything is inward and there is nothing exterior or objectified. Mysticism frees us from the natural and historical world which lies outside us, and brings the whole evolution of material nature and history within the sphere of the spirit. To live through anything mystically is to live through it spiritually and from within. In the practice of mysticism the whole objectified external world is blotted out in the night of sensibility, and it is only within the spiritual and divine world that anything is revealed. Final reality is only revealed in mysticism, in which man escapes from the secondary world of reflections and symbols. All that in religion, theology, and worship was symbolical and only prefigured in the flesh, becomes real in mysticism, and is revealed as the inner depths of life in its basic and original form. It is only in contemplation and mystical union that the divine life is achieved.

Mysticism presupposes a symbolical conception of the world while at the same time it transcends symbolism by abandoning symbols and turning to realities. Superficially it may appear that religion is more realistic than mysticism, but actually religion always admits an element of mysticism and in fact has its very origin here. There is no such thing as a religion entirely devoid of mystical contacts with reality. But positive religion is always concerned with the natural and historical life of peoples, it possesses social characteristics, it organizes the life of the masses and always presupposes the collective.[1] Religion establishes and organizes socially a relationship with God which implies a transcendent antithesis between God and man. Religion educates and guides, and, further, predicates an ordered system or hierarchy in the spiritual life, not only to facilitate man's ascent to God, but also the descent of God into the sinful world. In religion heteronomous elements are inevitable. Religion addresses itself to the whole of humanity, to small as well as great ; it brings truth and light to everybody, for it is not the sole prerogative of the spiritual aristocracy of the elect. Thus the religious experience which seems to us heteronomous and authoritarian is marked by piety and devotion. In each of us there are elements of this heteronomous religiosity.

The Church is wise when it condemns pride in mysticism. There

[1] Durkheim is right in regarding religion as a social fact and in placing it within society.

248

is in religion not only heteronomy but also exotericism ; it is not only a revelation but also mystery. These divine mysteries are revealed by degrees in proportion to man's spiritual growth and the receptivity of their minds. But beyond the exoteric there is always mystery. Mysticism is the esotericism of religion, which is only meant for certain people and for a minority, while religion must cater for all, and it is there that the difficulty of its task lies. The heteronomous and exoteric element of religion can, alas ! easily degenerate, and the true spirit of the religious life decays. Then it is essential to have recourse to mysticism, to the esoteric source. . . . This is one aspect of the relations between mysticism and religion.

But there is another. All mysticism is not necessarily good. It may also deteriorate and become corrupt, for an irreligious mysticism, in which the Logos is not present, easily degenerates, and may plunge man into even lower depths of darkness. There is a kind of mysticism in which the spiritual and " psychic," and even the corporeal, are confused and in which the spirit is no longer pure and unconfused. There are orgiastic types of mysticism in which the spiritual is swallowed up by the " psychical " or corporeal elements, and remains wedded to them. Such for instance was the mysticism of the ancient Dionysos cults, and that of the chlistis.[1] Pagan mysticism tried to achieve spirituality but failed. Even in Christianity itself we find the mystical ecstasy of the flesh in which the infinite spirit is made subservient to the finite. There is, in a word, a pseudo-mystical theophany.

Mysticism raises some big problems for the Christian world. Where mysticism begins, dogmatic precision and valid generalization end. The relations between mysticism and the Church are very complex. Neither the Orthodox nor the Roman Catholic Church have condemned mysticism, but they have been afraid of it and have distrusted certain of its tendencies. The official Church

[1] Members of a Russian orgiastic sect, the rites of which resemble those of the mysteries of Dionysos, and in which pagan and Christian elements are blended.

is habitually hostile to mysticism, and it is always difficult to find the least trace of the mystical in those whose Christianity is purely a matter of inherited tradition. The mystical basis of Christianity is denied in official theology and "rationalism" is very common among Church dignitaries. The mystical element of Christianity is denied while at the same time an endeavour is made to render it innocuous by the elaboration of officially recognized forms of mysticism. Both Orthodoxy and Roman Catholicism have an official mysticism. But there are different types of Christian mysticism which are regarded with suspicion or definitely condemned, notably Gnostic mysticism, which is always opposed to the theology of the established hierarchy, and prophetic mysticism.

There are two ways of looking at mysticism. It may be regarded as a peculiarly differentiated form of the spiritual life and as its crowning glory. In this case it presupposes the existence of a certain discipline and of a number of particular stages of growth. Its end is the contemplation of God and union with Him. The mysticism authorized by the Church is linked up with this conception. It is so closely bound up with asceticism that mystical and ascetical works are often confused. Thus the extracts from the patristic literature gathered together in "Philokalia" have a completely ascetic character. Asceticism explains the methods by which the passions can be mastered and the nature of the Old Adam overcome. It shows what man can do. Mysticism, on the other hand, which speaks of the contemplation of God and of union with Him, is a revelation of that which proceeds from God. Among the Eastern ascetics recognized by the Church there are certain of whom special mention may be made, for example, St. Macarius of Egypt, St. Maximus the Confessor, and St. Simon the New Theologian. But in the greater part of ascetic literature there is an absence of mysticism. In the case of St. John of the Cross, who is the classic model of orthodox Catholic mysticism, such works as "The Ascent of Mount Carmel" and "The Dark Night of the Soul" are primarily ascetic works, others like "The Living Flame of Love " are purely mystical. The mysticism approved by the Church is the highest point of the spiritual life, the very crown of life of the great and more specially gifted saints. The Roman Catholic Church, in which everything is so well organized, assigned to mysticism a particular place in the general scheme.[1] Mysticism must not be allowed to extend to every level within the Church's life, it must not be regarded as the foundation of our conception of the world, it must in fact recognize its own limitations.

But there is quite another way of looking at mysticism, which is of great importance. Mysticism may be considered as life at its deepest, as a form of consciousness which includes the whole universe ; it pervades everything. On every side we are surrounded by mystery and we are conscious of symbolism everywhere. The feeling which possesses us as we contemplate the profound mystery surrounding life is also a kind of mysticism. There are men of peculiar gifts who possess a mystical understanding of the world which is quite independent of any holiness. It is possible to be a saint without having any mystical gifts, just as it is possible to be mystically endowed without being a saint. We are always back at the old difficult problem of man's gifts, which are not merits, the genius which is not due to perfection or to sanctity. There are not only men who are favoured with mystical gifts, but there is also a mysticism inherent in human nature in general, for man is a spiritual being who does not belong merely to this world.

That is why the history of the spiritual life and culture of humanity includes mystics and a form of mystical creation which have no connection with any particular discipline or technique. Dostoievsky was a mystic in his feeling for life and in his understanding of it, although he knew nothing of any particular discipline. His mysticism belongs *par excellence* to the prophetic type.

[1] See, for example, Poulain : *The Graces of Interior Prayer : A Treatise on Mysticism.* Saudreau, who represents another school of thought, takes an opposite line, see *The Mystical State.*

Baader, Joseph de Maistre, Solovyov, and Léon Bloy were mystics, while at the same time far from being saints.

The following may be noted with regard to the different types of mysticism. There is a mysticism which is the perfection of the soul, a spiritual ascent leading to God, and there is another kind of mysticism which is a knowledge of the mysteries of being and of the divine. It is the former which has been predominant officially in the Church. It is the apotheosis of the moral and ascetic element. This form of mysticism is above all things a renunciation of " the world ", and an exclusive concentration upon God. But there is a Gnostic type of mysticism which has given to humanity its great creative geniuses. It is enough to mention the names of Plotinus, the Cabala, Eckhart, and Boehme. How can we classify them ? Gnostic mysticism has always provoked in the mind of the Church a certain suspicion. Theology has a certain jealousy of Gnostic mysticism, since it regards it as a false form of knowledge, and this is why one of the greatest gifts man has ever received is condemned. German mysticism, one of the most important manifestations of the human spirit, has been Gnostic in character. Here we find a form of spiritual knowledge and a perception of divine mysteries which rise above the distinctions created by metaphysics and theology.

The history of the human spirit and human culture testifies to the fact that the gift of mystical gnosis, of the contemplation of the mysteries of being, is a particular gift which cannot by any means be identified with sanctity. Jacob Boehme possessed this gift in an infinitely greater degree than St. Francis, St. Dominic, or even a philosopher like St. Thomas Aquinas. And if St. Seraphim of Sarov possessed the gift of contemplation of cosmic mysteries, that was due, not to his acquired sanctity, but to an individual charism. The question of gifts, aptitudes, and genius which are manifestations of the human spirit has not been entirely solved by Christian thought. We have an example of this in the matter of the mystical gift and the Gnostic genius. The prodigious gifts of a Plotinus or a Jacob Boehme cannot come save from God, and they are necessary to the cause of divine creation. The mind of the Church, actuated by pedagogic considerations, tried to submit mysticism to law, with the result that the greatest gifts were excluded.

II

Heiler makes a distinction between the mystical and prophetic types. The distinction is important but the terminology he suggests is conventional. It is not a question of putting one type in opposition to the other but rather of establishing a particular category of prophetic mysticism in which eschatological and apocalyptic elements predominate. It is that form of mysticism which penetrates the mysteries of the future and man's destiny in the world, which is, in fact, concerned with the end of things. Prophetic mysticism which is reformist in spirit is that which differs most from sacramental mysticism, which is *par excellence* conservative in character. In the history of Christianity prophetic mysticism has never been finally quenched. It has represented a tradition of a somewhat intimate character, and has been very closely united to the creative movement within the Church.

Christianity was born into the world through the agency of the eschatological mysticism of the first Christian community. A sense of the insufficiency of revelation and the incompleteness of the Church has been part of all prophetic mysticism, as has also been the idea of the possibility of a new revelation in Christianity and a creative movement which would operate within it. This form of mysticism is that which the mind of the Church has found it least possible to recognize, for the most orthodox type is not usually prophetic or Gnostic in character. It is the prophetic element in Christianity which is precisely its greatest problem. Is prophecy even possible under the New Covenant ? There is a widespread opinion that prophecy belonged to the Old Covenant, and was concerned only with the coming of the Messiah. But this would seem to imply a forgetfulness of the existence of the Revelation of St. John which forms part of the sacred canon of the New

Testament. There is a tendency to forget in Christianity the prophecy of Christ's Second Coming, of the transfiguration, illumination, and end of the world, of the new heaven and the new earth. Sacerdotalism has always tended to deny prophecy, which cannot from its very nature be dependent upon it. Prophecy is free and is attached to no hierarchic principle ; it represents a personal and individual inspiration and gift. The prophet unlike the priest does not belong to the angelic but to the human order. The central idea of Vladimir Solovyov was to defend the rights of the prophetic consciousness and function. He put the prophet on the same level as the priest and the king.

In Christianity the prophetic spirit is in conflict with the spirit of the law. All interest in Christ's Second Coming and in the Resurrection is evidence of the prophetic spirit. In this eschato-logical mysticism man's sense of infinite littleness is overcome. Prophetic mysticism is that of the Holy Spirit. It is Russian mysticism *par excellence*. It is inherent in the Russian people and it springs from the spiritual soil of orthodoxy though the official hierarchy may be hostile to it. . . . And it is this consideration which brings us to the question of the difference between Orthodox and Catholic mysticism.

The difference between Orthodoxy and Catholicism must be looked for above all in the sphere of mysticism, and in the different forms of spiritual experience and method. The whole realm of Christian experience and life is unique in its profundity. Orthodox and Catholic mysticism have equally a right to be called Christian. But these two worlds have developed along diverse lines, and have elaborated two different forms of spirituality while pursuing the same objective. Orthodox mysticism seeks to acquire the grace of the Holy Spirit, and here we find human nature transfigured, illuminated, and deified from within. It is the mysticism of the heart which is the centre of life. Therefore the mind must be united to the heart if there is to be any spiritual unity within. Christ enters the human heart and changes the whole nature of man. Man becomes another creature. For the idea of the divinization of

254

man is the fundamental concept of Orthodox mysticism, the object of which is the transfiguration of everything created. It presupposes the adventure of asceticism, and a heroic struggle against the Old Adam. And yet Orthodox mysticism is full of light and joy, and the mystery of divine creation lies revealed within it. The grace of the Holy Spirit is won by humility and not by suffering.

Catholic mysticism on the other hand is more Christocentric in character and more " anthropological." It is *par excellence* Eucharistic. Indeed it is not too much to say that in general Catholic mysticism tends to give a subordinate place to the work of the Holy Spirit. Frequently the Holy Spirit is actually identified with grace. Catholic mysticism is an imitation of Christ in which the sufferings of Our Lord are as it were lived through again. Hence the phenomenon of stigmata which is inconceivable to the Orthodox mind. Sacrifice, co-operation with the work of redemption by means of human suffering, and supererogatory merits are essential to Catholic mysticism. Here the upward march of the human spirit is organized and disciplined in the most elaborate manner. In its classical form such mysticism has defined three stages in man's spiritual pilgrimage, namely, the purgative, the illuminative, and the unitive ways. It insists that all who follow the mystical way must pass through what St. John of the Cross called " the dark night of the soul ", when the affections and the reason itself are overshadowed, and there is a real death to the world. Orthodox mysticism knows nothing of this " dark night " at least so far as it is considered as a particular stage in mystical progress. Orthodox asceticism, although of a very austere nature, does not involve an entering into " the dark night ", which would imply a more human conception of the mystical way. For the soul to be in " the dark night " is not the same thing as to be " in the Spirit ". In Catholic mysticism, as exemplified in the lives of its saints, suffering and sacrifice are surrounded by a kind of ecstasy. One cannot deny to this experience its original grandeur, and it is of course profoundly Christian in character, but it belongs to a type of mysticism different from ours, and certainly of a more " anthropological " type.

Of Russian Orthodox mysticism a classical example is to be found in St. Seraphim of Sarov, especially in a work, charming in its simplicity, which we owe to an unknown author, of which the title is " The true narrative of a ' strannik ' addressed to his Father in God." The practice of reciting the " Jesus Prayer " lies at the very heart of Orthodox mysticism. By means of this prayer Our Lord Jesus Christ Himself enters our hearts and enlightens our whole being. The Jesus Prayer (" O Lord Jesus Christ, Son of God, have mercy upon me a sinner ") is the point at which mystical concentration begins.

It is by passing through different stages, as for example through the " dark night of the soul ", that the Catholic mystic attains union with the divine, but in Orthodox mysticism the goal is reached by another road. For it cannot be maintained that it is by passing through such and such different stages of this mystical pilgrimage that man raises himself to union with God. Man is transfigured and deified only by an inward reception of the Holy Spirit. Moreover, another characteristic tendency of Orthodox mysticism is the supreme importance attached to the Holy Name. Our Lord Himself is present in the Jesus Prayer. The Holy Name contains within itself that divine energy which, when it is diffused throughout a man's being, penetrates and changes his heart. The Name possesses an ontological and in a sense *magic* significance. The distinction made by St. Gregory of Palama between the divine essence and the divine energy is very characteristic, and it enables us to understand more fully the nature of Orthodox mysticism. The glorification of the Holy Name, indeed all Platonism, is foreign to Catholicism. But nevertheless the divine energy working in man and in the world is transfused throughout creation. The gulf between the natural and supernatural does not exist for mystical and patristic writers of the East in the same sense that it does for Catholics, and especially for the schoolmen who in this direction have certainly left their mark upon Catholic mysticism.

The Eastern Fathers, who were steeped in the spirit of Platonism, have never regarded the non-divinity of the natural as absolute.

The humiliation of the creature can only be the humiliation of the sin present within it, and not that of the divine plan and creation. It is not the created world, the cosmos, or nature, but only sin and evil which are not divine and which are opposed to the divine. Our natural world is sinful and in a state of sin, it is non-divine. But the true world is the world as it is in God. Panentheism is the most perfect way of expressing the relation between God and the world. Pantheism, on the other hand, is a lie, though containing a fragment of truth found again in panentheism which confines itself to a description of the state of the transfigured world. The world, humanity, and cosmic life are divine in principle and divine forces are operative within them. "Naturlichkeit" can be transcended. The non-being with which it is associated can be overcome. The created world can be deified, but this deification can only take place through the work of grace and freedom. The initial creation of a deified world would have involved the absence of freedom. The victory over sin and evil is the deification of the created world. The natural world which is evil and a source of deception then ceases to exist, and nature is revealed in God. Thomism, which affirms both the supernatural and the element of sin and evil, tends also to invest nature with a neutral character fundamentally nondivine and opposed to the supernatural. The result of this is a fear of intuition which bridges the gulf between the natural and supernatural, a distrust of mysticism, and a condemnation of Platonic ontologism.

For such a conception the action of divine energy in the world and its transfiguration are inexplicable. A radical dualism between the natural and supernatural is not conducive to mysticism and it has its origin in an insufficient understanding of the nature of the Holy Spirit, the Third Hypostasis of the Holy Trinity. In the Spirit the divine nature of the world and of the natural is revealed, but it is nature illuminated, transfigured, and deified. It is because the nature of the Holy Spirit is incompletely revealed that the divine nature of the world is also obscured. The dualism inherent in Catholic mysticism portrays man in intensely tragic terms. But

Orthodox mysticism has nothing dramatic about it. It maintains a moral and religious but not an ontological dualism. It is more akin to German mysticism than to that of Latin Catholicism, while being less Gnostic. Most German mysticism is Catholic, as we can see from such names as Eckhart, Tauler, Suso, Ruysbroek and Angelus Silesius. But there is a real difference between them and the Spanish mystics. German Catholic mysticism has not received the approval of the Catholic Church in the way that Spanish mysticism has done. Jacob Boehme was a Lutheran, but he stands really above confessional differences, as in a certain sense all mystics do.

The great task achieved by German mysticism is the revelation of the nature of spirit in all its profundity ; it is *par excellence* a mysticism of the spirit. By penetrating to the very depths of the spirit it has succeeded in getting beyond the antithesis between the natural and supernatural. For Boehme the most fundamental antithesis is not that between the natural and supernatural, but between light and darkness. German mysticism stands apart from the classic distinction between Orthodox and Catholic mysticism. But the mysticism of prophetic and apocalyptic inspiration prefers the soil of Russian Orthodoxy because here there is a fuller revelation of the nature of the Holy Spirit. Neither Latin Catholic mysticism nor German mysticism are favourable to prophetism and apocalypticism.

The mysticism of the Church has always been organized and disciplined, and its object is the raising of the soul to God. But there is a form of mysticism which is indeterminate and unorganized, while yet a true mysticism both in substance and effect. It is this sort of mysticism which constitutes the basic foundation of life. But its potentialities have to be actualized by means of discipline and by insistence upon different stages through which the soul must pass in its mystical development. For contemplation presupposes a certain degree of inner purification and detachment, and asceticism is a necessary preliminary to this way of life. Without it recollection is impossible. It is only in freeing ourselves from the influence of this world and from that "multiplicity" which surrounds us on every side that we can rise to the pure contemplation of God alone. Man cannot immediately contemplate other worlds. That gift is not bestowed on him, and it is here that we find ourselves up against that fundamental paradox of mysticism, to which there is no ready-made solution, namely the eternal problem of human talents and endowments.

There is a gift of mysticism, which like all other gifts is freely bestowed on man by God. Mysticism is not acquired by laborious effort ; it is only asceticism that can be gained in this way. People who possess an intense spiritual life which is well ordered and disciplined may yet be lacking completely in mystical gifts and entirely devoid of higher sensibility and intuition. And it is here that we come to the paradox of the whole situation. On the one hand a mystical endowment is the free gift of God's grace, on the other hand mysticism presupposes in its acquisition the following out of a definite way of life and the observance of a certain discipline. What is called, sometimes in a depreciatory sense, "illuminism" is precisely this faith in the possibility of a sudden flash of inner illumination. The human intellect is certainly cognizant of two spheres of operation. There is the sphere of normal, ordinary, thinking, and there is another sphere where the mind receives special illuminations and intuitions. Here, then, is the chief problem of every system of religious philosophy, for such philosophy is always in the before-mentioned sense an "illuminism". St. Bonaventura, it may be recalled, as opposed to St. Thomas Aquinas, insisted that a true philosophy was dependent upon the illumination of the intellect by faith.

The Church, generally speaking, has not recognized the value of mysticism except for monks and nuns. Books on mysticism, both Catholic and Orthodox, had their origin in monastic circles and were intended for the use of monks, as manuals on the spiritual life. Is, then, a non-monastic form of mysticism possible ? To which we may reply that it is possible, that it exists in fact, and that it actually has a preponderating place in history. But it is instinct

I do not understand this at all.

with a spirit of distrust towards the Church, that is in so far as it is Gnostic or prophetic in character.

Mysticism indeed raises some special problems for the Christian consciousness. If there is ever to be a revival of Christian mysticism in the world, it will not be exclusively monastic. It will rather be a renewal and a deepening of the life of the world and a fresh understanding of it. And here is a question which concerns not only the future of mysticism within Christianity, but also mystical Christianity itself. There is, moreover, a danger which besets every attempt to follow the mystical way. Phantasy in this sphere of life may easily be mistaken for reality. Eastern mysticism has recognized and described this condition of being " charmed ". Mysticism indeed can be illusory. Man may not be a discerner of spirits, and the powers of darkness can appear to him in the guise of spirits of light. On the mystical path there may descend clouds of darkness and not illumination.

But it must be remembered that the spiritual life, generally speaking, is full of danger, for the absence of any spiritual life is in itself a source of security ; an ordinary existence and a religion which is merely traditional and external offers the maximum of peace and quietness. For all creative initiative conceals within itself a certain degree of danger ; and without it the spiritual life becomes atrophied. Mysticism is the new birth in the Spirit. That is what all the mystics teach us. Those forms of religion which are least dangerous are those which are adapted to the established order of society and to the " once-born ". Mysticism cannot become the organizing principle of the life of mankind or of whole nations. It is for this reason that it is often in conflict with the sort of religion upon which this task of organization devolves.

James' term

III

But mysticism contains other dangers too. It may take the form of the extinction instead of the illumination of man's *psyche*, that is to say, of the concrete multiplicity of human personalities. The problem which confronts us is that of the One and the many. Mysticism always moves from multiplicity towards the One ; it leaves the world and man in order to reach God. It is above all the way of detachment. Multiplicity is lost in unity and soul in spirit. But man's being is an aggregate in which spirit, soul, and body are unified. In Yoga, as in the system of St. Ignatius Loyola, mystical experience is to some extent " mechanized ", and the " psychical " element in man is eliminated. It was the same in Quietism, in which the individual human soul disappeared. The mysticism of the One in Plotinus and Eckhart does not solve the problem of the mystical meaning of human individuality and personality. The mystical theosophy of the Cabala, Boehme, St. Martin, and Baader is of quite a different nature.

The most delicate problem which faces mysticism is that of its attitude towards the problem of man and of the world, that is, of the world in all the multiplicity of its creation. This difficult problem arises whenever the mystics, including those who are attached to the Church, attempt a more profound treatment of the doctrine of love. They extol detachment from the world of created things. Impassibility and indifference towards creatures of every sort is the fundamental demand which mystical-ascetical discipline imposes. St. Isaac of Syria, for example, teaches that we must harden ourselves and make ourselves insensible towards all creatures in order that we may love God with all our hearts. The same idea is found in the writings of St. John of the Cross. Eckhart places detachment above love, and the spirit of love was certainly lacking in him. St. Basil the Great, in his precepts on the monastic life, warns the monks against all individual love and all friendship. Impassibility and indifference towards all human beings, and everything indeed which is human, seems to be the indispensable condition of asceticism. Man is a creature, and as such we cannot love him. We must be free from attachments to everything created.

There is an immense difference between the morality of the Gospels and the ascetic morality of the Fathers. Very few of them indeed were like St. Francis of Assisi or St. Seraphim of Sarov, who

261

knew how to combine ascetic detachment and mystical contemplation with the love of all creation and every divine creature.
Human nature seems incapable of holding on to the fulness of the
revelation given to us in the Gospels, to the love of God and the
love of our neighbour. In ascetical and mystical literature we often
find a plea put forward in favour of an impersonal and impassible
love which gives itself equally to all and knows nothing of individual preferences. As St. Maximus the Confessor declares,
" Happy is the man who can love every one with the same degree
of love." These words seem to be a denial of all individual choice
in love and of all friendship. Love in such a form is merely impersonal. Nor is this impersonality in love regarded simply as a
means to an end. It is the final end and the means to it is humility.

Here indeed is the most perplexing problem of Christian mysticism and asceticism, which seems at this point to be out of harmony
both with the Gospels and the Epistles by refusing to follow the
path which St. John, the beloved disciple, points out for us. The
Christianity of St. John is one of love and is opposed to that hardening of the heart which is commended by patristic writers and the
ascetical mystics. We are bound to love all created things, the
whole of God's creation, and every human being, and it is precisely
personality that we should love in God and through God. It is
not a question of humanistic love which is always impersonal and
abstract in character, but rather of the love of Christ. We find an
example of this in St. Seraphim. He is a living revelation of the
Holy Spirit in the life of man and of the world. Thus it is possible
to believe in a new type of mysticism with a different attitude
towards the world, which will unite detachment and contemplation
to an enlightened love of the whole divine creation and every
human personality. Here there is a big problem which mysticism
puts to Christianity. For there is a mysticism of love, the apostle
of which was St. John, and equally too St. Paul. Christianity is
the revelation of personality and of the absolute value of every
individual human soul ; it is the religion of love of to-morrow, and
it is born of the love of God Himself. But an asceticism which

hardens the heart and renders it insensible to creatures and to individual personalities, and which has been incapable of assimilating the light and truth of Christianity, comes very near to being not Christian but Hindu.

In Russia, Dostoievsky was the prophet of a totally different spirit and quite another form of mysticism. He belongs, like Solovyov, to the Russian tradition in Christianity. For there is a traditional mysticism of love. It is to be found, for instance, in the mythological speculations of Plato, in the Cabala, in Dante, in St. Francis of Assisi, in the " theosophy " of Jacob Boehme, in Baader, and in Solovyov. It is true that it has its origin in the doctrine of the " male-female " image of man, and there are often other confusing elements in it, yet in spite of that it has a real place in Christian symbolics. Christianity sets before us a spiritual form of love, but this love has for its aim the spiritualizing not the annihilation of the " natural " or " psychical " man.

IV

Mysticism and asceticism may pass through some very dark periods because of the concentration of the spirit on the evil and sin which are characteristic of the old nature. But a true mysticism overcomes the fear which Satan inspires. When we experience this fear and feel overcome by evil it shows that we are still in bondage to created nature in all its sinfulness and alienation from God. To rise above this is to conquer the fear of Satan and the obsession of evil which isolates the created world from God. The way to this victory is primarily that of asceticism, sacrifice, and holiness. But this is not all, for there is also the way of creation, and illumination, the surging ecstasy of human nature. But is there, after all, a mysticism of creation, and does mysticism lead to creation ?

This question also belongs to the sphere of Christian problematics. There is an eternal mysticism and Christianity must return to its fountain-head if it is not to become completely stereotyped. But

Error of
indifference
to the κοσμος
↓

in our days the mystical renaissance of Christianity will have a special task to perform. We have seen that, generally speaking, mysticism involves an absolute detachment from mankind and from the world, coupled with an exclusive orientation towards God. Mysticism must overcome the "world" in the bad sense of the word, that is, in the sense in which it is employed in Holy Scripture and the ascetic Fathers. Only pagan mysticism of an orgiastic nature is absorbed in the world of nature, but Christian mysticism always takes an opposite line. We find ourselves faced by the following problem : how is Christian mysticism to be related to the life of the cosmos and that of humanity ? Is such a thing possible ? To transcend the state of creatureliness does not mean the annihilation of the life of the cosmos or humanity, but rather its illumination and transfiguration. Pre-Christian mysticism, which reached its culminating point in Plotinus, involves a separation from multiplicity in order that there may be a concentration upon the One. Plotinus, the last great representative of the Greeks, rejected the dualism of the Gnostics who denied the beauty of the world, and perhaps to some extent anticipated Christianity. His greatness lies just in the fact that he abandoned the pagan world, with all its terrible corruption, in order to focus his attention upon a new spiritual world, and in doing this he took with him the Greek idea of the beauty of the cosmos. But he found no solution of this dilemma.

The problem that disturbs me may be expressed in the following manner, in the terms which I have adopted ; how can the natural world be transfigured and brought into the spiritual world as something real and not illusory ? How can the "psychical" be related to the spiritual ? So far as mysticism is concerned the question may be stated thus : how will man and the cosmos when spiritually transfigured be affirmed in mystical experience ? God does not merely desire His own existence. Man, the cosmos, and the divine creation are not merely for time but also for eternity. The deification of creation does not mean any loss in its significance, still less its extinction. Man and the world are not annihilated in

God, but illuminated and transfigured. They are now definitively part of being and are set free from non-being.

We must not love the " world ", in the Gospel sense of the word, but rather escape from its domination, though at the same time loving divine creation, the cosmos, and man himself. We must get beyond the monastic and ascetic attitude which despised and hated the world, for it is incapable of comprehending the full truth of Christianity ; indeed it is incapable of following Christ Himself. In fact it cannot be reconciled with the Gospel ethics. On the one hand man must live with his fellows and with the world, he must bear the burden of their tragic destiny, and on the other hand he must be freed from the world and its passions, a monk while living in the world. There is a certain kind of monastic and ascetic enmity towards mankind, a lack of understanding, and a profound lack of interest in all the movements which are taking place in the world. But there is in this attitude a self-sufficiency and a failure of love which, as Rosanov said, are adamantine. Such a type of monastic and ascetic mysticism is *par excellence* abstract and negative, and indeed, in the majority of cases, is not mysticism at all. For in God, and in union with Him, it is impossible for the world and man not to come to life again and for the fulness of being not to be achieved. St. Seraphim left the darker elements of monasticism behind in order to achieve a more luminous type of mysticism. Dostoievsky prophesied this state of things in the person of the elder Zossima.

In the practice of mysticism, as in everything else, means too often become ends. This type of asceticism, with its hostility to man and to the world, may obscure the true end of mysticism, which is transfiguration in God. It may place upon men burdens too heavy to be borne and also produce a great deal of tension in the soul. The difficulty of the spiritual life lies precisely in the necessity of combining detachment from the many and concentration upon the One, with the liberation and transfiguration in the Spirit of all the diverse elements of the world and of humanity. Two courses are possible and it is difficult to reconcile them. One involves a process of detachment from mankind and the world and a concentration upon God, the abandoning of the many for the One, the Eternal, and the Unchanging. The other has its orientation towards man and the world, towards the many and that which is subject to change. Greek philosophy was incapable of solving the problem, which is the result of the dualism between two worlds. Even Plato did not find a solution to it, though his conception of Eros was an approach to one. Greek thought was dominated far too much by the Parmenidean conception of the one changeless Being, which has exercised even upon Christian theology an influence of considerable importance. But Christianity does in principle admit a solution of this difficult problem and attempts to overcome the dualism involved in it. The fulness of Christian truth has been beyond the power of humanity to assimilate; in fact, even the mystics and saints have failed in this respect. Once again, then, we find ourselves face to face with the problem with which Plato, Plotinus, and other Greek philosophers had to grapple.

No solution indeed is possible except in the love of Christ and in the fulness of love. The creative energy of man is also a manifestation of love, of Eros, which brings unity and illumination. The task of the spiritual life is a particularly difficult one and is impossible so far as the natural man is concerned, for it consists in uniting by incessant prayer a free, spiritual, detachment and concentration upon the One and Eternal, with that love of mankind and of the world which illumines and transfigures everything. The supreme goal of mysticism is not only union with God, but also, because of this very union, a turning outwards of the self towards every creature. It is the realization of love and of creative energy, for love is creation. In this way the command of Christ to love God and man is fulfilled.

In Christian love every gift and charism conferred by God on man must be duly manifested. "There are diversities of gifts but the same Spirit . . . to one is given by the Spirit the word of wisdom; to another the word of knowledge, by the same Spirit. To one is given faith, by the same Spirit; to another the gifts of healing, by the same Spirit; to another the working of miracles;

to another prophecy ; to another the discerning of spirits ; to another the gift of tongues ; to another the interpretation of tongues." And St. Paul also tells us, " Quench not the Spirit ; despise not prophesyings ; prove all things ; hold fast that which is good." But monastic and ascetic Christianity sometimes leads to the quenching of the spirit and the denial of gifts, that is to say, to an intense dualism in which life, the creative energies, and indeed our whole attitude towards the world and mankind are left without any justification. Here, then, is the great problem which mysticism must face. Its mission is to free the human spirit from despondency and to justify its creative activity. Mysticism itself, however, has frequently been responsible for this condemnation of creative living. Mystical experience regarded this state of creaturehood as sin involving isolation from God. But in God natural being is transcended, and it is another kind of human nature the creative energies of which are rehabilitated.

In mystical experience the natural and human sphere is absorbed in that of the spirit and the opposition between mutually exclusive elements ceases. True mysticism frees us from the sense of oppression which arises from everything which is alien to us, and imposed, as it were, from without. In mysticism everything is experienced and lived out by me as a part of my self, as something in the profoundest sense " within myself ". Mysticism means a penetration into the innermost recesses of the spiritual world, where everything happens in a manner totally different from that of the natural world, for here there is no separation between things and no one thing is external to another. Nothing is external to me, everything is in me and with me, within the very depths of myself. But this mystical truth is in radical opposition to subjectivism of every kind, as well as to every species of psychologism, and solipsism ; it does not mean that nothing exists outside me, or that everything is simply part of my own individual personal condition or state. This truth implies, rather, that manifestation of the spiritual world in which everything lies, as it were, hidden in the profoundest intimacy ; it implies the internal as opposed to the external revelation of all that is real. I am in everything and everything is in me. The whole orientation of life is changed and transformed. To live, from the mystical point of view, is no longer to experience the state of oppression to which I am subjected by an externally opposed reality as in the natural world, but to be convinced that everything forms a part of my own inner destiny and transpires at a level so deep that it is nearer to me than my own self. Mysticism is the opposite of historical realism. Yet there is, nevertheless, a mysticism of history. The whole history of the world is the history of my spirit, for in the spirit these two histories cease to be externally opposed to one another. This, however, does not mean that the reality of myself is destroyed or that I lose my identity by being merged into all other objects. It means, rather, that I only acquire being, reality, and personality when everything about me has ceased to be external, strange, impenetrable, or lifeless, and when the kingdom of love is realized.

We are entering upon a period of new spirituality, which will be the counterpart of the present materialism of our world. There will also be a new form of mysticism corresponding to this new period in Christian history. It will be henceforth impossible to oppose the conception of a higher life by pointing to the sinfulness of human nature which must be overcome. There is no longer any room in the world for a merely external form of Christianity based upon custom. It is precisely the mystical and spiritual life which leads to victory over sin. The world is entering upon a period of catastrophe and crisis when we are being forced to take sides and in which a higher and more intense kind of spiritual life will be demanded from Christians. The sort of Christianity which is purely outward in character and never rises above the level of mediocrity is to-day on the decline ; while that which possesses eternal significance and an inner mystical quality is growing more intense and stronger. Moreover the Church herself will have to change her attitude towards mysticism and the spiritual life. It is only during periods when custom and external tradition are obstinately insisted upon that religion lacks a mystical element.

This is inevitably recovered during periods when tradition and custom are being subjected to catastrophic disturbance. It is then that mysticism of the type associated especially with the work of the Holy Spirit becomes dominant. A period of revived spirituality within Christianity is bound to be one in which there will be hitherto unprecedented manifestations of the Holy Spirit.

CHAPTER EIGHT

Theosophy and Gnosis

I

WORDS often provoke a false association of ideas which do not correspond to their ontological meaning. "Theosophy" is a word of this kind, for it may mean very different things. Contemporary theosophical movements have given to it a debased significance and have made us forget the existence of an authentic Christian theosophy, and a genuine knowledge of the divine. The theosophical tradition runs right through Christian history. The first Christian theosophist, in the profoundest meaning of the word, and the first representative of Christian gnosis (as opposed to the pseudo-Gnostics) was St. Paul himself. Clement of Alexandria and Origen were also theosophists and Christian Gnostics. The works of the Areopagite and mediæval mysticism, the writings of the great Boehme, in spite of certain defects, admit a true Christian theosophy of a very different kind from that associated with the name of Steiner or Annie Besant. The same might be said of Baader and Solovyov at a period nearer our own. The Cabala is theosophical in character and has exercised a considerable influence on Christian mysticism. Heraclitus and Plato were great theosophists of the ancient world, which, even in its decline, produced a Plotinus. These men were, if we may so put it, "intoxicated" with the divine wisdom. Mystical theology, as opposed to scholastic theology, has always been theosophical, as indeed is all contemplation in which there is a synthesis between philosophy and religion.

But it is clear that contemporary theosophy is different from that of other ages. The spirit of Mme. Blavatsky or Mrs. Besant differs considerably from that of Heraclitus, Plotinus, Origen, the pseudo-Dionysius the Areopagite, Master Eckhart, Jacob Boehme, Baader, or Solovyov. Its form is quite different ; they belong to another type altogether. Contemporary theosophical writings are devoid of divine and creative inspiration. They betray no talent ; they are frankly boring ; they are, moreover, written in a style which would be more appropriate to a manual of mineralogy or geography ; in fact they are almost impossible to read! The students of modern theosophy learn its " geographical " terms by heart and are, therefore, constantly obliged to consult these mystical Baedeckers in order to avoid confusing the mountains and rivers of the spiritual world. It is easy to make a slip over the succession of incarnations, to confuse Jupiter, Venus, and Mercury, for it is difficult to translate these avatars into the language of a living spiritual experience. The majority of theosophists and anthroposophists have no " clairvoyance " of their own. They do not see cosmic evolution in the memory of the world, but they have recourse to Steiner's *Akashic Chronicle* or some other work which they learn by heart. In this way a spiritual orientation is begun of which even the starting point is false.

Theosophy misuses names which it has no right to employ. It is, moreover, as difficult to find God in the theosophy of Annie Besant as it is to find man in the anthroposophy of Rudolph Steiner. If you open a few books on theosophy you will find much about the foundation and evolution of the cosmos, the complex structure of man resulting from this evolution, and re-incarnation ; but the name of God is not mentioned. Cosmosophy would be a much better name for it than theosophy, for it deals with nothing but the composition and development of the cosmos, and in this it is completely monistic. So far as it is concerned God does not exist, there is only " the divine " which is simply the cosmos with its numerous different planes. In such a system man disappears and is entirely subject to cosmic processes.

Contemporary theosophy bears the indelible marks of the

271

intellectual period from which it had its origin, a period in which naturalism, evolutionism, rationalism, and materialism were predominant. The modern theosophical movement begun by Mme. Blavatsky has from the outset affirmed a particular form of spiritual naturalism and evolutionism. It made no attack upon the intellectual habits of nineteenth-century man and made no demand for any act of faith on his part or for any spiritual revolution. The spiritual world is to be won by peaceful means, by a process of evolution. The intellectualism of modern man, and in fact his whole mentality, was both accepted and justified. Theosophical knowledge is to be assimilated to the naturalism, evolutionism, and, we might almost say, to the materialism of contemporary science.

Steiner is a disciple of Haeckel whom he reveres as his master. Theosophical thought adopts monism in its crudest form which a more refined philosophy has already discarded. It is striking to notice that while theosophy associates itself with the most simplist movements in philosophy it avoids those which are more complex and profound ; it has from its inception taken on a popular character. It addresses itself to those already contaminated by evolutionism, positivism, and naturalism, that is to say, to currents of thought manifestly inferior to contemporary philosophy and to the spiritual culture of to-day. Theosophists attempt to justify the vulgarization of their literature by this very fact. Anthroposophists may even be heard to say that Steiner, the most eminent of the theosophists, wrote his books for fools, but that he reserves his profounder utterances for the initiated.

Nevertheless in spite of the very low level of popular theosophical literature and in spite of the charlatanism with which it is so often associated, theosophy is not to be taken lightly and we must recognize it as an important symptom. Its growing popularity is bound up with the crisis which has overtaken both science and Christianity. It is symptomatic of a profound unrest in modern man and of a return to the spiritual. Moreover, neither science nor the official Church are attaching sufficient importance to theosophy and the occultism connected with it. The popularity of theosophy is easily explainable in these syncretistic days. Theosophy in choosing evolutionism took the easiest way of escape from contemporary atheism, materialism, and naturalism, towards the discovery and actual knowledge of the spiritual world. Theosophy helps to bridge the gulf which separates the two worlds. It inculcates the way of perfection and the development of fresh organs of receptivity, but its precepts differ radically from those of religion and mysticism. Theosophy does not demand the renunciation of the wisdom of the age. It adapts itself to the instincts of the average man who would like to broaden his environment and multiply his riches by a merely superficial contact with the spiritual world. Theosophy will never be able to satisfy the deep spiritual longing of the peoples of the earth who can only live by religious faith. As for the real aristocracy of the spirit it too can find no place in contemporary theosophy.

Popular theosophy is based upon the contradiction inherent in the exoteric treatment of what is claimed to be esoteric. Its essential task is the revelation of the esoteric. But it stirs no emotion in the presence of the deepest of all mysteries, for its esotericism offers a secret rather than a mystery. True esotericism is innocent both of dissimulation and enigma, it predicates the mysterious which is revealed at a greater or lesser depth according to what is given, or to the spiritual level attained. The distinction between the esoteric and the exoteric is a real and eternal one which we find referred to even by St. Paul. There is both a deeper and a more superficial understanding of Christianity. Esotericism in Christianity almost coincides with mysticism. Christian mystics have been truly esoteric. But the contemplation to which they devoted themselves, though beyond the reach of simple Christians, has nothing of the enigmatic about it. To understand them completely it is only necessary to possess an experience similar to theirs. To comprehend the esoteric element in Christianity our minds must be directed towards the other world. But in theosophy and occultism, which claim to have a religious character, esotericism presents somewhat equivocal features.

The difference between the exoteric and the esoteric is a relative one. Esotericism claims to protect the secret truth and mystery from profanation at the hands of the uncomprehending masses who are unable to assimilate them. But what is there of the esoteric in contemporary theosophy ? Is it divine wisdom or naturalistic monism ? To which of the more important beliefs is this esotericism opposed ? Is it opposed to the Christian Church, or to present-day materialism and positivism ? Perhaps the mystery lies in the fact that God does not really exist at all and that there is nothing but the infinite cosmos ? Theosophical literature certainly gives us good grounds for regarding its esotericism in this light. In this matter Mme. Blavatsky and Steiner differ radically from Jacob Boehme and St. Martin. When pagan polytheism flourished monotheism was regarded as an esoteric truth to be hidden from the masses who were unable to reach such a high level. In the days of the ascendency of Church Christianity it was naturalistic monism that was regarded as esoteric. But what still remains to be discovered is what constitutes esotericism in an age of confusion like the present one, which is without any unique, integral, and predominant belief.

To the mind of the Church no less than to that of materialists theosophy seems to conceal something, yet when one penetrates to the bottom of its esotericism it is always a spiritualist form of naturalism, evolutionism, or monism that one discovers. Steiner is a monist just as Haeckel was, and he naturalizes divine mysteries. But his monism is linked up with a particular form of Manichean dualism.

What is true in occultism is that the difference between the esoteric and the exoteric is to be found in the variation of degrees of consciousness. Its dynamic conception of consciousness is also a right one, for a static conception, with no clearly marked limits, can only be fleeting and transitory. We are surrounded by invisible and unknown forces, and it is only for a time that we are immune from their influence. The sphere of the occult and the magical certainly exists and the world is subject to its action. This must be recognized apart from any judgment as to the value of these forces. Positive science itself more and more recognizes the existence of the metapsychical.[1] But scientific occultism has little in common with the religious pretensions of occultism and theosophy.

II

In their conception of man Christianity and theosophy differ radically and profoundly from one another. There is no kind of similarity between Christian anthropology and that of popular theosophy. It is essential to trace the opposition between these two conceptions of human destiny to its furthest point. Christianity is anthropocentric and anthroposophic in the truest sense of the words. According to Christianity man is the highest order of being and is superior even to the angelic hierarchy. The Son of God became incarnate in a man and not in an angel. Man is from all eternity and he also inherits eternity ; he is created in the image and likeness of God, he is not a product of cosmic evolution nor is he re-absorbed by it ; he is not the child of nature nor that of processes which are accomplished in it. Man is "the child of God." The human species cannot be eclipsed by a new race, whether of supermen, angels, or demons. No evolution can transform our grade in the hierarchy into another. The divine plan for man cannot be modified ; it can only be realized, or destroyed. Man inherits eternal and divine life ; through Christ, the God-Man, he is rooted in the very heart of the divine life. Man can put himself in immediate contact with God and no cosmic evolution can separate them. If there is anything esoteric in Christianity it is certainly not the notion that man is a product of cosmic evolution, that he can be surpassed by it, and that a new universal aeon will arise bearing the sign of a new super-human race, but rather the idea that man is more than a simple creature, that the Second Hypostasis of the Trinity is Man born in eternity.

[1] See, for instance, the work of Charles Ricket, *A Treatise on the Metapsychical*, in which the existence of all occult manifestations is recognized, including that of materialization.

In the Cabala there was a theosophy, an anthroposophy, and an esotericism which were genuine. This esotericism is unknown to modern theosophy. Whatever its forms and different shades of meaning might be it possesses its own esotericism, which, while a sop to the pride of man in time, gives him less importance so far as eternity is concerned. The Christian conception of man is hierarchical and not evolutionist. Man is not a transitory fragment of the cosmos, a mere step in its evolution; he is superior to the cosmos, independent of its infinity, and in principle embraces it completely.

The theosophical consciousness, though it admits cosmic subordinations, is entirely evolutionist ; every grade in the hierarchy of being is capable of transformation into another. The main currents of theosophical thought are a radical denial of the Christian idea of man. According to them man has not existed from all time nor does he inherit eternity. The cosmos is eternal but man is only something temporary and fleeting, corresponding to a single aeon of cosmic evolution. He had no existence in former periods, nor will he have in those which are to come. Man is overwhelmed by the worlds above and below him. He has his roots in time and not in eternity, in the cosmos and not in God.

The theosophical consciousness is monistic and monophysite ; it recognizes the existence of only one nature, the divine impersonal cosmos. Man is the product and instrument of evolution, in the process of which he comes into being and then is dissolved again. He is an entity composed of three bodies (the physical body, the etheric, and the astral) and of the impersonal spiritual " ego." He is only a temporary synthesis of cosmic forces. His structure resembles that of those Easter eggs which fit inside one another ; he is devoid of any concrete spiritual nucleus, and, if there is one, it is impersonal and cosmic. Anthroposophy, though the name is derived from the word " man," presupposes that a single universal aeon underlies the outward sign of man and that this will itself suffer eclipse. This cosmic period is in some sense man in dissolution and the world of this aeon is composed of fragments of him. But this apparent exaggeration of the value of man does not mean that he has any absolute or eternal significance, for there is nothing here but the play of the cosmic forces. The periods which follow will not bear man's sign ; another species will be found and it will not be human. There is a hierarchy of spirits superior to man who direct him.[1] Between God and man there is a complex gradation of angels and demons, who make immediate communion impossible. But for that matter God is really non-existent, being merely a cosmic hierarchy which is regarded as divine. Theosophy re-establishes the old demonolatry and man remains subject to the genii.

The freedom of the human spirit achieved by Christianity is no more and we are confronted with a return to ancient, semi-Christian, semi-pagan, Gnosticism. Man disappears, and his image is lost in the various cosmic hierarchies and stages of evolution, in the infinite succession of aeons. Theosophy and anthroposophy of every variety deny personality, and combat this principle in the interests of a sort of cosmic communion. They complicate the problem by failing to observe the distinction between personality and individuality. For Christian thought personality is a spiritual category while individuality is a biological one.

Personality for the theosophists as for philosophers of Hartmann's school is only in reality the result of the imprisonment of spirit in matter, in the physical body, and therefore it is a stage to be super-seded by further evolution. The doctrine of re-incarnation borrowed from India destroys the integrality of being. The temporal synthesis of cosmic forces, of the planetary fragments of different stages of evolution, breaks up into constituent parts and a new synthesis takes place. But the unity and integrality of per-sonality disappears.

Theosophists are right when they insist on the complex structure of man and that there are within him various cosmic levels super-imposed upon one another. They are equally right when they refuse to see in the natural man the intangible and immutable substratum of personality. Personality is God's idea of man, and

---

[1] See R. Steiner, *Die Geistige Führung des Menschen und der Menscheit*, in which his Christology is also developed.

man's eternal destiny is indissolubly linked with this unique and divine thing. Its image remains in God and not here below in the world, in natural substantiality. But for the theosophist there is an infinite evolution of spiritual worlds between the divine and human beings. In reality this infinite evolution is just the Divine Being.

Mystical experience of communion with God is considered by theosophists as unrealizable. Theosophy is forced to deny that the integral and unique image of man is in God and that it is a divine idea ; it regards it always as the result of complex processes which take place in the world. Theosophical and anthroposophical thought alike deny that man is a design of God, or that he is eternal, and in this they resemble Communism. Popular theosophy is a form of naturalism transferred to the spiritual sphere, a naturalistic monism of the type of Haeckel's. It is for this reason that Steiner permits himself the assertion that Haeckel corrected Boehme and gave his principles their further development. But though we find in Boehme a Christian doctrine of man, of the First Adam, there is no trace of such a conception in Steiner, who was, as we saw, a disciple of Haeckel. Schuré claims that man proceeds from a being who is half-fish and half-serpent—a theory of man's origin which has no very clear connection with Christianity. The naturalistic evolutionism of the theosophist is in conflict with the Platonic doctrine of ideas, species, and the hierarchy of being. Theosophy is anti-hierarchical like all evolutionist theories, for it admits the existence of only one species which is both from all eternity and to all eternity. It is, besides, a denial of man, a sort of spiritual Darwinism. According to the hierarchical thought of Christianity man does not come from the animals nor can he develop into superman. He may suffer decline just as he can also develop and rise in the scale, but he will remain man even in the Kingdom of God.[1]

[1] The distinction between the theosophy of Mme. Blavatsky or Mrs. Besant and the anthropology of Steiner, so freely exaggerated on both sides, is not essential to an understanding of their fundamental principles ; but Steiner is the more interesting.

We have already shown how anthropology varies with our Christology. Our attitude towards man is determined by our attitude towards Christ. Man only becomes conscious of himself, in the absolute sense, through Christ, the God-Man. Theosophical Christology is elaborated in such a way that it cannot help leading to a denial of man. Or else theosophy bases itself upon the pre-Christian thought of Hinduism which only sees in Jesus Christ one initiate among many, or else evolves a naturalistic Christology and sees in Christ simply a cosmic impulse. But all forms of theosophy alike make a distinction between Jesus and Christ and deny the existence of the God-humanity. Mme. Blavatsky could not endure Christianity and regarded Brahmanism as a higher form of the religious consciousness.[1] There was, it is true, in Brahmanism a pre-Christian religious truth but it is absent from modern theosophy. Steiner considers his theosophy Christian ; he recognizes the fact that a new period in world-history has begun with the coming of Christ and he is even prepared to speak of Eastern theosophy as reactionary. Nevertheless, his Christology is naturalistic and evolutionist in character, and this affects his anthropology in an adverse sense.

Man is made up of fragments of planetary evolutions, and both he and the earth are but stages of this cosmic evolution. Man is reincarnated and thus loses his image, the substratum of personality. The very earth itself is subject to these peregrinations ; the unique and integral entity, the ontological core of things, can be found nowhere. Personality comes together and then dissolves, only to reappear in other personalities. The whole of humanity also passes through an analogous process and is reincarnated in a species which is no longer human. Man possesses a physical body which corresponds to the mineral kingdom, an etheric body which corresponds to that of plants, an astral body which corresponds to that of animals, and a spiritual Ego which has an affinity with God.[2] All these

---

[1] There may be found in a book of Mrs. Besant's called *Esoteric Christianity* a whole series of truths relating to the mystical interpretation of Christianity, and this work is less antichristian than the others.

[2] Cf. Steiner : *Die Geheimwissenschaft im Umrisse.*

constituent parts are then dissolved and so personality itself disappears. The spiritual Ego does not in itself constitute personality, which is only formed in union with the physical, etheric, and astral bodies as an evolutive and transitory synthesis of elements capable both of union and dissociation. Jesus and the Christ are distinct and are united only at the moment of His Baptism, but even the image of Jesus dissolves, for, according to Steiner, there are two infant Jesuses. The Christ, in so far as He is the Logos and a cosmic agent, reincarnates Zoroaster in Jesus.

The Christology of Steiner is an original and modernized reconstruction of the ancient heresies of Manicheism and Nestorianism in which the two natures of Christ remain distinct. Steiner denies the mystery of the divine humanity in Christ and the integrality of His Image. Christ is not a Personality, but a cosmic impulse or agent. For other theosophists Jesus Christ is part of the same succession of great initiates which includes Buddha and Zoroaster. Theosophy and anthroposophy see the Christ not in God nor in the divine Trinity, but in nature and the cosmic process. Cosmic infinity swallows up the Image of Christ and also the image of man who shares His destiny.

These then are the characteristics of that " cosmosophical " consciousness which arrogates to itself without any right the names of theosophy and anthroposophy. For this type of thought recognizes neither God, man, nor personality but only the cosmic impersonal which is identical with the divine impersonal. There is no clearly defined hierarchy with well marked intervals between the different grades within it and in consequence no integrality in any being whatsoever ; everything is confused, all is in all and passes into all. Here we find once more the old Hindu philosophy by which theosophical thought is dominated. The truth of mysticism, namely that of unity and of the profound character of the spiritual world, is here both naturalized and popularized.

Theosophy finds itself forced to deny the eternal value of the individual soul ; it cannot recognize the indefectible significance of the human name. It finds no place within its system for the

Christian revelation of personality, for it is really pre-Christian. And even Steiner, who speaks freely of the impact of Christ and Christianity on world history, knows nothing of this revelation. Christianity is personalist ; and, so far as it is concerned, every being constitutes a unique and concrete personality. Theosophy and anthroposophy are anti-personalist, for the anthroposophical doctrine of the spiritual Ego is not a doctrine of personality. This Ego is completely impersonal and is an aggregate of bodies which belong to other planes, and which afterwards separate. Human personality is only a temporary conglomeration. What theosophy really believes in is a sort of basic and original collectivism, a kind of anti-hierarchical communism of being. The human image is obscured and disintegrated by the bad infinity of different worlds. This is the reason why theosophy knows nothing either of the mystery of Christian love or of Hindu philosophy and religion.

The mystery of love is the mystery of personality, which penetrates into another in a unique never-to-be-renewed identity. It is the vision of another's image in God. Only the lover can contemplate the face of the beloved. The image of man is always distorted and obscured for one who does not love. It is only through love that we can see the beauty of the human face. Love is not the confirmation of an identity, the discovery of a single principle in myself and another—*tat tvam asi*, as Indian thought would have it. If " you " and " I " are but one then my love for you is only the love of myself. There is no longer another being. The loving subject and his love always imply the existence of another and presuppose a going-out of the self towards this other person, the mystery of the union of two beings who enjoy independent and distinct reality. The absolute image of love for all time is given us in the divine Trinity and it cannot be found either in abstract monotheism or pantheism. Indeed theosophy denies both the " you " and the " me ". Yet love is always a relationship between personalities. If there is no such thing as personality there can be no place for love. Immortality, resurrection, the eternity of personality are the vindication of love, the affirmation of the beloved in God, that is, in eternity.

It is clear that for theosophy, which believes in the cosmic aggregation and dissolution of personality and its composite and ephemeral character, personality cannot be eternal. Personality, love, and immortality are united and indissolubly connected in spiritual experience. Love possesses an eternal significance if its object is eternal, and if it asserts this eternity with all its force. The mystery of uniqueness, of that which cannot be repeated, is as inconceivable, so far as theosophy is concerned, as it is for Indian religious thought. Theosophy regards everything as capable of being reproduced and multiple in character. The unique personality of Jesus Christ does not exist. The Christ is reincarnated many times. Man and indeed the whole earth have to submit to these reiterated peregrinations. There is no such thing as a unique event in history, which might thus give it a unique significance. The meaning and individuality of history are, however, bound up with the uniqueness of the events which comprise it, and above all with the unique coming of Christ. All concrete spiritual life depends likewise on this same uniqueness. Pre-Christian Hindu thought as well as theosophy has no place for personality and through omitting this essential fact fails to grasp the significance of history.

Theosophy refuses to envisage the final goal in that divine eternity which gives significance to all that is unique and personal. This denial of the divine goal is closely bound up with the denial of any absolute mystery. Mystery envelops us in the divine Absolute. The denial of this mystery leaves us immersed in the infinitude of the universal process. Personality, uniqueness, eternity, and mystery are all inseparably connected. To assert the existence of mystery is not the same thing as to be an agnostic. In the sphere of knowledge the exploration of the deepest levels is an endless process. But all gnosis ends in mystery, which means that it all ends in God. God is a mystery in which all things have their ending.

But theosophical gnosis never succeeds in reaching God, for it is completely occupied with the world and cosmic evolution. Either the world has its end in God or the world itself is infinite. If its final end is in God then the ultimate solution of things is lost in mystery, which we must contemplate in the spirit of devout recollection. If, on the other hand, the world is infinite then there is no solution, no final mystery, and no place for religious awe and veneration. Theosophy in its popular literary expression asserts the infinitude of the world, regards God as a product of it, has no place for mystery, and simply means the possession of a secret. But when this secret is partly revealed we can see nothing in it but the various evolutions of infinite worlds, and the divinization of the world itself. There is neither human nor divine personality, but only an impersonal cosmic divinity. Theosophical gnosis refuses to recognize the antinomy inherent in the religious consciousness and puts in its place an evolutive continuity. Christianity is above all things historic, it frees the knowledge both of God and man from the crushing incubus of cosmic infinity, it asserts the existence of a unique beginning which cannot be repeated, on which history is based, and which differentiates it from nature.

Theosophy knows nothing of the mystery of that freedom, upon the basis of which the world rests. This is the reason why it fails to understand evil, which it considers simply from the angle of evolutionism. Steiner, at the beginning of his activity, wrote a book called *The Philosophy of Freedom*. But there is nothing about freedom in the book ; or, rather, the freedom of which it does treat is simply the result of necessity. Man comes to freedom through evolution, but he does not originate in freedom. Steiner had no conception of this initial liberty, and one cannot help noticing in his words the influence of Haeckel and Max Stirmer. For that matter no theosophical works really deal with this subject of initial freedom, because for them the human spirit is imprisoned in cosmic evolution. It is freed in the process, it is true, but this just goes to show that freedom is only the result of evolution. Man is not created in the divine image, and that is why freedom does not belong inherently to him as the initial and eternal principle of his being.

Man being the offspring of the universal process, necessity must be the force which drives him forward. Steiner affirms, it is true, that man must be free and that he will be so. But that is only a brief moment in the cosmic process, for man is doomed to disappear. He has not always existed and he will not always exist, his place will be taken by higher grades in the hierarchy ; a new aeon will be substituted for him. With this conception of being, in which the spiritual impersonal Ego is only one constituent element, one may well ask what need man has of freedom.

Because it denies freedom theosophy is bound to deny evil too. It has also adopted in this connection the evolutionist point of view, to which it sometimes adds a certain element of Manicheism. If freedom does not exist neither does evil. Theosophists waver between a naturalistic and evolutionist monism and a Manichean dualism. But monism and dualism are alike unable to solve the problem of evil or even to state it. In effect dualism also conceives evil from the naturalistic point of view, for it only regards it as a particular and independent sphere of being, as a base and lower form of nature. The spiritual interpretation of evil is always linked up with the idea of freedom. Evil has its origin in freedom and not in nature, and that is why it is irrational. That is the Christian point of view about it. But theosophy, on the other hand, derives evil from cosmic evolution and asserts that it can be overcome in the process. The problem of evil as well as that of man and of God is thus lost in cosmic infinity. Ultimately there is neither freedom nor evil, God nor man, but only the cosmic process, an unending succession of aeons, an aggregation and a dissolution of different universal planes. There is a potential infinity but not an actual one, a cosmic infinity but not one that is divine or eternal.

III

The fundamental difference between Christianity and theosophy is that while the former is the religion of grace, the latter ignores grace altogether. The theosophical conception of the world has upon it the imprint of law and not of grace. The path of development professed and practised by theosophists is exclusively one leading from the lower to the higher. The natural man makes superhuman efforts to reach the spiritual world ; he toils upwards in darkness, but no ray of light shines from above to illuminate the obscurity of his progress. Man travels towards the light through the shadows without assistance of any kind.

Human destiny is controlled by law and not by grace, and this naturalism even invades the very depths of the divine and spiritual life. Justice is identified with this naturalistic law, with the law of spiritual nature. Karma is precisely one of these laws of human destiny from which man cannot escape, before he has redeemed by endless reincarnations the consequences of an endless series of previous ones. The past extends indefinitely into the future and cannot be overcome. Karma is, on the one hand, the natural law of spiritual evolution which shows that human destiny is regulated by law and not by grace, and, on the other hand, it is the law of justice, the reward which has been deserved, the harvest which has been sown, the redemption of errors previously committed. For theosophy the natural law and the moral law are the same.

One can regard the prospect of this series of transmigrations in a gloomy, not to say sinister, light, yet the teachings of theosophy themselves are based upon an optimistic hypothesis which sees in the natural evolution of spiritual worlds the manifestation of an equitable law and the triumph of cosmic and divine justice. Theosophy does not envisage the incursion into the life of the universe of a free irrational evil ; and therefore sees no need to be delivered from it by grace. Everything has to be worked for, nothing is given freely. But grace is free, and is therefore incomprehensible so far as theosophy is concerned. The justice of Karma, by subordinating man to natural cosmic evolution, is also a denial of the superabundance of creation. Human nature is not called to create, but to develop, to evolve, to redeem the past in the future.

Christianity is radically different from theosophy in all this, for it is the religion of free and superabundant grace. In the mystery

285

of Redemption, the law and justice of Karma which control human destiny are transcended. Christianity is the religion of love ; it triumphs over the law of nature and that of justice. The man who has partaken of the mystery of Redemption, who has received Christ into himself, and who is of the seed of Christ, can no longer be subject to the law of Karma or be compelled to redeem the past through a series of endless transmigrations and a long judicial process in obedience to the law. The crucified thief who spontaneously and suddenly turned to Christ was no longer subject to the law of Karma ; he entered at once upon that spiritual path which he could never have reached according to the law of evolution and justice except by passing through an interminable series of incarnations. He who had lived a life of sin and crime was to be with Christ in Paradise, in the bosom of the Heavenly Father.

From the theosophical point of view the happy fate of the penitent thief is inconceivable, though theosophists do sometimes envisage the possibility of a mitigation of the law of Karma. But in what happened to this thief the law of Karma is abrogated. It is in this abolition of Karma and in the victory of grace over human destiny as subject to law that the deepest element in Christianity is revealed. Christianity frees man from the domination of time and temporal processes while theosophy maintains their hold upon him. There is no theosophical work in which there can be found even a statement of the problem of time and eternity, much less its solution. Theosophy seems to know the infinite while being ignorant of eternity. Man remains separated from God by the infinitude of the cosmic process ; he can have no immediate contact with eternity and the life of the divine, for he remains imprisoned in the life of the cosmos.

The Christian Church puts man face to face with God and opens up the way to communion with Him. This way is revealed above all in prayer. Here man stands before God without the intervention of any hierarchies or series of evolutions, he leaves time to enter eternity, he leaves behind him the life of the world to penetrate into the divine. The experience of communion with God

286

which is achieved in prayer cannot be justified on theosophical principles. Prayer has quite a different meaning in theosophy and it is only one of the forms which meditation can take.

By subordinating man to cosmic evolution, by refusing him the absolute light of eternity, theosophy renders the meaning or the Logos of the life of humanity and of the universe unintelligible. Evolution does not give us the clue to the meaning of things; on the contrary, evolution itself presupposes a meaning and a plan behind each succeeding temporal process. There must be light at the beginning, not simply the end, for man's path requires illumination. Theosophy leads man through a process of cosmic evolution the meaning of which is inexplicable, which remains obscure, and of which the issue is unknown. If there is no light except at the end of an infinite process of evolution then it cannot illuminate our way or explain its significance. Man thus finds himself the instrument of cosmic agencies which are quite unintelligible to him. The Logos, being Himself one of these agents, does not control the cosmic process in any way, and man has no possibility of communion with Him. But the meaning of things can only be grasped in eternity, it is incapable of being realized in that infinity where all meaning is lost. Man is refused a place in eternity and is left stranded in an infinite time series. The absence of grace in theosophy makes it impossible to find an intelligible meaning for the world and human life. For the sake of whom, or what, must man pursue the path of his evolution? The real fact is that theosophy has no place for revelation in its system, and this is the factor which determines all its peculiarities.

Christianity is less optimistic because it recognizes the irrational principle of evil in the world, and because it does not take for granted that the law of spiritual evolution is necessarily good. But it is an infinitely more joyous and more illuminating creed than theosophy because it believes in the good news of deliverance from evil and the coming of the Kingdom of God. The idea of this Kingdom has no part in theosophical doctrine. Eschatology is not dealt with either, for Karma, the endless series of reincarnations and evolutions, and even fusion with impersonal divinity, offer no solution of the final destiny of man. So far as theosophical thought is concerned, Redemption might as well be non-existent or at least have no more importance than it has in Hinduism, although theosophists live in the Christian era. For them the world remains still under the power of magic and necessity. Their conception of the world is magical, not mystical. Theosophy is a reaction in the Christian world towards pre-Christian spiritual principles, but as it is syncretistic in character it absorbs within itself a certain number of Christian elements, though inevitably distorting the Christian conception of man, freedom, and grace. Theosophists will naturally consider such an interpretation of their teaching as inaccurate. They will try to prove that theosophy expounds an ancient form of divine wisdom which is anterior to the whole evolution of our world, the science of the great initiates who directed it all. I know these objections already, but they will not make me admit that the meaning of the evolution of the universe is revealed to man in this way or that it possesses eternal significance. The relation of theosophy to ancient wisdom and the great initiates is an arbitrary one, of which presumably theosophists alone possess the secret.

IV

Theosophy and occultism, which are becoming increasingly popular, raise for Christians the problem of gnosis, and in this lies their positive significance. Christianity itself, or to put it more exactly Christendom, is responsible for their popularity. Theosophy has an attraction because of its denial of the doctrines of eternal punishment and hell which the moral consciousness of the modern man refuses to entertain. Another attractive feature in theosophy is the attempt it makes to resolve the problem of the origin, development, and destiny of the soul, a problem which has no fixed solution so far as the mind of the Church is concerned. Yet another attraction is the reconciliation which it effects between faith and knowledge, religion and science.

Theosophy and Gnosis

Those who think that the problem of gnosis can be solved by the official theology of the Church must go more deeply into the question. In the mind of the Church there is a strong agnostic element which is the result of its fight against Gnosticism. The conviction that there is an authorized gnosis, which is crystallized in the orthodox theology of the Church, and that all other forms of gnosis are heretical and forbidden, is the view which predominates officially in the Christian world. But in fact theology by its very methods and nature is not a form of gnosis. In theology results are known beforehand, and are not obtained by a process of knowledge, and theology is only appealed to in order to provide them with some kind of justification. In theology there is no complete doctrine of the cosmos and the doctrine of man is also one-sided. Cosmology has always been suspect in Christianity. The doctrine of Wisdom (*Sophia*) was an attempt to bridge this gap. It is curious to observe that all cosmological teaching in theology and Christian philosophy has in every age been regarded with a certain distrust. Official theology has preferred scientific positivism and a mechanistic theory of nature to any form of cosmological gnosis. Better a godless world than one regarded as divine.

In contemporary Christianity a concordat has been established between religion and science. The main current of Christian thought to-day regards our world as having lost its sense of the cosmos and even the very faculty of contemplating it. The mediæval world, like that of antiquity, had a vision of the cosmos and the hierarchy of nature. Modern man has lost this faculty of contemplating the cosmos, and nature, so far as he is concerned, is simply the object of scientific knowledge and of practical mechanical control.

The mind of the Church in our day is losing more and more its cosmic nature. The Church is beginning to be regarded as a community of believers, as an institution ; dogmas are being interpreted from the moralistic standpoint, and the psychological aspect of the sacraments is stressed at the expense of their cosmic significance. Nominalism is getting the better of realism in the Church's thinking.

The reality of the cosmos is disappearing through exclusive concentration upon the reality of psychical and social life. Religion is valued from the practical standpoint as a social, organizing, force. In theology the doctrine of the Church as the mystical body of Christ and as a cosmic and not merely a social entity is disappearing. Almost unnoticed a positivist spirit is beginning to overtake Christianity and the consciousness of the Church. This theological positivism is of a very peculiar nature, and is characterized by a complete lack of any mystical understanding of life. It is curious to observe that positivism in regard to the conception of nature has for a long time made its way into Christian thought and that it even had its roots in this soil.

The work of St. Basil the Great which deals with the interpretation of Genesis is an example of this sort of positivism *sui generis*. It is a naturalistic treatise which, allowing for the difference in scientific outlook between his age and ours, might be compared with the works of Haeckel. The positivism and naturalism of this particular work are very striking if one compares it with Boehme's *Mysterium Magnum*, which is also an interpretation of Genesis. In St. Basil we find descriptive physics, in Boehme cosmological gnosis. But this gnosis has not been recognized by the mind of the Church, which remains on the defensive in relation to its doctrines. In modern Christianity and science the knowledge which former generations possessed is lost, and the occultists are right in re-affirming it. But the question is, how can Christian thought conceive of the relations between Gnosticism and agnosticism?

It is only in our own day that the final consequences of the controversy between Gnosticism and agnosticism have come to light. The predominant official theology rejects both systems and tries to occupy a middle position. But this is not possible for long. The dogmatic thought of the Church has been elaborated in the course of its struggle with gnosticism and from this fact a number of things became inevitable. Antignosticism, for instance, became in some measure agnosticism. Knowledge of the mysteries of cosmic life was forbidden. The dogmatic work

of the Doctors of the Church and the œcumenical councils
cannot be called gnosis ; formulas were elaborated with an eye to
what was considered normative religious experience, and this was
accompanied by the refutation of erroneous doctrines. The mind
of the Church connected gnosis with the distortion of religious
experience.

The Christian Church had as its primary mission the rescue of
man from the domination of nature and his deliverance from the
power of demonic elements. The agnosticism of the Church
guarded the spirit of man from the power of the natural elements,
and of that cosmic infinity which threatened to engulf him. In all
this we can see a struggle for the preservation of man's image, as
well as for the freedom of his spirit. It is for this reason that we
must not regard the agnosticism of the Church with scorn, nor too
lightly criticize it. We must try and understand its significance.
The mind of the Church comes to terms more easily with a
mechanistic conception of nature and scientific positivism than it
does with Gnosticism and Gnostic cosmology, because it fears the
power of magic over the human soul and seeks to free his spirit
from it.

The ancient Gnostics were in many respects remarkable thinkers.
The Doctors of the Church were, without any sort of doubt, unjust
to them and they often distorted their ideas.[1] Valentinus was a
man of genius, a fact which may be discerned even in the very
biased treatment of him by St. Irenæus. But in Gnosticism, with
its still pagan attitude towards the cosmos, man was not liberated
from the power of spirits and demons, and remained as before
under the influence of magic. In fact the Gnostics were not really
Christian heretics but pagan initiates who had absorbed some
elements of Christian wisdom in a syncretistic manner. But they
never grasped the fundamental mystery of Christianity, the
redemption of man and the transfiguration of the lower into the
higher nature. In reality they had a static conception of the world
and could not conceive the true dynamic quality of Christianity.

[1] Cf. E. de Faye : *Gnostics and Gnosticism.*

Elements of evolutionism may be discovered among them in a rudimentary form ; they speak of epochs and periods of history. Their ideas have a certain interest but they are very far from the real dynamic of Christianity which asserts the transubstantiation or transfiguration of the lower natural elements. For the Gnostics the image of God and the image of man are dissolved in the cosmic process. The cosmos with its extremely complex hierarchic structure and its endless succession of aeons destroys not only man but God also.

The consciousness of the Church rose in revolt in the name of God and man against this form of Gnosticism and refused to allow man to become the prey of cosmic forces. Spiritual deliverance and liberation from these forces was the significant task achieved by the thought of the Church. To understand the mystery of the transfiguration of the lower into the higher it is necessary to free man from the law of the cosmos. Therefore until man was spiritually emancipated from the natural element and until his spiritual nature was united to God the Church limited the attempts made by Gnostics to penetrate the mysteries of cosmic life. Gnosticism exalted the pride of " spiritual " men and their presumed superiority over those who belonged to the " natural " and " carnal" category ; but they were unable to find out how to sanctify the soul and body and how to effect their transfiguration into the realm of the spirit.

In the history of man's intellectual development the result of a Church's agnosticism has appeared in the rise of science, of mechanical invention, and the mechanization of nature. Christianity liberated forces in man which then proceeded to turn against him. And even to-day those who remain true to the general mind of the Church often show a preference for positivist mechanics and physics, which, according to them, present no danger to Christianity, rather than to the Gnostic cosmology which appears to them a rival as before. But the linking up of Christianity with the mechanistic conception of nature is not in principle necessary.

We should be wrong in concluding that Christianity has no

place for gnosis and permits no kind of knowledge of cosmic mysteries. The dogmatic consciousness of the Church makes no such claims. Clement of Alexandria, Origen, St. Gregory of Nyssa, and St. Maximus the Confessor were Christian Gnostics. A Christian gnosis is possible. Christianity cannot countenance a return to the pagan conception of nature, to demonolatry, to the domination of magic over the human spirit, and to the dissolution of the image of man through the agency of the spirits of the elements.

It has been said, " Be ye wise as serpents and harmless as doves." Here the wisdom of the serpent, gnosis, has its justification. But this wisdom is not incompatible with simplicity of heart. Christianity denies that man can come to God and to divine mysteries by the way of a ceaseless evolution of thought ; it asserts that in the search for divine knowledge man suffers a spiritual catastrophe which changes both his consciousness and his thinking, that he goes through the experience of faith in which the world of invisible things is revealed. In this experience the possibility of knowledge is opened up. Faith does not deny gnosis, but it prepares the way for it through spiritual experience.

This question presents itself to us who are members of the Orthodox in a manner totally different from that in which it arises in Roman Catholicism. For the latter God may be known not only through revelation, but also through natural human reason. This idea is the corner-stone of Thomism. It is a form of rationalism which refuses to admit that so far as the reason is concerned a contradiction is involved in all knowledge of God. The Vatican Council pronounced an anathema on all who affirm that the one true God, our Creator and Master, cannot be known through created things by the natural light of human reason. This decree which condemns fideism, and Catholic thinkers such as Pascal and Joseph de Maistre, establishes in the centre of Catholic thought a rationalistic naturalism and a mode of thought about God dominated by rational categories. Natural theology is thus recognized as obligatory.

For Orthodoxy the question arises in a different form, because it has no compulsory rational doctrine like Thomism. This rationalistic naturalism is the product of agnosticism and it is opposed to gnosis in every form. God and the mystery of life are unknowable, but in nature and creation we can find proofs of the existence of God by rational and naturalistic means. A *modus vivendi* is thus established between revelation and the natural knowledge of God, between religion and science. This concordat between the natural and supernatural orders does not, however, increase the sphere of gnosis, but on the contrary restricts it ; it is the result of a lack of faith in the possibility of the illumination of reason and of a form of knowledge in the Spirit which is divine-human. But if a Christian gnosis is possible it can only be a spiritual and mystical form of knowledge and not a natural or rational one.

The Orthodox East has expended a less intense energy in the sphere of thought than has the Catholic West. Orthodoxy has not elaborated a precise system of doctrine and the East is more inclined to Gnosticism than the West, for it has a greater belief in the possibility of mystical gnosis, often regarded as heretical in the West. The Doctors of the Eastern Church are more Gnostic than those of the West, and thus Christian gnosis can more easily develop on the spiritual soil of Orthodoxy than on that of Catholicism. Russian religious and philosophical movements are evidence of this. But Christian agnosticism, which is in integral relationship with Catholic rationalism, was not without its justification.

But a day may come when this kind of agnosticism will disappear from Christianity, for it is becoming a danger. It has meant what is virtually a pragmatic ignorance. Man's ability to receive impressions must be limited so that he is neither deafened nor blinded by the thunder and lightning of the cosmos. We are protected by our insensibility and lack of perception from all that might prove dangerous to us, and for the revelation of which we are as yet unprepared. Lack of knowledge can be a safeguard as well as knowledge. If we could see and know everything in the world which is at present hid from us, we should be unable to stand the strain and the elemental forces of the world would prove our undoing. Clairvoyance is dangerous and is meant only for the few, for it demands considerable spiritual preparation. Man would not be able to bear the vision of the *aura* which surrounds various beings.

But a time may come when ignorance may be more dangerous than knowledge and the receptive faculties of the senses are. The pragmatism of ignorance may cease to be valuable, and it is then that the pragmatism of knowledge comes into its own. Knowledge is useful in so far as it is a protection against the hostile forces of the world. It is not only the mechanical knowledge of nature which provides us with useful inventions which is indispensable to us, but also the knowledge of the inner life of the cosmos and of the structure of the world. Man must be spiritually prepared for it; he must acquire the wisdom of Christ, which is not merely that rational and natural intelligence which has the sanction of the Vatican Council, but rather an illuminated type of intelligence. Man will then no longer run the risk of dissolution by the cosmic elements or of falling into the hands of the demons. Christian gnosis rests upon the acquiring of Christ's widsom, and on a divine-human knowledge in and through Christ. False gnosis must be banished by the true gnosis of Christ. That is what the Christian mystics tell us. The time has come when science can no longer remain neutral ; or, rather, when it will have to become either Christian or a department of black magic.

We find in theosophy certain ancient truths and elements of knowledge. Theosophy is connected with occultism, which is not a modern movement but has a long tradition behind it going back right through the history of the development of man's spirit. The so-called occult sciences are only a form of charlatanism. The sphere of the occult and magic, in so far as it is real, belongs to the natural world. These secret forces, which have yet to be studied by science, act both upon man and the cosmos. In the course of the last few decades modern science has turned more and more to the study of occult phenomena in man and in nature. The sphere of the subconscious, of which the ancients were well aware but which seemed closed to more modern generations, is now being gradually opened up. Science is beginning to admit into the sphere of its researches magical phenomena which were for a long time regarded as mere survivals of superstition and imposture. Du Prel, who stood for a scientific occultism, said long ago that science must inevitably return to the truths of magic and that magic is just unknown physics.[1] Such phenomena as telepathy, clairvoyance, animal magnetism, somnambulism, materialization, etc. are becoming the objects of scientific analysis. Science is compelled to recognize certain facts which it had previously denied. The Society of Psychical Research in England has for a long time studied these facts and numerous discoveries have been made in this sphere by psychiatrists and neuropathists.[2]

The predominant opinion in official circles which puts final limits to the scope of knowledge, and would like to determine beforehand what can or cannot form part of experience, is no longer tenable, and we can now see the dogmatic, not to say superstitious, character of such a point of view. At the present day we realize that the field of experience has no limits, and there is no longer any faith in the sort of restrictions which have their origin in rationalistic empiricism. We have avoided accepting in quite an artificial manner a whole category of occult phenomena, which were recognized in earlier periods of history when the mind was unclouded by the limitations of rationalism. Science has had to see the horizon of its researches retreat indefinitely and to study all sorts of occult and miraculous phenomena, however incredible they might appear. The nature of the universe and that of man are infinitely richer than science believed it was in the period of the " illuminati." The sphere of the subconscious is definitely a part of scientific research and this sphere is inexhaustible.

The whole of man's creative powers come from the subconscious.

[1] See du Prel's book, *Die Magie als Naturwissenschaft*, in which he stoutly insists that science is the product of magic.

[2] Particularly by the school of Freud, Coué, and Baudouin.

The development of science in this direction confirms the statement of occult tradition. Primitive magic has not been finally crystallized in the science which it has produced, for it possesses its own peculiar line of development. Civilized man, as well as the savage, has his magic, and this has a line of development parallel to that of science. But the time is coming when these parallel lines will converge and when science, having reached its final perfection, will again be one with magic. At the present day we are actually assisting at this process. The popularity of occultism is only a symptom of it.

Occultism, in so far as it means an enlargement of the sphere of our knowledge of man and the world, is reconcilable in principle with Christianity, which is really no more opposed to it than it is to science. Occultism is no more in opposition to Christianity than are physics and psychology. But there is a strong opposition and conflict between it and Christianity whenever occultism claims to be a substitute for religion. Occultism as a religion is indeed at the opposite pole to Christianity. The same may be said of spiritism, which may either be a scientific study or a false religion, as with Alan Kardec. So far as Christian thought is concerned this pseudo-religious occultism is exposed to the same objections as the teaching of the Gnostics was. Our knowledge of God, our Christology, our conception of the function of man cannot be the result of occult knowledge. The occult sciences have made researches into the hidden forces of nature but they cannot resolve the final problems of being. We see in theosophical contemplation of cosmic life the dangerous side of an occultism which has passed beyond its proper field.

Theosophy gives us the anatomy of man and of the cosmos, and by dissecting the living, organic, whole is reduced to contemplating the world as if it were nothing but a corpse. There is nothing vital in theosophical knowledge. Life disappears at the first touch of those theosophists and occultists who claim to have knowledge of the final mystery of things. Their observations are confined to mere fragments of existence and they have no vision of it as a whole. Theosophy claims to be a vast synthesis, whereas in fact it is an

297

analysis ; it performs an autopsy on the living tissues of the body of the universe and then proceeds to arrange them in order. Its elaborate schematizations, which its disciples must learn by rote, smack of the dissecting room and the dead-house. Theosophy only gives us the mortal remains of the world after they have been completely dissected and analyzed. It knows nothing of the mystery of the living whole. Theosophy is not a synthesis of religion, philosophy, or science, but rather a confused jumble in which neither true religion, philosophy, or science are to be found. Occultism must be transferred completely to the sphere of science where it will enlarge the field of research. But religion can in no way be dominated by it. True Christian gnosis presupposes a positive religious basis and its effective power is due to the fact that it has its origin in genuine revelations of the spiritual world ; it unites religion, philosophy, and science in an effective manner without subordinating faith to a pseudo-scientific outlook.

Man's consciousness and personality can and must be developed ; and with this enlargement of their scope there will come a new interpretation of nature which will cease to be regarded from a static point of view. But to affirm the existence of a cosmic consciousness also brings with it certain dangers. An emancipation of personality which permits of it reaching out into the whole cosmos may mean the loss of its proper limitation or its absorption by cosmic infinity. Thus Christian thought can only admit a cosmic gnosis in which the nature of personality remains exactly defined, and in which it will be neither confused nor dissociated by this infinity. The problem of gnosis, so far as the Christian consciousness is concerned, is two-sided. To forbid gnosis means to put a premium on a false gnosis and to encourage theosophy in which a number of scattered truths are given a highly artificial synthesis. False theosophy then must be countered by a genuine Christian form of theosophy.

Occultism is right in insisting that nature is not a mechanism but a hierarchy of spirits ; it is also right in denying the uniqueness, isolation, and stagnation of our own aeon. Not only positivism but even the consciousness of the Church in some measure identifies the universe, and creation with the aeon of our own world. But actually there are no precise limits separating what goes before from what follows.

In the dawn of universal history nature was less materialized and condensed than it has been subsequently in the course of the evolution of our aeon. Occult traditions tell us of this incandescent state of the world, and include truths which have been forgotten both by religion and science. At the beginning of the life of our universe man's consciousness was far from fully awake, and corresponding to this condition there was an absence of precise limits between our own world and others. Even the Akashic Chronicle contains certain elements of truth in this connection. The "rigidity" of material nature is not the final truth about it. In Christian thinking the materialist conception of nature will inevitably undergo a radical change. At the present moment men are already beginning to doubt the mechanistic view. Occultism has lost its way in the contemplation of living nature, but the problem which it states is a right one.

The philosophers and theosophists of the Renaissance were in closer contact with the mysteries of nature than our own generation. Boehme considers that the life of the cosmos proceeds in terms of the categories of good and evil, sin and redemption, light and darkness, that is to say, in terms of spiritual categories ; Paracelsus, who was full of profound ideas, had already pursued this line of thought, and we should do well to have frequent recourse to him and to Boehme. Their theosophy and their cosmology are infinitely superior to those of Mrs. Besant or Steiner. The cosmos can only be conceived as a living organism. We must be able to see the spirit in nature and nature in the spirit, the objective in the subjective, the natural in the spiritual, and the cosmic in the anthropological. Cosmology has always been based on the inner identity of spirit and nature, that is to say, on a conception of nature which regards it as a spiritual phenomenon.

Russian sophiology is an attempt to restore to Christianity a cosmic consciousness, and to make room for cosmology and cosmosophy among the things of Christ. It is valuable as a symptom, for it tries to overcome the positivism of the Church. It is one form of the expression of Christian Platonism, the penetration into the consciousness of the Church of the world of Ideas, of the doctrine of the universal soul, and of Platonic realism which is opposed to the nominalist degeneracy of Christianity. It must be recognized that the official mind of the Church does not believe in the reality of the cosmos and that it looks upon the world from a positivist angle because of its adoption of a moralistic interpretation of Christianity. The cosmic nature of the Church is something utterly beyond the grasp of such a type of thought, which only sees its social implication. But the characteristics of sophiology are such that the problem of the cosmos threatens finally to overshadow completely the problem of man. Human freedom and creative activity disappear. Nevertheless, to-day the main religious problem is that of man, not of *Sophia* or the cosmos. Sophiology must be linked to the problem of anthropology. Boehme is in this sense the great precursor, and for our age is of more value than Plato. His doctrine is also less pantheistic than that of the adepts of Russian sophiology, and we may do well to recall here briefly what has been said about this doctrine of Boehme's and try to draw our conclusions from it.

Sophia is the Virgin of man, his *Virginität*.[1] Man is " male-female " in character as long as his Virgin remains with him, that is, when he is himself a virgin, chaste and integral. The Fall of " male-female " man means the loss of the Virgin who returns to Heaven, while on earth woman appears in order to redeem his sin through motherhood. Feminine nature everlastingly attracts and beguiles the masculine principle once it is bereft of its integrality, and the former tries to unite itself to the latter but without ever achieving satisfaction. Man comes under the sway of the sexual element and is in bondage to natural necessity. Furthermore the

[1] The doctrine of *Sophia* in Boehme is to be found in all his principal writings.

loss of the Virgin means for him the loss of liberty. The natural world is not virginal and it is not the wise female element which controls it. But the heavenly Virgin comes again into this natural world in the form of the Virgin Mary and from her is born in the spirit the New Adam in whom a wise virginity and a holy motherhood are to triumph over the wrong kind of femininity. The veneration of *Sophia*, of the heavenly Virgin, is closely linked with that of the Mother of God. From her the God-Man is born, in Whom, for the first time in the history of the natural world, absolute virginity and integrity, that is to say, " male-female " humanity, appears.

The universal soul is feminine and it is also fallen, but as in the case of the human soul the restoration of virginity is possible. The Virgin Mary appears as the virginal principle, that is, of eternal beauty. *Sophia* is beauty. Beauty is the heavenly Virgin. The illumination and transfiguration of the natural created world is the manifestation of Beauty. And when art, in the widest sense of the word, penetrates the beauty of the cosmos, it sees beyond the ugliness of the natural world the world's virginity, the divine idea of what it should be. But the wisdom of the world is bound up with the virginity of man. Russian sophiology seems to deny that man is at the centre of the world and that the cosmos is in him ; it is therefore not a really virile form of doctrine, for it places the masculine spirit in subordination to the feminine soul.

We must return in some entirely new way to a sense of the cosmos. The task of Christian gnosis is to establish an ideal balance between theosophy, cosmosophy, and anthroposophy. For mysticism, occultism, and religion do exist side by side in human consciousness. Mysticism is immediate communion with God, the contemplation of God and union with Him. Occultism is union with the secret forces of the cosmos and it is also cosmic development. Religion is the attitude of man towards God in an organized form, it is the hierarchical and normative method of communion with Him. Boehme, more than all the other Gnostics, knew how to unite in himself the mystical, occult, and religious moments ; thus his gnosis, in spite of certain errors, is nearest to a true Christian gnosis. Esotericism and exotericism do not exclude one another ; exotericism must be comprised within esotericism.

Theosophy is religious syncretism. Similar movements have arisen before in periods of spiritual crisis. Fragments of ancient knowledge and occult tradition are combined with a modern outlook and contemporary naturalism and rationalism. The most distressing feature of theosophy and anthroposophy is their presumption, the claim to a knowledge which they do not possess, the taking up of a particularist attitude towards their own writings, and the certainty with which they assert that the uninitiated cannot understand their teachings. The spiritual attitude of theosophists is not Christian ; it is self-sufficient. Theosophy attracts people by the idea of the brotherhood of men and peoples which it cannot realize. Nevertheless movements of thought of this kind are always the precursors of real spiritual illumination.

CHAPTER NINE

Spiritual Development and the Eschatological Problem

I

IT is difficult to discuss certain questions even in principle because of a certain association of ideas which prevent us from grasping the exact nature of the problem. Mankind is by no means free in its thinking, and we are biased by emotion. Thus it comes about, for example, that religious thought refuses to make an impartial examination of the problem of spiritual development, because the very idea of a " development " recalls by association the particular theories of evolution and progress which were current in the nineteenth century. These theories of evolution and progress have made it almost impossible for us to grasp the idea of the creative development of the spirit. The introduction of the principle of development into religious life is characterized as " modernism " and is regarded as a compromise with contemporary non-religious evolutionism. But it is essential to make the following point : one may reject the theory of evolution but it is impossible to deny the fact of development in the world. It is necessary also to make a distinction between the development of spirit and the evolution of nature. We rightly criticize that theory of progress in which may be seen a false religion seeking to substitute itself for Christianity.[1]

But it is necessary to remember that the idea of religious progress

[1] I have made a radical criticism of the theory of progress in my book, *The Meaning of History*.

303

is Christian in origin and that it is only a secularized and distorted version of the Messianic idea of the Christian search for the Kingdom of God. The idea of progress belongs to the sphere of religious teleology which regards history as having an absolute meaning and goal. Seen from the angle of positivism this idea is in reality void of all interest and presents an obvious contradiction. Positivism has no room for a conception of evolution save one which has neither goal nor meaning. This is a long-established and elementary truth. But insufficient attention is paid to the fact that the idea of progress, that is to say, of movement, of the march of history towards an absolute and supreme goal, has only been made possible by Christianity, and that the idea could never have arisen in ancient Greece.

History moves towards a central event of absolute importance, namely, the Coming of Christ. And from this point it moves further towards the climax which is to end world history, namely, the Second Coming of the Saviour. This is the factor which determines the creation of the various periods of world history and spiritual progress. It is in this way that the inner spiritual dynamic of history is brought into being. For history is not merely an external evolution without meaning, that is to say, a re-division of the elements of the world in which there is no absolute value ; in world history there is a dynamic quality of meaning, namely the Logos, and this determines its inner movement. Christianity is Messianic and eschatological, that is to say, dynamic and progressive in the spiritual or deepest sense of the word. It is a movement towards a goal in which all things are resolved. It is not a process of evolution in the modern sense of the word for it is not subject to a development determined by natural necessity. Christianity has not appeared as a static and immutable truth requiring a definitive form ; it came into the world as a dynamic truth, unfolding itself irresistibly. Christ was not immediately recognized, nor the dogmatic system of the Church suddenly revealed ; neither the liturgy nor the organization of the Church were complete from the beginning. The Church of Christ is itself the result of a development

and it evolved from the primitive eschatological idea of the
Kingdom of God ; it went through various stages and periods
of development. This is a truth which must be regarded as finally
established and there is no reason to be afraid of it. It does not
affect the absolute character of Christianity in any way, nor does it
rule out the possibility of further development.

The Christian revelation contains innumerable potential riches
capable of actualization in history and in the world. Each word
of the Gospel is but the hidden spring of an infinite process of
development. If Christianity in the past has been to a very high
degree dynamic, it can be so in the future too. An arrest in its
dynamic quality is only the effect of spiritual sloth and weakness.
There can be, and indeed there must be, a dogmatic development
in the Church, as Cardinal Newman and Solovyov so rightly
insisted. Every question has not yet been settled and Christianity
is not a finished product, nor will it be finished till the end of
time ; its fulfilment corresponds to the coming of the Kingdom
of God. But if we are looking for this Kingdom of God and
moving towards it, we cannot be in a static condition. The existence of a static Orthodoxy or Catholicism is a pure fiction, a piece
of mere auto-suggestion, and it arises from the objectification and
" absolutization " of what are simply temporary periods in Church
life.

When there is no sense of creative mission in the Church,
spiritual decadence follows. All men of marked activity in the
Christian world were " modernists " in their time, though this
does not mean that they accommodated themselves to the spirit of
their time or to its current thought, but rather that they attempted
to solve the essentially creative problems of their particular epoch.
St. Thomas Aquinas was a modernist in his time and so was St.
Athanasius the Great. Modernism [1] in Christianity, that is to say,
conformity to a given spiritual period, is always connected with

---

[1] I use the word " modernism " not in the specific sense of Catholic
Modernism, which is quite foreign to me, but in the sense of a possibility of
innovation.

the really deep currents of contemporary life and not with its superficialities ; at the same time it links the future to the past. The very idea of development or progress involves the existence of different religious periods and varying degrees of revelation. Even the distinction between the Old and the New Covenants, between paganism and Christianity, shows the existence of a true spiritual development. The Gnostic idea of aeons is itself a fruitful one and makes possible a philosophy of history. The coming of Christ divides world history into two main periods of fundamental importance, into two cosmic aeons each capable of a variety of subdivision. But this very fact, this original phenomenon of the process of universe, implies the existence of a spiritual development and a dynamic process in history. The static interpretation of the world makes Christ's coming, which is a cosmogonic fact, completely incomprehensible and impossible, and it springs from a static conception of the structure of consciousness.

The static ontology or metaphysics to which theology is wedded is the result of allowing the mentality of a particular period to become stereotyped as if it possessed immutable significance. But the real nature of the spiritual life cannot be grasped when it is approached from this angle, because the spiritual life means dynamic development, not in the evolutionist sense of a redistribution of purely external elements, but in an interior, spiritual, creative sense. There is no immutable, universal, order, established for all eternity as the upholders of a static system of philosophy suppose. Being is life and spirit. Spirit is fire, a kindling of life which is eternally active. The static conception of the universe regards the world as nothing better than an extinct volcano.

Heraclitian not Parmenidean

But the creation of the world is not finished, and man co-operates actively in the process, the results of which we see in the form of a development. The Old Testament gives us an incomplete view of the creation of the world ; but because of its limitations, it regarded this view as representing the whole truth, and it thought of creation as a completed process. This cosmogony has been inherited by Christianity and it is a difficult task to effect a separation. The biblical cosmogony leaves no room for the mystery of freedom or for creative development, for it always regards the world as a mystery which is fulfilled and as an order incapable of change.

But a creative development in the world is possible because freedom springs from a deep and ineffable source, and because man bears the image of his Creator, and of His freedom, and creative energy. Creativity arises from the deep potentialities of spirit and freedom. Development implies potential existence. But it is a very different kind of development from that which Darwin, Spencer, or Haeckel envisaged. It is not a naturalistic evolution, but a development which proceeds from the spirit. Such free development has indeed nothing in common with that which derives from necessity, for it is creative rather than determined action. It is only the outward expression of that which transpires within ; for there is a creative expansion which has its origin in freedom. There is no universal law of development or progress. The optimistic theory of a continuity of development and universal progress is fundamentally naturalistic and unspiritual, nor can it be reconciled with the freedom of the human spirit and of creation.

There is in the world a basic irrational freedom which is anterior to it and that is why there is bad as well as good development. The triumph of the divine principle of good in the world is not achieved by gradual stages. The good is the result of freedom, not of necessity. Various elements, principles, and organisms, taken in isolation, develop and progress, but development and progress are not an obligatory law for the life of the universe as a whole.

The theories of evolution and progress which predominated in the nineteenth century simplified the problem too much and interpreted it in a spirit of naturalistic optimism. This optimism entirely misunderstood the connection between real evolution, freedom, and creativity and entirely lost touch with the authentic sources of spiritual development. Evolutionism by ignoring the subject of evolution virtually denies the existence of that which evolves. It is a static conception and throws into the past the hierarchy of nature as we see it to-day by arranging the various degrees of this hierarchy in chronological order ; it fails to grasp the mystery of genesis. The savages, as well as the animals and the plants, are our contemporaries. In the dawn of universal life everything was quite different and infinitely more mysterious.

The various periods in the life of humanity and of the human spirit do not necessarily point to a steady spiritual improvement or to the progressive realization of the Kingdom of God in the world. Even the passing of the world from the pre-Christian to the Christian era does not in itself constitute a moral improvement ; it does not mean that men have conquered evil and are gradually nearing the Kingdom of God. It proclaims the coming of a new spiritual epoch for man, the revelation of new spiritual forces, a fresh struggle between good and evil, and the emergence of a new good ; but it also means fresh evil. The ancients were more peaceful, balanced, and more resigned to fate than are the people of the Christian era, who have lost the measured harmony and classical forms of expression which the Greeks once possessed. Many things have been discovered and there has been progress, but on the other hand some things have been forgotten and there has also been regression. Certain ancient forms of knowledge have been lost, and parallel to this new forms have been developed about which the ancients knew nothing. Several faculties which men enjoyed in antiquity seem to have disappeared completely for ever. Man to-day appears to be less capable of endurance, less virile, and more fearful than he was in earlier ages. In fact we are faced with a very complex process and we cannot regard it simply as a gradual growth of what is of positive value coupled with the disappearance of what is negative.

The spiritual development of man proceeds amidst contradiction and opposition. It is a tragic process which neither the theory of evolution nor that of progress can comprehend. Freedom is the constant background of spiritual development and it complicates the whole process to an infinite degree. We can only see the external aspect of evolution, but within the depths of the spiritual life there is a creative process at work in which freedom moves now towards the good, now towards evil, now to God, now to Satan. We can estimate the complexity of all this by studying the development of modern history and the fate of Christianity. Deep changes are taking place, a new period is beginning, there is spiritual development, but there is no such thing as progress, in the nineteenth-century sense of the word. Progress is inevitably accompanied by regress, and evolution by dissolution. A new and more refined type of spirituality is beginning to arise, while spirituality, generally speaking, is on the wane and the world is becoming more materialistic. But the universe, the creation of God, is a process of becoming, an absolute which is becoming, as opposed to an absolute which is.

II

Is it possible, then, to speak of a law of evolution ? This law certainly does exist in the sense in which it is employed by those who believe in a naturalistic evolutionism. True evolution, as we have already remarked, is determined from within not from without ; its starting-point is spirit and freedom, not nature and necessity. Behind the external aspect of evolution there is a creative process ; but this process is subject to no law. Nevertheless something analogous to the dialectic principle might be applied to development of all kinds. It is in this way that the method by which all growth and enrichment in the life of the universe takes place is discovered.

The source of this development lies in the experience of what has been lived through. The fundamental truth about the mystery of development is expressed in the aphorism of Léon Bloy which was quoted in the introduction of this book, namely, " There is an end to suffering, but no end to the experience of having suffered." Suffering may be overcome, but one can never forget the fact that one has suffered. Every experience is an enrichment, even if enrichment involves the negation of this experience. Thus the experience of evil when it has been overcome and unmasked is an

enrichment which conduces to the realization of a higher good.
The experience of the world when it has been victoriously sur-
mounted brings in like manner a higher quality of faith. The
experience of contradiction too can lead in the same way to a higher
unity. After the experience of revolution it is impossible to return
to the state which preceded it. After absorbing the philosophy of
Kant, I am incapable of adopting a pre-Kantian system. Similarly
the effects of humanism cannot be eliminated and romanticism
makes the return to ancient classicism impossible. Above all the
experience of freedom cannot lead me to accept necessity.

Unity is achieved through contradiction. Without experience
there is no movement, no life, for movement cannot be constrained
by *a priori* standards. A refusal to learn the lessons of experience
means a denial of development in the world, and an affirmation of
its static immutability. We must " try the spirits ". Man and the
world have to pass through great times of testing, for such is the
method of their development. The real value of German idealism,
with its strong mystical foundation, lies in its revelation of the
dialectic of the spirit. The meaning of the experience of contraries
has a definite relation to the problematics of Christian thought ;
it is the problem of overcoming the original naïveté of the religious
life, of relating sound knowledge to unshakable faith.

But does Christianity recognize the function of such testing, or
is it a static *a priori* system, which is unrelated to creative development ? I am well aware that the static point of view is predominant
in Christianity, that the experience of movement is regarded with
suspicion and fear because of its possible fatal consequences, and I
suffer personally as a result of this attitude. But this suffering is
also an experience from which something must necessarily result.
In the history of Christianity there has been too much of the policy
of not offending the weaker brethren. Creative development has
been held up for the sake of " these little ones ". But the " little
ones " have not been safeguarded in practice, for there is no power
on earth capable of finally restricting experience or inhibiting life,
and the attempt to do so has merely resulted in the ossification of

Christianity. As a matter of fact it is precisely " these little ones " whom a static conception of Christianity has caused to stumble, by its hostility towards every fresh movement in life. It is impossible to get away from fresh experiences and contradictions by trying to put up artificial barriers ; it is impossible to keep mankind in a state of somnolent, traditional, inertia.

Development in the world is inevitable because the creative freedom of man stirs within it, because human experience becomes more complex, and because the contradictions of life must emerge. The world is not a system isolated in itself, for the infinite is operative within it at every point, and this leads to fresh experience, continually bringing to light fresh contradictions which must be overcome in experience. The inexhaustible riches of the infinite require illumination. Man's destiny is to explore the infinite and make it intelligible, to bring light to bear upon the mysterious origin of things. Development is determined by the existence of an initial void. Man is not predestined to remain within a static order which has been established for ever ; his mission is to experience forces of all kinds so that he may exercise his freedom. What sense is there in freedom if it is to remain inactive, and if it is not to reveal itself in every possible way ? Freedom brings us to experience, to the test of contradiction, that is to say, to creative action and spiritual development. The denial of creation and spiritual development in Christianity always implies the denial of freedom. The system of St. Thomas Aquinas is in reality forced to reject freedom as being an imperfection ; it is compelled to reduce everything to the necessity of truth and, consequently, to refute creative development.

We approach the heart of the problem of development in Christianity as well as that of freedom if we look at it from the point of view of the relation between God and creation. Does God desire that man and the world should experience their freedom, and reveal their powers in experience, or does He intend that creation should observe His laws in a spirit of formal obedience ? The solution of this question depends upon our breaking free from a servile conception of God and of our attitude to Him, as well as from all traces of idolatry. An idolatrous religion based upon fear means a denial of creative development, a fear of all fresh experience, and the creation of barriers which thwart the processes of life.

Static conceptions in metaphysics and ethics are exoteric in character and only reflect a passing experience, a transitory period in the history of Christianity. But man, because of his limitations, erects the relative and temporal into the absolute and eternal. That is one of the forms of self-affirmation and human self-sufficiency which accepts its own limitations and is afraid of being lost in the infinite and the spiritual. Creative activity is precisely a transition from isolation and limitation. The infinite and spiritual are esoteric ; the finite and the limited are exoteric. The static conception of the world belongs to the same category, and so does the evolutionist conception in the sense in which it is affirmed by positivism and modern science. Evolutionism denies liberty, creative activity, and new experiences lived out in the depths of being, in exactly the same way as they are denied by the static conception of the world.

Hegel gets nearer the truth in his theory of an evolution by way of contradictions and their resolution in a higher phase of development ; but his theory of the natural development of spirit involves an isolation or naturalization of the spiritual life in its mysterious and infinite profundity. But the naturalization of spiritual life is always exoteric and is never really profound. We can express the truth about development only in terms of spiritual experiences and not in metaphysical categories. It is impossible to elaborate a metaphysic of development, for it always means a limitation of spiritual experience, which is by nature unfathomable and infinite in character while at the same time possessing a quality of intimacy. The one incontrovertible truth is this : whatever experience may have been, whether good or bad, it is never useless, and it always forms part of the next stage of development. Man is never put to the test without results, and there can never be a return to an earlier stage. We must go forward all the time, and even reaction itself in the spiritual life is innovation and not repetition.

III

Christian thought is concerned not only with the development of the individual, but also with his historical, social, and universal development. Christianity itself is a stage, and that the most important one, in universal revelation. Our world is one of the phases of being and of basic and original life itself. Only from an exoteric point of view can this world be conceived as summing up the entire universe and the whole of divine creation. According to mediaeval thought, notably in the circles connected with St. Thomas Aquinas and Dante, the idea of order (*ordo*) concealed the idea of development and of the creative process. The world was regarded as an eternal order created by God.

To-day the idea of development has taken the place of the idea of order and of an immutable cosmic hierarchy. To reach the complete truth the idea of a cosmic hierarchy must be reconciled with that of development. The world is not only the cosmos, it is also cosmogony ; our universal aeon is a cosmogonic process, and even the world has anthropogonic aeons which exist not only in the history of the universal religious consciousness, but also in the history of Christianity. The Coming of Christ into the world is the central fact of anthropogony, the flowering-time of humanity. But man's self-consciousness was not immediately revealed in Christianity, and it too had to pass through stages of development, nor is there any reason to suppose that this process is finished. Development in time exists, were it only because the fulness of truth cannot be comprised within time (or can only be partially disclosed) and requires eternity for its expression. Christianity has not been finally actualized and has immense potentialities. The conservative element in Christianity cannot tolerate even the idea of a potential creative energy, because, so far as it is concerned, everything has been finally actualized. Thus the content of Christianity is impoverished, and it almost looks as if men wanted to limit it for fear of its possibilities. Our task is certainly not to adapt Christianity to modern naturalistic evolutionism, as certain

313

" modernists " do, but rather to discover in its depths a principle independent of development.

If the Christian Church is God-humanity then the new experience which is revealed in the struggles of the spirit, and in the contradictions by which human freedom is tested, must have their place in a new Christian era. It is in this way that man is revealed, and is called by God to reveal himself freely. But what makes this question particularly difficult is our ignorance as to what comes from God and what from Satan. For the whole mystery of freedom lies precisely in this, that it may be directed either towards God or against Him. And modern history is singularly complex in this respect.

The creative development of the spirit and the free exercise of man's powers cannot be understood from a juridical point of view as the attempt to reach certain external standards or as submission to an established order of eternal significance. It must be conceived as the free co-operation of man with the work of God. In creative spiritual development there is a new principle which means an offering of human freedom to God, an offering, moreover, which God expects from us. The life of the spirit is not the eternal prolongation of the natural order, but a creative and dynamic process. Spiritual development is possible because there is freedom. The origin of development is not to be found in transcendent being conceived as an immutable standard, but in the void (*Ungrund*) which requires illumination and from which the light comes. An intellectual conception of the nature of spirit means a denial of the possibility of development, because it tends to recognize the established order as final. It regards development simply as a species of quantitative transposition which occurs in the material world in the form of a purely external evolution. But development in the true sense of the word is spiritual growth, the bringing to birth of those hidden forces which lie hidden in the inner depths of existence, not a movement on the plane of the exterior world.

In the religious life there is clearly no evolution in the modern sense of the word, for Christianity does not evolve and there is no

314

progress in the sense of a process which is necessarily good directed towards some absolute and supreme end in the future. Spiritual development is dynamic in character and has its origin in freedom, not in necessity. So far as the theory of evolution is concerned, development is a natural necessity. According to the theory of progress the development of man is the moral necessity of the progressive realization of a fixed standard, of an inevitable movement towards the final goal. But this is a denial both of the freedom of the spirit and of creation. Development in Christianity is not an inevitable process; it is a manifestation of the freedom of the spirit which comes from within, a penetration of the natural world by the spiritual. Spiritual development in the world manifests itself, moreover, as the intervention of a transcendent principle. Spiritual development is not an immanent revelation of nature which is self-inspired. In the immanent processes of nature there is only a redistribution of existing matter and energy. Spiritual development means the victory of spirit over nature, which can only be the result of liberty and not of necessity.

The hope of development in Christianity lies in the possibility of overcoming the dominating influence of the natural world and in a fuller manifestation of the spirit in freedom. The denial of the possibility of development in Christianity is the result of subjecting the spirit to natural forms, and shows ignorance of the true nature of spirit, which is that of fire. Heraclitus, Jacob Boehme, and Dostoievsky understood this truth about the nature of spirit better than many others. There is more in what they have to say than in Parmenides, St. Thomas Aquinas, Hegel, or Spencer. Nevertheless for Christian thought the primary idea is not that of progress or development, but of illumination and transfiguration.

IV

The spiritual world is like a torrent of fire in its free creative dynamism. But in the natural world the movement of the spirit is retarded and takes the form of evolution. A true creative movement is always vertical in direction, a movement from the depths to the heights. It is only projected and objectified as a horizontal line upon the surface of things. Moreover the source of creative development is always to be found in the depths of the spirit. The movement becomes horizontal because the point towards which the vertical movement is directed is changed. One of the saddest mistakes of evolutionism has been to seek for the origin of movement and development in external factors. Nineteenth century evolutionism was always unable to penetrate to the heart of being, and failed to see in it the energy which produces all development. Evolutionist methods consist in more and more attention being paid to the surface of things and in placing the origin of life in something outside itself, in a principle which bears no resemblance to it whatever. But even when the origin of life and movement has been traced to something external, the inner cause of it all has still to be discovered, and then one must go further and further afield in order to find something external by which to explain development. The theory of evolution only touches upon a secondary not upon an original sphere, and can therefore account only for the projection and not the initiation of the creative process. To admit the principle of development in Christianity does not imply its subordination to evolution in the horizontal sense, which is determined by factors outside and apart from the Christian spirit. In this sense Christianity *is* anti-evolutionist. But the principle of development in Christianity may exist as a function of the free creative and dynamic nature of spirit. Deep down within, there is always a creative process at work which originates in freedom, and that which appears to us as development is really only an external process projected horizontally.

Development is an exoteric category, for it takes place on the inert and static plane of our world. But in the spirit, in the inner world, there is nothing inert and all is movement, though there is no development or evolution in the superficial sense of the word. In the spiritual world nothing is determined by external factors and everything is derived from the inner depths of being. The process

316

of development in Christianity, in the sense in which I understand it, means this, and this only ; there is no cleavage between the two worlds of time and eternity, for eternity is capable of entering time, and time, eternity. To regard the world as static always means that it is conceived as isolated, shut up within itself, within limits which have been fixed for all eternity.

When we speak of a development in the Church's dogma we mean that in the inner depths a new form of religious experience has come to light, that the fire of the spirit seeks new forms of expression in the external world. From an external point of view this process looks like a development, for when a creative movement of the spirit takes place in a vertical direction, that is from the inner depths, development horizontally is inevitable and cannot be stopped. A new wine of the spirit always requires new bottles.

There are periods in which there is, as it were, a process of re-incarnation in the world, and our present age is one of them. The historic forms in which things have been embodied are no longer regarded as satisfactory, and fall into decay. The world becomes " disincarnated ", if we may so phrase it, and it is difficult to see in what form it will re-incarnate itself. This process of dis-incarnation is accompanied by the loss of plastic beauty, and life becomes formless and often ugly ; the loss of style in architecture is one of the characteristic symptoms of this. Beauty disappears not only in life but in art, of which futurism is a particularly glaring example. Aesthetic receptivity is intensified during periods of division and disincarnation, but its object perishes.

The materialization and mechanization of modern civilization is precisely a process of disincarnation in which the historic embodi-ment of things is disappearing. The concrete form of the organic aggregate is perishing. The materialization of human life is not an incarnation but the reverse. The machine is separating spirit from flesh. In our mechanical civilization the organic synthesis of soul and body disappears. The machine is destroying the plastic historical forms of things and is substituting mechanical for organic elements. The whole organization of the life of the Christian world is collapsing, and many who are wedded to the existing state of affairs and identify it with being itself, imagine that the end of Christianity and of the world is at hand. In reality it is herd-Christianity which is going under. The very basis of the social order on which historic Christianity rests is shaken. But below the outward convulsions of a system supposedly everlasting a real spiritual experience is concealed. Christianity of a merely customary order is disappearing, because the spirit has departed from it. But the eternal truth of Christianity has not been shaken by this. Christianity cannot always be linked with the temporary historic forms of the social structure. We cannot, however, regard this process of the disincarnation and re-incarnation of the world in the same light as the supporters of the theory of progress do, for whom every transition is necessarily good. In reality we are confronted by a double process ; if the powers of evil are at work in it, the spirit is also not inactive and is gaining a measure of positive victory.

From the point of view of the theory of evolution we are obliged to recognize that a mechanical civilization leads to regression in the sphere of the human organism. In earlier periods man was much better armed from the anthropological standpoint, he was stronger and his organism was more developed than it is at the zenith of our present civilization. Side by side with social progress there goes biological and anthropological regression. Progress towards perfection becomes social rather than strictly speaking human. Without the aid of mechanical inventions man is powerless and defenceless. Consequently if evolution is regarded objectively from the anthropological point of view a double process must be recognized in it and the question becomes singularly complex if one considers each historical period in isolation.

Thus there is a profound dualism in the process of modern history. Its development and progress are accompanied by a corresponding decrease of interest in the spiritual, coupled with a growth of interest in what is merely fleeting and terrestrial. The nations of the world have become less religious and are now incapable of the wild fervour characteristic of the Middle Ages. Reason has destroyed the spiritual world in man ; the desire to profit by the life of this world and its goods is a ruling passion of modern humanity. This is one aspect of the process, but not the only one.

Modern history and the development which is taking place within it constitute an enormous wealth of new experience for mankind. The human soul has become more complex and at the same time more fully developed. The harshness and cruelty of earlier periods have been diminished and there is much greater humanity ; there is a new compassion abroad in the world not only towards men but even towards animals. There is more refinement and sensitiveness of conscience in the world, a greater opposition to cruelty, falsehood, and violence, and more demand for love and liberty.

But why has Orthodox and Catholic Christianity not sought to modify social relationships in the spirit of Christian love, and why has it so often supported a system founded on the anti-Christian principles of violence and cruelty ? Why has it so often in its history defended the rich and powerful at the expense of the poor and weak ? To which we can only reply that it is not Christianity but Christians who are responsible for these things. The human soul, cruel, limited in its outlook, and animated by ferocious instincts has distorted Christianity and set its mark upon it. This distortion of Christian truth has sometimes taken the form of a solicitude for the eternal salvation of the soul. The fear of eternal damnation not only for oneself but for one's neighbour has been the cause of violence and cruelty through which it was hoped to win deliverance and salvation.

But in the course of a long historical process the human soul has been transformed by the mysterious and almost imperceptible action of Christianity, even though from an outside point of view it often seems to be far removed from it. The positive development of the human soul is the work of Christianity. But humanistic progress, while diminishing cruelty, suppressing violence, and affirming the dignity of personality, has also led to new cruelties and new

319

acts of violence, to the dragging down of all individuals to a common level, to an impersonal civilization, to atheism, to the suppression of the soul, and the denial of the existence of " the inner man ". A new soul has been effectively created which demands more compassion and a greater kindness towards all that lives. New feelings have been developed.

Modern Christians have difficulty in reconciling themselves to the idea of hell and eternal punishment. The continual recollection of these torments had a certain value in the Middle Ages, given the education and discipline of the period, and helped to keep men loyal to the Church, but it is impossible to educate modern people or to attract them to the Church along such lines. On the contrary, from the strictly pedagogic point, it is better to-day to mention these subjects as little as possible, for the idea of hell has become a stumbling-block in the way of those who desire to join the Church. The modern man prefers theosophy and the doctrine of re-incarnation. But when one compares the soul of man at the present day with that of earlier periods of history, it is clear that to-day the human soul is less integral and more divided, that it has passed through many contradictions, that it has less faith, and is weaker and more superficial than it was formerly.

At the present day Christianity is confronted by souls of a very different kind and this fact requires a modification of its methods. The human soul in these last days of the modern period has experienced every form of doubt and temptation ; it has been subjected to every kind of testing, passed through all life's contradictions, and has gone down into the lowest depths of darkness. But the Orthodox and Catholic Churches, whether through inertia or tradition, persist as in the past in the attempt to preserve their flock, the mass of humanity, against temptation, against dangerous experience of all kinds, against everything which makes for complication in the life of the soul, and against too much intellectual development.

The fundamental practical problem which faces Christianity to-day is no longer that of warning men against temptations and preserving them from trials, but on the contrary in helping them out of such things, and in the achieving of spiritual results which will bear fruit. No power on earth can stop evolution with all the contradictions which it brings in its train. God Himself wills it, and desires the realization of every sort of possibility ; He wills that human freedom should be put to the test and that experience should be widened and deepened. The Christian Church is eternal but it must take account of the evolution which is taking place in the world, of the modifications which transpire in the human soul, and the coming to light of fresh states of consciousness. If a Christian renaissance is possible, it will not be achieved by the preservation of souls from temptation, but rather by a return to the Christianity of " new " souls which have passed through trial and temptation. The Christian renaissance will mean the bringing back of the prodigal son to the Father. We have not got to face the danger of a defection from Christianity (for that happened long ago and the world is beguiled by every kind of temptation) but a desire to return to Christianity. The world is no longer Christian and Christianity no longer dominates it outwardly. We must see things as they really are and recognize the *fait accompli*. That is our first task. Our century is in no sense of the word concerned with the question of preserving something. The fear of dangerous and attractive ideas can only be regarded as childish in an age when these ideas predominate. In the future, domination and consequently " preservation " will be the function not of Christianity but of the hostile forces of atheism, Communism, and mechanized civilization.

The predominating attitude of the Church seems to indicate that it has yet to grasp what has taken place in the world, and it appears to be several centuries behind the times. Christian apologetics are so out of date in their methods that they are positively harmful and a hindrance to those who would return to Christianity. The Christian renaissance can only take place through the medium of a youthful and creative sentiment. It is difficult to frighten modern people with anything, for they have already experienced the strongest temptations of every kind, to the deification of man, the religion of humanism, Marxism, Nietzscheanism, Socialism, anarchy, atheism, and occultism. For such the return to God and to Christianity does not involve the " preservation " of something, but rather a spiritual revolution. It is from the depths of an un-fathomable freedom that the soul comes to Christ and to God. This movement of the soul in modern man was well understood by Dostoievsky. The whole of Russian literature depicts for us this search for God on the part of the soul which has been overcome by temptations, and which then strives to make them known for what they really are. Spiritual development cannot be stopped. It must go on at all costs.

The soul of man undergoes a certain change as a result of its tragic experience of humanism ; it is aware of fresh aspirations and suffers in new ways. Christianity in its ancient form is no longer suited to the structure of the modern soul, which, however, still looks to it for eternal truth. The relations between God and man are no longer determined by external forces, by a horizontal movement, but by an inner power, that is, by a vertical movement. The attitude towards evil is changing ; it is regarded from a spiritual rather than a juridical standpoint. People no longer believe that evil can be overcome by means of external compulsion, but only by a positive spiritual force which must check it from within. Moreover our will must be directed to securing the highest degree of spiritual development, for if it is not attained we cannot escape the ordeal of evil and its consequences which have a providential significance. Herein lies the meaning of all revolutions. We can-not oppose them simply with an arbitrary conservatism, for this attitude to life is doomed. The only possible way to oppose revolu-tion is through a positive and creative spiritual force which will change life and transfigure it. It is the same where the individual man is concerned ; if his life is not spiritual and creative he will inevitably succumb to the blandishments of revolution.

It is out of the question to protect man from " the world " and its temptations by coercive means applied from without, for he is surrounded by " the world " and its temptations and must therefore overcome them from within and in freedom. It is nowadays impossible to keep anyone in a spiritual hot-house, for the hot-houses have all been destroyed. Each one of us shares in the destiny of the world and of humanity, and must accept his own portion of the general responsibility, working here below for his regeneration. And the grace of God acting within the freedom of man is responsible for our inward transfiguration.

V

With the problem of spiritual development there is closely bound up that of eschatology, of the final destiny of the human soul and of the world. The modern Christian attitude cannot reconcile itself with primitive eschatology on moral grounds. It is very difficult to accept a metaphysical system which makes the eternal destiny of the soul dependent on this temporal life, which exists merely from the cradle to the grave. According to this point of view our brief life on earth is a mere trap, and our fitness for eternity is determined by an experience whose duration is entirely insignificant. In modern Christianity the fear of eternal punishment can no longer determine the whole of life to the same degree in which it did in the Middle Ages. That is one of the results of the spiritual process through which we have passed. So far as we are concerned to-day this question is primarily a moral and spiritual and not a dogmatic one, nor does it consist in elaborating a theory of apocatastasis as Origen and St. Gregory of Nyssa did. The whole problem has now been removed from the theological and metaphysical sphere, in which the final mysteries of human destiny are resolved with the aid of rational categories,[1] to the sphere of our present spiritual orientation and our moral will. We must not only strive for our own personal salvation, but for the salvation and transfiguration of everything and everybody. The question of knowing whether all men will be saved, and how the coming of the Kingdom of God will be brought about, is the final mystery which is in-

[1] Origen tried to produce a rational eschatology.

soluble by reason ; but we must strive with all the force of our spirits for the salvation of all men. We must all be saved together, with the whole universe, in *sobornost* and not in isolation.

This idea corresponds to the spirit of Orthodoxy, and particularly to Russian Orthodoxy. N. Feodorov in his doctrine of the resurrection and of the conditional nature of apocalyptic prophecy has brilliantly described the orientation of our will towards universal salvation. There is a very great moral advance in this and a real victory over transcendent religious egoism. The desire for universal salvation is a manifestation of love. We are not elaborating a form of ontology in which universal salvation is necessary. We recognize that the greatest difficulties here are those raised by the problem of freedom. The idea of hell does not receive its justification from the judgment of God nor from the punishments which He awards, nor yet from the idea of justice, but rather from human freedom. God cannot save man against his own will, and cannot force him into Paradise. God cannot violate human liberty. Man is free to choose torment without God rather than happiness in God ; he has a right to hell, as it were. But hell means the impossibility of loving God because of a certain orientation of human freedom, of a certain estrangement from God and separation from Him, through self-isolation.

The idea of eternal punishment was born of the experience in virtue of which all suffering felt in this life appears to us as eternal. Torment which was not eternal would not be the torment of hell. Hell is precisely this sense of infinity, this ignorance of the end, this eternity of suffering contained not in its prolongation but in a single instant. A transcendental ontology of heaven and hell is only an objectification of spiritual experience through the medium of the categories of the natural world ; it is a naturalistic concept. The doctrine of posthumous sanctions is only the product of a cruel and barbaric age which saw earthly justice in terms of punishment and torture. The idea of heaven and hell is a conception which reduces the spiritual life to the sphere of naturalism. Dante's Inferno is full of pre-Christian and pagan elements. But eschatology must be freed from every sort of naturalism and must be expressed in terms of the spiritual life. And we must envisage the spiritual life in terms of a creative dynamism which has an entirely different conception of the realization of the Kingdom of God and the truth of Christ. The Kingdom of God is not an existence in the naturalistic sense of the word any more than hell. The Kingdom of God is the ⟵ life of the spirit and hell is only a form of spiritual experience ; it is an impasse, an obstacle, which appears to be eternal, infinite, and unescapable ; it represents the tragedy of human freedom. If the solution of the eschatological problem given us by traditional theology is exoteric and rationalistic, the theory of development and infinite evolution is no better. It involves a sort of rarification of life which hinders spiritual intensification.

There is no more difficult problem in religion than that of eschatology. Man is haunted by three nightmares : the religious nightmare of the eternal punishment of hell ; the occultist and theosophical nightmare of evolution and reincarnation in an infinitude of worlds ; and the nightmare of mysticism, which is the annihilation of human personality in God. It is hard to say which of the three is the worst. It sometimes looks as if man is ready to admit the existence of hell in order to escape from an infinite series of evolutions or the final dissolution of himself in God.

" In the religious idea of hell there is at least a strong affirmation of personal being. We are face to face here with an antinomy, to that fundamental " ἀπορία " to which the eschatological problem brings us. If we logically affirm personality and freedom, we are bound to assert the possibility of hell. It is easy to get rid of the idea of hell, but it is at the price of personality and freedom. On the other hand, our personality and our freedom cannot be reconciled with eternal punishment ; our moral consciousness protests against it. I can still admit the possibility of these torments for myself, and I may even have a foretaste of them. But it is difficult for me to conceive of them for others. It is possible still to admit punishment from man's standpoint, but not from God's. Already in Origen we find the belief that Christ would not accept the

damnation of even one single human being, and that His sufferings
on the Cross opened the way to universal salvation.[1]

Another difficulty arises in connection with the following
problem. Personality must have the opportunity of infinite
development for the manifestation of its eternal and creative nature ;
but infinite development and the absence of a definite goal is
regarded with horror as involving the impossibility of attaining the
Kingdom of God. This difficulty shows us that the eschatological
problem is insoluble if it is looked at from the angle of naturalistic
rationalism. It can only be solved in the Kingdom of God itself.

The problem of the origin, destiny, and final end of the soul has
not yet found a definitive dogmatic solution within Christianity.
Not only its final destiny but even its origin is mysterious. The
traditional theological opinion, according to which each human soul
is created by God at the moment of physical conception, is such a
lamentable one that we need not stop to consider it seriously. There
is, on the other hand, an eternal element of truth in the Orphic
doctrine of the soul put forward by Plato. The pre-existence of
the human soul in the spiritual world is an indispensable truth, for
the soul is not the child of time but of eternity.

But the doctrine of reincarnation on the earth is incompatible
with Christianity. It involves the splitting up of personality and
introduces a naturalistic conception into the spiritual life. Here
we are up against a limit to the possibility of including a principle
of development within Christianity. When this principle is
considered as a solution of the mystery of the origin and final
destiny of the human soul, it becomes a naturalistic principle which
is necessarily hostile to Christianity. Nevertheless the denial of
spiritual development is a denial of the necessity for man to perfect
himself and to attain a perfection like that of the heavenly Father ;
it is a denial of the search for and realization of the Kingdom of
God. The limit of the principle of development is a mystery which
safeguards the divine life. The eschatological problem helps us to
realize the distinction which must be made between infinity and

[1] See Denis : *The Philosophy of Origen.*

326

eternity. The idea of the infinity of reincarnation and of punishment in hell belongs to the natural world ; but eternity belongs to the spiritual world and to the Divine Being. It is, moreover, impossible to admit that an eternity of an evil, diabolical, and infernal type exists side by side with the eternity which is divine.[1]

[handwritten marginal note: This distinction between infinity and eternity is very important.]

---

[1] In Holy Scripture the expression is " of the age of the ages " (τοῦ αἰῶνος τῶν αἰώνων). But the question as to whether the aeon of aeons is eternity remains an enigma and a mystery. Hell is the aeon and the aeon of aeons, but that does not mean that it is eternity, and that no new aeons are possible.

CHAPTER TEN

The Church and the World

I

IS the Church an ontological reality ? The catechisms give us no information on this point. The ontology of the Church is still scarcely revealed. It is a task which belongs to the future. The essence of the Church has not yet become sufficiently real and actual to permit of its ontological elaboration. Besides this, is a definition of the nature of the Church possible ?

The Church cannot be understood when seen merely from the outside ; it cannot be rationally defined, or reduced to concepts. The Church can only be understood by those who live within it. Its life must actually be experienced, for it is not a reality of the external kind. Its intrinsic nature cannot be apprehended by those who stand apart from it. The Church is not a temple built of stone, neither is it a community of believers, nor a parish consisting of human beings, nor yet an institution juridically determined—though all these things are elements in its composition. It does not possess definite limits and external marks which determine its inner nature and differentiate it from the rest of existence. The Church possesses physical, psychical, and social elements, yet none of these define its nature. The Church is not a tangible substance belonging to the world of visible things, nor is it an empirical reality analogous to that of minerals, plants, or animals. It belongs to the world of invisible things which can only be demonstrated by faith, for it is an inner reality.

It is true that the Church exists for everyone as an empirical reality, that everyone has to determine their attitude towards it, and that its enemies, who do not believe in it, fight against it as against something real. But such people recognize its reality in a sense which is quite different from that in which it is accepted by those who believe in it and live in it. For from the outside all that can be seen is bricks and mortar, ceremonies, an institution, and a hierarchy. But the true reality of the Church, its being, is inward and mystical, and is something beyond buildings, clergy, rites, councils, etc.[1] Its nature is spiritual, for it belongs to the spiritual rather than to the natural world.

This does not mean that the Church is not incarnate in the natural and historical world, or that it remains invisible. I see the Church in experience, but this experience commences when I begin to overcome my limitations and the isolation of my psychical world with all its division and disharmony, and when I enter into the unity of the great spiritual world and pass beyond both time and space. This spiritual world and the experience of it are supra-individual and supra-" psychical " ; they virtually belong to the Church. The spiritual life is metaphysically social and not individualistic, and the Church has a spiritually social nature in the deepest sense of the word. The experience of the Church is *soborny,* for *sobornost* is one of its ontological qualities. In this experience I am not alone, for I am one with all my brethren in the spirit in whatever place or time they may have lived.

I am myself limited as regards the extent of my knowledge ; my experience is restricted and cannot pretend to cover the diversity of existence in all its fulness ; I have not myself known a great number of spiritual contacts of a determining character. I have written this book ; but in this book I have only been able to reach a certain degree of illumination and have only seen certain aspects of the truth. But I can get outside myself, and I can, metaphysically speaking, pass beyond my own limitations and have contact with experience of a supra-personal kind. In the religious experience of the Church, and in his contact with Christ, man is not alone and

[1] Peter Lippert, S. J., has treated this question in an excellent manner in *Das Wesen des Katholischen Menschen.*

confined within his own limitations, for he is drawn near to all others who have known this experience, to the whole Christian world, to apostles, saints, and to all who are in Christ whether living or departed.

It is not only the living who belong to the Church ; all the generations which have gone before are equally part of it, all of them are living in the Church, and I am in real union with them all. That is one of the essential characteristics of the Church, in which in *sobornost* all men come to the self-same Christ, and draw from Him a unique and unifying power. We all form part of one Christian race, the spiritual seed of the New Adam.

This new race possesses the mind of Christ, by which we apprehend that which is beyond our own intelligence. The man who lives in the Church enters upon a new order of being, his nature is changed and he becomes more spiritual. Moreover, in the Church it is not only the mind but also the love of Christ which is at work, and His freedom too, of which the natural world and the children of the Old Adam know nothing. The Church is the order of love and freedom, and represents their union. In the natural world freedom and love are dissociated ; freedom is opposed to unity and asserts itself in disunion ; unity, on the other hand, appears to be synonymous with arbitrary constraint. But the order of the Church knows nothing of constraint, nor of the freedom which is opposed to unity and love.

The Church, in the process of actualization and incarnation in the natural and historic world, may clothe itself in the forms of this world, and even borrow from it the principle of coercion and violence, but these elements are foreign to its inner nature and to its essence. The Church is the mystical body of Christ ; to belong to it is to be a member of Christ's body, that is, to be a cell within it, an organ of this mystical organism. In belonging to the mystical body of Christ we partake of His mind, His love, and His freedom, of which we were unaware in the natural world of our " psychical " isolation.

The life of the Church rests upon holy tradition and succession.

330

It is through tradition that in each new generation man enters into the same spiritual world. Tradition is a supra-personal and *soborny* experience, the creative spiritual life transmitted from generation to generation, uniting the living and the dead and thereby overcoming death. Death reigns in the world indeed but it is vanquished in the Church. Tradition is the memory which brings resurrection, the victory over corruption, the affirmation of eternal life. The tradition of the Church is not an authority imposed from without. It is a real and intrinsic victory over the division created by time ; it is a glimpse of eternity in the mortal flight of time, a union of past, present, and future in the oneness of eternity. Life in the tradition of the Church is life in eternity ; it is the perception and recognition of inward realities. The past is not known externally from remains of its monuments which have been subjected to historical analysis, but from within, through sacred memory, through inner contacts with it, through the life in *sobornost* which transcends the breaches made by time. Tradition is not authority ; it is the creative life of the spirit. Authority is a category only applicable to the natural world of division and hatred. In the spiritual world it has no meaning ; or, rather, it means simply a certain humility and submission which precede freedom. The phrase " authoritarian tradition " is only the translation of spiritual phraseology into the language of the natural and historical world.

The Church is not a reality existing side by side with others ; it is not an element in the historic and universal whole ; it is not a separated objective reality. The Church is all ; it constitutes the whole plenitude of being, of the life of humanity, and of the world in a state of Christianization. It possesses a cosmic nature, and to forget this means decadence. A conception of the Church which would regard it as a hospital to which souls come for treatment would be truly lamentable. Those who only see in the Church an institution deny its cosmic significance. It is in the Church that the grass grows and the flowers blossom, for the Church is nothing less than the cosmos Christianized. Christ entered the cosmos, He was crucified and rose again within it, and thereby all things were

331

made new. The whole cosmos follows His footsteps to crucifixion and to resurrection.

Beauty is the Christianized cosmos in which chaos is overcome ; that is why the Church may be defined as the true beauty of existence. Every achievement of beauty in the world is in the deepest sense a process of Christianization. Beauty is the goal of all life ; it is the deification of the world. Beauty, as Dostoievsky has said, will save the world. An integral conception of the Church is one in which it is envisaged as the Christianized cosmos, as beauty. Only a differential conception can transform it into an institution.

But the Church, until the realization of the Kingdom of God, also leads a divided existence. It has to rise above those elements of the world which lack illumination and it cannot be confused with them. The Church is, above all, something invisible, inward, and mystical. It belongs to the spiritual and not to the natural order. So far as this quality is concerned the Church is still only incompletely actualized. In the philosophy of Aristotle and St. Thomas Aquinas potentiality, considered in relation to action, is always identified with imperfection, with matter, and with incomplete being ; true being is perfect and is that which is wholly action. Nothing in God exists in a state of potentiality, for He is *actus purus*. Hence Thomist and Catholic thought has been forced to recognize the historic actualization and incarnation of the Church as though it were its true being. The mystical Church seems to be non-existent, for being merely potential it is one with imperfection, matter, and incomplete being. Aristotle has a tendency towards making absolute historic incarnations and subordinating the infinite to the finite.

But another conception of potentiality is possible, one on which mysticism and German philosophy, especially Boehme and Schelling, throw some light. According to this point of view virtuality is regarded as the deepest element in being, as its inner mysterious origin in fact ; it is presumed that it is always richer than its actual manifestation. This conception admits potentiality in God ; He is not wholly in action. In the Church too there is an element of the potential. The Church is virtually infinitely greater than its actualized elements. The true origin of the Church is mystical ; it is lost in the unfathomable and the infinite. The historic Church does not exhaust the fulness of the virtual, mystical, Church. It is only with such a conception of potentiality, as is manifested by the infinite unfathomability of being, that the oppressive limitations of the finite can be transcended.

Christianity has risen above these limitations and has discovered the infinite and the unfathomable. In Christian thought matter predominates over form, and this is the essential distinction between Christianity and Hellenism. Scholasticism tried to impose Hellenic form upon the Christian substance of life, that is to say, to limit its infinite potentiality and creativity ; it had no desire to recognize as authentic being anything but action and matter as finally subjected to form.

Christianity in the East escaped the Aristotelian revival and the domination of Hellenic form. The Platonic tradition which has existed for all time in the East opened up other lines of development. But even in Orthodoxy the mind of the Church has been too much hampered by the limitations of actualized form, and it has been afraid of potentiality ; there has been a spirit of inert conservatism in the East. If the relationship between potentiality and action is construed differently from the manner in which Aristotle or St. Thomas Aquinas have done it, we are not thereby compelled to reject the necessity of actualization and incarnation ; we need only enlarge the sphere of possible actualization by admitting that the sphere of actuality does not exhaust the fulness of being.

The Church belongs not only to the realm of the mystical and potential ; it is also visible and actualized. The Church incarnates itself in history, as Christ became incarnate. But the inner being cannot be confined to what we see of it historically in its incarnation. The Church is visible in the life of Christ, in the lives of the saints, in the sacraments, in its hierarchy, communities, councils, etc.

The actualization, the form, while being a positive advantage, an enrichment, and a real victory, does not imply the denial of an unfathomable infinity ; it does not mean that the exoteric contains more than the esoteric. The line followed by Boehme was not sufficiently orthodox and his doctrine was confused, but he was at least more of a Christian than Aristotle. The Hellenic world was afraid of the infinite and tried to protect itself against it. In the Christian world the infinite was precisely revealed, as well as the substance of life. Boehme was completely lost in this infinity, which has been unveiled since the Christian revelation.

In the consciousness of the Church there are two opposed principles ; the ancient Hellenic and Aristotelian principle of restrictive form and of achieved actuality, and the Christian principle, which is mystical, and always susceptible of new creative actualization. We must not forget that actualization and incarnation even of the Church in history arises from the reactions of human nature, from the limitations of a mobile and dynamic consciousness, and the spiritual orientation of man. The visible Church is only the partial actualization of the invisible Church ; it is only an incomplete form of its substance and of the life of humanity and of the world. The Church is not manifested and revealed in all the fulness of its being and does not realize all the possibilities contained within itself. Its complete actualization and incarnation will mean the transfiguration of the cosmos, the coming of a new world, the setting up of the Kingdom of God. The inward is far richer than the outward.

Roman Catholics make a distinction between the soul and body of the Church. The soul is greater than the body. All those whose wills are directed to God and to the divine belong to it even if they are not consciously Christian and if they take no part in the incarnate and visible life of the Church. Those who belong to the body of the Church are those who participate in its sacraments and are obedient to its hierarchy. This doctrine acts as a corrective to the Roman Catholic conception of the Church, which means the damnation of the majority of mankind. But this doctrine must lead men to recognize that the Church is potentially bigger and richer than that which is contained within the orbit of the actualized Church.

There are two points of view on this subject ; either one recognizes that the absolute and infinite, in penetrating the relative and finite, create round them a closed circle of sanctification, or one admits that the relative and finite aspire to the absolute and infinite and thus give rise to a creative movement. The first opinion is exclusively conservative and sacramental, the second is creative and prophetic. A full-orbed Christianity has room for both points of view within itself.

Incarnation is symbolization ; the visible Church is the symbolization of the Church invisible, the earthly hierarchy of the heavenly. But the symbol necessarily presupposes the infinity which lies beyond it. The Church as actualized and incarnate in history does not constitute its whole unfathomable depth and fulness ; for its infinity lies beyond its boundaries. It is impossible to imprison the infinite in the finite. It is the knowledge of this truth which distinguishes symbolic from naïve realism.

The Church is the body of Christ which embraces the whole infinity of cosmic life, for it is itself cosmic. The sacraments and dogmas of the Church are the visible expression of the mysterious life of the cosmic body of Christ. Nevertheless dogmas, as we have already observed, are only the symbolic formulas of truths of spiritual experience, of essential contacts between man and God. The sacraments are only the chief visible points in which the action of God in cosmic life is focussed. Christ, the Son of God, is eternally crucified in the cosmos and His eucharistic sacrifice is eternally offered. The Church leads us to these mysteries of the divine life, but they remain beyond the grasp of rationalism and the juridical spirit. The Church is bi-lateral by its very nature and cannot be regarded from a monophysite standpoint. It has not only a divine origin ; it has also a cosmic origin. It bears not only the signature of God, but also the trade-mark of the world. The Church is the God-world, the God-humanity.

The cosmic terrestial foundations of the Church must be purity,

335

innocence, and chastity achieved in cosmic life and in the world. If this purity and chastity had not been achieved, then the birth and incarnation of God and the coming of the Son to this earth would have been impossible. The power to receive God and to bring Him into the world would not have existed. The coming of God cannot be the result of compulsion exercised upon the world from outside, for the world must itself welcome God. The world had been developing slowly in the direction of the birth and incarnation of the Son, and it had to create a nature sufficiently pure and chaste to receive God into itself. The Virgin Mary is precisely this pure nature of the world, its natural deification, which constitutes the cosmic foundation of the Church. The Church does not rest only on Christ, on divine grace, but also on the Virgin Mary, the Mother of God, on the soul of the cosmos, which, having achieved purity and chastity, conceived in the spirit instead of through sinful nature.

In the Virgin Mary the world and humanity attain to a free deification, not by any particular act of grace which exempted them from original sin as the Roman Catholic dogma of the Immaculate Conception teaches, but by the free wisdom of the creature itself. God could make all men chaste by an act of His almighty Will. But He desires that the chastity and integrality of human nature, which was only attained in an absolute manner in the case of the Virgin Mary, should be freely acquired. In her the world and humanity responded to the divine appeal. The Church possesses a unique universal nature not only in its divine element, but also in its cosmic human element. The Virgin Mary is the female cosmic soul of humanity.

The universal Church has not been entirely actualized in the visible historic Church; otherwise the variety of churches and confessions would be inexplicable. The universal Church is above and beyond all divisions. If, on the one hand, the actualization of the Church in history constitutes a process of enrichment, namely, the fulfilment of the universal historic rôle which Christianity has to play, on the other hand it implies a process of diminution, an inevitable adaptation to the average level of the mass of humanity.

336

In the Church " economy " has played a preponderating part. All historic bodies have been created to serve the interests of collectives and they bear the imprint of them. Religion in the world is a creation in which the mass of the people, as well as religious teachers and prophets, have all collaborated. That is why the religious life contains at one and the same time popular and spiritually aristocratic levels.

The visible Church cannot consist only of a minority of the elect for it has a message for the whole of mankind and of the universe. From this fact there springs the whole of its negative aspect, the whole poignant tragedy of its destiny, the whole repulsive attraction of its history. The Church must descend to the depths of the world's life and cannot remain on the heights as the Gnostics, Montanists, and other sectarians wish.

The human world, in which the Church must act, is dominated by pagan naturalism, dissension, and limitation. The universal truth of the Church acting in the world and in humanity is distorted by the limitations of their pagan particularism. The great error of history has lain in the fact that man has too often mistaken his own limitations for the Divine Word, and that he has conferred a sacred and absolute value upon particular historic embodiments. The Church is an ontological reality, a spiritual organism. In this real being, which belongs not only to earth but also to heaven, and which is not only in time but also in eternity, two natures are joined together, namely, God and the world, God and humanity. That is the reason why the Church, as an organism and a real being, shares the destiny of the world and of humanity, and also undergoes the process of suffering and development. The Church belongs to the order of love and freedom, but it acts in the natural world of discord and compulsion. The Church belongs to the spiritual order, but it is placed within the natural order which it is called upon to transfigure.

The sacraments of the Church are the prototypes of the trans-figuration of the whole universe. It is only through the sacraments in general, and through the liturgy in particular, that the people have access to the very depths of the spiritual life. The sacraments operate at the deepest levels of cosmic life where the sacrifice of Christ is effected. It is true that this sacrifice is operative in every phenomenon of life, but the sacraments are visible expressions of it, and are concentrated within the mystery of the Church, and are there revealed to all men. Popular religion is liturgical and symbolic.

I cannot belong to the Church on condition of accepting only the heavenly Church or the Church which has realized perfection on earth. I cannot accept the Church in the outward sense of the word. I can only accept it inwardly. There can, therefore, be no contractual relationships between it and me. I desire creative development, I cannot accept stagnation and inertia ; but I cannot draw up an agreement with the Church about this matter. Only an integral conception of the Church which regards it as the Christianized cosmos, as the heavenly and eternal Church, as opposed to a merely temporal and historic body, can free me from a sense of being oppressed by it or can prevent me from exercising my critical faculty in relation to it. To come into the Church is to enter upon the eternal and divine order of the world. This does not mean that we have to make a break with the world or with history, but rather that we participate in their transfiguration.

The Church is dynamic, it is a creative process ; an arrest of this process is a mark of human weakness and sin. In the Church there is, besides the Petrine principle, that of St. John and St. Paul. The esoteric tradition of St. John has never died out in the Church, and there is enshrined within it the eternal Gospel as well as the purely historic and temporal Gospel. Christ taught us to expect the coming of the Kingdom of God and called us to seek for it above everything else ; He did not at first institute a historic Church with an earthly organization.[1] The primitive Christian community lived in an

---

[1] We find many ideas in historical criticism which are very just in this respect, though there seems to be little comprehension of the religious bearing of these statements. There are great truths in Zome, Sabatier, and Heiler, but they only see historic truth in some sort of separation from the consciousness of the Church.

atmosphere of eschatology in expectation of the Second Coming
of Christ and the advent of the Kingdom of God ; the organization
of a Church, in the historic meaning of the word, was unnecessary.
The foundation of the Church for an earthly existence only became
essential when men first became conscious of the long period of
history which lay ahead of them, the moment for the setting-up of
the Kingdom of God having not yet arrived. This necessitated an
elaborate organization adapted to a prolonged existence in history.
The charismatic gifts began to die out, and canons were formulated
according to which it was recognized that the grace of priesthood
has been transmitted by Apostolic Succession. Instead of the
Kingdom of God there was the Church on earth. But the Church
on earth must never be confused with the Kingdom of God, still less
identified with it, for the Church is only the means by which we
are brought to the Kingdom. The idea of the Kingdom of God
remains an eschatological and not a historical idea. The Kingdom
of God is bound up with the invisible, heavenly, and mystical
Church.

II

Christ was the manifestation of the God-Man, of perfect man, of
two natures united in one Person. This is why Christianity is said
to be the religion of God-humanity, a non-monist form of religion.
In the Church also two natures are united in one organism,
namely, God and humanity. The Church is an organism, a divine-
human process ; human freedom and activity operate within it as
well as the grace of God. The monophysite conception of the
Church denies the reciprocal action of God and of humanity ; this
conception hinders, above all, the true comprehension of that
fellowship of men in love which is so important a part of the
positive content of Christianity. It means the exaltation of the
angelic at the expense of the human principle, and leads to
the exclusive dominance of the ecclesiastical hierarchy and of
the priesthood in the life of the Church. Clericalism is a form
of monophysitism, a depreciation of the value of humanity. It is

considered that in the Church the hierarchy should dominate, that is, the angelic and not the human order. In this way human creativity is rendered impossible and is unchurched. In actual fact, however, human creativity has existed in the life of the Church and cannot be stopped, but it has been disguised because of the pre-dominance of sacerdotalism. The Papacy is an intensely human activity, but it has never wanted to consider itself as something purely human.

A monophysite view of the Church is contradicted by the fact that God is revealed in Christianity by his Son the God-Man, that is to say, that revelation itself presupposes the human activity and freedom which are manifested in Christ. The Christian Church has its origin not only in the divine, but also in the divine-human ; it cannot exist without humanity and human nature ; and this humanity is not only an object of the activity of divine power, it is also itself an active, free, creative subject which responds to the divine call.

In the Church there is always a movement from God to man and from man to God ; it is in this way that the dynamic of the historical life of the Church is determined. There must be a firm divine foundation upon which the priesthood can be based, for it cannot rest upon unstable human nature. But as the historic life of the Church must also be a dynamic and creative process, it must rest upon a human foundation as well, and it presupposes the activity of humanity within it. The experience of knowledge, moral experience, and in fact the experience of life in its fullest sense, is only possible if one shares in the destiny of man and of the world. The Church is not a principle extrinsic to humanity and to the world ; it is an actual experience ; if it is the divine-human life, it must involve both an experience of the tragic destiny of the world and a sharing in it. That is an elementary truth above dispute which is recognized by all churchmen and by the theologians of all denominations, but the systematic, radical, deductions which are to be drawn from it are ignored by many, or regarded as merely problematical.

The movement from man to God, in other words, the manifestation of freedom and human creation, takes forms which are regarded as outside the specific sphere of the visible Church. A great many creative processes belong only to the invisible Church, to its soul. The life of God-humanity is singularly complex and many aspects of the divine-human process are not assimilated by the Church and are not considered as forming part of it ; its consciousness remains *par excellence* differential and not integral. Only the " sacerdotal " element of Christianity is officially recognized ; as for the " prophetic " element it seems to be relegated to a position outside the visible Church altogether. The greater part of our life is in this way put outside the pale, and we are condemned to a divided existence in which we have to move backwards and forwards between the rhythm of the Church and that of the world. The whole of our creative life belongs to the world instead of the Church. For can it really be said that it is in the sphere of the Church that we gain knowledge, create works of art, contemplate the beauty of the cosmos, effect moral valuations, or make new discoveries ? Or is it again within the sphere of the Church that romantic love flourishes, that true freedom is acquired, or that justice and real brotherhood are realized ?

Nevertheless we must admit that everything which constitutes true being in all its fulness *is* part of the Church, and that only non-being is outside it. All true creation by man belongs to the Church in the full cosmic sense of the word. The problem consists in knowing whether man is called simply to salvation, or whether he has also a mission to create. The creative process of life is not indispensable for the salvation of the soul ; the creative freedom of man is necessary not for salvation, but for the sake of the Kingdom of God ; and for the transfiguration of the world. It is difficult to discover the real limits of the Church, because in practice the doctrine on this subject has received insufficient elucidation in Christianity. The unveiling of the Church's true nature presupposes a development of religious anthropology, a revelation of the religious doctrine of man. The problem is still further complicated by the fact that in human creation and activity being and non-being are confused, and our whole task consists in discovering and then separating what derives from being from that which derives from non-being in the divine-human process. This confusion is the cause of the difficulty which the consciousness of the Church experiences in recognizing human creativity, and it has its origin in the freedom of man.

The discovery of the life of God-humanity in the Church springs from the Christian doctrine of the New Adam and the new spiritual race which has its origin in Christ. But the dominant school of thought in the Church only recognizes the existence of the Old Adam, and the natural race of mankind ; it seems to be unconscious of the fact that, in and through Christ, man is already a new creature in whom a new freedom and power are revealed. Since the time of Christ original sin has no longer absolute power over man, for man and the cosmos do not belong exclusively to the natural order any more, the breach between the natural and supernatural having been brought to an end. Spiritual life and creation are now possible within it, and belong to the divine-human life of the Church.

The whole of the life-process takes place within the Church, it is there that the beauty of cosmic life flowers. It is within the Church that the creation of a Goethe, or a Pushkin has been achieved, that Boehme reached the furthest heights of gnosis, that Nietzsche experienced the tragedy of Dionysos crucified ; it is within the Church that human creativity has taken place, that is, when it had its origin in being and when it was so destined. In Christ man has received a power which is both human and divine ; he has become entirely man, a spiritual being, a new and eternal Adam. Man is only revealed in God-humanity, that is to say, in the Church, even though he may be unconscious of the fact. Goethe, for instance, could not conceive that the whole of his authentic creation lay within the sphere of the Church and was actually a manifestation of it.

To conceive of Christianity exclusively as the religion of personal salvation is to restrict the area of the Church's consciousness, and to obscure the true life of God-humanity and the divine-human creative process of the world. In fact this conception of Christianity is pure nominalism which contradicts the very idea of a Church and involves the rejection of the ontological reality, not only of the Church itself, but also that of humanity, God-humanity, and the cosmos as well. Only a conception of Christianity as the religion which illuminates and transfigures the world enables us to recognize that the creative life of humanity really belongs to the Church. Our problem does not consist in asking whether one can, from the Church's point of view, justify the creative life of humanity, but rather whether this creative life is the life of the Church itself in spite of the fact that we may be unconscious of it.

The present age has produced an unprecedented dualism between the Church and the world, between the sacred and the profane, between religion and life ; it has dissolved the ancient historical unity in which Christianity and the life of society were both comprised. This situation is an intolerable one for religious thought ; life becomes godless and has neither justification nor sanctification, religion being relegated to a mere corner of existence. Yet even this unhappy occurrence is fraught with new possibilities, for it is due to this that Christianity is breaking free from certain of the pagan traditions of natural humanity, and that a new spirituality is coming to birth in the world. In the visible Church the old sinful nature of man is at work, and often brings with it a distorted and reduced version of Christianity, for up to the present the full implications of Christology have still to be worked out. The tragic element of corruption in the historic life of the Church comes from this same unenlightened and unchristianized human nature. But in the history of the Church's life, as in that of the world at large, the majority rule over the minority, that is to say, the least spiritual elements in humanity dominate those that are most spiritual. Moreover, this evil influence of human activity in the life of the Church has been a prodigious obstacle in the way of the perception of its divine-human nature, and the inner sanctification of the creative process accomplished within it.

343

III

St. Thomas Aquinas placed man with his intelligence among the lower grades of the hierarchy of spirits. According to him purely intellectual knowledge is beyond man's reach, it demands sensible experience. The knowledge possessed by angels is purely intellectual and is superior to that of man. According to this conception human beings do not occupy a central place in the hierarchy of the cosmos, and it is indeed difficult to see why on this theory Christ should not have belonged to the category of God-Angel rather than to that of God-Man. Christian metaphysics have to face the difficult problem of the relation between the angelic and the human hierarchies. Must the human be subordinated to the angelic as to a superior principle ?

The historic destiny of man is intimately bound up with the answer given to this question. The clerical and hierocratic view of the Church, the State, and the social and cultural life of mankind is one in which the angelic principle is placed above the human. Hierocracy in its extreme form is in conflict with the idea of the God-Man, for which the idea of the God-Angel is substituted. The hierocracy of the Roman Catholic Church contradicts the idea of man as the centre of the hierarchy of being, an idea of which the truth is revealed in the coming of the God-Man ; this doctrine further impedes the realization that life of the Church is really the life of God-humanity. " Papo-cæsarism " just like " cæsaro-papism " subordinates the human to the angelic principle, and such a system could only be justified had Christ been the God-Angel rather than the God-Man. But the humanity of Christ must involve the rejection of such a point of view.

In this connection eastern " cæsaro-papism " is exactly on the same level as western " papo-cæsarism." The Emperor, who belongs to the priestly order and who receives particular charisms conferring power upon him, is no longer part of the human order, but belongs to that of the angels. In him the human element has

344

no more importance than it has in the case of a priest, for it is not to him that the charisms are granted ; they are only symbolized in the world, while in reality they are granted to the angelic order. The Pope and the Emperor are mediators whose power is more than human, and who are regarded as if they were nothing short of a theophany ; the man in them is in truth only an accidental phenomenon. Thus the active element belongs to the angelic or mediatorial principle, while the human element must remain passive.

But in reality the hierarchy established by Christ is entirely the reverse of this. Man, and not the angels, are at the centre of being, and it is man who has his origin in the very heart of the Trinity. Christ is the absolute heavenly Man and cannot be subject to any angelic hierarchy. The angelic principle is passive and mediatorial, while the human, on the contrary, is active and creative. The angelic hierarchy of the priesthood is necessary to the life of the Church precisely because it is passive and does not depend on the free activity inherent in the human principle, and because the power to administer the sacraments belongs to it. It is through the intervention of this angelic hierarchy that man receives divine grace and power.

But though the angelic hierarchy of the priesthood has a mission to fulfil, this cannot be extended to the whole of man's life and creativity in society and in culture. In fact the angelic order, in the strict sense of the word, means the monastic state in so far as it involves the extinction of human nature. This throws a flood of light on the nature of the hierarchical principle. In the spiritual and religious life symbolism is substituted for realism. The hierocracy which produces " papo-cæsarism " and " cæsaro-papism " is always a form of symbolism in which the true elevation of the human spirit is not revealed. The predominant rôle in life is not that of sanctity, which is a real acquisition of human perfection, it is, rather, that of priesthood, which is only a symbolization in human terms of the hierarchy of heaven. Thus the Emperor, as a member of the sacred order, as a sort of " external bishop " of the Church, is neither a great man, nor a powerful leader whose value is determined by his human qualities, but only the symbolic reflection of the angelic hierarchy.

Such historical phenomena are the results of the union between Church and State, of the confusion of the Kingdom of God with the kingdom of Cæsar ; they arise from the introduction into Christianity of a false principle of monarchy which is alien to it, and which really belongs to paganism and primitive totemism. " Papo-cæsarism " and " cæsaro-papism " offer a false solution of the problem of anthropology, a doctrine of man, in which his value, his active and creative mission, are denied, and the angelic is substituted for the human principle. The degeneration of Christianity is the result of an exclusive hierocracy and a symbolism which impedes the final triumph of realism. Hierocratic domination is the result of Christianity becoming entangled with racialism, within which it developed, and through which it was distorted by becoming the religion of the herd.

It is the hierocratic principle, the symbolism of the angelic hierarchy, which maintains the racial characteristics of Christianity. This element is now passing through a metaphysical crisis and is being shaken to its foundations. In the future Christianity will no longer be merely the religion of a race, nor can faith be a matter of mere inheritance. It is becoming a personal issue. Christianity is ceasing to be a popular religion in the old sense of the word, and is becoming the religion of intellectuals throughout the world. This involves a change in the very nature of Christianity, and the end of the symbolic, hierocratic, consciousness.

The final eschatological idea of Christianity is a universal royal priesthood, not a hierocracy, nor even a papal or imperial theocracy, nor yet a symbolic reflection of the heavenly world, but rather a religious transfiguration of humanity and this world. Humanity is moving by way of hierarchical development towards the universal kingdom of freedom, towards religious transfiguration ; it is subject to the action of divine energy and receives the gifts of grace through the mediation of the priesthood. The royal priesthood of

346

which St. Peter and St. Macarius of Egypt [1] speak is a hierarchical kingdom, but it is that of the human hierarchy and not the angelic, though this does not imply a denial of the rôle played by the hierarchic principle in history. In fact, humanity is very deeply indebted to this principle for without it mankind could never have escaped from the chaos of spiritual barbarism.

IV

The Church is by its nature one ; it is like personality a unique reality. It is conscious of itself as universal, for universalism is its constitutive principle. The Church cannot be determined by geographical or ethnographical limitations ; it is not national, it is neither eastern nor western.

But universalism itself may be understood in a variety of senses. It may mean, for example, a merely " quantitative " distribution over the whole globe which demands a unity of exterior organization. This is what may be called a " horizontal " conception, and it is particularly dear to Roman Catholicism. But there is another view more typical of Orthodoxy. Universalism is qualitative, not quantitative ; it is a matter of depth ; the universal Church does not demand the establishment of an external unity of organization. *Sobornost* can exist in the inwardness of each diocese. This " vertical " conception of universalism is that which best affirms the unity and œcumenicity of the Church in spite of its external divisions.

In the human element, in the natural world, Christianity can only be individualized, and this is a good thing ; but it is also to be found in a state of division and dissension, and that is evil and a sin. The Church is not divided, neither in its ontological nature which is always *soborny*, nor in respect of divine truth, but in humanity which has been incapable of accepting the fulness of Christianity and which

---

[1] St. Macarius of Egypt says, " Just as in the time of the prophets anointing was necessary because the anointed were kings and prophets, so now spiritual men, consecrated by a heavenly anointing, become Christians by grace, so that they may be kings and prophets of heavenly mysteries ".

has only assimilated fragmentary aspects of the truth. The division has taken place in the kingdom of Cæsar, for the Kingdom of God can only be one. The hostility between different confessions is the enmity of the kingdom of Cæsar, and of humanity as absorbed by this natural world. The spiritual world, on the other hand, knows nothing of this animosity and division, but is itself less powerful in this natural world.

In this visible world there is no external unity in the Church ; its œcumenicity is not completely actualized. Not only the division of the Churches and the multiplicity of Christian confessions but the very fact that there are non-Christian religions in the world at all, and that there is, besides, an anti-Christian world, proves that the Church is still in a merely potential state and that its actualization is still incomplete. Only a completely Christianized human race and cosmos can give eternal expression to the Church's universal character. In fact this process of Christianization is only partially achieved. The true universality of the Church still remains concealed, and only its divisions can be seen. It is only by assimilating and identifying the part with the whole that the visible unity of the universal Church can be affirmed. But although there is no apparent unity that does not mean that the principle of universality is not active in the visible sphere.

It is not the Church which lacks unity, but the kingdom of this world, for what belongs to God and what to Cæsar have been confused in the course of history. The division of the Church was determined by motives which belong to " Cæsar's " world and there are certain movements making for its unity which are guided by similar principles. But though flesh and blood may divide, it is only the spirit which can unite. Up till the present most of the schemes for uniting the Churches have been " Cæsarist," and therefore useless and harmful.[1] It is not on this plane that union will be effected ; it will be accomplished only in the spirit and by the action of the Holy Ghost.

Eastern and Western Christianity are to be distinguished not by

[1] I am speaking here of the various " Uniat " movements, or contemporary movements of a purely external or social character.

differences in dogma and ecclesiastical organization, but by the character of their spiritual experience due to the divergence between various human elements which have accepted and then distorted Christianity. Spiritual experience is a deeper thing than dogma and precedes it in time ; the organization of the Church is determined by the spiritual orientation of the life of nations. It is these differences of a primary, vital, character which have determined the development of the East and the West. Here we have two spiritual orientations of the Christian world, the existence of which is predetermined by the divine plan for the world's history. Vital experimental spiritual differences were manifested well before the division of the Churches and need not necessarily have provoked it. Christianity should be capable of existing in a variety of forms in the universal Church.

The writings of the Eastern Fathers are always very clearly distinguished from those of the Western Fathers. In the East the Platonic tradition remained strong, it was more mystical, its interests were more ontological and speculative. Dogma especially owed its elaboration to the Doctors of the Eastern Church. It was in the East that all the Gnostics and heretics appeared, and this fact witnesses to the intense interest with which gnosis and questions of a dogmatic and religious-metaphysical nature were regarded. An Origen or a St. Gregory of Nyssa could never have arisen in the West, where the traditions of Stoicism and Roman legalism predominated. In the West the main topics of interest were the organization of the Church and the question of grace, freedom, and redemption. Western patristics have not furnished the name of a single great thinker except that of St. Augustine. The West merely produced remarkable writers, of whom Tertullian and St. Jerome were the most notable.

In Eastern Christianity the fundamental question has been the transfiguration of the nature of the world and of man ; in a word, of " theosis." This is linked up with the much more cosmic character of Orthodoxy, and with its more particular interest in the Second Coming of Christ and the Resurrection. The Doctors of the

349

Eastern Church, Clement of Alexandria, Origen, St. Gregory of Nyssa, St. Gregory Nazianzen, and others, would not by themselves have elaborated a conception of Christianity as a religion of personal salvation, nor yet the doctrine of the beatitude of the elect in Paradise and the eternal damnation of the whole of the rest of the human race. Eastern thought is less attracted by the ideas of justification and salvation than it is by those of transfiguration and deification ; and from this fact the origin of its doctrine of " apocatastasis " is to be treated.

In the West, in Catholicism first and then in Protestantism, the primary questions are those of justification, of salvation by works or by faith, and the attempt to estimate the part played by freedom and grace, respectively, in the work of salvation. That is why the question of the criterion of authority acquires such importance, and in all this there is obviously a juridical and social conception of salvation. This question will never provoke any particular interest in Eastern theological circles. When attention is focussed upon the criterion of authority it assumes that nature is not transfigured, that it is separated from God and in opposition to Him ; the natural is separated from the supernatural, and is untransfigured and not Christianized, requiring to be disciplined by external means.

In reality the natural as an independent sphere of being does not exist ; for it is only a state of sin and of separation from God. The true being of man and of the world is rooted in God. That is how Orthodoxy regarded the matter and in this it was nearer the truth than Catholicism, which was intensely dynamic but which did not imply the transfiguration of nature and its deification. Catholicism does not seem to expect the Christianization of the cosmos and the human race, and that is why it always possesses a more juridical character than Orthodoxy.[1]

---

[1] There are quite clearly in Catholicism not only mystics but even theologians possessed of a quite different spirit, especially in German Catholic theological circles. In Moehler, Scheeben, and, among contemporary writers, in Guardini, a more organic and mystical conception of the Church may be found.

Orthodox and Catholics have a different conception of grace. In Orthodoxy grace is the gift of the Holy Spirit. In Catholicism the action of grace is too limited by the legalistic organization of the Church, and the doctrine of the Holy Spirit and that of grace are almost identified. The nature of the Holy Spirit, as an independent Hypostasis of the Trinity, is not given much prominence. On the other hand Orthodox thought sees the action of the Holy Spirit everywhere. Orthodoxy deep down is essentially the religion of the Holy Spirit ; the idea of sacrifice and of " buying back " so dear to Catholicism remains alien to it. From this fact there comes too quite a different conception of the action of the Holy Spirit which is regarded as the transfiguration of human nature, as illumination, the birth of a new creature, and not as reconciliation with God or as the justification of man in God's sight.

In reality grace can change man but not justify him, because it is the free action of divine power working upon human nature. For the rest, we may well ask is the justification of man necessary so far as God is concerned ? It seems as if we are faced here with a juridical notion created by the limitations of human thought, which were incapable of accepting the divine truth of Christianity. Even in Orthodoxy the theology of the schools is infected with this idea of justification, although to a lesser degree than in Catholicism. Theological doctrine holds that man is saved by Christ and that he is reconciled to God by the sacrifice of Christ.

But if we go into the matter more deeply we shall see that many are not saved *by* Christ but *in* Christ, in the new spiritual race which Christ began, in the new nature, and in the new spiritual life. Christ is above all the revelation of this new life, and of the kingdom of God. Justification and salvation are only secondary moments in the path of spiritual progress—a truth which Orthodoxy grasps more easily than Catholicism. The West tends to separate God and humanity more than the East, while at the same time laying more emphasis on the mission of mankind in its state of isolation. This is the origin of the intense and original activity of the anthropological principle in the institution of the Papacy. From the same source we may also trace the development of humanism, which makes a definitive separation between man and God. Here we have, as it were, a special kind of Nestorianism. It is easy to criticize the dogmatic system of the Papacy, but one is apt to forget that it is a myth created in history by Western Christendom, and that this myth became the driving force of the historical process and was by no means entirely negative in its results.

The Christians of the East are in spirit Platonists, while those of the West are Aristotelians. This is not a difference of doctrines or theories, but a difference of life and experience. The natural order according to the Aristotelian and Thomist conception is not penetrated by divine forces ; it lives according to its own laws, and is only subject to the organized action of external grace. We have already shown that the whole development in the West, not only of Catholicism but of culture generally, is based upon the Aristotelian conception of the relation between form and matter, between potentiality and action. Less attention is paid to the importance of the substance and potentiality of being. Matter, or substance (in the Greek sense of the word), or potentiality, constitutes non-being. True being is only matter as subjected to form. Perfect life is all action ; potentiality in life is an imperfection. The actualization, achievement, and organization of Catholicism and the whole of Western culture spring from this.

In the East, in Orthodoxy, the forces of the spirit are not all actualized or achieved ; they have no particular determined form ; they are still in a state of unrealized, latent, potentiality. Moreover, we do not consider this as an imperfection or as non-being. The East is even inclined to believe that what is latent constitutes being to a greater degree than that which is openly manifested. This is one of the great differences between the East and the West. The spiritual development of the East cannot be thought of in terms of Aristotelianism. For Eastern religious thought the natural is rooted and grounded in the supernatural ; the divine energy comes into the world and makes it divine. The empirical world is rooted in the world of ideas and the world of ideas rests upon God. That is why there is a heavenly cosmos, a heavenly humanity, and a heavenly Church, a world of intelligible essences, a world of ideas uniting the Creator and creation, God and the world.

The militant character of Catholicism represents the triumph of the completed form and the finished act ; it is the organization of being through the subjection of matter to form and by the actualization of that which is potential. The life of humanity is envisaged as so much matter which must be reduced to a pre-determined form. The Catholic Church in its hierarchy conceives itself as a principle of form to which matter, and the chaos of life, is to be subjected. All the potential forces of life are to be actualized ; it is then alone that authentic being appears ; the whole object of life lies in this ceaseless actualization. The West regards life as action, as reality ; hence the value attributed to organization in Catholicism and Western culture. Organization is the triumph of form, it represents the actualization of potential forces. The hierarchy is regarded as an army, the Church as a fortress, and therefore the human soul must submit to organization. It is the function of this army and this fortress to preserve us from the chaos of matter, and subject life to the control of form. Such is the spirit of Latin Catholicism. The West, it is true, is full of infinite variety, but this is the spirit which predominates.

Orthodoxy is not militant and is not actualized. It has more belief in inner spiritual forces which are not organized. The predominance of form and action over substance and potentiality, which is half being and half non-being, is part of the pathos of antiquity. The Greeks were afraid of the infinite in the shape of matter and chaos, and the Catholic world and Western culture are equally suspicious of it.

We find here the explanation of the identification of the Kingdom of God and the life of the Church in its historic earthly destiny. The Kingdom of God takes shape and is organized and actualized in the life of the Church. The historic consciousness stifles the eschatological. The Kingdom of God is no longer sought for nor expected as a miraculous transfiguration of the world to be accom-

plished at the end of time. Orthodoxy has preserved the eschatological view of the Kingdom of God better than Catholicism ; the
Church is not yet the Kingdom of God so far as Orthodoxy is
concerned, for the Kingdom will only be set up at the end of time
and is connected with the Second Coming of Christ. That is why
we find at the very heart of Orthodoxy these three things : faith
in the Resurrection, the festival of Easter, and a real expectation of
the transfiguration of the world. The Catholic Church is less
concerned with the Coming of Christ in power and glory than it is
with the power and glory of Christ in the Church apart from the
transfiguration of the world.

Orthodoxy and Catholicism both affirm the ontological reality of
God, the cosmos, man, and the Church. When Orthodox or Catholics use the somewhat roundabout expression " faith in God " the
accent falls on the word " God." God is prior to my faith in Him
and more real than it is. The Church is an ontological reality and
not a community of believers. This realism and this objectivism
has begun to degenerate in Catholicism into a formalism and
external authoritarianism which tends to be substituted for a vital
ontologism.

Protestantism was the revolt of man's subjectivity against an
externally imposed coercive authority ; the centre of gravity in
religion became faith, or man's inner attitude towards God, and
there was certainly an element of truth in this. But in making this
protest there was a failure to rise above the antithesis between
subject and object. In Luther we find a predominant tendency to
nominalism and individualism. Religious forces have been
secularized and have been diverted to cultural creation. The
cultural results of the Reformation were singularly important and
in the eighteenth and nineteenth centuries the religious consequences
of it no longer bore much relation to the religious power and genius
of Luther himself. In the religious life the process of disintegration
set in. In Liberal Protestantism the Christian religion suffers
" deformation " and becomes merely a science of religion. Protestantism rightly fought against authoritarianism and heteronomy

in the religious sphere and asserted the freedom of the spirit and liberty of conscience ; but, for the rest, Protestantism began to break with the traditions of the Church, and the element of protest predominated at the expense of creative religion.

It must, however, also be noted that individualism is inherent not only in Protestantism, but in the whole of Western Christianity. The idea of the salvation of the individual soul, as well as the idea of the predestination of a small number to salvation, is a species of celestial, metaphysical, individualism. The spirit of *sobornost*, the idea of the collective character of the ways of salvation, is opposed to this sort of individualism. In the Church we are saved with our brethren, all together. We hope for a universal salvation, that is to say, for the transfiguration of the whole cosmos. The spirit of *sobornost* is better expressed in Orthodoxy than it is in Catholicism. Orthodoxy is resolutely anti-individualistic, though Catholics do not understand this. But this cosmic *sobornost* has not found its proper expression in the theology of the schools, nor in ascetic literature. It can be found only in the religious thought of the nineteenth century, in Khomiakov, Dostoievsky, Bukharev, Solovyov, and Feodorov.

V

It is impossible for us not to desire earnestly a reunion of the Churches, in which the sinful divisions of Christendom may be brought to an end. But does this mean that we must abandon our own confession for a state of interconfessionalism ? To which we would reply, " By no means," for such a condition would, in fact, be to surrender ourselves to an abstraction as devoid of real existence as internationalism. The term " inter " has no meaning ; it refers to no known sphere of being. There is no creative religious force in the interconfessional spirit. It is only by remaining in one's confession, and by deepening and broadening it, that one can work towards universalism or supra-confessionalism. This means that one must go deeper and higher rather than attempt to move on the surface of things.

That is why the difficult problem of the unity of the Christian world must be approached not from an external point of view, but from within. The churches will never be united by treaties signed by their respective governments or by mutual conventions and concordats. In order to achieve a real union of the churches it may even perhaps be necessary to avoid having union as our objective. At the present day Vladimir Solovyov's point of view is out of date, and in any case Solovyov never really experienced Catholicism spiritually from within. Attempts to secure reunion have only increased conflict and deepened antagonisms. Only the Holy Spirit can unite the Churches ; reunion can only be the result of grace and cannot be secured by purely human efforts. Least of all can the various governing bodies of the Church bring about the union of Christendom, for they have always been the cause of division.

But there is another way to unity and that is through the inward and spiritual union of Christians of all confessions, through an attitude animated by love which permits of mutual recognition of other confessions as also living in the same spiritual world. Only this inner way of *spiritual* union can bring about the reunion of Christendom which will not be effected by that more outward method of approach which is concerned with dogma and organization. Above all we must try to change the mutual relationships between Orthodox, Catholics, and Protestants rather than those of their churches.

It is in this way that the groundwork of a new universal Christianity will come into being. Beyond the diversities of Christian confession the one universal Church is in process of affirmation, and of this fact we may become aware even while we still remain faithful to our own confessions. The limits of the universal Church do not coincide with those of the visible historic churches ; the soul of the Church is one, and to it there belong, not only the members of the different churches, but even those who are outside the visible Church altogether. There is a great spiritual brotherhood composed of Christians to which not only the Churches of the East and West belong, but also all those whose wills are directed towards God and the divine, all in fact who aspire to some form of spiritual elevation.

I wish to be united with Joan of Arc, but not with Bishop Cauchon who burnt her ; I wish to be united with St. Francis of Assisi but not with the ecclesiastics who persecuted him. I can be in union with Jacob Boehme, that great mystic who had the heart of a child, but not with the Lutheran clergy who condemned him. And it is the same everywhere and throughout Christendom. In the task of the reunion of the Christian world, the most important factor is the work of deepening the mystical life of Christendom so that the positivism and materialism of the churches may be transcended.

VI

The religious life of humanity has two sources, namely, the great mass of religious people and the innovators or prophets. It is through these two channels that divine power is transmitted to mankind. The whole history of religion teaches us this. The first stage of the religious life is social, embodying itself in the tribe and in the nation ; religion is, as it were, grafted on to the corporate life of whole races and peoples, to the life of the natural world. But in the historic destiny of the religious life a subjective period follows in which individual religious personality makes its appearance and frees itself from the dominance of the social conscience to which it is opposed. Then for the first time a religion of the spirit, as distinct from a religion of nature, appears.

The great religious doctors and prophets have been pioneers of the religion of the spirit. This form of religion has its origin in prophetic individuals and not in the great mass of religious people, which always tends to prevent religion progressing from the objective and naturalistic stage. The genius of the prophet frees religion from purely natural and collective elements, and breaks the bonds which tie it to the State. In the prophet both religious individualism and universalism are always indissolubly connected.

357

One of these great prophetic individuals and one of the first religious teachers was Zoroaster ; in his religion spirit began to predominate over nature. But the greatest prophetic individuals were undoubtedly the seers of the Old Testament who marked a new step forward in biblical revelation.

The prophet, as opposed to the sacrificing priest, is always a solitary figure, who has had to make a painful break with the religion of the masses. The prophet, according to the spiritual type to which he belongs, is the bearer of the subjective principle in religion, while the religious collective is the upholder of the objective principle. It is only later that spiritual principles, expressed in the first place by the prophets, acquired objective value, and that the religious life passes into an objective stage. While the religious life is stimulated by prophetism it grows weaker under priestly influence. Prophetic individuality is by its very nature interested in the future rather than in the present or the past. The seer is always dissatisfied with the present, he discerns the evil in his surroundings and awaits the triumph of that higher spiritual principle which is revealed to him in prophetic vision.

There is always a certain millenarianism, an expectation of the coming of the Kingdom of God in this world, about the prophetic spirit. The prophet waits for the Day of Judgment and the triumph of justice. The prophetic element is the eternal element of the spiritual life of the world ; it is the source of creative movement which will tolerate no sort of stagnation in religion. The prophet can only breathe the air of liberty, he finds the hardened world about him oppressive, he keeps his eyes always fixed upon the spiritual world which is to penetrate the stifling atmosphere of this lower world of ours. The prophet foresees the destiny of man and of the world, the developments which will take place in the empirical world through the contemplation of things spiritual. Prophetic gnosis is always a philosophy of history which is indeed an impossibility apart from the free spirit of prophecy.

The prophet, as distinct from the saint, is immersed in the life of the world and shares the destiny of its inhabitants. But he denies the life of the world and condemns it, predicting for it a fatal end. It is this which constitutes the element of tragedy in the life of the prophet. He is condemned to suffer, he is always unhappy, and often stoned. He is distinguished from the priest in that he lives amid the storm of revolt and knows no rest.

The prophetic element is often hostile to the priestly for it recks little of ceremonial and priestly functions. The prophet is also distinguished from the priest by the fact that he belongs to the human order ; he is a man inspired by God. The prophet does not aspire to perfection, to sanctity, and to personal salvation, although he may have reached the highest degrees of spiritual perfection ; he may be a saint, or on the other hand he may not be. He does not abandon the world in order to save his own soul, but he desires the perfection of mankind, and not merely that of the individual.

In prophetism there is always something of the revolutionary spirit which is not to be found in priesthood. The prophet does not bring peace to the soul ; there is necessarily an element of discontinuity somewhere in his psychology. Moreover, the prophetic element can never be the only or the predominating element in the life of religion. The world would not be able to bear such " a burning and a shining light ", and therefore is forced to protect itself from its exclusive predominance. Yet without it the spiritual life would be finally extinguished in the world. Luther had a prophetic nature and his spirit was greater than his conception of religion in the limited sense of the word. In the nineteenth century the prophetic element is to be found in Dostoievsky, Solovyov, Feodorov, de Maistre, Carlyle, Nietzsche, Léon Bloy, and Kierkegaard. Without men of this type all spiritual progress would come to a standstill.

There is a prophetism in the world which is outside the Church, and this is one of the most difficult problems with which the mind of the Church is confronted. How can the prophetic mission be justified ? Perhaps it is necessary for the purposes of divine Providence in this world that it should not be recognized as within the

Church ; yet in reality it is as much a function of the Church as priesthood. It is only on the surface that the prophet is in conflict with the religion of the masses or with the *sobornost* of the Church, for deep down it is clear that prophetism is one of the Church's functions. This is a fact which it is often difficult to see clearly.

Genius is intimately associated with the prophetic spirit. Its destiny is as tragic and unhappy as that of the prophet since both are condemned to solitude though animated by a spirit which is universal. But prophetic solitude has nothing in common with individualism. The prophet is social, as well as solitary.

The whole future of Christianity and the possibility of its renaissance depends on whether prophetism will or will not be recognized and revealed within it. The Christian renaissance presupposes not only the priestly spirit of the sanctification of life, but also the prophetic spirit of real transfiguration. The Christian movement has its origin not only in the popular and the collective, but also in prophetic individualities of every degree. The priestly hierarchy is the indispensable element in Christianity, but it cannot dominate exclusively at the expense of the prophetic element. The expectation of Christ's Second Coming is the prophetic element of Christianity which cannot be removed from it. Christianity in the course of centuries of objectification has hardened into a collective, hereditary, and national religion under the exclusive control of the priesthood, with the result that the prophetic spirit has been quenched to such an extent that it is actually regarded as heretical. In Catholicism the prophetic spirit is represented entirely by women, such as St. Hildegarde, Marie de Vale, Catherine Emmerich, etc.

Naturalistic elements, belonging to natural rather than spiritual religion, have lingered on in Christianity, and prophecy which stands for the religion of the spirit has always been opposed to them. There are those who, while belonging to a Christian confession, are scarcely Christians at all in the spiritual sense of the word ; they have accepted their faith in a purely outward fashion. Such people are the greatest opponents of the prophetic spirit, for it is a menace to their naturalistic and traditional religion of authority with all its externalism.

Even the Book of Revelation, the prophetic book of the New Testament, may be interpreted not as symbolic of the spiritual but from a naturalistic standpoint which really amounts to materialism. The prophetic and creative spirit in these apocalyptic visions is obscured by such a method of interpretation and all that is left is superstition and a virtual negation of life.

Two figures stand out in the spiritual life of mankind, namely, those of the saint and of the prophet, nor has mankind been able to supersede them. Both are necessary to the work of God in the world and to the coming of His Kingdom. These two pathways of the spirit, the way of holiness and the way of prophetism, have both their contribution to make to the final coming of God-humanity, are integral to the life of the Church, and participate in its fulfilment. For a time, owing to some inscrutable divine plan, prophetism has been able to function outside the visible body of the Church ; but the hour is at hand when this spirit will be recognized as belonging to the Church, and as having its origin within it. It is through tragedy, through intestine conflict, and through terrible struggles, that the religious destiny of man is accomplished. But mankind is moving forward to fulness of life, to its ultimate deification, and to the Kingdom of God.

Two conflicting ways of life are to be found here below ; there is the Kingdom of God and the kingdom of this world, and it is essential to make a real spiritual distinction between them. Millenarianism may be taken in a materialistic sense with the result that it becomes the dream of an earthly utopia. The building of the Tower of Babel was of this kind ; it is in reality the kingdom of Antichrist, that false millenarianism which is to be found at the present day in Communism. But in the hopes of millenarianism there is to be found as well a real expectation of the New Jerusalem, of a positive consummation of the world process, and of the realization of the Kingdom.

The prophets of Christianity are not optimistic, they give no support to the theory of progress, they condemn with severity the evil from which there is no escape in this world. But neither are they pessimistic, for the fact is that they are far beyond human optimism or human pessimism.

They look constantly for the coming of Christ in all the fulness of His power and glory.